新世纪商务英语专业本科系列教材（第二版）／总主

国际管理学
简明教程

A SHORT COURSE IN
INTERNATIONAL MANAGEMENT

主编　张家瑞

编者　张家瑞　尹筱艺　陈佳兵　熊忠淑
　　　王艳慧　杨思羽　陈　欢

上海外语教育出版社
外教社　SHANGHAI FOREIGN LANGUAGE EDUCATION PRESS

图书在版编目（CIP）数据

国际管理学简明教程 / 张家瑞主编. -- 2版. -- 上海 : 上海外语教育出版社, 2022
新世纪商务英语专业本科系列教材 / 王立非总主编
ISBN 978-7-5446-7222-1

Ⅰ.①国… Ⅱ.①张… Ⅲ.①国际商务-英语-高等学校-教材 Ⅳ.①F740

中国版本图书馆CIP数据核字 (2022) 第144749号

出版发行：**上海外语教育出版社**
（上海外国语大学内）邮编：200083
电　　话：021-65425300（总机）
电子邮箱：bookinfo@sflep.com.cn
网　　址：http://www.sflep.com
责任编辑：仝　琳

印　　刷：上海华教印务有限公司
开　　本：850×1168　1/16　印张 22.5　字数 605千字
版　　次：2022年9月第2版　2022年9月第1次印刷

书　　号：ISBN 978-7-5446-7222-1
定　　价：70.00元

本版图书如有印装质量问题，可向本社调换
质量服务热线：4008-213-263　电子邮箱：editorial@sflep.com

总 序

截至 2020 年，全国已有 403 所高校开办了商务英语本科专业，有 500 多所高校的英语类专业开设了商务方向或课程，商务英语专业的发展进入内涵建设与质量提升的新常态。2018 年教育部颁布了《普通高等学校本科外国语言文学类教学质量国家标准》，先后出台了《关于加快建设高水平本科教育 全面提高人才培养能力的意见》(简称"新时代高教 40 条")、《关于实施一流本科专业建设"双万计划"的通知》《关于一流本科课程建设的实施意见》和《教育部办公厅关于开展 2019 年线下、线上线下混合式、社会实践国家级一流本科课程认定工作的通知》等一系列重要文件，2020 年外国语言文学类专业教学指导委员会发布了《普通高等学校本科商务英语专业教学指南》(以下简称《教学指南》)，给商务英语人才培养和专业建设指明了方向，提出了更高要求。

为了认真贯彻落实国家有关文件精神，上海外语教育出版社与部分教育部国家级一流商务英语本科专业院校合作，对入选"十二五"普通高等教育本科国家级规划教材的"新世纪商务英语专业本科系列教材"进行全面修订。修订后的"新世纪商务英语专业本科系列教材(第二版)"体系更加完整，全方位覆盖专业核心课程、专业方向课程和实践教学环节，英语语言技能和专业知识并重，很好地体现出《教学指南》对商务英语专业学生知识和能力的要求。

本系列教材中，英语语言技能课程包含《商务英语综合教程》《商务英语视听说教程》《商务英语阅读教程》《商务英语写作教程》《商务英语论文写作》《商务英语口译教程》《商务英汉翻译教程》《商务汉英翻译教程》等。

商务专业知识与技能模块包含《国际贸易实务》《国际商业伦理》《国际商业文化》《国际商务礼仪》《国际商务合同》《国际经济学》《国际商务谈判》《国际知识产权》《国际营销》《国际支付》《国际贸易单证》《国际管理学》等简明教程。

本系列教材具有以下四个鲜明的特色：

第一，完全对接《教学指南》规定的培养目标和课程体系，突出打牢英语基本功，拓宽国际视野，提升人文素养，培养商务意识和素养，着重提高英语应用能力、商务实践能力、跨文化交流能力、思辨与创新能力、自主学习能力。

第二，编写理念先进，选材新颖地道，充满时代感，坚持语言、文化、商务三者有机结合，充分体现国际化、人文性、复合型、应用性的特点和全人教育的理念。

第三，体系完整，覆盖商务英语专业核心课程、部分方向课程，以及实践教学环节，语言技能教材突出听、说、读、写、译、跨文化交际等技能训练导向；商务知识与技能教材理论体系完整，知识讲解简明扼要，语言原汁原味，配套练习实用性和可操作性强，注重中外真实案例分析，培养思辨和创新能力。

第四，课堂任务设计多样化和立体化的特色鲜明，突出网络多媒体技术的应用，提供丰富的视频材料和多模态教学资源，加大了英语学习的趣味性和输入的有效性。

本系列教材由多所教育部国家级一流商务英语本科专业院校的专家和老师合作编写，可供商务英语专业本科生、英语专业商贸方向学生、财经类院校本科生以及各类经管专业本科生使用，同时也可作为大学英语ESP课程模块的商务英语教材，以及各类企事业单位培训和社会商务英语学习者的参考书。本套教材的修订得到上海外语教育出版社领导和编辑的大力支持，在此表示衷心感谢。

北京语言大学教授、博士生导师

王立非

前 言

　　《国际管理学简明教程》是上海外语教育出版社"新世纪商务英语专业本科系列教材(第二版)"中"专业核心课程·商务专业知识与技能"板块的一本。本书的编写以最新颁布的《普通高等学校本科商务英语专业教学指南》(以下简称《教学指南》)为指导,培养《教学指南》提出的"掌握国际商务的基础理论与实务,具备较强的跨文化能力、商务沟通能力与创新创业能力,能适应国家与地方经济社会发展、对外交流与合作需要,能熟练使用英语从事国际商务、国际贸易、国际会计、国际金融、跨境电子商务等涉外领域工作的国际化复合型人才"。本书致力于达到《教学指南》提出的"知识要求"——掌握商务活动的基本工作内容和运行机制;熟悉商务组织治理结构、战略规划、运营管理等方面的基本理论和基础知识;了解经济学、管理学、法学等相关学科基础知识。此外,本书将有助于实现《教学指南》提出的"能力要求"——具有良好的商务英语运用能力和跨文化商务沟通能力;具有基本的商务分析、决策和实践能力;具有良好的团队合作能力,较强的领导、管理、协调和沟通能力。

　　《国际管理学简明教程》共16章,涵盖全球化、国际管理中的文化语境、国际管理伦理、国际贸易理论、外国直接投资、外汇市场、国际货币系统、全球资本市场、国际企业的战略、国际企业的组织、进入战略和战略联盟、进出口和对等贸易、全球化生产、业务外包和物流、全球营销、全球人力资源管理、国际商务中的会计和金融等主题。

　　《国际管理学简明教程》各章结构如下:本章概要、学习指南、正文文本及注释、知识链接、巩固练习、案例分析、拓展阅读。本书具有以下特色:

　　1. 涵盖国际管理学的主要理论,反映最新发展动态。教材内容丰富,囊括了当代国际管理学的重要领域。通过本课程的学习,学生将能清晰地了解现代国际管理学的概况和发展态势,对未来学习更加专业的国际管理学课程打下坚实的基础。

2. **经典文献和案例相得益彰。**教材选文不乏各领域有影响力的经典理论原文,例如霍夫斯泰德的文化维度理论、特朗皮纳斯的七维文化架构理论、绝对优势理论、产品生命周期理论等。案例部分紧扣主题,精选真实、典型的商务案例,既有可口可乐、联合利华、IBM、劳斯莱斯等国际知名大公司的案例,也有海尔、联想、字节跳动、传音科技等中国知名公司的案例。

3. **兼顾英语语言能力和商科思维训练。**课后练习既有阅读练习、拓展阅读等旨在培养英语语言能力的任务,也有案例分析、讨论等旨在培养学生商科思维能力的任务。

本书适用于高等院校商务英语、经济管理等专业的双语或者全英文课程,也可作为各类企事业单位人员的培训材料或任何感兴趣人士的学习资料。

本书的编写得到了上海外语教育出版社编辑的悉心指导和大力支持,对出版社编辑的辛勤付出表示衷心的感谢!本书的编写成员为:西南财经大学经贸外语学院的研究生尹筱艺、陈佳兵、熊忠淑、王艳慧、陈欢和四川旅游学院的杨思羽,全书由西南财经大学经贸外语学院院长张家瑞教授审校。

张家瑞

2021年4月于成都

Table of Contents

Globalization

CHAPTER 1

全球化

本章概要

本章主要介绍全球化的含义、机制、特点、主要方面及相关争议,以及以可口可乐、TCL 等跨国公司为代表的全球化推动者。

学习指南

古老的贸易路线丝绸之路是早期全球化的一个例子。自20世纪90年代,人类全球化进入加速阶段,这个含义丰富的国际术语得到广泛使用。促进全球化发展的三大因素:一是技术进步带来了国际活动的增加,二是政府对国际活动的阻碍减少,三是管理技术的进步和日益统一。跨国公司是全球化的重要推动者,他们关注品牌和品牌管理,由此产生了创新的广告活动、大型商场和企业校园,同时也改变了全球就业形势。

通过本章学习,希望大家能够实现以下目标:

(1)基本目标(Text-based Goals)

- 掌握本章涉及话题的基本专业术语及词汇,如全球化、跨国公司、全球扩张等;
- 掌握本章的主要知识点,即全球化的含义、机制、特点、主要方面及相关争议。

(2)拓展目标(Extended Goals)

- 思考本章引言,为什么埃马纽埃尔·马克龙认为"全球化可以是绝佳的机遇"?
- 通过学习背景知识、拓展阅读、案例分析进一步了解全球化产生的主要背景、内涵及影响。

全球化并非鲜闻。自文明伊始，人们就与邻里进行商品交易。丝绸之路是欧洲、北非、东非、中非、南亚和远东之间古老的贸易路线网，是早期全球化的一个例子。全球化最常被提及的两大驱动力是有益于推动国际活动的技术进步和政府对国际活动阻碍的减少。一些人指出第三个因素是管理技术的进步和日益统一。

Globalization is not new. Since the start of civilization, people have traded goods with their neighbors. The silk road, an ancient network of trade routes used between Europe, North Africa, East Africa, Central Africa, South Asia and the Far East, was an example of early globalization. Beginning in the 1990s, human globalization entered an accelerative phase in which the process gained widespread usage as an international term with many interpretations.

Why globalization? The two most often cited driving forces of globalization are technological advancements that are conducive to an increased international activity and a reduction of government induced barriers to international activity. A third factor pointed to by some is the advancement and growing uniformity of management techniques.

Multinational corporations are agents of globalization. They have begun to focus principally on brands and brand management, believing that while products are made in factories, a brand is made in the mind and bought by the consumers. A brand is an idea, a lifestyle, and an attitude. The result is innovative ad campaigns, superstores and corporate campuses, but also a change in the face of global employment. Super brand companies focus on first creating the "soul" of companies and then removing the burdensome bodies of employees, factories and machines. If you want to explore how globalization is vividly reflected in multinational companies, Coca-Cola deserves our close attention.

Coca-Cola

可口可乐

　　如今，可口可乐是世界上最知名的跨国品牌之一。该公司借助饮料行业的迅速发展并凭借其全球最大的饮料公司的地位，继续保持增长势头。事实上，可口可乐采取的三个关键战略：全球营销战略、产品差异化和技术，在支持其全球化快速成长和扩张的过程中发挥了重要的作用。

Today, Coca-Cola is one of the most well-known brands in the world. This company has continued to gain momentum and growth, capitalizing on the rapidly expanding beverage industry and ranking as the largest beverage company in the world. With its push for global market share, Coca-Cola now operates in over 200 countries with over 84,000 suppliers. Currently, over 70% of Coca-Cola's business income is generated from non-U.S. sources (Coca-Cola Company, 2012). In over a century, Coca-Cola has grown the company into a multi-billion dollar business.

COCA-COLA'S JOURNEY TO GLOBALIZATION

Founded back in the 1880's, Coca-Cola was developed by John Pemberton as an American iconic brand known for high quality and

consistency. During this period in history, storekeepers demanded pre-packaged products with brand name recognition. Coca-Cola met these demands with its iconic red and white logo and brand marketing to instill confidence in the consumers that the Coca-Cola product would taste the same everywhere it was purchased. These strategies soon became the foundation for Coca-Cola's plan to expand globally.

In the early 1900's, Coca-Cola started to globalize. Bottling plants were initially built in Cuba and Panama as the U.S. military spread to these regions, causing a rise in demand for the Coca-Cola brand. These plants proved to be successful, reducing shipping and delivery costs typical in these regions. Soon after, additional bottling plants opened in Hawaii, Puerto Rico, and the Philippines. These efforts launched Coca-Cola's investment in testing foreign markets for future expansion opportunities. By 1926, Coca-Cola had established foreign relationships and plants around the world in support of its newly created center of global operations. Coca-Cola continued on its path of mass production and rapid expansion for the next several decades. Local branches along with local partnerships to produce and distribute the signature Coca-Cola products were established throughout the world. The ending of World War II and the Cold War marked the signature period in which Coca-Cola had established itself as a true global corporation known for its efficiency and worldwide capabilities.

Next, let us take a look at three key strategies employed by Coca-Cola to support rapid growth and expansion across the globe: global marketing strategies, product differentiation, and technology.

GLOBAL MARKETING STRATEGIES

Coca-Cola's marketing strategies played a significant role in successfully globalizing the company. The company's popular advertising slogans and **catchy** jingles played into the hearts and minds of people around the world. Some of the most remembered advertising slogans include:

"Drink Coca-Cola."
"Things go better with Coke."
"Good 'til the last drop."
"It's the real thing."
"Always Coca-Cola."
"Enjoy."
"Life tastes good."

Coupled with these slogans, songs were used to have consumers remember the brand. One of the company's most popular jingles was known as "I want to buy the world a coke", produced in 1971 by Billy Davis. The commercial featuring this song portrayed a world of hope

Word Study

consistency
/kən'sɪstənsɪ/ n. 一
致性
catchy /'kætʃi/ adj. 悦
耳易记的

3

and love produced by a group of multicultural teenagers on top of a hill. This commercial went down in history as one of the most well-known commercials of all time.

In addition to Coca-Cola's advertising efforts, Coca-Cola became the first commercial sponsor of the Olympic Games in Amsterdam in 1928. Coca-Cola continues to be an Olympic Games sponsor today. Coca-Cola has also sponsored many other sporting events such as the International Federation of Association Football (FIFA), National Hockey League (NHL), National Basketball Association (NBA), National Football Association (NFL), Major League Baseball (MLB), NASCAR, and Cricket World Cup.

PRODUCT DIFFERENTIATION

Another key factor that has supported Coca-Cola's globalization vision is the company's ability to customize the product to meet the needs and wants of individual markets. For example, Coca-Cola has been able to **tailor** its product line to meet the needs of the younger consumers by offering Powerade and flavored Coke products, such as Cherry Coke and **Vanilla** Coke. Additionally, the company is meeting the needs of the health conscious, older consumers with Diet Coke, Vitamin Water, and Odwalla products. Coca-Cola has invested significant time and money into researching and understanding different marketing segments based on lifestyle, age, and income in order to accurately develop and market its products. Packaging differentiation has also played a key role in how adaptable the Coca-Cola product is to various market segments. Functional packaging has been used to make the products available in different sizes and forms, including glass and plastic bottles, **aluminum** cans, and fountain drink **dispensers**. The company considers various shapes and sizes of the bottles and cans to ensure easy stacking and vending machine dispensing. To promote the company's **commitment** to environmental sustainability, all packaging materials are designed to be recyclable and labeled accordingly for easy consumer identification.

TECHNOLOGY

Technological advances contributed to Coca-Cola's ability to globalize rapidly throughout the 20th century. Product transportation became more efficient and cost effective with the development of bigger and faster semi-trucks, cargo ships, jet aircraft, and trains. Coca-Cola was able to **manufacture** and ship products quicker and farther to market segments that were unreachable before these transportation improvements. In addition, technological advances became the driving force behind the ease and speed at which information was available. **Distributors** and **warehouses** were able to more accurately track inventory

Word Study

tailor /'teɪlə/ v. 定制
vanilla /və'nɪlə/ adj.
　香草味的
aluminum /ə'ljuːmɪnəm/
　n. 铝
dispenser /dɪs'pensə/
　n. 自动取货机
commitment
　/kə'mɪtmənt/ n.
　承诺, 保证
manufacture
　/,mænjʊ'fæktʃə/ v.
　生产, 制造
distributor /dɪs'trɪbjʊtə/
　n. 经销商
warehouse /'weəhaʊs/
　n. 仓库

levels and fill order shipments, resulting in lower overall operating costs. Computerization also led to **slashed** product costs and improved efficiencies. Computerized and automated manufacturing equipment increased the speed and volume in which products were produced. These technological advances enabled Coca-Cola to compete on a global scale, selling the well-known brand of products across the world at competitive prices.

What Is Globalization?

Globalization is the spread of products, technology, information, and jobs across national borders and cultures. In economic terms, it describes an interdependence of nations around the globe fostered through free trade.

On the upside, it can raise the standard of living in poor and less developed countries by providing job opportunity, modernization, and improved access to goods and services. On the downside, it can destroy job opportunities in more developed and high-wage countries as the production of goods moves across borders.

Globalization motives are idealistic, as well as opportunistic, but the development of a global free market has benefited large corporations based in the Western world. Its impact remains mixed for workers, cultures, and small businesses around the globe, in both developed and emerging nations.

Globalization is the **integration** of national economies through trade, investment, capital flow, labor migration, and technology. Jagdish Bhagwati, a highly regarded economist on international trade, defines globalization as the "integration of national economies into the international economy through trade, direct foreign investment (by corporations and multinationals), short-term capital flows, international flows of workers and humanity generally, and flows of technology." Typical examples of economic globalization are the global supply chains now standard for the manufacture of many devices, ranging from cars to smart phones; the processes surrounding raw materials, components, and assembly may take place across multiple countries.

How Does It Work?

Globalization results from the removal of barriers between national economies to encourage the flow of goods, services, capital, and labor. While the lowering or removal of **tariffs** and **quotas** that restrict free and open trade among nations has helped globalize the world economy, transportation and communication technologies have had the strongest

Word Study

slash /slæʃ/ v. 大幅削减
integration /ˌɪntɪˈɡreɪʃən/ n. 整合，一体化
tariff /ˈtærɪf/ n. 关税
quota /ˈkwəʊtə/ n. 配额

什么是全球化？

全球化目前有诸多定义，从广义上来说，全球化是产品、技术、信息和就业跨越国界和文化的传播。它具有两面性。

全球化的定义涉及多个角度，从经济角度来讲，备受推崇的国际贸易经济学家贾格迪什·巴格瓦蒂将全球化定义为"通过贸易、外国直接投资（由公司和跨国公司）、短期资本流动、国际工人和人员的流动，以及技术流通，将各国经济融入国际经济。"经济全球化的典型例子是全球供应链，它如今已成为从汽车到智能手机等诸多设备生产的标准；原材料、部件和组装的流程可能在多个国家进行。

它是怎样运作的？

全球化起因于国家经济之间壁垒的消除，以鼓励商品、服务、资本和劳动力的流动。运输和通信技术对加快

全球化步伐的影响
最大。技术的使用
使大型跨国公司等
企业，能够在全球范
围内维护客户、供应
商甚至竞争对手。

在全球化进程
中，一些组织已发展
成为关键角色。例
如，世界银行和国际
货币基金组织主要
处理发展中经济体
的自由贸易问题和
国际货币政策，包括
发展中国家和工业
化国家之间的债务
和贸易平衡。世界
贸易组织和关税贸
易总协定一直致力
于消除贸易壁垒和
降低贸易成本。

impact on accelerating the pace of globalization.

Thomas L. Friedman describes the "flattening" of the world economy through globalized trade, **outsourcing**, supply-chaining and political liberalization. The use of technologies allows businesses, such as large multinational corporations, to maintain customers, suppliers and even competitors on a world-wide basis. The breakdown of businesses into components along its value-chain creates opportunities for multiple businesses located at various spots on the globe to participate in the production of a single good or service. This global network, even for a single enterprise, is part of globalization.

Several organizations have either been created or have evolved into key roles in the process of globalization. The World Bank and the International Monetary Fund, for instance, deal primarily with issues of free trade in developing economies and with international monetary policy, including debt and trade balances between developing and industrialized countries. The World Trade Organization, along with the General Agreement on Trade and Tariffs (GATT), has been involved with removing trade barriers and reducing the cost of trading.

Features of Globalization

EFFICIENT USE OF RESOURCES

全球化的特点

全球化有许多
特点，包括世界资源
能更有效利用；技术
创新快速转移；在自
然灾害期间，各国提
供及时的救援；金融
市场一体化；世界更
联通，人们的旅行和
交往更便利；整个世
界变成一个大舞台，
人们可以在全世界
施展才华。

Globalization leads to a more efficient use of world resources because every country has different set of natural and human resources which which allow it to produce a particular product at a lower cost than any other country. If there was no globalization, these raw material and human resources would have been **diverted** to some other work which would have resulted in **inefficiency** and wastage of resources and hence globalization by opening them up to world markets forces the nations to produce products which **yield** them the maximum profits.

QUICK TRANSFER OF INNOVATION

Globalization leads to faster transfer of any invention or discovery made in one country from another. Gone are the days where one country had to wait for many months to get better and new technological advancement from other countries. Nowadays countries get new technological advancement discovered in other countries almost instantly which in turn leads to higher efficiency.

IMMEDIATE HELP

Another feature of globalization is that all countries are connected and during times of natural **calamities** like floods, earthquakes, famines,

Word Study

outsource /'autsɔːs/ v.
　将……外包
divert /dar'vɜːt/ v. 转
　移，改变用途
inefficiency /ˌɪnɪˈfɪʃənsi/
　n. 效率低，无能
yield /jiːld/ v. 出产，
　产生
calamity /kəˈlæmɪti/
　n. 灾难，灾害

all other countries send immediate help to the affected country. Thus in a way it helps in reducing the deaths due to shortage of basic **amenities**. With globalization, the whole world has become a family where countries will always have differences but in times of need, they help each other just like family members do.

INTEGRATION OF FINANCIAL MARKETS

Integration of financial markets is another important feature of globalization. Due to globalization, all financial markets of the world are interconnected and hence one event leads to reaction in not only home market but it has implications over other global markets, too. This connection is not limited to the stock market only; rather it covers the **commodity** market, the **currency** market and the **bond** market.

MOVEMENT ACROSS THE WORLD

Due to globalization people are able to travel and explore other countries and experience and discover new culture, food, tradition and many other things. Hence one can say that it in a way helps removing cultural barriers because as people travel they tend to discover new facts about the other countries and remove many misconceptions they used to have. Few decades back if you have told people of developed countries to visit countries in Asia and Africa they would have said no but nowadays people go happily to these countries for vacation as well as adventure. In short, globalization has reduced the distance between nations and in the minds of people.

WHOLE WORLD IS A STAGE

Due to globalization, the whole world is open for talented people to show their skills. Whether an individual is an actor or a businessperson or a sportsman or in any other field, he or she can show his or her skills and make name and money all over the world, which was not possible a few decades back. The whole world is a stage, a platform for people irrespective of their age, religion, ethnicity, and background to make most of their talent.

Key Aspects of Globalization

ECONOMIC GLOBALIZATION

Economic globalization is the increasing economic interdependence of national economies across the world through a rapid increase in cross-border movement of goods, services, technology, and capital. Whereas the globalization of business is centered around the **diminution**

Word Study

amenity /əˈmenəti/ *n.*
便利设施
commodity /kəˈmɒdɪti/
n. 商品
currency /ˈkʌrənsɪ/ *n.*
货币
bond /bɒnd/ *n.* 债券
diminution
/dɪmɪˈnjuːʃən/
n. 减少，缩减

全球化主要包括哪几个方面？

　　全球化体现在很多方面，其中主要包括三个方面：经济全球化、文化全球化和政治全球化。

of international trade regulations as well as tariffs, taxes, and other impediments that suppresses global trade, economic globalization is the process of increasing economic integration between countries, leading to the emergence of a global marketplace or a single world market. Economic globalization can be viewed as either a positive or a negative phenomenon. Economic globalization comprises: globalization of production, which refers to the obtainment of goods and services from a particular source from different locations around the globe to benefit from difference in cost and quality. Likewise, it also comprises globalization of markets, which is defined as the union of different and separate markets into a massive global marketplace. Economic globalization also includes competition, technology, and corporations and industries.

International standards have made trade in goods and services more efficient. An example of such standard is the intermodal container. **Containerization** dramatically reduced transport of its costs, supported the post-war **boom** in international trade, and was a major element in globalization.

CULTURAL GLOBALIZATION

Cultural globalization refers to the transmission of ideas, meanings, and values around the world in such a way as to extend and intensify social relations. This process is marked by the common consumption of cultures that have been **diffused** by the Internet, popular culture media, and international travel. This has added to processes of commodity exchange and colonization which have a longer history of carrying cultural meaning around the globe. The circulation of cultures enables individuals to partake in extended social relations that cross national and regional borders. The creation and expansion of such social relations is not merely observed on a material level. Cultural globalization involves the formation of shared norms and knowledge with which people associate their individual and collective cultural identities. It brings increasing interconnectedness among different populations and cultures.

Music has an important role in economic and cultural development during globalization. Music **genres** such as jazz and reggae began locally and later became international phenomena. Globalization gave support to the world music phenomenon by allowing music from developing countries to reach broader audiences.

POLITICAL GLOBALIZATION

Political globalization refers to the growth of the worldwide political system, both in size and complexity. That system includes national governments, their governmental and intergovernmental organizations as well as government-independent elements of global civil society such

8

as international non-governmental organizations and social movement organizations. One of the key aspects of the political globalization is the declining importance of the nation-state and the rise of other actors on the political scene.

Increasingly, non-governmental organizations influence public policy across national boundaries, including humanitarian aid and developmental efforts. **Philanthropic** organizations with global missions are also coming to the **forefront** of humanitarian efforts. For example, the Bill and Melinda Gates Foundation projects include a current multibillion-dollar commitment to funding immunizations in some of the world's more **impoverished** but rapidly growing countries.

Globalization: Controversial?

PROS

Globalization brings the advanced economies of the world together.

Globalization provides an opportunity for the most significant economies and countries in the world today to work together to accomplish big things. Whether we are building space stations that orbit our planet, sending missions to the moon, or developing ways to counter hunger that every family can afford, this process frequently tries to make the world become a better place. The price on these massive efforts are often too high for one country to manage by itself. Through the spirit of cooperation, humanity can use its strength of diversity to tackle big problems.

It stabilizes the politics of the world.

Even though there is a wave of **populism** and **elitism** growing around the world lately, the processes of globalization still encourage more cooperation than isolation. Economies do not grow as efficiently when they are isolated from one another as they do when they work together. That means there is always a certain level of import-export opportunities that are available because there is no other way to maintain the quality of life.

It opens up more opportunities for free trade.

Globalization makes goods and services available to many people often at lower prices. When we concentrate on the national borders that exist in our world, we limit our access to goods and services. Even when they exist between allies, duties and tariffs limit the number of import opportunities available. Even if the high fees are solely applied to luxury goods, it encourages buyers to evade the rules that prevent them from getting what they want at a reasonable price. Currently, there

有争议的全球化？
好处：
　　全球化给全球经济、政治、文化等方面带来的好处主要包括：1. 凝聚世界发达经济体；2. 稳定世界政治局势；3. 创造更多自由贸易机会；4. 促进信息和技术传播；5. 创造更多就业机会。

freelancer /ˈfriːˌlænsə/
n. 自由职业者,特
约人员

entrepreneur
/ˌɒntrəprəˈnɜː/
n. 企业家

offshoring /ˈɒfˌʃɔːrɪŋ/
n. 离岸,离岸外包

distribution
/ˌdɪstrɪˈbjuːʃən/ n.
分布,供应

borderless /ˈbɔːdəlɪs/
adj. 无边界的,没
有边际

intervention
/ˌɪntəˈvenʃən/ n. 介
入,妨碍

are more than 1,500 different trade barriers in existence that have an impact on global trade. Globalization helps us to focus our energies on what we require rather than enforcing standards that we have devised for ourselves.

It facilitates the spread of information and technology.

In a worldwide society, art and culture aren't the only things that spread more easily. Information and technology are in the same boat. Consider the emergence of mobile banking in Kenya or the practice of microlending as examples. Civil society organizations can draw inspiration from other countries, and successful ideas can spread more quickly.

It creates more employment opportunities for the average person.

Over the next generation, the number of **freelancers** and self-employed individuals is expected to increase to over 50% of the overall labor force. About one-third of workers are already earning an income outside of the traditional employment contract. When we reduce restrictions to access for these **entrepreneurs**, then it adds another level of value to the overall economy.

Although there could be skill-based shortages in some industries that occur because of globalization, especially with **offshoring** issues that may occur, this advantage makes it possible for anyone with a good idea, a special talent, or a useful skill to build a life for themselves.

弊端:
    全球化给世界
带来的不利影响主
要包括:1. 分销网络
集中化导致的效率
低下和浪费;2. 使发
达经济体产生更多
的离岸外包;3. 促使
文化同质化。

CONS

Globalization would centralize distribution networks.

Even with an emphasis on infrastructure building in the developing world, we still don't have many countries that match what Europe, North America, or Oceania can provide to consumers already. That means an effort to go **borderless** must use centralized distribution networks to ensure product access is available to everyone.

The only problem with this structure is that it creates more inefficiencies. We are already losing hundreds of thousands of tons of food every day because of waste that is built into the domestic systems. This issue would only get worse if there are more people to serve using the same processes that we currently use.

It creates more offshoring from the advanced economies.

The advanced economies of the world have the highest labor costs, the highest manufacturing costs, and the highest distribution costs unless there are specific government **interventions** that prevent them from increasing.

The threat of offshoring is a threat that enforces specific employment behaviors in the advanced economies that reduce wages and benefits. If we were to reduce borders and improve living conditions around the world, the developing world would see a rise in their standard of living. In the advanced economies, there would be the risk of reducing the financial strength of the average household.

It has the potential to promote cultural homogeneity.

As people's preferences **converge** and products can't compete with cheaper multinational ones, globalization may lead to increasing cultural homogeneity. Near future, we may lose valuable cultural customs. Some critics of globalization believe due to this goods are becoming homogeneous and people will use the same kind of things from cars to food habits. Homogenization is something that is imposed on people by market forces and it treats people as a product. Due to this, the global tendency could eliminate cultural diversity, and thus, it creates a popular **monoculture**.

VERDICT ON THE PROS AND CONS OF GLOBALIZATION

Globalization gives us all an opportunity to live, work, and communicate in ways that bring all of us closer together. This structure gives everyone an opportunity to create a world for themselves where any dream becomes possible. It can improve the safety of the workplace, encourage innovation, and give us more access to the goods and services that we need. It is a process that provides more competition than what border **enforcement** creates.

When we reduce the restrictions that are in place between nations, then we can also create more security issues that require more intelligence and communication to solve. Individuals with ill intent can move with greater freedom in a globalized world.

That's why the pros and cons of globalization are critical to review. It can put us on a path toward economic freedom, but this structure can also encourage the rich to get wealthier at the expense of the poor.

Word Study

homogeneity /ˌhəʊməʊdʒəˈniːəti/ n. 同质
converge /kənˈvɜːdʒ/ v. 汇集，趋同
monoculture /ˈmɒnəˌkʌltʃə/ n. 单一文化社会
verdict /ˈvɜːdɪkt/ n. 结论，裁定
enforcement /ɪnˈfɔːsmənt/ n. 执行，实施

Key Terms
专业术语

globalization 全球化
global market share 全球市场占有率
global marketing strategy 全球营销策略
trade barriers 贸易壁垒
cultural barriers 文化障碍

multinational corporation 跨国公司
product differentiation 产品差异化
national economy 国家经济
global economy 全球经济
cultural homogeneity 文化同质化

全球化与逆全球化

曾几何时，全球化一度被视为经济繁荣和政治正确的代名词；然而近年来随着希腊主权债务危机、英国脱欧、中美贸易摩擦等事件的爆发，原本围绕在全球化上的金色光环已然消失，与之相反的逆全球化趋势则日趋明显。

当今世界面临着两种截然不同的全球化发展路径：中国主张建立人类命运共同体，在国际合作中坚持共商共建共享的原则；美国则继续坚持一家独大的制度构建原则，且正在向贸易保护主义的方向行进，与全球化渐行渐远。美国在十九世纪所保护的是处于上升期的新兴产业，而现在保护的却是处于滑坡期的落后产能。这种消极的保护主义从长期看只会阻碍美国经济结构优化，且与整个世界的利益背道而驰。

旧的全球治理体系引起广泛不满，总的原因是各国在历史、文化、现实国情等各方面的显著差异，以及国家利益至上和国内政治诉求优先（如减少失业、缩小收入差距、维护高水平社会福利）在全球化面前所展现出的刚性。因此，一个让人乐于选择的全球治理新制度体系有赖于中国的奋斗，中国奋斗的成功意味着在世界范围内良币驱逐劣币。中国的奋斗所要解决的问题是如何确立自由贸易与国家利益之间的平衡，合理的平衡点意味着中国应该承担起作为一个大国的责任。在美国正在放弃这一责任的情况下（如美国退出了防止全球气候变化的《巴黎协定》），中国更应该积极提供全球公共品，并且中国主导的全球化需时刻与资本主义国家主导的霸权主义全球化拉开距离，后者既不符合中华传统的天下观，从历史的教训看也是不可持续的。

文献来源：
汪毅霖."逆全球化"的历史与逻辑［J］.读书,2020（02）: 14-23.

A. Compare the pros and cons of globalization and list the key points.

B. According to the text, fill in each of the following blanks with an appropriate word or phrase.

1) _____ is the spread of products, technology, information, and jobs across national borders and cultures.

2) Globalization results from the removal of barriers between national _____ to encourage the flow of goods, services, capital, and labor.

3) Cultural globalization refers to the transmission of ideas, meanings, and values around the world in such a way as to extend and intensify _____.

4) One of the key aspects of the political globalization is the _____ importance of the nation-state and the _____ of other actors on the political scene.

5) The _____ organizations influence public policy across national boundaries, including humanitarian aid and developmental efforts.

6) Through the spirit of cooperation, humanity can use its strength of _____ to tackle big problems.

7) Over the next generation, the number of freelancers and self-employed individuals is expected to increase to _____ of the overall labor force.

8) The advanced economies of the world have the highest _____ costs, the highest _____ costs, and the highest _____ costs.

9) The threat of _____ is a threat that enforces specific employment behaviors in the advanced economies that reduce wages and benefits.

10) Globalization can put us on a path toward economic freedom, but this structure can also encourage the _____ to get wealthier at the expense of the _____.

C. Read the text and decide whether the following statements are True (T) or False (F).

1) The silk road cannot be regarded as an example of globalization because a number of nations are not involved.   (   )

2) The concept of globalization appears in the 21st century.   (   )

3) Product differentiation is one of the three key strategies by Coca-Cola to support the rapid growth and expansion across the globe.   (   )

4) The impact of globalization remains always positive for workers, cultures, and small businesses around the globe, in both developed and emerging nations.   (   )

5) The use of technologies allows businesses, such as large multinational corporations, to maintain customers, suppliers and even competitors on a world-wide basis.   (   )

6) The connection of financial markets is an important feature of globalization. However, it is limited only to the stock market.   (   )

7) Globalization gives us all an opportunity to live, work, and communicate in ways that bring all of us closer together.   (   )

8) Globalization makes goods and services cheaper and available to many people.   (   )

9) Few decades back if you have told people of developed countries to visit countries in Asia and Africa they would have said yes.   (   )

10) Even though there is a wave of populism and elitism growing around the world lately, the processes of globalization still encourage more cooperation than isolation. ( )

1) What are the driving forces of globalization?
_____
_____

2) What do you learn from Coca-Cola's journey to globalization?
_____
_____

3) Can you give some examples of globalization in your daily life?
_____
_____

4) In addition to the key aspects covered in the text, please find more aspects of globalization and discuss with your partner.
_____
_____

5) Do you think globalization has brought us more benefits or adverse effects? Please give your reasons.
_____
_____

Case Story

TCL Marks 40th Anniversary with Global Activities

TCL, a global leading intelligent technology company, is celebrating its 40th anniversary. The past four decades have witnessed TCL's extraordinary growth from a small cassette tape manufacturer into one of the world's leading consumer electronics players, covering 160 countries and regions.

To mark its 40th anniversary, the company is hosting a wide array of events for its employees, customers, partners and communities around the world, starting with notable advertisements in landmark cities in key markets including Dubai, Los Angeles, Paris, Sao Paulo and Sydney.

These five cities are located on continents where TCL has experienced continuous expansion.

Chairman and CEO of TCL Li Dongsheng remarked, "Over forty years, the three key driving forces of innovation, globalization and strategy have helped TCL to forge ahead."

40 Years of Innovation and Globalization

Thanks to its commitment to innovation over the years, TCL has shaped its core competences around a comprehensive global layout of its three main businesses: smart devices, semiconductor displays, and semiconductor photovoltaics and semiconductor materials.

Starting from the production of audiotapes, TCL has continuously improved and pushed the boundaries of possibilities for display and audio technology to provide consumers around the world with a smart and connected lifestyle fulfilled through a diversified product portfolio covering TVs, smartphones, audio and smart home products. In 2020, TCL ranked third in terms of market share by sales volume of its TVs in the global TV market and ranked second in the global LCD TV market.

TCL further expanded its business from smart devices to semiconductor areas, which strengthens its capabilities in the vertical integration of the industry chain. The establishment of TCL CSOT in 2009, now a world-leading panel supplier, and the acquisition of Zhonghuan Semiconductor in 2020 have enhanced TCL's strategic reserves in semiconductor displays, semiconductor photovoltaics and semiconductor materials. With this strategic move, TCL has grown into a leading high-tech industrial group.

Since it was founded, TCL has always been strategically focused on global markets. The company entered Vietnam in 1999, marking the first step in its international expansion. The acquisition of Thomson TV and Alcatel's mobile phone business in 2004 was also a significant milestone in TCL's globalization. In the following 22 years, through continuous transformations and adaptions, TCL has established 42 research and development (R&D) centers and 28 manufacturing bases around the world and operates in over 160 countries and regions. In the first half of 2021, over 52% of TCL group's revenue was contributed by its overseas markets. It has grown to become a leading international company with a truly global influence.

40 Years of Commitment to Communities

Besides its ongoing innovation and globalization, TCL brings happiness and excitement to consumers around the world through its ever-expanding sponsorship of leading international sporting and entertainment events and associations. To name a few, TCL has twice been an official partner of Copa America and is a long-term global partner of

FIBA. TCL also became the first company to own the naming rights for the world-famous TCL Chinese Theatre in Hollywood, California.

As a socially responsible corporation, TCL adheres to the concept of sustainable development of itself and the communities it serves. For example, showcasing its commitment to empowering women and girls worldwide, TCL became the Global Promotional Partner of FIBA's "Her World, Her Rules" program. In response to climate change, TCL is spearheading efforts to move towards green manufacturing processes throughout the entire production and operation process cycles assisted by digitalization. In recognition of its sincere efforts, TCL received a Silver Rating in the EcoVadis Business Sustainability Ratings this year.

Partnering with some of the leading global industry players, TCL will strive to co-build ecosystems based on its three core competences, spearhead innovation and support industrial upgrading.

Case Discussion

1) Please name a few international cities where TCL has expanded its business.

_____

_____

2) What are the specific strategies that TCL has applied when going global?

_____

_____

3) How does TCL enhance its brand impact around the globe?

_____

_____

Case Summary

在过去的40年里,TCL从一家小型盒式磁带制造商,发展成为覆盖160个国家和地区的全球领先消费电子产品制造商。TCL董事长兼首席执行官李东生指出,创新、全球化和战略三大关键驱动力引领TCL不断前进。TCL围绕其三大主要业务的全面全球布局塑造了其核心竞争力:智能设备、半导体显示器、半导体光伏和半导体材料。

TCL自成立以来,一直以全球市场为战略重点。TCL于1999年进入越南,标志着其国际扩张的第一步。2004年并购汤姆逊公司和阿尔卡特公司的手机业务也是TCL全球化的重要里程碑。在接下来的22年里,通过不断的转型和适应,TCL在全球建立了42个研发中心和28个制造基地,业务遍及160多个国家和地区。

2021上半年，TCL集团超过52%的收入来自海外市场。TCL已经成长为一家具有真正全球影响力的国际公司。未来，TCL将在全球范围内与同行业头部企业合作，致力于引领创新和产业升级。

Reading
Expansion
拓展阅读

Reading I

Globalization Is Close to Its "Holy Cow" Moment

Globalization has changed.

The globalization we knew and understood for most of the 20th century resembled more the globalization that emerged from the Industrial Revolution than it did the globalization we experience today. That globalization was based on the movement of goods across borders — measurable, limited by physical infrastructure, and parried by policies such as tariffs. But globalization today is about more than trading goods; it's about trading ideas and, increasingly, services. Our 20th-century paradigms of globalization are ill-equipped to understand what cross-border trade means for the present and near future. Globalization has changed, but the way we think about it hasn't.

The New Globalization

Globalization is arbitrage. What is arbitrage? It's taking advantage of a variation in price between two markets. When the relative prices of some goods are cheap in Mexico, that's what they sell to us, and when other goods are relatively cheap in the U.S., that's what we sell to them. A two-way, buy-low/sell-high deal — that's arbitrage, and trade theory is all about what the direction of arbitrage, and especially arbitrage in goods, is.

But goods aren't the only thing that can move across borders; there can also be an arbitrage in know-how, and there can be arbitrage in labor. The new globalization has to do with knowledge crossing borders. Future globalization will have to do with labor crossing borders — not people, but labor services.

Globalization as arbitrage is constrained by three costs: trade costs, or the cost of moving goods; communication costs, or the cost of moving ideas; and face-to-face costs, or the cost of moving people. In the pre-globalized world, production and consumption were geographically bundled. In particular, people were tied to the land since the land was what provided most people's living, and if they needed anything — candles, horseshoes, clothes, whatever — it had to be made within walking distance because it was too expensive and dangerous to move anything anywhere.

New globalization's impact is more sudden than old globalization's because it's driven by information and communication technology (ICT), not by tariff cuts or the construction of new ports and container ships. It's more individual because it's no longer felt across entire sectors and skill groups, but in individual stages of production. It's more unpredictable. It's hard to know which of these stages will disappear and why. And it's more uncontrollable because governments have very good policies for controlling people and goods crossing borders, but they don't have good policies for controlling firm-specific know-how crossing borders.

So there has been a generalized feeling in goods-producing sectors that no matter what job or skill set you have, you can't really be sure whether your job won't be next. There has been a sense of fragility, of vulnerability — an economic insecurity that's been generalized, and this has been going on for two decades.

The Future of Globalization

To date, the gains and pains of globalization and automation have been felt mostly by the manufacturing sector. In the future, the gains and pains will be felt by professional and service-sector jobs. That's because digital technology is going to lower the third constraint to globalization as arbitrage: the cost of moving people around, or facilitating face-to-face interaction.

Service jobs have been shielded from globalization because they require people to be face-to-face, or at least near each other. For most services, you can't put them into a container and ship them from China to New York. So global competition was deflected by the shield of high face-to-face costs.

Digital technology, however, is opening a pipeline for direct international wage competition. In other words, labor from countries such as Kenya, Nigeria, or the Philippines can come and work in G7 offices directly through telecommunications. There are a number of ideas and technologies that are making this increasingly feasible:

Telemigration

Many people work from home on a regular or semi-regular basis. Does it matter if they're working from home in Chicago or if they're working from home in Beijing? As remote work becomes more technologically and culturally mainstream, perhaps we won't be offshoring entire jobs, but rather the stages of production of white-collar jobs — specific tasks that can be done remotely for cheaper than they're done locally.

Machine translation

Many of us have become, or at least have the ability to be, multilingual, thanks to the computing power of our phones. An English speaker can sit down in a restaurant in France, Germany, China, Spain, and many other countries and order dinner using Siri as a translator. For more conversational applications, Skype Translator can provide real-time voice translation in eight languages.

Advanced telecommunication technologies

A final technology that's helping to close the distance between collaborators in different countries is "telepresence" — immersive videoconferencing environments that use high-resolution, life-size screens, dozens of speakers and microphones, and often tables that look the same on both sides, so a group in New York and a group in Mumbai, India, could have the feeling that they're almost in the same room. There are even telepresence robots, which make it possible for someone operating remotely to actually move around an office or other workspace and have a physical presence there. So far this hardware is pretty expensive, and therefore only used at the high end of industries such as consulting and banking — or, in the case of robots, medicine — but all it has to do is get cheaper, and it will change things.

Reaching Epiphany

Humans have brains that are built to think about things linearly — to understand motion in nature, to look at two points and calculate how long it would take to walk from one to the other. But technological growth is exponential. That mismatch gives rise to the cognitive pattern known as Amara's law, which states that we have a tendency to first overestimate and then underestimate the significance of new technologies. For instance, we landed on the moon, and people assumed the next step would be colonizing Mars. We've still never set foot on Mars, but in the meantime, we've put countless technologies into space that have changed the experience of life on earth.

There's a point at which the exponential path of technological growth crosses the straight line of human expectation, and it's the point at which the real power of this technology that we've alternately over- and underestimated fully dawns on us. I call it the "holy cow" moment. We haven't quite reached it yet with ICT and its meaning for globalization. When we do, it will not be the result of a single, sudden event.

Second Thoughts

For each of the following statements, choose one (or more than one) answer to fill in the blank.

1) New globalization's impact is more sudden than old globalization's because _____.

   A. it is driven by information and communication technology

   B. it is driven by tariff cuts or the construction of new ports and container ships

C. it is easier to make predictions

D. it is harder to control

2) The gains and pains of globalization will be felt by the professional and service-sector jobs, due to the development of _____.

A. tourism

B. digital technology

C. agriculture

D. social relations

Reading II

Global Leaders Require Global Intelligence

In recent years, researchers have begun to emphasize the importance of these three "new" intelligence: Emotional Intelligence, Digital Intelligence and Global Intelligence.

The concept of Global Intelligence (GQ) was first introduced to me at graduate school by none other than Bill George, the bestselling author of *Discover Your True North*. GQ is the intelligence needed to manage the world. As the world becomes more and more globalized, people, products, investment and technology will continue to cross national borders and cultures, making people and business more connected than ever before. GQ requires the same universal set of principles such as compassion and caring that we feel for our own family and community members.

Having a good GQ requires having the experience and the ability to have unique experiences dealing with different cultures, customs and languages, not to mention a general in-depth understanding of differences. Having a healthy GQ is key to being a great leader, especially in globalized and diverse markets. A lot of failures derive from leaders lacking the six elements that make for a high GQ.

These six elements are as follows:
- Adaptability
- Awareness
- Curiosity
- Alignment
- Collaboration
- Empathy

Adaptability

Adaptability in GQ is understanding the world and predicting the changes that are bound to happen in the coming years. Leaders should be able to adapt to the ever-changing global context quickly and be prepared to change tactics overnight to accommodate any changes necessary to stay competitive in today's globalized market place.

Awareness

Have a strong sense of awareness in GQ is the ability to understand yourself and the world around you. This includes understanding your strengths, weaknesses and prejudices to predict how you're going to react to significant cultural differences in the new economy.

Curiosity

The ability to be curious when it comes to the cultures and differences you encounter along the way is key in developing a GQ. We're talking about personal passion and an insatiable desire to learn more about other cultures. It's important to remain humble and acknowledge that there are different cultural norms and ways of doing things. In Denmark, we've chosen to incorporate symbolic policies like forcing people to shake hands when receiving their citizenship. That's supposedly how "we" show one another respect. I disagree. We display one another respect by embracing the fact that some people would instead prefer to bow, hug, kiss your cheek or even fist pump.

Alignment

One of the challenges of globalization will be ensuring that people continue in the same direction in spite of their differences. Norms and customs differ from one country to the next and having the ability to work and get everyone on the same page and in the right direction is what makes for great leadership.

Collaboration

In a global context, the ability to build horizontal networks across geographical borders and bring people together for a cause will be paramount.

Empathy

Empathy is the ability to walk a mile in someone else's shoes. This requires humility and an ability to engage with people from different cultures on a personal level. In the new economy, there will be no room for judgment. Without empathy, you will never achieve remarkable results. Even people in positions traditionally characterized by their introverted and internally oriented nature are now required to interact with others, so it's essential that we all work toward improving our abilities to connect with others. Without it, we won't be able to inspire trust which is a key element to securing a solid professional life.

Do you know why people don't hire you, why your customers don't buy your products, or why voters don't vote for your party? If you want to find out why, you need to look beyond your skill set, the price of the product or your resume and focus on whether or not people like you. Do you know what kind of emotions you inspire in other people?

Second Thoughts

1) What is GQ? Can you define GQ in your own words?

_____

_____

2) Think about the questions in the last paragraph, and write down your ideas.

_____

_____

Cultural Context in International Management

CHAPTER 2

国际管理中的文化语境

本章概要

本章主要介绍跨文化管理、文化多样性的作用,以及霍夫斯泰德的文化维度理论、特朗皮纳斯的七维文化架构理论等。

学习指南

  每个文化群体对于价值观、信念、态度和行为都有不同的看法。人类学和跨文化交流领域的主要思想家,例如特朗皮纳斯和吉尔特·霍夫斯泰德,已经明确指出反映在不同文化中的众多价值,例如身份、交流、力量、不确定性、时间的使用、合作和竞争等。文化价值观的差异将体现在我们在工作场所中如何进行互动。这也是跨文化管理中一个值得重点考虑的问题。

  通过本章学习,希望大家能够实现以下目标:

(1)基本目标(Text-based Goals)

- 掌握本章涉及话题的基本专业词汇,如跨文化管理、国际经济、文化敏感、文化适应性等;
- 掌握本章的主要理论,即霍夫斯泰德的文化维度理论以及特朗皮纳斯的七维文化架构理论。

(2)拓展目标(Extended Goals)

- 思考本章的文化理论,文化还可以包括哪些不同的维度?
- 通过学习背景知识、拓展阅读、案例分析进一步了解文化多样性以及跨文化管理的意义。

> Intercultural dialogue is the best guarantee of a more peaceful, just and sustainable world. 跨文化交流是世界和平、公正、可持续发展的最佳保障。
>
> —Robert Alan Aurthur(罗伯特·艾伦·亚瑟)

市场日益全球化,对美国经济以及希望在国外开展业务的公司都具有巨大的影响。屡获殊荣的教育家和作家 Elizabeth A. Tuleja 博士在圣母大学门多萨商学院教授跨文化管理和跨文化交流课。本文作者与 Tuleja 谈论全球经济中美国企业和企业领导者面临的一些挑战,以及跨文化管理和文化多样性的作用。

The increasing globalization of the marketplace carries immense implications for the U.S. economy and for companies hoping to do business abroad. In 2018, exports of U.S. goods and services were at $2.2 trillion and supported almost 11 million jobs, according to the International Trade Administration and the U.S. Census.

With manufacturing operations and supply chains spanning national borders, intercultural skills and knowledge are assuming a growing importance for many firms.

Award-winning educator and author Elizabeth A. Tuleja, PhD, teaches Intercultural Management and Intercultural Communication courses for the online and campus-based MBA and Executive MBA programs at the University of Notre Dame's Mendoza College of Business. Tuleja also is a fellow at Notre Dame's Kellogg Institute for International Studies and its Institute for Asia and Asian Studies.

As a **consultant**, Tuleja has shared her expertise in management communication with the U.S. Marine Corps, Merrill Lynch, HSBC, Bank of America and China Development Bank, among other clients. She previously taught at The Chinese University of Hong Kong and The Wharton School at the University of Pennsylvania, where she earned her master's and **doctorate** degrees.

Tuleja is the author of *Intercultural Communication for Business* and her research has focused on global leadership and intercultural communication. Her *Global Business Leader* website offers guidance to professionals seeking to understand the complexities of global communication.

We spoke with Tuleja recently about some of the challenges facing U.S. businesses and corporate leaders in a global economy, and about the role of intercultural management and cultural diversity.

WHAT DO YOU FIND TO BE THE MOST INTERESTING PART OF INTERCULTURAL MANAGEMENT?

The most interesting part of intercultural management is learning something new each day. When interacting with people from other cultures there is always something to learn, so there is an ongoing learning challenge. Even if you have lived in another culture for years, you discover

Word Study

consultant /kən'sʌltənt/
  n. 顾问,咨询师
doctorate /'dɒktərɪt/
  n. 博士学位

您认为跨文化管理中最有趣的部分是什么?

跨文化管理中最有趣的部分是每天学习新知识。与来自

new things every day. This learning process keeps us on our toes and there are always new possibilities around every corner.

There is a Chinese proverb that says, "Observers can see the chess game more clearly than the players." Chinese proverbs are profound because their simplicity is rooted in wisdom that is based on observation of familiar circumstances and situations. When I talk with business people about intercultural issues in management, it's important to understand that we don't really see our culture unless we bump up against the behavior, language, situations, etc., of another culture. Then we start to notice differences. We naturally assume that everyone else thinks the same way that we do, communicates the same way that we do and behaves the same way that we do. We are too busy being engaged in our "game" to have a proper perspective.

Social psychologists tell us that it's a natural process of **socialization** for people to see things based upon their own experiences and world views — that is **ethnocentrism**. However, to be able to engage socially on a deeper level, it is necessary for us to develop **ethnorelativism**, which opens our eyes to other perspectives. It's our ability to view the values and behaviors of others as cultural and not simply universal (i.e., if we behave a certain way, others will also). This doesn't mean losing one's core values; rather it is a way to step outside of one's vantage point and try to see things from someone else's perspective.

It's common for Europeans to know several languages and have experience with different cultures. Does this place U.S. businesses and professionals, who are frequently not multilingual or multicultural, at a disadvantage in a global economy? If so, how can they overcome it?

Europeans have an advantage because the cultural norm is that they grow up needing to speak several languages due to their geographical **proximity** to other countries. With that comes the added advantage of experiencing the norms of other cultures on a daily basis. But simply being in contact with or experiencing other cultures does not necessarily mean a person will be culturally sensitive. Humans naturally default to ethnocentrism (the attitude that one's group is superior) and we need to be reminded that flexibility, patience and adaptability are necessary.

For example, recent research in the intercultural field regarding study abroad has shown that it is not the length of time spent abroad, the study of a language or even living with a host family that determines whether a person will become culturally sensitive and adaptable. Rather, it is the constant and conscious reflection on what is happening and why it is happening that helps a person become interculturally competent.

As business professionals, we can take a strong lesson from this in that whether we have had a lot of experience working across cultures, a little or none, all of us need to be aware that cultural differences exist. We

其他文化的人互动时，总是需要学习一些东西，因此，学习方面的挑战一直存在。即使你已经在另一种文化中生活了多年，你每天仍会发现新事物。这种学习过程使我们保持警觉，生活中处处都有新的可能性。在跨文化交流中，要相互理解，留意不同文化的差异。

Word Study

socialization
/ˌsəʊʃəlaɪ'zeɪʃən/
n. 社会化
ethnocentrism
/eθnəʊ'sentrɪzəm/
n. 民族中心主义
ethnorelativism
/eθnəʊ'relətɪˌvɪzəm/
n. 民族相对主义
proximity
/prɒk'sɪməti/ n. (空间)接近,邻近

expertise /ˌekspəˈtiːz/
n. 专门知识，专门
技术

merger /ˈmɜːdʒə/ *n.*
合并，并购

acquisition /ˌækwɪˈzɪʃən/
n. 收购

assignment /əˈsaɪnmənt/
n. （分派的）工作，
任务

accountant /əˈkaʊntənt/
n. 会计

need to develop a deeper understanding of the values, beliefs, attitudes and behaviors of those with whom we work and/or live, and then do something about it. By that I mean self-monitoring and examining our behaviors and interactions by reflecting on what went well and what didn't go well. We also need to be open and ask someone from that particular cultural background how they might have interpreted the interaction, all the while realizing that culture is fluid and, even though we can make generalizations about certain aspects of any given culture, all people are different to some extent.

We need to remain open and flexible versus rigid and fixed. When we do this, coupled with our growing knowledge of other cultures, we can develop a repertoire of responses for any situation in which we find ourselves.

WHAT DO YOU CONSIDER TO BE THE BIGGEST MISTAKE U.S. BUSINESSES MAKE WHEN ENGAGING IN INTERCULTURAL COMMUNICATION?

您认为美国企业在进
行跨文化交流时最大
的错误是什么？

在跨文化交流中
最大的错误是认为专
业领域的知识就足
以成功开展跨文化
业务了。

乍一看，全球领
导者指的是能够熟
练地进行并购、能轻
松应对全球供应链
管理的复杂情况，或
能理解国际会计惯
例的众多细节的人。
但是，仅具备职能性
业务技能是无法成
功应对全球业务环
境的。

另一个常见的
误解是，认为在自己
文化中运用自如的
领导才能可以自然
而然地转移并应用
于另一种文化背景。

The biggest mistake is thinking that your area of **expertise** is enough to be successful in doing business across cultures.

At first glance, the notion of a global leader usually denotes someone who is able to deftly perform a **merger** and **acquisition**, or easily navigate the intricacies of global supply chain management or comprehend the myriad details of international accounting practices. However, it is simply not enough to possess the functional business skills in order to navigate successfully in the global business environment.

Another common misconception is that successful leadership skills practiced in one's own culture are naturally transferable when applied in another cultural setting. We learn of many cross-border deals and negotiations that fall flat simply because not enough due diligence has been performed or key players are unable to adapt readily to the challenges found in cross-cultural relations — even though such high performers may have performed well with their previous **assignment**. Research into cultural intelligence (CQ) by Christopher Earley and Soon Ang has shown that there are many differences involved in the transfer of such leadership capabilities because what may be meaningful and appropriate in one context could be insulting and improper in another based upon the cultural norms for living.

For example, let's say you are an **accountant** and have risen through the ranks within your organization. Because of your expertise, you are selected to go to Chile to work on a partnership with another company. You figured that you would easily adjust to Chilean culture because you enjoy the Latin culture overall — you had studied Spanish in high school, spent a semester in Seville, Spain, during college and now enjoy vacationing in

Mexico with your family. However, once you get to Chile and have to set up your household, get your family settled and learn to adapt daily to another way of thinking and behaving as you manage a team of junior accountants, you realize that what you signed up for was not what you expected. Your expectations for efficiency, consistency and accuracy are not the same as your employees or colleagues. It becomes harder and harder to accomplish the goals of the **joint venture** because of the day-to-day struggles to communicate and fit in with your counterparts.

Global leaders today are required to readily adapt to changes and deal with complexities within interpersonal relationships in order to flourish in an environment of **ambiguity**. Global leadership means that a person possesses intercultural competence, also known as CQ, or cultural intelligence. Cultural intelligence is the ability to both recognize and understand the beliefs, values, attitudes and behaviors of others, and then be able to apply that knowledge by adapting your behavior accordingly.

This is what makes a business person successful when working across borders or with people in their offices who hold different world views.

DO DIFFERING CULTURAL VIEWS ABOUT COMPETITION PLAY A ROLE IN AN INCREASINGLY GLOBAL MARKETPLACE?

Yes, differing cultural views about competition or any other cultural value will affect how we interact in today's side-by-side global marketplace.

Every culture group has different views about values, beliefs, attitudes and behaviors. Key thinkers in the field of **anthropology** and intercultural communication, such as Edward T. Hall and Geert Hofstede, have identified numerous values that are reflected across cultures, such as identity, communication, power, uncertainty, use of time, cooperation and competition. Differences in cultural values will manifest themselves in how we interact in the workplace. So, whenever you get a group of diverse people working with each other, you will find that there are many challenges that you will encounter — people simply look at the world in fundamentally different ways.

Let's look at the cultural values of competition and cooperation. Competition can be defined as being motivated by the opportunities to achieve and exceed goal expectations, and value is placed on material achievement and assertiveness. Cooperation is based on trust and **collaboration** with an emphasis placed on long-term relationships, and value is placed on quality of life and interdependence.

So, let's say your group of Executive MBA students from the United States is working with a global team as part of their international **immersion** project. On your team are members from the United Kingdom, Canada, France, India and China. You have your first meeting and get right down to business, discussing the project, assigning roles and

Word Study

joint venture 合资企业
ambiguity /æmbɪ'ɡjuːɪti/
　n. 模棱两可
anthropology
　/ˌænθrə'pɒlədʒi/ n.
　人类学
collaboration
　/kəˌlæbə'reɪʃən/ n.
　合作
immersion /ɪ'mɜːʃən/
　n. 沉浸,浸入

在竞争日益激烈的全球市场中,关于竞争的不同文化见解是否会发挥作用?

关于竞争或任何其他文化价值的不同文化观点都将影响我们在当今全球市场中的互动方式。

每个文化群体对于价值观、信念、态度和行为都有不同的看法。人类学和跨文化交流领域的主要思想家,例如爱德华·T·霍尔、吉尔特·霍夫斯泰德,已经明确指出在不同文化中的众多价值,例如身份、交流、力量、不确定性、时间的使用、合作和竞争。

defer /dɪˈfɜː/ v. 服从，听
从，遵从

tact /tækt/ n. (处事等)
老练，得体

hypothesis /haɪˈpɒθəsɪs/
n. 假设

heuristic /hjʊəˈrɪstɪk/
adj. (教学或教育)
启发式的

responsibilities, as well as constructing a timeline for deliverables. After all, as U.S. Americans, you don't want to waste time. You notice halfway through your meeting that your Indian classmates are listening to the discussion but not participating in the conversation and you get frustrated.

What happened here? In cooperative cultures, such as in India, people will generally sit back, listen and observe the dynamics of the group, taking in the context of the situation. There is a need to learn about the people of the group and you do this by observing — it would be rude to cut in and interrupt. It would be equally rude to rush to any decision-making during your very first meeting, which should be reserved for getting to know each other. Anything that happens must be based upon the developing relationship and it should be done together. To rush in and take over would be disastrous to the overall goal of the group project — the goal is to cooperate and not compete.

Do all Indian people interact like this when meeting for the first time? Of course not. We talk about these cultural values in general because we have to take into account that not all U.S. Americans would jump to interact with strong personalities, nor would all Indians **defer** to the other people in the group as they begin to form relationships through politeness and **tact**.

When we talk about cultures we often think in terms of a national culture, for example, "The French do this" and "The Germans do that." As we try to make sense out of the differences between these national cultures, we are often drawn to generalizations in order to categorize unfamiliar information — cognitive psychologists tell us that this is called creating a "mental model" or "schema" (representation of the surrounding world or our experiences). Another interculturalist, Milton Bennett, explains that using generalizations wisely can be a good way for global managers to make sense of the complexities that often confuse and confound us. However, generalizations must be based upon combining cultural knowledge with openness to individual differences.

Here's why: while in every culture there are dominant cultural patterns that can generally describe the standard values, practices and behaviors of any given group of people, there are also many sub- and co-cultures within that dominant culture. These could be ethnic, religious and social-class influences, among others. So, you use generalizations as a **hypothesis** to be tested and observed. Danielle Medina Walker, creator of the Cultural Orientations Model (COM) and author of the book *Doing Business Internationally: The Guide to Cross-Cultural Success*, says that generalizations are **heuristic** statements, subject to review and change about what is expected, rewarded and reinforced in any given social environment.

Knowing some of these cultural values — and how people from

different national cultures, in general, might approach work situations based upon their norms for interaction and behavior — can help you to understand what is happening without passing judgment. Otherwise, both parties would be frustrated with each other as they wondered why one was being overly **assertive** and the other passive.

Word Study

assertive /əˈsɜːtɪv/ *adj.* 坚定自信的

Key Terms
专业术语

intercultural management 跨文化管理
global leadership 全球领导力
core values 核心价值观
geographical proximity 地理邻近
cultural values 文化价值观

intercultural communication 跨文化交流
cultural diversity 文化多样性
cultural norm 文化规范
cultural intelligence (CQ) 文化智商
cultural patterns 文化模式

Information Link
知识链接

跨文化冲突在国际企业管理中的表现

跨文化冲突表现在国际企业管理的各个方面,其中某些特定的管理职能对文化更加敏感些,主要表现在管理理念、员工激励、协调组织、领导职权和人力资源决策等方面。

在管理理念方面,根植于不同的国家社会文化,受到地域文化的影响,各国企业的管理理念有较大差异。中国及东南亚企业的管理中,带有中国传统古典哲学思辨和思想启蒙色彩的儒家、道家、法家等学说已经深深地嵌入属于东方文化体系的企业道德、企业哲学与企业精神体系中,形成独创的管理理念,而西方的管理理念的形成则是随着管理理论的发展步伐,更多地从管理大师们的管理思想中汲取营养。因此,西方企业管理理念中更多地渗透着科学管理与行为管理的思想精髓。这些差异在合资企业推行企业文化、制定企业战略过程中形成了较大的冲突。

在员工激励方面,由于文化背景、理念的不同,激励可能会表现为各种不同方式。比如,在美国文化中,人们对工作的态度多是积极热情的,而在墨西哥文化中,人们多认为工作是为了维持所期望的生活水平而不得不采取的一种谋生手段。相应地,文化不同的国家对员工激励方面的态度和政策也不同。

在协调组织方面,文化背景不同可能会导致组织协调方式选择的不同。如在日本的企业中,组织协调可能会采用"和风细雨"的商谈式方法,而在美国企业中可能会采用严格的制度管理与约束方法。

在领导职权方面,西方管理中往往对企业部门及负责人有较为严格、明确的职责、职权、职务解析,并按照科学管理的原则,遵循一系列授权规则使企业规范运行,形成有序、配套、系统的各职级行使原则。而在东方文化体系中,以人为本的理性追求、重视情感联系的信誉氛围、崇尚礼遇礼节的风尚,可形成具有自身特点的领导职权分配与运用方式。

在人力资源管理方面,在东方文化体系背景中,往往遵循"以人为本、以德为先、人为为人"的原则,而在西方文化体系中,更多主张奉行一系列严格、科学的人事管理制度。

文献来源:
李艳宏,刘帆.国际企业的跨文化冲突与管理〔J〕.西安石油学院学报2001(03):41-44.

Workbook
练一练

A. How to understand "The biggest mistake is thinking that your area of expertise is enough to be successful in doing business across cultures"?

_____

_____

_____

B. According to the text, fill in each of the following blanks with an appropriate word or phrase.

1) There is a Chinese proverb that says, "_____ can see the chess game more clearly than the _____".

2) Europeans have an advantage because the _____ is that they grow up needing to speak several languages due to their geographical proximity to other countries.

3) As business professionals, we need to be aware that _____ exist.

4) Global leaders today are required to readily adapt to _____ and deal with _____ within interpersonal relationships in order to flourish in an environment of ambiguity.

5) Edward T. Hall and Geert Hofstede, have identified numerous _____ that are reflected across cultures.

6) Competition can be defined as being motivated by the opportunities to achieve and exceed _____.

7) Cooperation is based on trust and _____ with an emphasis placed on long-term relationships, and value is placed on quality of life and _____.

8) In cooperative cultures, to rush in and take over would be _____ to the overall goal of the group project — the goal is to cooperate and not compete.

9) Using _____ wisely can be a good way for global managers to make sense of the complexities that often confuse and confound us.

10) While in every culture there are dominant _____ that can generally describe the standard values, practices and behaviors of any given group of people, there are also many sub- and co-cultures within that dominant culture.

C. Read the text and decide whether the following statements are True (T) or False (F).

1) In 2018, exports of U.S. goods and services were at $2.2 trillion and supported almost 11 million jobs, according to the International Trade Administration and the U.S. Census. ( )

2) Tuleja is the author of *Intercultural Communication for Business* and her research has focused on global trade. ( )

3) The most interesting part of intercultural management is learning something new each day. When interacting with people from other cultures there is always something to learn. ( )

4) Social psychologists stated that it's a natural process of socialization for people to see things based upon their own experiences and world views — that is ethnocentrism. ( )

5) Simply being in contact with or experiencing other cultures will make a person culturally sensitive. ( )

6) It is the constant and conscious reflection on what is happening and why it is happening that helps a person become interculturally competent. ( )

7) We need to remain open and flexible versus rigid and fixed, to develop a repertoire of responses for any situation in which we find ourselves. ( )

8) The biggest mistake U.S. businesses make when engaging in intercultural communication is thinking that successful leadership skills in one's own culture can be applied natually in another. ( )

9) Elizabeth A. Tuleja is an educator, author and politician. ( )

10) Every culture group has different views about values, beliefs, attitudes and behaviors. ( )

Discussion
讨论

1) What is the most interesting part of intercultural management according to the text?

_____

_____

2) What is the determining factor for cultural sensitiveness and adaptability?

_____

_____

3) Are there any other factors to determine one's cultural adaptability?

_____

_____

4) What are the common misconceptions when engaging in intercultural communication according to the text?

_____

_____

Case Story

Why Learning About Intercultural Management Is Important

Today's business environment is increasingly diverse. Managers in multinational companies work across continents and time zones on global projects, connecting with colleagues spreading out across the world.

Management consulting firm The Boston Consulting Group, for example, has 90 offices in 50 countries. It combines its global focus with efforts to increase diversity within the workplace — BCG has set up advocacy groups like Women@BCG, Pride@BCG and Diversity@BCG.

Companies have realized that diversity is not just a moral consideration; it makes business sense too. McKinsey research has found that diversity is clearly correlated with profitability.

For Thomas Allanic, director of the Master in Management at ESCP Europe — a leading proponent of Intercultural Management — knowing how to manage cultural diversity has become a strategic advantage. To be successful, he says businesspeople "need an understanding of how cultural diversities impact the structure and operation of organizations."

At the same time, there's something of a skills gap when it comes to managing these diverse teams. In its 2018 Skills Gap Survey, the *Financial Times* lists "the ability to influence" and soft skills like teamwork among the most important and difficult-to-recruit skills for employers today.

Employers want to hire business school graduates who can work with and lead people from diverse international backgrounds. Above all, they're looking for graduates skilled and experienced in intercultural management.

What Is Intercultural Management?

More than just awareness, intercultural management is an understanding and respect of other cultures within an international context. In practice, it means cultural differences being acknowledged and managed openly, rather than ignored.

Culture shapes management practices. In the United States, for example, the approach to work is very practical and task-orientated, where niceties can be left out in email communication among colleagues for the sake of time-saving efficiency.

In China, by contrast, silence is an important part of discussion, indicating good listening and contemplation, and not seen as something needing to be filled. A focus on Guanxi — developing personal as well as professional connections with colleagues and partners — is often found in business in China.

Intercultural management is about opening the conversation around the nuances of different cultural approaches in business, so managers are aware of — and can respond to — these differences in attitude and behavior.

"Intercultural managers are not only sensitive to the differences; they know how to work towards adjusting behaviors to maximize results", Thomas explains.

Why Is Intercultural Management Important?

Intercultural management is important because companies today work across countries and cultures. Few organizations can work solely within their own cultural context. With the internet, even small startups can connect with customers or suppliers thousands of miles away.

To understand intercultural management, Thomas continues, people need to be "open-minded and adaptable to new situations and people from different countries and curious to learn about how different cultures communicate, live, and work together."

Lorenzo Saudino is a current student on the Master in Management at ESCP Europe. He's half Iranian, half Italian, and he's lived in Morocco, Italy, Iran, and Nigeria. He speaks four languages fluently and is currently learning French while he studies at ESCP Europe's Paris campus. The school has campuses in Paris, Berlin, London, Madrid, Turin, and Warsaw.

For Lorenzo, intercultural management is about overcoming cultural preconceptions. "Being biased in decision-making is one of the biggest threats to being a good manager", Lorenzo asserts.

"You need to broaden your mind through multicultural immersion so that you have an objective outlook which doesn't favor your cultural approach over another."

Based in Berlin, professor Marion Festing leads ESCP Europe's Chair in intercultural management and is head of the excellence center devoted to it. Intercultural management is also taught at ESCP Europe through the newly-developed business game "Moving Tomorrow — An Intercultural Journey". Created by Marion, it enables students to deepen their intercultural understanding by playing along with an interactive story of a simulated company.

Lorenzo has found such experiences at ESCP Europe useful as he targets a career in consulting after his degree. Master's students at the school also get the opportunity to live and learn in up to four different countries during the two or three-year program, with Europe offering maximum cultural diversity at minimal geographical distances.

In the future, intercultural management will only become more important as students explore a variety of career paths. Nearly 50% of ESCP Europe Master in Management students develop their career outside their home country.

For Lorenzo, it's the diverse community environment at the school that means students can practice intercultural management throughout their degree.

"There is a union between students, faculty and alumni across the European campuses", Lorenzo explains, "and a sense of ownership concerning what we are a part of, and the kind of intercultural business we want to support."

Case Discussion

1) Why is intercultural management so important for many international companies?

_____

_____

2) What can students do to improve their intercultural consciousness and ability?

_____

_____

3) According to what Thomas Allanic said, how can intercultural managers do to maximize results?

_____

_____

Case Summary

当今的商业环境越来越多样化。跨国公司的经理在全球项目中跨大洲和时区工作,并与分布在世界各地的同事保持联系。

管理咨询公司波士顿咨询集团(Boston Consulting Group)在50个国家/地区设有90个办事处。它结合了全球关注点和努力提高工作场所内的多样性,成立了多个倡导小组,例如Women@BCG、Pride@BCG和Diversity@BCG。

公司已经意识到多样性不仅仅是道德上的考虑,它同时也具有商业意义。麦肯锡的研究发现,多样性与获利能力高度相关。

欧洲管理学院管理学硕士课程的主管Thomas Allanic是跨文化管理的主要支持者，他认为知道如何管理文化多样性已成为一项战略优势。他说，要取得成功，商人"需要了解文化多样性如何影响组织的结构和运作。"他对跨文化管理的概念及其重要性做了详细解释。

有机构致力于跨文化管理研究，并开发出相关的游戏，比如商业游戏"Moving Tomorrow — An Intercultural Journey"。

一些学生来自多元文化背景，他们通过在校学习、课外实践学习跨文化管理，更趋向于寻找国外的工作。

Reading I

Geert Hofstede's Cultural Dimensions Theory

Professor Geert Hofstede developed the Cultural Dimensions Theory through his studies of how the values of a workplace can be influenced by culture. Under Hofstede's definition, culture is considered to be the collective programming of the mind, which allows each member of a group or category of people to be distinguished from one another.

Under this theory, there are six dimensions of national culture that have been identified. Here is a look at those six dimensions and what it means for the modern workplace.

Power Distance

This cultural dimension is an expression of how people without power in a society accept and even expect unequal distribution. How does a society handle inequality when it is discovered amongst its people? When there is a large amount of this dimension within a society that has a hierarchy, then people accept their place and role within that society without complaint.

If there is a low amount of this dimension within a society, then people will work to create an equalization of power amongst all members of that society. They will demand that any inequality discovered be either rectified or justified.

Individualism

This cultural dimension requires individuals to take care of themselves and their families. It creates a close-knit network of similarly-minded individuals who are accomplishing tasks in a similar (or opposite) way so that everyone can enjoy a better standard of life. When there are high levels of this dimension, then people work hard for themselves.

When there are low levels of individualism within a society, then collectivism begins to take shape. The framework in society becomes a need for an individual to be taken care of by family and friends. This is done in exchange for loyalty to the collective. Instead of "me", society focuses on "we".

Masculinity

This cultural dimension looks at the preference a society has for certain achievements that are generally associated with me. This may include heroism, assertiveness, and other forms of achievement. It is a measurement of success. With high levels of masculinity, these traits will be emphasized and treasured, creating a competitive way of life.

With low levels of masculinity, there is more of a preference toward modesty and cooperation. The society is more orientated toward consensus results and caring for those who may need some level of assistance.

Uncertainty Avoidance

This cultural dimension focuses on how often and how much the members of a society become uncomfortable with events that are strange, uncertain, or ambiguous. If there are high levels of this dimension operating within a society, then there will be rigid behavioral codes that will be enforced and anyone "thinking outside of the box" will be harshly criticized.

When there are low levels of this dimension in a society, then the goal is often to control the future instead of letting it happen. Attitudes are more relaxed toward creative ideas because the end that is achieved is more important than the processes that were used to reach the end of the journey.

Long Term Orientation

This cultural dimension is a reflection of how a society looks at the past. Do they use the lessons learned from before to make challenges in the present easier? Are there future plans being initiated from current situations? Or is the society ignoring the past completely?

When a society focuses on this dimension at a high level, it will typically take an approach that can only be described as pragmatic. They will encourage greater education and learning opportunities while reducing spending to create a better future.

With low levels of this dimension present, any change to society is considered to be suspicious. The people who complete tasks based on traditions and previous best practices are often celebrated.

Indulgence

This cultural dimension looks at how often the members of a society are able to purchase or receive items that go beyond their basic needs. It is a reflection of how an individual may pursue their personal enjoyment of life and be able to have fun. With societies that have a high indulgence level, spending often reflects the individual's wants and virtually anything within reason is allowed.

When there is a low level of this dimension in a society, then indulgence is often regulated by policies, procedures, or even laws. The goal is to suppress the desire to find individual gratification and it will often be enforced through the creation and enforcement of very strict norms within the society.

In Conclusion

Geert Hofstede's Cultural Dimensions Theory offers us a glimpse at how we can expect a group of individuals to behave within a society of any size and scope. Whether it's at work, in a community, or even on a national level, these six dimensions help to define who we are and who we will plan to be.

Second Thoughts

For each of the following statements, choose one (or more than one) answer to fill in the blank.

1) _____ doesn't belong to the six dimensions of culture.
   A. Personal thought
   B. Long term orientation
   C. Individualism
   D. Masculinity
2) People with low levels of masculinity tend to be _____.
   A. modest
   B. confident
   C. selfish
   D. outgoing

Reading II

Trompenaars Cultural Dimensions — The 7 Dimensions of Culture

Trompenaars Cultural Dimensions Model, also known as The 7 Dimensions of Culture, can help you to work more effectively with people from different cultures.

Business is becoming ever more global, and as a result of this, teams are becoming more diverse. Thus, we are likely to need to work with people from other countries and cultures.

Most of the time things will go well when you work with people from other cultures. But when things don't, and misunderstandings arise, Trompenaars Cultural Dimensions Model can help.

The model was first described in the book, *Riding the Waves of Culture: Understanding Diversity in Global Business*, written by Fons Trompenaars and Charles Hampden-Turner in 1993. To create the model, they surveyed over 40,000 managers from 40 countries.

The book won't help you to learn cultural etiquette. If that is what you're looking for then you need a different book. The real advantage of this book and the model is that it allows you to step outside of your own biases and stereotypes. In doing so you can see how another culture might approach a problem. This can then prompt you with ideas to resolve any misunderstanding.

The 7 Dimensions of Culture Model (Trompenaars Cultural Dimensions Model) works by differentiating cultures based on their preferences in the following 7 dimensions:

1. Universalism vs. particularism.
2. Individualism vs. communitarianism.
3. Neutral vs. affective.
4. Specific vs. diffuse.
5. Achievement vs. ascription.
6. Sequential time vs. synchronous time.
7. Internal direction vs. external direction.

Now let's examine each of Trompenaars Cultural Dimensions in turn.

1. Universalism vs. Particularism

This dimension can be summarized by asking what matters more, rules or relationships?

Cultures based on universalism try to treat all cases the same, even if they involve friends or loved ones. The focus is more on the rules than on the relationship. Universalist cultures include Canada, the U.S., the U.K., and Australia.

Cultures based on particularism will find relationships more important than rules. You can bend the rules for family members, close friends, or important people. Each case has to be examined in light of its special merits. Particularist cultures include Latin America, Korea, China, and Russia.

Tips for working with universalist cultures:
Keep your promises.
Be consistent.
Explain the logic behind why you have made a certain decision.

Tips for working with particularist cultures:
Invest in building relationships so you can understand the particular needs of others.
Respect these needs as much as possible in your decision making.
Call out specific important rules that must be followed.

2. Individualism vs. Communitarianism

This dimension can be summarized by asking "Do we work as a team or as individuals?" Do people desire recognition for their individual achievements, or do they want to be part of a group?

Individualistic cultures believe that your outcomes in life are the result of your choices. In these cultures, decision makers make decisions and they don't need to consult to do so. Thus, decision makers can make decisions at speed. It is your responsibility to look after your happiness and fulfillment. Individualistic cultures include Canada, the U.S., the U.K., and Australia.

Cultures based on communitarianism believe your quality of life is better when we help each other. Thus, these cultures organize themselves around groups. There is a strong sense of loyalty within the group. As a result of this group tendency, decision making is slower as everyone gives input. Job turnover will be lower due to high group loyalty. The group gets rewarded for high performance, not the individual. Communitarian cultures include Japan, much of Africa, and Latin American countries.

Tips for working with individualistic cultures:
Reward and issue praise based on a person's individual performance.
Encourage people to use their own initiative.
Align the individual's need with those of the organization.

Tips for working with communitarian cultures:
Reward the group for high performance.
Praise the group in public, but praise individuals for their contribution in private.
Include the whole team in decision making.

3. Neutral vs. Affective

This dimension can be summarized by asking "Do we show our emotions?"

In a neutral culture, people tend not to share their emotions. Emotions are of course felt by the individual, but they are kept in check and controlled. Observing these people you would consider them cool and rational. Neutral cultures include Germany, the Netherlands, and the U.K.

In an affective culture, people tend to share their emotions, even in the workplace. In an affective culture, it considered normal that people share their emotions. Examples of affective cultures include Italy, Spain, and Latin America.

Tips for working with neutral cultures:
Keep your emotions, both what you say and what your face says, in check.
Remember that people are less likely to express their true emotions. So try to read between the lines of what people are telling you.
After initial chit-chat, stay on topic in meetings.

Tips for working with affective cultures:
Use emotion to communicate what you want and your goals.

Share how you feel to strengthen your workplace relationships.

Learn some techniques to diffuse situations where emotions run high.

4. Specific vs. Diffuse

This dimension of Trompenaars Cultural Dimensions Model can be summarized by asking how separate our personal and professional life is.

In a specific culture, people tend to keep their personal and work life separate. These cultures don't see an overlap between the two spheres. These cultures tend to be schedule focussed and direct and to the point in their communications. They focus more on the goal than the relationship. Examples of specific cultures include Germany, the U.S., the U.K., and the Netherlands.

In a diffusive culture, people tend to see their personal and work life as interconnected. These cultures believe that objectives can be better achieved when relationships are strong. As such, in these cultures work colleagues socialize with each other outside of work more. These cultures are courteous and respect age, status, and background more. Examples of diffusive cultures include China, India, Argentina, and Spain.

Tips for working with specific cultures:

Organize agendas for your meetings.

Stick to your agenda as best as you can.

Focus first on setting objectives for people. Your relationship comes later.

Tips for working with diffusive cultures:

Build your relationship before you start setting objectives.

Expect invitations to more social occasions from colleagues. Commit to attending them.

Expect to discuss business in social situations and personal matters in the workplace.

5. Achievement vs. Ascription

This dimension of Trompenaars Cultural Dimensions Model can be summarized by asking, "Do we prove ourselves to get status or is it given to us?"

In an achievement culture, you earn status through knowledge or skill. Job titles are earned and reflect this knowledge and skill. Anyone can challenge a decision if they have a logical argument. Examples of achievement cultures include the U.S., the U.K., Germany, and Scandinavia.

In an ascription culture, you are given status based on who you are. This could be because of your social status, your education, or your age. You earn respect in these cultures because of your commitment to the organization, not your abilities. A decision will only be challenged by someone with higher authority. Examples of ascription cultures include Japan, Italy, and France.

Issue praise to an individual in front of their peers.

Avoid using titles.

Reward individual performance.

Use titles to refer to peers.

Pay extra care to show respect to your superiors. If you wish to challenge the decision of a superior, handle this delicately.

6. Sequential time vs. Synchronous time

This dimension can be summarized by asking, "Do things get done one at a time or do many things get done at once?"

In a sequential time culture, time is very important. People like projects to be completed in stages. Time is money, and so it is important that each stage is finished on time. It is rude to be late for meetings in these cultures. Examples of sequential time cultures include the U.S., the U.K., and Germany.

In a synchronous time culture, people see the past, present, and future as interwoven. Because of this people do several things at once, as time is interchangeable. This results in plans and deadlines being flexible. It also explains why punctuality is less important. Examples of synchronous time cultures include Japan, India, and Mexico.

Tips for working with sequential time cultures:

Keep to deadlines and commitments.

Try not to deviate from the set schedule.

Show up on time.

Tips for working with synchronous time cultures:

Allow people some autonomy within the schedule.

Allow time for people to arrive late to meetings.

Be explicit, calling out any deadlines that are not flexible and must be reached.

7. Internal direction vs. External direction

This dimension of Trompenaars Cultural Dimensions Model can be summarized by asking "Do we control our environment or are we controlled by it?"

In an internal direction culture, people believe that they can control their environment to achieve their goals. The focus is selfish (one's self, one's team, and one's organization). Winning is important in these cultures and aggressive personalities are thus prevalent. Examples of internal direction cultures include the U.S., the U.K., and Australia.

In an external direction culture, people believe that they must work with their environment to achieve their goals. In these cultures winning isn't as important as maintaining a strong relationship. They emphasize environmental factors to achieve their goals. Examples of external direction cultures include China, Russia, and Saudi Arabia.

Tips for working with internal direction cultures:
Allow people to set their own (within reason) learning development plans.
Allow a degree of constructive criticism.
Set clear goals and objectives.

Tips for working with external direction cultures:
Rather than set goals, give feedback so as people can correct their course en route.
Allow people autonomy to use their relationships to achieve results.

How to Use the Model

Unfortunately, Trompenaars Cultural Dimensions Model has no clear and consistent way to use it. But here is a very simple process you can use to start using the model:

First, self-evaluate that any misunderstanding is, at root, caused by cultural differences.

Second, score the person (not the country they are from) against each of the 7 dimensions.

Third, examine those dimensions with the biggest score. Select from the tips provided for that dimension to attempt to resolve the problem.

Note that we score the person, rather than the country he/she is from to avoid overgeneralizing, in view of the existence of cultural differences within even the same country.

Second Thoughts

1) What do you think is the most important dimension? And why?

_____

_____

2) Are there any other tips for working with individualistic cultures? Please write your ideas.

_____

_____

Ethics in International Management

CHAPTER 3

国际管理中的伦理

本章概要

本章主要介绍全球商业伦理的概念、起源、演变及其在国际管理活动中的意义与重要性。

学习指南

伦理学领域是寻求美德和道德的哲学分支,解决各种环境下人们"正确"和"错误"行为的问题,它是告诉人们应该如何行动的行为标准。商业伦理是将伦理原则应用于业务关系和活动。国际管理伦理对于企业的发展和管理有着重要意义。

通过本章学习,希望大家能够实现以下目标:

(1)基本目标(Text-based Goals)

● 掌握本章涉及话题的基本专业术语及词汇,如全球商业伦理、企业社会责任等;

● 掌握本章的主要知识点,即全球商业伦理的概念、起源、演变及其在国际管理中的意义与重要性。

(2)拓展目标(Extended Goals)

● 思考本章内容,为什么在国际管理活动中要强调伦理的重要性?

● 通过学习背景知识、拓展阅读、案例分析进一步了解伦理在不同国际管理场景中的体现。

A business that makes nothing but money is a poor business.（只会赚钱的企业是一个糟糕的企业。）

—Henry Ford（亨利·福特）

Global Business Ethics

伦理学领域是寻求美德和道德的哲学分支,解决各种环境下人们"正确"和"错误"行为的问题,它是告诉人们应该如何行动的行为标准。伦理学影响许多领域,除了商业,还包括医学、政府和科学等等。

The field of ethics is a branch of philosophy that seeks virtue and morality, addressing questions about "right" and "wrong" behavior for people in a variety of settings; the standards of behavior that tell how human beings ought to act. Ethics impacts many fields — not just business — including medicine, government, and science, to name a few. We must first try to understand the "origins of ethics — whether they come from religion, philosophy, the laws of nature, scientific study, study of political theory relating to ethical norms created in society or other fields of knowledge." The description below on the field of ethics shows how people think about ethics in stages, from where ethical principles come from to how people should apply them to specific tasks or issues.

This approach will be used in this chapter to help you understand global business ethics in a modern and current sense.

This section on global business ethics is less about providing you with a tangible list of dos and don'ts than it is about helping you understand the thinking and critical issues that global managers must deal with on an **operational** and strategic basis.

Where Do Our Values Come From?

我们的价值观从何而来?

正如人们依靠历史来了解政治、技术和社会变革一样,思想和哲学的变革也可从历史中寻找。思想的变迁有其历史可循。一百年前人们可以接受或不可以接受的东西,如今可能已经截然不同,包括人们如何表现自己,以及他们如何按照习俗、价值观和信念做事并互相影响。

Just as people look to history to understand political, technical, and social changes, so too do they look for changes in thinking and philosophy. There is a history to how thinking has evolved over time. What may or may not have been acceptable just a hundred years ago may be very different today — from how people present themselves and how they act and interact to customs, values, and beliefs.

Ethics can be defined as a system of moral standards or values. Cultural beliefs and programming influence our values. A sense of ethics is determined by a number of social, cultural, and religious factors; this sense influences us beginning early in childhood. People are taught how to behave by their families, exposure to education and thinking, and the society in which they live. Ethical behavior also refers to behavior that is generally accepted within a specific culture. Some behaviors are universally accepted — for example, people shouldn't physically hurt other

Word Study

operational
/ˌɒpəˈreɪʃənl/ *adj.*
(公司等)运作上的,经营上的

people. Other actions are less clear, such as **discrimination** based on age, race, gender, or ethnicity.

Culture impacts how local values influence global business ethics. There are differences in how much importance cultures place on specific ethical behaviors. For example, bribery remains widespread in many countries, and while people may not approve of it, they accept it as a necessity of daily life. Each professional is influenced by the values, social programming, and experiences encountered from childhood on. These collective factors impact how a person perceives an issue and the related correct or incorrect behaviors. Even within a specific culture, individuals have different ideas of what **constitutes** ethical or unethical behavior. Judgments may differ greatly depending on an individual's social or economic standing, education, and experiences with other cultures and beliefs. Just as in the example of bribery, it should be noted that there is a difference between ethical behavior and normal practice. It may be acceptable to discriminate in certain cultures, even if the people in that society know that it is not right or fair. In global business ethics, people try to understand what the ethical action is and what the normal practice might be. If these are not consistent, the focus is placed on how to encourage ethical actions.

While it's clear that ethics is not religion, values based on religious teachings have influenced our understanding of ethical behavior. Given the influence of Western thought and philosophy over the world in the last few centuries, many would say that global business has been heavily impacted by the mode of thinking that began with the Reformation and post-Enlightenment values, which placed focus on equality and individual rights. In this mode of thinking, it has become accepted that all people in any country and of any background are equal and should have equal opportunity. Companies incorporate this principle in their employment, management, and operational guidelines; yet enforcing it in global operations can be both tricky and inconsistent.

What Are the Reformation and Enlightenment?

Modern political and economic philosophies trace their roots back to the Reformation and Enlightenment. The Reformation was a period of European history in the sixteenth century when Protestant thinkers, led by Martin Luther, challenged the teachings of the Roman Catholic Church. As a result of the Reformation, the Catholic Church lost its control over all scientific and intellectual thought. While there were a number of debates and discussions over the **ensuing** decades and century, the Reformation is widely believed to have led to another historical period called the Age of Enlightenment, which refers to a period in Western philosophical, intellectual, scientific, and cultural life in the eighteenth century. The

Word Study

discrimination /dɪsˌkrɪmɪˈneɪʃən/ n. 歧视，区别
constitute /ˈkɒnstɪˌtjuːt/ v. 被视作，被看作
enlightenment /ɪnˈlaɪtnmənt/ n. 启蒙，启发
ensuing /ɪnˈsjuːɪŋ/ adj. 随后的

什么是改革与启蒙？
现代政治和经济哲学的根源可以追溯到宗教改革与启蒙运动。宗教改革指的是十六世纪的欧洲历史时期，马丁·路德（Martin Luther）领导的新教思想家对罗马天主教的教义提出了挑战。改革的结果是，天主教教会失去了

Enlightenment, as it is commonly called, promoted a set of values in which reason, not religion, was advocated as the primary source for **legitimacy** and authority. As a result, it is also known as the Age of Reason.

It's important to understand the impact and influence of these two critical historical periods on our modern sense of global business ethics. The **prevailing** corporate values — including those of institutional and individual equality; the right of every employee to work hard and reap the rewards, financial and nonfinancial; corporate social responsibility; and the application of science and reason to all management and operational processes — have their roots in the thoughts and values that arose during these periods.

Impact of Ethics on Global Business

At first, it may seem relatively easy to identify unethical behavior. When the topic of business ethics is raised, most people immediately focus on corruption and bribery. While this is a critical result of unethical behavior, the concept of business ethics and — in the context of this book — global business ethics is much broader. It impacts human resources, social responsibility, and the environment. The areas of business impacted by global **perceptions** of ethical, moral, and socially responsible behavior include the following:

- Ethics and management
- Ethics and corruption
- Corporate social responsibility

ETHICS AND MANAGEMENT

Ethics impacts various aspects of management and operations, including human resources, marketing, research and development, and even the corporate mission.

The role of ethics in management practices, particularly those practices involving human resources and employment, differs from culture to culture. Local culture impacts the way people view the employee-employer relationship. In many cultures, there are no clear social rules preventing discrimination against people based on age, race, gender, sexual preference, **handicap**, and so on. Even when there are formal rules or laws against discrimination, they may not be enforced, as normal practice may allow people and companies to act in accordance with local cultural and social practices.

Culture can impact how people see the role of one another in the workplace. For example, gender issues are at times impacted by local perceptions of women in the workplace. So how do companies handle local customs and values for the treatment of women in the workplace?

If you're a senior officer of an American company, do you send a woman to Saudi Arabia or Afghanistan to negotiate with government officials or manage the local office? Does it matter what your industry is or if your firm is the seller or buyer? In theory, most global firms have clear guidelines **articulating** anti-discrimination policies. In reality, global businesses routinely self-censor. Companies often determine whether a person — based on their gender, ethnicity, or race — can be effective in a specific culture based on the prevailing values in that culture. The largest and most respected global companies, typically the Fortune Global 500, can often make management and employment decisions regardless of local practices. Most people in each country will want to deal with these large and well-respected companies. The person representing the larger company brings the **clout** of their company to any business interaction. **In contrast**, lesser-known, midsize, and smaller companies may find that who their representative is will be more important. Often lacking business recognition in the marketplace, these smaller and midsize companies have to rely on their corporate representatives to create the professional image and bond with their in-country counterparts.

Cultural norms may make life difficult for the company as well as the employee. In some cultures, companies are seen as "guardians" or paternal figures. Any efforts to lay off or fire employees may be perceived as culturally unethical. In Japan, where lifelong loyalty to the company was expected in return for lifelong employment, the decade-long recession beginning in the 1990s **triggered** a change in attitude. Japanese companies finally began to alter this ethical perception and lay off workers without being perceived as unethical.

Global corporations are increasingly trying to market their products based not only on the desirability of the goods but also on their social and environmental merits. Companies whose practices are considered unethical may find their global performance impacted when people boycott their products. Most corporations understand this risk. However, ethical questions have grown increasingly complicated, and the "correct" or ethical choice has, in some cases, become difficult to define.

For example, the **pharmaceutical** industry is involved in a number of issues that have medical ethicists **squirming**. First, there's the well-publicized issue of cloning. No matter what choice the companies make about cloning, they are sure to offend a great many consumers. At the same time, pharmaceutical companies must decide whether to **forfeit** profits and give away free drugs or cheaper medicines to impoverished African nations. Pharmaceutical companies that do donate medicines often promote this practice in their corporate marketing campaigns in hopes that consumers see the companies in a favorable light.

Tobacco companies are similarly **embroiled** in a long-term ethical

Word Study

articulate /ɑ:'tɪkjʊleɪt/
v. 清楚地表达
clout /klaʊt/ n. 影响力，
势力
in contrast 相反
trigger /'trɪgə/ v. 触发，
引起
pharmaceutical
/,fɑ:mə'sju:tɪkəl/
adj. 制药的
squirm /skwɜ:m/ v. 羞
愧难当
forfeit /'fɔ:fɪt/ v.（因犯
错）丧失，被没收
embroil /ɪm'brɔɪl/ v.
使卷入（困境）

debate. Health advocates around the world agree that smoking is bad for a person's long-term health. Yet in many countries, smoking is not only acceptable but can even confer social status. The United States has banned tobacco companies from adopting marketing practices that target young consumers by exploiting tobacco's social **cache**. However, many other countries don't have such regulations. Should tobacco companies be held responsible for knowingly marketing harmful products to younger audiences in other countries?

ETHICS AND CORRUPTION

To begin our discussion of corruption, let's first define it in a business context. Corruption is "giving or obtaining advantage through means which are illegitimate, immoral, and/or inconsistent with one's duty or the rights of others. Corruption often results from **patronage**.

Our modern understanding of business ethics notes that following culturally accepted norms is not always the ethical choice. What may be acceptable at certain points in history, such as racism or sexism, became unacceptable with the further development of society's mind-set. What happens when cultures change but business practices don't? Does that behavior become unethical, and is the person engaged in the behavior unethical? In some cultures, there may be conflicts with global business practices, such as in the area of gift-giving, which has evolved into bribery — a form of corruption.

Paying bribes is relatively common in many countries, and bribes often take the form of grease payments, which are small inducements intended to **expedite** decisions and transactions. In India and Mexico, for example, a grease payment may help get your phones installed faster — at home or at work. Transparency International tracks **illicit** behavior, such as bribery and **embezzlement**, in the public sector in 180 countries by surveying international business executives. It assigns a CPI (Corruption Perceptions Index) rating to each country. New Zealand, Denmark, Singapore, and Sweden have the lowest levels of corruption, while the highest levels of corruption are seen in most African nations, Russia, Myanmar, and Afghanistan.

Even the most respected of global companies has found itself on the wrong side of the ethics issue and the law. In 2008, after years of investigation, Siemens agreed to pay more than 1.34 billion euros in fines to American and European authorities to settle charges that it routinely used bribes and slush funds to secure huge public-works contracts around the world. Officials said that Siemens, beginning in the mid-1990s, used bribes and **kickbacks** to foreign officials to secure government contracts for projects like a national identity card project in Argentina, mass transit work in Venezuela, a nationwide cell phone network in Bangladesh and a United Nations oil-for-food program in Iraq. "Their actions were not an

伦理与腐败

开始讨论腐败之前,首先要在商务语境下对其进行定义。腐败是"通过非法、不合伦理和/或与某人的职责或他人的权利相抵触的手段提供或获得利益。腐败往往源于资助关系。"

Word Study

cache /kæʃ/ n. 隐藏物,隐藏处

patronage /ˈpætrənɪdʒ/ n. 赞助,资助

expedite /ˈekspədaɪt/ v. 促进,加快

illicit /ɪˈlɪsɪt/ adj. 违法的,不正当的

embezzlement /ɪmˈbezlmənt/ n. 侵占,挪用

kickback /ˈkɪkbæk/ n. 回扣

anomaly", said Joseph Persichini Jr., the head of the Washington office of the Federal Bureau of Investigation. "They were standard operating procedures for corporate executives who viewed bribery as a business strategy."

Each year Transparency International analyzes trends in global corruption. The following is an excerpt from their 2010 Global Corruption Barometer report.

"Corruption has increased over the last three years, say six out of 10 people around the world. One in four people report paying bribes in the last year."

The 2010 Barometer captures the experiences and views of more than 91,500 people in 86 countries and territories, making it the only world-wide public opinion survey on corruption.

Views on corruption were most negative in Western Europe and North America, where 73 per cent and 67 per cent of people respectively thought corruption had increased over the last three years.

"The fall-out of the financial crises continues to affect people's opinions of corruption, particular in North America and Western Europe. Institutions everywhere must be resolute in their efforts to restore good governance and trust", said Huguette Labelle, Chair of Transparency International.

In the past 12 months one in four people reported paying a bribe to one of nine institutions and services, from health to education to tax authorities. The police are cited as being the most frequent recipient of bribes, according to those surveyed. About 30 per cent of those who had contact with the police reported having paid a bribe.

More than 20 countries have reported significant increases in petty **bribery** since 2006. The biggest increases were in Chile, Colombia, Kenya, FYR Macedonia, Nigeria, Poland, Russia, Senegal and Thailand. More than one in two people in Sub-Saharan Africa reported paying a bribe — more than anywhere else in the world.

Poorer people are twice as likely to pay bribes for basic services, such as education, than wealthier people. A third of all people under the age of 30 reported paying a bribe in the past 12 months, compared to less than one in five people aged 51 years and over.

Most worrying is the fact that bribes to the police have almost doubled since 2006, and more people report paying bribes to the judiciary and for registry and permit services than five years ago.

Sadly, few people trust their governments or politicians. Eight out of 10 say political parties are corrupt or extremely corrupt, while half the people questioned say their government's action to stop corruption is ineffective.

"The message from the 2010 Barometer is that corruption is **insidious**.

透明国际组织每年都会分析全球腐败的趋势。其《2010年全球腐败晴雨表》报告显示：

"全世界每10个人中就有6个人认为，在过去三年中，腐败现象有所增加。去年有四分之一的人报告有过行贿行为。"

Word Study

anomaly /əˈnɒməli/ *n.* 异常现象，反常现象

bribery /ˈbraɪbəri/ *n.* 行贿，受贿

insidious /ɪnˈsɪdiəs/ *adj.* 暗中为害的，不知不觉间加剧的

It makes people lose faith. The good news is that people are ready to act", said Labelle. "Public engagement in the fight against corruption will force those in authority to act — and will give people further courage to speak out and stand up for a cleaner, more transparent world."

Gift-giving and connections

Gift-giving in the global business world is used to establish or pay respects to a relationship. Bribery, on the other hand, is more commonly considered the practice in which an individual would benefit with little or no benefit to the company. It's usually paid in relation to winning a business deal, whereas gift-giving is more likely to be ingrained in the culture and not associated with winning a specific piece of business. Bribery, usually in the form of a cash payment, has reached such high proportions in some countries that even locals express disgust with the corruption and its impact on daily life for businesses and consumers.

The practice of using connections to advance business interests exists in just about every country in the world. However, the extent and manner in which it is institutionalized differs from culture to culture.

In Western countries, connections are viewed informally and sometimes even with a negative **connotation**. In the United States and other similar countries, professionals prefer to imply that they have achieved success on their own merits and without any connections. Gift-giving is not routine in the United States except during the winter holidays, and even then gift-giving involves a modest expression. Businesses operating in the United States send modest gifts or cards to their customers to thank them for business loyalty in the previous year. Certain industries, such as finance, even set clear legal guidelines restricting the value of gifts, typically a maximum of $100.

In contrast, Asian, Latin American, and Middle Eastern cultures are quick to value connections and relationships and view them quite positively. Connections are considered essential for success. In Asia, gift-giving is so ingrained in the culture that it is formalized and structured.

For example, gift-giving in Japan was for centuries an established practice in society and is still taken seriously. There are specific guidelines for gift-giving depending on the identity of the giver or **recipient**, the length of the business relationship, and the number of gifts exchanged. The Japanese may give gifts out of a sense of obligation and duty as well as to convey feelings such as **gratitude** and regret. Therefore, much care is given to the appropriateness of the gift as well as to its aesthetic beauty. Gift-giving has always been widespread in Japan.

Today there are still business gift-giving occasions in Japan, specifically *oseibo* (year's end) and *ochugen* (mid-summer). These are must-give occasions for Japanese businesses. *Oseibo* gifts are presented in the first

Word Study

connotation
/ˌkɒnəˈteɪʃən/ n. 含义,隐含意义
recipient /rɪˈsɪpɪənt/ n. 接受者
gratitude /ˈɡrætɪtjuːd/ n. 感谢,感激

half of December as a token of gratitude for earlier favors and loyalty. This is a good opportunity to thank clients for their business. *Ochugen* usually occurs in mid-July in Tokyo and mid-August in some other regions. Originally an occasion to provide consolation to the families of those who had died in the first half of the year, *ochugen* falls two weeks before *obon*, a holiday honoring the dead.

Businesses operating in Japan at these times routinely exchange *oseibo* and *ochugen* gifts. While a professional is not obligated to participate, it clearly earns goodwill. At the most senior levels, it is not uncommon for people to exchange gifts worth $300 or $400. There is an established price level that one should pay for each corporate level.

Despite these guidelines, gift-giving in Japan has **occasionally** crossed over into bribery. This level of corruption became more apparent in the 1980s as transparency in global business gained media attention. Asians tend to take a very different view of **accountability** than most Westerners. In the 1980s and 1990s, several Japanese CEOs resigned in order to apologize and take responsibility for their companies' practices, even when they did not personally engage in the offending practices. This has become an accepted managerial practice in an effort to preserve the honor of the company. While Japanese CEOs may not step down as quickly as in the past, the notion of honor remains an important business characteristic.

Long an established form of relationship development in all business conducted in Asia, the Arab world, and Africa, gift-giving was clearly tipping into **outright** bribery. In the past two decades, many countries have placed limits on the types and value of gifts while simultaneously banning bribery in any form. In the United States, companies must adhere to the Foreign Corrupt Practices Act, a federal law that specifically bans any form of bribery. Even foreign companies that are either listed on an American stock exchange or conduct business with the U.S. government come under the purview of this law.

There are still global firms that engage in questionable business gift-giving; when caught, they face fines and sanctions. But for the most part, firms continue with business as usual. Changing the cultural practices of gift-giving is an evolving process that will take time, government attention, and more transparency in the awarding of global business contracts.

Companies and their employees routinely try to balance ethical behavior with business interests. While corruption is now widely viewed as unethical, firms still lose business to companies that may be less diligent in adhering to this principle. While the media covers stories of firms that have breached this ethical conduct, the **misconduct** of many more companies goes **undetected**. Businesses, business schools, and governments are increasingly making efforts to deter firms and professionals from making and taking bribes. There are still countless less visible gestures

Word Study

occasionally
/əˈkeɪʒənəlɪ/ *adv.*
偶尔地；间或
accountability
/əˌkaʊntəˈbɪlɪti/ *n.*
责任
outright /ˈaʊtˈraɪt/ *adv.*
毫无保留地
misconduct
/mɪsˈkɒndʌkt/ *n.*
不端行为，不诚
实行为
undetected /ˌʌndɪˈtektɪd/
adj. 未被发现的

that some would argue are also unethical. For example, imagine that an employee works at a firm that wants to land a contract in a foreign country. A key government official in that country finds out that you went to the business school that his daughter really wants to attend. He asks you to help her in the admission process. Do you? Should you? Is this just a nice thing to do, or is it a potential conflict of interest if you think the official will view your company more favorably? This is a gray area of global business ethics. Interestingly, a professional's answer to this situation may depend on his or her culture. Cultures that have clear guidelines for right and wrong behavior may see this situation differently than a culture in which doing favors is part of the normal practice. A company may declare this inappropriate behavior, but employees may still do what they think is best for their jobs. Cultures that have a higher tolerance for ambiguity, may find it easier to navigate the gray areas of ethics — when it is not so clear.

Most people agree that bribery in any form only increases the cost of doing business — a cost that is either absorbed by the company or eventually passed on to the buyer or consumer in some form. While businesses agree that corruption is costly and undesirable, losing profitable business opportunities to firms that are less ethically motivated can be just as **devastating** to the bottom line. Until governments in every country consistently monitor and enforce **anticorruption** laws, bribery will remain a real and very challenging issue for global businesses.

CORPORATE SOCIAL RESPONSIBILITY

Corporate social responsibility (CSR) is defined in Wikipedia as "the corporate conscience, citizenship, social performance, or sustainable responsible business, and is a form of corporate self-regulation integrated into a business model. CSR policy functions as a built-in, self-regulating mechanism whereby business monitors and ensures its active **compliance** with the spirit of the law, ethical standards, and international norms."

CSR emerged more than three decades ago, and it has gained increasing strength over time as companies seek to generate goodwill with their employees, customers, and stakeholders. "Corporate social responsibility **encompasses** not only what companies do with their profits, but also how they make them. It goes beyond philanthropy and compliance and addresses how companies manage their economic, social, and environmental impacts, as well as their relationships in all key spheres of influence: the workplace, the marketplace, the supply chain, the community, and the public policy realm." Companies may support nonprofit causes and organizations, global initiatives, and prevailing themes. Promoting environmentally friendly and green initiatives is an example of a current prevailing theme.

Coca-Cola is an example of global corporation with a long-term

Word Study

devastating
/'devə,steɪtɪŋ/ adj.
毁灭性的,破坏性
极强的
anticorruption
/'æntɪ,kərʌpʃən/ n.
反腐败
compliance
/kəm'plaɪəns/ n. 顺
从,服从,符合
encompass /ɪn'kʌmpəs/
v. 包含,包括

企业社会责任
　　企业社会责任
(CSR)在维基百科
中的定义为"企业良
知、公民身份、社会绩
效或可持续发展的
负责任的经营,是一
种整合到商业模式
中的企业自我监管
形式。CSR政策是一
种内置的自我调节
机制,企业可以借此
监视并确保其积极
遵守法律精神、伦理
标准和国际准则。"

commitment to CSR. In many developing countries, Coca-Cola promotes local economic development through a combination of philanthropy and social and economic development. Whether by using environmentally friendly containers or supporting local education initiatives through its foundation, Coca-Cola is only one of many global companies that seek to increase their **commitment** to local markets while enhancing their brand, corporate image, and reputation by engaging in socially responsible business practices.

Companies use a wide range of strategies to communicate their socially responsible strategies and programs. Under the auspices of the United Nations, the Global Compact "is a strategic policy initiative for businesses that are committed to aligning their operations and strategies with ten universally accepted principles in the areas of human rights, labor, environment and anti-corruption."

Enforcement of Ethical Guidelines and Standards

伦理准则和标准的执行

The concept of culture impacting the perception of ethics is one that many businesspeople debate. While culture does impact business ethics, international companies operate in multiple countries and need a standard set of global operating guidelines. Professionals engage in unethical behavior primarily as a result of their own personal ethical values, the corporate culture within a company, or from unrealistic performance expectations.

关于文化影响伦理认知的概念是许多商人争论的话题。文化确实会影响商业伦理，但跨国公司在多个国家/地区开展业务，需要一套标准的全球运营准则。专业人士参与不合伦理的行为，主要原因在于他们自己的个人伦理价值观、公司内部的企业文化或不切实际的绩效期望。

In the interest of **expediency**, many governments — the U.S. government included — may not strictly enforce the rules governing corporate ethics. The practice of gift-giving is one aspect of business that many governments don't examine too closely. Many companies have routinely used gifts to win favor from their customers, without engaging in direct bribery. American companies frequently invite **prospective** buyers to visit their U.S. facilities or attend company conferences in **exotic** locales with all expenses paid. These trips often have **perks** included. Should such spending be considered sales and marketing expenses, as they are often booked, or are these companies engaging in questionable behavior? It's much harder to answer this question when you consider that most of the company's global competitors are likely to engage in similarly aggressive marketing and sales behavior.

Governments often do not enforce laws until it's politically expedient to do so. Take child labor, for example. Technically, companies operating in India or Pakistan are not permitted to use child labor in factories, mines, and other areas of **hazardous** employment. However, child labor is widespread in these countries due to deep-rooted social and economic challenges. Local governments are often unable and unwilling to enforce national rules and regulations. Companies and consumers who purchase goods made by children are often unaware that these practices remain unchecked.

Word Study

expediency
/ɪkˈspiːdɪənsɪ/ n.
权宜，私利
prospective
/prəˈspektɪv/ adj.
可能的，潜在的
exotic /ɪgˈzɒtɪk/ adj.
异国风情的
perk /pɜːk/ n.（工资之外的）补贴，津贴
hazardous /ˈhæzədəs/
adj. 有危险的，冒险的

The Evolution of Ethics

Ethics evolves over time. It is difficult for both companies and professionals to operate within one set of accepted standards or guidelines only to see them gradually evolve or change. For example, bribery has been an accepted business practice for centuries in Japan and Korea. When these nations adjusted their practices in order to enter the global system, the questionable practices became illegal. Hence a Korean businessman who engaged in bribery ten or twenty years ago may not do so today without finding himself on the other side of the law. Even in the United States, discrimination and business-regulation laws have changed tremendously over the last several decades. And who can know what the future holds? Some of the business practices that are commonly accepted today may be **frowned** on tomorrow.

It's clear that changing values, as influenced by global media, and changing perceptions and cultures will impact global ethics. The most challenging aspect is that global business does not have a single definition of "fair" or "ethical". While culture influences the definitions of those ideas, many companies are forced to navigate this sensitive area very carefully, as it impacts both their bottom line and their reputations.

Word Study

frown /fraʊn/ v. 皱眉

Key Terms
专业术语

global business ethics 全球商业伦理   ethical norms 伦理规范
the Reformation 宗教改革   the Enlightenment 启蒙运动
grease payment/slush funds 贿赂/行贿基金
corporate social responsibility 企业社会责任
ethical guideline 伦理准则   ethical standard 伦理标准

Information
Link
知识链接

培育商业伦理精神

商业伦理精神的培育,从根本上说,就是要破除所谓的"商业无道德神话",改变"利润至上"的商业环境和商业观,塑造"价值优先"的商业文化。

"商业无道德神话"支持这样一种观点:"商业行为与道德无关。商业活动无需考虑道德问题。对企业来说,追求经济利益才具有实质意义,谈论道德问题就是不务正业。"这种说法尽管有违人们在直觉上的道德感,但它却是商业社会中"牢固的成见"。现代西方主流经济学既是这一观点在理论上不自觉的辩护者,同时也自然地借由这种理论造成的实证结果得到辩护。为了破除这一根深蒂固的"业界神话",近半个世纪以来,商业伦理学一直在艰难的环境中苦口婆心地争辩着"企业为什么要讲道德"和"企业如何讲道德"。但实事求是地说,商业伦理学在今天之所以受到人们的重视,在很大程度上并不取决于伦理学家们提供的各种理由和方法,而是因为屡屡发生的企业失德行为一次比一次危害大,一次又一次突破社会道德的底线,使得人们不得不重新审视企业追求经济价值的意义,不得不在更高的价值层面上重新评价和规范商业行为。

历史地看,现代商业社会不自然的"无道德"特征是与现代商业文明起源于伦理观念这一事实和传统背道而驰的。在现代商业文明发起的源头,伦理观念不但孕育了新的商业精神,还通过这种商业精神带来了持续而稳定的商业繁荣。有趣的是,大约在16—17世纪这段时间里,这一现象同时发生在中国和欧洲。

明清之际,处于"四民"之末的商人阶层缔造了中国社会一度的商业繁荣。而在背后起重要推动作用的,恰恰是被称为"贾道"的伦理观念。有学者指出,明清之际的商人大多原是儒生。"弃儒就贾"后便不自觉地把儒家的义利观念带入商业活动,渐渐有意识地生发出作为"道统"之一的"贾道"。王阳明讲"四民异业而同道"的时代,说的就是商业活动被纳入"正统"、经商也被视为"正道"的年代。正是带着经商也是"弘道"的信念,明清之际的儒商不仅有着高度的敬业精神和事业心,还乐于承担一切重要的社会公益事业,如编族谱、建宗祠、设义庄、疏通河道、开路修桥、建书院寺庙等,甚至连属于士的阶层所做的文化事业如整理文献和刊行丛书也乐此不疲。儒商的种种义举受到社会的广泛认可和政府的褒奖,在"若有德业,则为铭文"的感召下,他们愈发看重自己的名德。

大约在相同的时间段里,西方社会经历了宗教改革。基督教世界摇摇欲坠,世俗世界的兴盛伴随着科技革命的浪潮推动了商业社会的崛起。马克斯·韦伯在《新教伦理与资本主义精神》一书中认为,正是在加尔文宗诸派宗教伦理孕育的资本主义商业精神的感召下,大量的清教徒投身商业活动为资本主义原始积累赚取了"第一桶金"。这种资本主义精神可称之为禁欲主义天职观,即从事商业活动不再是低贱的行为,而是符合上帝要求、为上帝劳作的天职。

不难看出,无论是明清商人的"贾道"理念,还是欧洲清教徒的"天职观",它们之所以能成就一种商业文明或塑造一种商业精神,关键就在于它们能把个体的经济行为和某种公认的崇高价值结合起来,从内在和外在两个方面使人获得超越性,形成了一种在个体和社会之间的良性互动。在这种双向的互动过程中,个体既获得了超越自身利益的自我认同,社会也从中受益并对个体进行良性反馈。相反,如果经济行为的动机是单纯的自利,而社会成就评价只是建立在效果主义基础上的福利标准,那么个体和社会之间就不再是一种相互推升的递进关系,而是一种相互掣肘的制约关系。从这个意义上讲,要走出"商业无道德神话"的困境,就要在根本上实现个体行为动机与社会成就评价之间的良性互动。这两者相辅相成、不可分割。如果只是强调在个体层面改善行为动机而不调整社会成就评价体系,那么道德的个体就有可能在社会压力系统下面临"劣币驱除良币"的道德风险。如果社会成就评价的调整不能起到改善个体行为动机的效果,那么,再好的评价系统也会流于形式而无人问津。更为重要的是,这种良性互动不但在说理层面和社会教育系统内需要经济学、管理学和伦理学以更加开放的姿态和视野吸收对方有益的东西,更需要金融家、企业家、社会活动家和一切有志于从事这项事业的人通过一定的机制、措施、路径把这种良性互动现实地建立起来并一直推动下去。这种良性的互动机制就是所谓的伦理法。按照黑格尔的概念，它是主观和客观相统一的自在自为的法。只有在这种法的形式中，才能形成作为共同存在方式的伦理精神。

资料来源：
中国文明网.张霄,中国人民大学哲学院伦理学教研室主任

A. How does ethics impact international management practices? Please write your answer.

_____

_____

_____

_____

B. According to the text, fill in each of the following blanks with an appropriate word or phrase.

1) Ethics is a branch of philosophy that seeks _____ and _____, addressing questions about "right" and "wrong" behavior for people in a variety of settings.

2) Ethics can be defined as a system of _____ or values.

3) Ethical behavior also refers to behavior that is generally accepted within a _____.

4) In global business ethics, people try to understand what the _____ is and what the _____ might be.

5) Modern political and economic philosophies trace their roots back to the _____ and _____.

6) The Reformation was a period of European history in the sixteenth century when _____ thinkers, led by _____, challenged the teachings of the Roman Catholic Church.

7) The age of Enlightenment is also known as the Age of _____.

8) Ethics impacts various aspects of management and operations, including human resources, marketing, research and development, and even the corporate _____.

9) In Japan, where lifelong _____ to the company was expected in return for lifelong employment, the decade-long recession beginning in the _____ triggered a change in attitude.

10) Global corporations are increasingly trying to market their products based on both the _____ of the goods and on their social and environmental merits.

C. Read the text and decide whether the following statements are True (T) or False (F).

1) It's rarely seen that many companies have routinely used gifts to win favor from their customers, without engaging in direct bribery.　(　　)

2) Technically, companies operating in India or Pakistan are not permitted to use child labor in factories, mines, and other areas of hazardous employment.　(　　)

3) The Global Compact is a strategic policy initiative for businesses that are committed to aligning their operations and strategies with ten universally accepted principles in the areas of human rights, labor, environment and anti-corruption.　(　　)

4) In many developing countries, Coca-Cola promotes local economic development through a combination of philanthropy and social and economic development.　(　　)

5) Corporate Social Responsibility emerged more than eight decades ago, and it has gained increasing strength over time as companies seek to generate goodwill with their employees, customers, and stakeholders.

　(　　)

6) Bribery in any form only increases the cost of doing business — a cost that is either absorbed by the company or eventually passed on to the buyer or consumer in some form, which is rarely agreed.　(　　)

7) Corporate social responsibility encompasses not only what companies do with their profits, but also how they make them.　(　　)

8) Asians tended to take a very different view of accountability than most Westerners in the 1980s.　(　　)

9) There are still business gift-giving occasions in Japan nowadays.　(　　)

10) In Europe, gift-giving is so ingrained in the culture, particularly in Italy, that it is formalized and structured.　(　　)

Discussion
讨论

1) Where do our values come from?

_____

_____

2) What values do you think are the good ones?

_____

_____

3) How does ethics impact global business?

_____

_____

4) What do Asians think about gift-giving?

_____

_____

5) What kind of ethics should businesses obey in international management?

_____

_____

Case Story

Cultural Values and Leadership Preferences of Immigrants

Scholars have been studying the link between culture and leadership for decades. Cultural values influence leadership significantly, in both the perception of leadership and how behavior is controlled or influenced. People's most fundamental values form during the first 10 years of life. Culture and socialization experiences form lay theories that help people understand, act, and react to situations in their environment and behave accordingly. These experiences and settings are different across nations and even when countries neighbor each other. Cross-cultural researchers have demonstrated that leadership preferences vary from one country to another and that the meaning of leadership is rooted in, and changes according to the culture where it is used. Individuals who grow up in a culture-specific rich environment tend to embrace such culture and learn to interpret the world from that perspective, regardless of where they live.

As people migrate to other parts of the world, they bring with them their unique perspective and may have a hard time understanding a different view. People assume those with whom they interact will behave according to their expectation, and when that is not the case, misinterpretation and miscommunication may occur, which could lead to conflict. In most of the cross-cultural research studies, researchers compared work-related values and leadership preferences across nations, assuming there is a consensus of beliefs within each nation, and often failing to consider acculturation as a factor.

Culture, as defined in most cross-cultural studies, relies on the notion that people within a societal group share similar values. Hofstede (2001), for example, defined culture as "the collective programming of the mind that distinguishes the members of one group or category of people from another". In this definition, Hofstede referred to the mind as the way people feel, think, and act, resulting in attitudes, beliefs, and abilities.

Culture includes a set of imperceptible values that manifest as behavior. This construct is useful for comparing cultures across societies as it relies on the assumption that a consensus on the importance of values exist within societal groups and differs from other groups. In largely diverse countries the assumed consensus of values may be nonexistent, except for culturally linked values. This notion indicates that to compare cultural groups within the same society requires research at the value level of the individual.

Culture does not influence the values of people the same way; people form and internalize values differently according to experiences and personal goals. In countries with a large immigrant population, the internalized values could vary drastically among the various members of society. People from complex cultures tend to be self-reliant, independent, and self-actualizing, whereas people from non-complex cultures tend to be collectivist, follow norms, and be obedient. When these two different cultures coexist in one country, there are bound to be differences of opinion. Immigrants tend to hold on to the culture from their country of origin after migration and pass it on to their descendants. This process tends to prolong the acculturation process.

Although research shows that the core values of immigrants change slowly over time, the process of acculturation is not linear, and several variables affect it such as family, length of time in host country, school and work environment, age at migration, and exposure to local and home country culture. It may take three generations for immigrants to acculturate entirely to a new country. Additionally, acculturation studies revealed that acculturation is reciprocal; immigrants and natives exchange elements of their cultures with one another. Immigrants and non-immigrants unknowingly learn from one another, creating a blend of two or more cultures. In this study, I examined how acculturation affects the work-related values and leadership preferences of immigrants. First- and second-generation immigrants may display and prefer leadership styles reflective of their cultural values, which acculturation may affect. Because followers determine leadership effectiveness and not the leader, managers may be using the wrong management or leadership style for the workforce they manage.

Despite all the research in cross-cultural leadership, a gap in knowledge exists in the literature to explain the relationship between the cultural values of immigrants and their leadership preferences. This gap may exist because most of the research on cross-cultural leadership focuses on national culture and compares the differences among countries or clusters of nations. Few researchers have examined the intranational cultural differences and their effects on leadership preferences. Most of these researchers have overlooked the contextual factors that may influence leadership preferences and the cultural values of the participants. Their studies also focused on leadership theories that align with Western views, which tend to classify leadership as either authoritarian or democratic, and often ignore paternalistic leadership as it does not neatly fall into either category. A problem with this approach when comparing intranational cultural differences in leadership preference is that researchers leave out leadership styles that do not align with Western views. Paternalistic leadership, which many consider the ideal leadership style in collectivistic and high power distance societies, such as Mexico, is one of the styles often not included. Organizations may benefit from understanding how to create leadership development programs that not only embrace diversity but also gain a competitive advantage by developing leaders based on the relationship between their cultural identity and leadership preferences.

Case Discussion

1) What do you think is the link between culture and leadership?

_____

_____

2) What can immigrants do to adapt to the local culture?

_____

_____

Case Summary

数十年来，学者们一直在研究文化与领导力之间的联系。文化价值观在领导力的感知以及行为的控制或影响方式方面都对领导力有重大影响。文化和社会化经验形成了可帮助人们理解、采取行动并对环境中的状况做出反应并据此行事的基础理论。这些经验和环境在不同国家甚至邻近国家之间也有所不同。跨文化研究者证明，领导偏好在一个国家与另一个国家之间是不同的，领导的含义根植于其所处的文化，并随着文化的变化而变化。在某种文化环境中成长的个人倾向于拥抱这种文化，并学会从那个角度解释世界，无论他们身在何处。

当人们迁移到世界其他地方时，他们带着自己独特的视角，可能很难理解另一种观点。人们认为与他们互动的人会按照自己的期望行事，如果事与愿违，就可能会发生误解和沟通错误，从而可能导致冲突。在大多数跨文化研究中，研究人员比较各个国家与工作相关的价值观和领导偏好，假设每个国家内部对信仰有共识，并且往往没有考虑文化适应这个因素。在关于跨文化领导力的研究中，尚缺乏对移民文化价值观及其领导偏好之间关系的研究。

在充分考虑文化身份及领导偏好的基础上培养领导者，拥抱多样性，这将为企业组织带来竞争优势。

Reading I

The Utility of Offshoring: A Rawlsian Critique

Most prominent arguments favoring the widespread discretionary business practice of sending jobs overseas, known as "offshoring", attempt to justify the trend by appeal to utilitarian principles. It is argued that when business can be performed more cost-effectively offshore, doing so tends, over the long term, to achieve the greatest good for the greatest number. This claim is supported by evidence that exporting jobs actively promotes economic development overseas while simultaneously increasing the revenue of the exporting country.

The Goal of Greatest Global Growth

Proponents of offshoring tend to defend it on the grounds that it is the surest and fastest way to increase the GDP (Global Domestic Product) of every nation worldwide. In other words, it maximizes global average and median GDP. It is therefore generally said to be a "win-win game". Such assessments of course overlook the possibility of facilitating human rights and environmental abuses as a result of outsourcing to on-site facilities in lesser-developed countries with little or no regulatory oversight. Furthermore, in the absence of social safety nets for stabilizing the boom and bust patterns of the free market, offshoring might come at too great a human cost. But such situational contingencies notwithstanding, if offshoring can generally be shown to maximize global economic value, it can be justified on purely economic utilitarian grounds. For although offshoring obviously creates immediate job-winners at the expense of immediate job-losers, so long as it tends to increase global average and median economic value over the long term, it continually stimulates job growth. And since, according to utilitarianism, everyone's interests should be taken into consideration equally, being American grants no greater moral claim to gainful employment than does being Indian, Malaysian, Chinese, Vietnamese, Cambodian, or Bengali.

The Goal of Genuine Impartiality

Rawls insightfully demonstrates, in *A Theory of Justice*, that utilitarianism "mistakes impersonality for impartiality". What he means by this is that instead of defining impartiality, as utilitarians do, from the perspective of a sympathetic observer of everyone's interests, one should define it from the perspective of the persons themselves with their own individual preferences, in an original position of equality. Only then can genuine impartiality be achieved by guaranteeing that no individual will have to bear a greater sacrifice than absolutely necessary for the establishment of a just society. If we apply this standard of impartiality to the case of offshoring, we immediately arrive at some interesting results. Imagine being in the Rawlsian "original position" of determining the norms of a just society, not knowing what particular socioeconomic status one's fortune will bring. From this standpoint, everyone would make sure to set up a society in which no one would be more disadvantaged than absolutely necessary to insure equal opportunity. Inequalities would thus be allowed so long as they worked to the greatest interest of the least advantaged, by for example, instituting differentials on the basis of merit. Now, imagining oneself in this position, Rawls would ask if anyone would welcome being born at random into a society such as ours in which the dramatic aforementioned offshoring trends occurred? If we think seriously about the economic hardships, the instability and the insecurities incurred broadly across the middle class from lives of constant retraining, I think it's quite clear such a prospect would be rather unappealing. Indeed, it becomes apparent that the utilitarian goal of greatest global growth disproportionately benefits a smaller number of upper-class stockholders at the expense of a much larger number of working-class stakeholders facing the prospect of job-loss. And as for poor families that will benefit from lower priced goods, they would clearly trade that in for a more secure professional future, especially since it is mostly their less desirable jobs which are ripe for offshoring.

The Capitalist Social Contract

Interestingly, the more socialist-leaning economies of Europe, unified by the Euro (the UK conspicuously excluded) have little or no share of the offshoring market. Naturally, those might expect those economies are much more regulated by the hand of government. One therefore might expect those governments to mutually choose to inhibit the export of jobs to other countries outside the European Union. And indeed, this generally seems to be the case at present. By contrast, the more capitalist-leaning economies of the world such as the U.S., the U.K. and Japan have relatively liberal trade regulations and are thus, not surprisingly, the leading exporters of jobs.

Now, if we agree with Rawlsian contractarianism that discretionary offshoring is unjust, how should the more capitalist-leaning economies of the world work to minimize the trend? Obviously, they could erect new regulatory measures such as implementing a tax on offshoring companies proportionate to the value of the labor offshored and revoke the right of those companies to count the costs of offshoring as a non-taxable business expense. But given the amount of value still to be gained from offshoring even under those conditions, it is doubtful the trend would subside. In any case, capitalism constitutes a social contract that places a particularly strong moral obligation on corporations themselves to refrain from offshoring, in which the major portion of the economy is in private hands. Thus, contrary to socialism, in which the government retains a significant degree of ownership of economic value, capitalism leaves ownership and hence distribution much more in the hands of the private sector. As a result, business has a much greater degree of responsibility to voluntarily uphold its obligations to the collective social contract justice requires. For if it does not meet this responsibility it risks inviting governmental regulatory controls that will diminish its autonomy and profitability.

Second Thoughts

For each of the following statements, choose one (or more than one) answer to fill in the blank.

1) Proponents of offshoring tend to defend it on the grounds that _____.
   A. it is the surest and fastest way to increase the GDP of every nation worldwide
   B. it is fair and just to every nation worldwide
   C. it can help lesser-developed countries
   D. it can create more jobs in every nation worldwide

2) The leading exporters of jobs in the world include _____.
   A. the U.S.
   B. the UK
   C. Japan
   D. the EU

Reading II

Management Ethics

Management is a systematic way of doing work in any field. Its task is to make people capable of joint performance, to make their weaknesses irrelevant and convert them into strengths. It strikes harmony in working equilibrium, in thoughts and actions, goals and achievements, plans and performance, products and markets. Lack of management will cause disorder, confusion, wastage, delay, destruction and even depression. Successful management means managing men, money and material in the best possible way according to circumstances and environment.

Management ethics is related to the social responsiveness of a firm. It is "the discipline dealing with what is good and bad, or right and wrong, or with moral duty and obligation. It is a standard of behavior that guides individual managers in their work".

"It is the set of moral principles that governs the actions of an individual or a group."

When managers assume social responsibility, it is believed they will do it ethically, that is, they know what is right and wrong.

Types of Management Ethics

Three types of management ethics or standards of conduct are identified by Archie B. Carroll.

1. Immoral management

It implies a lack of ethical practices followed by managers. Managers want to maximise profits even if it is at the cost of legal standards or concern for employees.

2. Moral management

According to moral management ethics, managers aim to maximise profits within the confines of ethical values and principles. They conform to professional and legal standards of conduct. The guiding principle in moral management ethics is "Is this action, decision, or behavior fair to us and all parties involved?"

3. Amoral management

This type of management ethics lies between moral and immoral management ethics. Managers respond to personal and legal ethics only if they are required to do so; otherwise there is a lack of ethical perception and awareness.

There are two types of amoral management.

a. Intentional

Managers deliberately avoid ethical practices in business decisions because they think ethics should be followed in non-business activities.

b. Unintentional

Managers do not deliberately avoid ethical practices but unintentionally they make decisions whose moral implications are not taken into consideration.

Guidelines for Ethical Behavior

Though every individual and group has a set of ethical values, the following guidelines are prescribed by James O'Toole in this regard.

1. Obey the law

Obeying legal practices of the country is conforming to ethical values.

2. Tell the truth

Disclosing fair accounting results to concerned parties and telling the truth is ethical behaviour of managers.

3. Respect for people

Ethics requires managers to respect people who contact them.

4. The golden rule

The golden business principle is "Treat others as you would want to be treated". This will always result in ethical behavior.

5. Above all, do no harm

Even if law does not prohibit use of chemicals in producing certain products, managers should avoid them if they are environment pollutants.

6. Practice participation — not paternalism

Managers should not decide on their own what is good or bad for the stakeholders. They should assess their needs, analyze them in the light of business needs and integrate the two by allowing the stakeholders to participate in the decision-making processes.

7. Act when you have responsibility

Actions which cannot be delegated and have to be taken by managers only (given their competence and skill) must be responsibly taken by them for the benefit of the organization and the stakeholders.

Approaches to Management Ethics

There are three approaches to management ethics.

1. Utilitarian approach

In this approach, managers analyze the effects of decisions on people affected by these decisions. The action rather than the motive behind the action is the focus of this approach. Positive and negative results are weighed and managerial actions are justified if positive effects outweigh the negative effects. Pollution standards and analysing the impact of pollution on society is management ethics code under utilitarian approach.

2. Moral rights approach

In this approach, managers follow ethical code which takes care of fundamental and moral rights of human beings; the right to speech, right to life and safety, right to express feelings etc. In the context of business organizations, managers disclose information in the annual reports necessary for welfare of the people concerned. The nature, timing and validity of information is taken into account while reporting information in the annual reports.

3. Social justice approach

According to this approach, managers' actions are fair, impartial and equitable to all individuals and groups. Employees are not distinguished on the basis of caste, religion, race or gender though distinction on the basis of abilities or production is justified. For example, all employees, males or females with same skills should be treated at par but it is justified to treat employees who produce more differently from those who produce less.

Barriers to Management Ethics

James A. Waters describe three "organizational blocks" of management ethics.

1. Chain of command

If employees know that superiors are not following ethical behavior, they hesitate in reporting the matter up the hierarchy for the fear of being misunderstood and penalized. The chain of command is, thus, a barrier to reporting unethical activities of superiors.

2. Group membership

Informal groups lead to group code of ethics. Group members are strongly bonded by their loyalty and respect for each other and unethical behavior of any member of the group is generally ignored by the rest.

3. Ambiguous priorities

When policies are unclear and ambiguous, employees' behavior cannot be guided in a unified direction. It is difficult to understand what is ethical and what is unethical.

Solutions to Barriers

The following measures can improve the climate for ethical behavior.

- Organizational objectives and policies should be clear so that every member works towards these goals ethically.
- The behavior of top managers is followed by others in the organization. Ethical actions of top managers promote ethical behavior throughout the organization.
- Imposing penalties and threats for not conforming to ethical behaviour can reduce unethical activities in the organization. Formal procedures of lodging complaints help subordinates report unethical behavior of superiors to the concerned committees.
- Educational institutions also offer courses and training in business ethics to develop conscientious managers who observe ethical behavior.

Values of Managers

There are many ways in which the basic human values — truth, righteousness, peace, love and non-violence can be practiced in the day-to-day conduct of business. There are different aspects of management such as marketing, finance, industrial relations, etc., but the most important aspect is "man-management."

For example, most of the Indian enterprises today face conflicts, tensions, low efficiency and productivity, absence of motivation, lack of work culture, etc. This is perhaps due to the reason that managers are moving away from the concept of values and ethics.

The lure for maximizing profits is deviating managers from the value-based managerial behavior. There is need for managers to develop a set of values and beliefs that will help them attain the ultimate goals of profits, survival and growth.

1. Optimum utilization of resources

The first lesson in the management science is to choose wisely and utilize optimally the scarce resources to succeed in business venture.

2. Attitude towards work

Managers have to develop visionary perspective in their work. They have to develop a sense of larger vision in their work for the common good.

3. Work commitment

Managers have to work with dedication. Dedicated work means "work for the sake of work". Though results are important, performance should not always be based on expected benefits. They should focus on the quality of performance. The best means for effective work performance is to become the work itself. Attaining the state of *nishkama karma* is the right attitude to work because it prevents ego and the mind from thinking about future gains or losses.

4. Detachment

Managers should renounce egoism and promote teamwork, dignity, sharing, cooperation, harmony, trust, sacrificing lower needs for higher goals, seeing others in you and yourself in others etc. The work must be done with detachment. De-personified intelligence is best suited for those who sincerely believe in the supremacy of organizational goals as compared to narrow personal success and achievement.

5. Vision

Managers must have a long-term vision. The visionary manager must be practical, dynamic and capable of translating dreams into reality. This dynamism and strength of a true leader flows from an inspired and spontaneous motivation to help others.

Second Thoughts

1) What does management ethics mean? Can you define management ethics in your own words?

_____

_____

2) What do value-based managers do to perform their duties well?

_____

_____

International Trade Theory

国际贸易理论

CHAPTER
4

本章概要

本章主要介绍国际贸易相关理论,利用国际贸易理论分析德国如何在全球贸易中取得成功,并详细介绍绝对优势理论和产品生命周期理论。

学习指南

国际贸易从欧洲航海探险、殖民扩张一直发展到今年,已有几个世纪的历史。在此过程中,众多学者对此做了研究,也发展出了很多国际贸易相关的理论。相对而言,国外的理论发展时间较长,国内的理论近年来也有快速的发展。

通过本章学习,希望大家能够实现以下目标:

(1)基本目标(Text-based Goals)

- 掌握本章涉及话题的基本专业术语及词汇,如绝对优势、相对优势、产品生命周期等;
- 掌握本章的主要知识点,即国内外国际贸易理论发展情况、绝对优势理论、产品生命周期理论等。

(2)拓展目标(Extended Goals)

- 思考不同国际贸易理论的优缺点;
- 通过学习背景知识、拓展阅读、案例分析进一步了解影响当今全球贸易的主流理论以及如何用理论来解释贸易现象。

> All theories are legitimate, no matter. What matters is what you do with them.（所有理论都是合理的，这不要紧。要紧的是你拿这些理论做什么。）
>
> —Jorge Luis Borges（豪尔赫·路易斯·博尔赫斯）

International trade theories are simply different theories to explain international trade. Trade is the concept of exchanging goods and services between two people or entities. International trade is then the concept of this exchange between people or entities in two different countries.

People or entities trade because they believe that they benefit from the exchange. They may need or want the goods or services. While at the surface, this may sound very simple, there is a great deal of theory, policy, and business strategy that constitutes international trade.

In this section, you'll learn about the different trade theories that have evolved over the past century and are most relevant today. Additionally, you'll explore the factors that impact international trade and how businesses and governments use these factors to their respective benefits to promote their interests.

What Are the Different International Trade Theories?

"Around 5,200 years ago, Uruk, in southern Mesopotamia, was probably the first city the world had ever seen, housing more than 50,000 people within its six miles of wall. Uruk, its agriculture made prosperous by sophisticated irrigation canals, was home to the first class of middlemen, trade **intermediaries** ... A cooperative trade network ... set the pattern that would endure for the next 6,000 years." Matt Ridley, "Humans: Why They Triumphed", *Wall Street Journal*, May 22, 2010, accessed December 20, 2010,

In more recent centuries, economists have focused on trying to understand and explain these trade patterns. Thomas Friedman's flat-world approach segments history into three stages: Globalization 1.0 from 1492 to 1800, 2.0 from 1800 to 2000, and 3.0 from 2000 to the present. In Globalization 1.0, nations dominated global expansion. In Globalization 2.0, multinational companies **ascended** and pushed global development. Today, technology drives Globalization 3.0.

To better understand how modern global trade has evolved, it's important to understand how countries traded with one another historically. Over time, economists have developed theories to explain the mechanisms of global trade. The main historical theories are called classical and are from the perspective of a country, or country-based. By the mid-twentieth century, the theories began to shift to explain trade from a firm, rather than a country, perspective. These theories are referred to as modern and are firm-based or company-based. Both of these categories, classical and modern, consist of several international theories.

Classical or Country-based Trade Theories

古典或基于国家的贸易理论
主要包括重商主义、绝对优势理论、比较优势理论、赫克歇尔·俄林理论、列昂惕夫悖论。

MERCANTILISM

Developed in the sixteenth century, mercantilism was one of the earliest efforts to develop an economic theory. This theory stated that a country's wealth was determined by the amount of its gold and silver holdings. In its simplest sense, mercantilists believed that a country should increase its holdings of gold and silver by promoting exports and discouraging imports. In other words, if people in other countries buy more from you (exports) than they sell to you (imports), then they have to pay you the difference in gold and silver. The objective of each country was to have a trade surplus, or a situation where the value of exports are greater than the value of imports, and to avoid a trade deficit, or a situation where the value of imports is greater than the value of exports.

A closer look at world history from the 1500s to the late 1800s helps explain why mercantilism flourished. The 1500s marked the rise of new nation-states, whose rulers wanted to strengthen their nations by building larger armies and national institutions. By increasing exports and trade, these rulers were able to **amass** more gold and wealth for their countries. One way that many of these new nations promoted exports was to impose restrictions on imports. This strategy is called **protectionism** and is still used today.

Nations expanded their wealth by using their colonies around the world in an effort to control more trade and amass more riches. The British colonial empire was one of the more successful examples; it sought to increase its wealth by using raw materials from places ranging from what are now the Americas and India. France, the Netherlands, Portugal, and Spain were also successful in building large colonial empires that generated extensive wealth for their governing nations.

Although mercantilism is one of the oldest trade theories, it remains part of modern thinking. Countries such as Japan, Singapore, and even Germany still favor exports and discourage imports through a form of neo-mercantilism in which the countries promote a combination of protectionist policies and restrictions and domestic-industry **subsidies**. Nearly every country, at one point or another, has implemented some form of protectionist policy to guard key industries in its economy. While export-oriented companies usually support protectionist policies that

Word Study

mercantilism
/ˈmɜːkəntaɪlɪzəm/
n. 重商主义
amass /əˈmæs/ v.
（尤指大量）积累，积聚
protectionism
/prəˈtekʃənɪzəm/
n. 保护主义
subsidy /ˈsʌbsɪdi/ n.
补贴

favor their industries or firms, other companies and consumers are hurt by protectionism. Taxpayers pay for government subsidies of select exports in the form of higher taxes. Import restrictions lead to higher prices for consumers, who pay more for foreign-made goods or services. Free-trade advocates **highlight** how free trade benefits all members of the global community, while mercantilism's protectionist policies only benefit select industries, at the expense of both consumers and other companies, within and outside of the industry.

ABSOLUTE ADVANTAGE

In 1776, Adam Smith questioned the leading **mercantile** theory of the time in *The Wealth of Nations*, or *An Inquiry into the Nature and Causes of the Wealth of Nations* (London: W. Strahan and T. Cadell, 1776). Recent versions have been edited by scholars and economists. Smith offered a new trade theory called absolute advantage, which focused on the ability of a country to produce a good more efficiently than another nation. Smith reasoned that trade between countries shouldn't be regulated or restricted by government policy or intervention. He stated that trade should flow naturally according to market forces. In a hypothetical two-country world, if Country A could produce a good cheaper or faster (or both) than Country B, then Country A had the advantage and could focus on specializing on producing that good. Similarly, if Country B was better at producing another good, it could focus on specialization as well. By specialization, countries would generate efficiencies, because their labor force would become more skilled by doing the same tasks. Production would also become more efficient, because there would be an **incentive** to create faster and better production methods to increase the specialization.

Smith's theory reasoned that with increased efficiencies, people in both countries would benefit and trade should be encouraged. His theory stated that a nation's wealth shouldn't be judged by how much gold and silver it had but rather by the living standards of its people.

COMPARATIVE ADVANTAGE

The challenge to the absolute advantage theory was that some countries may be better at producing both goods and, therefore, have an advantage in many areas. In contrast, another country may not have any useful absolute advantages. To answer this challenge, David Ricardo, an English economist, introduced the theory of comparative advantage in 1817. Ricardo reasoned that even if Country A had the absolute advantage in the production of both products, **specialization** and trade could still occur between two countries.

Comparative advantage occurs when a country cannot produce a product more efficiently than the other country; however, it can produce

Word Study

highlight /'haɪlaɪt/ *v.*
    强调, 突出
mercantile /'mɜːkəntaɪl/
    adj. 商业的, 贸易的
incentive /ɪn'sentɪv/
    n. 激励
specialization
    /ˌspeʃəlaɪ'zeɪʃən/ *n.*
    专门化

productivity
/ˌprɒdʌkˈtɪvɪti/ *n.*
生产力,生产率
concentrate
/ˈkɒnsentreɪt/ *v.* 集
中(注意力),全神
贯注
abundance /əˈbʌndəns/
n. 富足,富裕
labor-intensive
/ˈleɪbə.ɪnˈtensɪv/
adj. 劳动密集型的

that product better and more efficiently than it does other goods. The difference between these two theories is subtle. Comparative advantage focuses on the relative **productivity** differences, whereas absolute advantage looks at the absolute productivity.

Let's look at a simplified hypothetical example to illustrate the subtle difference between these principles. Miranda is a Wall Street lawyer who charges $500 per hour for her legal services. It turns out that Miranda can also type faster than the administrative assistants in her office, who are paid $40 per hour. Even though Miranda clearly has the absolute advantage in both skill sets, should she do both jobs? No. For every hour Miranda decides to type instead of doing legal work, she would be giving up $460 in income. Her productivity and income will be highest if she specializes in the higher-paid legal services and hires the most qualified administrative assistant, who can type fast, although a little slower than Miranda. By having both Miranda and her assistant **concentrate** on their respective tasks, their overall productivity as a team is higher. This is comparative advantage. A person or a country will specialize in doing what they do relatively better. In reality, the world economy is more complex and consists of more than two countries and products. Barriers to trade may exist, and goods must be transported, stored, and distributed. However, this simplistic example demonstrates the basis of the comparative advantage theory.

HECKSCHER-OHLIN THEORY (FACTOR PROPORTIONS THEORY)

The theories of Smith and Ricardo didn't help countries determine which products would give a country an advantage. Both theories assumed that free and open markets would lead countries and producers to determine which goods they could produce more efficiently. In the early 1900s, two Swedish economists, Eli Heckscher and Bertil Ohlin, focused their attention on how a country could gain comparative advantage by producing products that utilized factors that were in **abundance** in the country. Their theory is based on a country's production factors — land, labor, and capital, which provide the funds for investment in plants and equipment. They determined that the cost of any factor or resource was a function of supply and demand. Factors that were in great supply relative to demand would be cheaper; factors in great demand relative to supply would be more expensive. Their theory, also called the factor proportions theory, stated that countries would produce and export goods that required resources or factors that were in great supply and, therefore, cheaper production factors. In contrast, countries would import goods that required resources that were in short supply, but higher demand.

For example, the Philippines and India are home to cheap, large pools of labor. Hence these countries have become the optimal locations for **labor-intensive** industries like textiles and garments.

LEONTIEF PARADOX

In the early 1950s, Russian-born American economist Wassily W. Leontief studied the U.S. economy closely and noted that the United States was abundant in capital and, therefore, should export more capital-intensive goods. However, his research using actual data showed the opposite: the United States was importing more capital-intensive goods. According to the factor proportions theory, the United States should have been importing labor-intensive goods, but instead it was actually exporting them. His analysis became known as the Leontief Paradox because it was the reverse of what was expected by the factor proportions theory. In subsequent years, economists have noted historically at that point in time, labor in the United States was both available in steady supply and more productive than in many other countries; hence it made sense to export labor-intensive goods. Over the decades, many economists have used theories and data to explain and minimize the impact of the paradox. However, what remains clear is that international trade is complex and is impacted by numerous and often-changing factors. Trade cannot be explained **neatly** by one single theory, and more importantly, our understanding of international trade theories continues to evolve.

Word Study

paradox /'pærədɒks/
  n. 悖论
neatly /niːtlɪ/ adv. 整
  齐地,恰如其分地.
intraindustry
  /'ɪntrə'ɪndəstrɪ/ adj.
  行业内的,产业内的

Modern or Firm-based Trade Theories

In contrast to classical, country-based trade theories, the category of modern, firm-based theories emerged after World War II and was developed in large part by business school professors, not economists. The firm-based theories evolved with the growth of the multinational company (MNC). The country-based theories couldn't adequately address the expansion of either MNCs or **intraindustry** trade, which refers to trade between two countries of goods produced in the same industry. For example, Japan exports Toyota vehicles to Germany and imports Mercedes-Benz automobiles from Germany.

Unlike the country-based theories, firm-based theories incorporate other product and service factors, including brand and customer loyalty, technology, and quality, into the understanding of trade flows.

COUNTRY SIMILARITY THEORY

Swedish economist Steffan Linder developed the country similarity theory in 1961, as he tried to explain the concept of intraindustry trade. Linder's theory proposed that consumers in countries that are in the same or similar stage of development would have similar preferences. In this firm-based theory, Linder suggested that companies first produce for domestic consumption. When they explore exporting, the companies often find that markets that look similar to their domestic one, in terms of

现代或基于企业的
贸易理论
    与传统的基于
国家的贸易理论相
反,现代的基于公司
的理论类别是在第
二次世界大战之后
出现的,并且在很大
程度上是由商学院
教授而不是经济学
家发展起来的。 基
于公司的理论随着
跨国公司(MNC)的
发展而发展。 基于
国家的理论无法充
分解决跨国公司或
行业内贸易扩张问
题,后者是指两个国
家在同一行业生产
的商品之间的贸易。
例如,日本向德国出
口丰田汽车,并从德
国进口奔驰汽车。

Word Study

per capita 人均
maturing /məˈtjʊərɪŋ/
  adj. 成熟的
substantial /səbˈstænʃəl/
  adj. 大量的，重大的
rivalry /ˈraɪvəlrɪ/ *n.*
  竞争（对手）
optimize /ˈɒptɪmaɪz/ *v.*
  使最优化，使完善

customer preferences, offer the most potential for success. Linder's country similarity theory then states that most trade in manufactured goods will be between countries with similar **per capita** incomes, and intraindustry trade will be common. This theory is often most useful in understanding trade in goods where brand names and product reputations are important factors in the buyers' decision-making and purchasing processes.

PRODUCT LIFE CYCLE THEORY

Raymond Vernon, a Harvard Business School professor, developed the product life cycle theory in the 1960s. The theory, originating in the field of marketing, stated that a product life cycle has three distinct stages: (1) new product, (2) **maturing** product, and (3) standardized product. The theory assumed that production of the new product will occur completely in the home country of its innovation. In the 1960s this was a useful theory to explain the manufacturing success of the United States. U.S. manufacturing was the globally dominant producer in many industries after World War II.

It has also been used to describe how the personal computer (PC) went through its product cycle. The PC was a new product in the 1970s and developed into a mature product during the 1980s and 1990s. Today, the PC is in the standardized product stage, and the majority of manufacturing and production process is done in low-cost countries in Asia and Mexico.

The product life cycle theory has been less able to explain current trade patterns where innovation and manufacturing occur around the world. For example, global companies even conduct research and development in developing markets where highly skilled labor and facilities are usually cheaper. Even though research and development is typically associated with the first or new product stage and therefore completed in the home country, these developing or emerging-market countries, such as India and China, offer both highly skilled labor and new research facilities at a **substantial** cost advantage for global firms.

GLOBAL STRATEGIC **RIVALRY** THEORY

Global strategic rivalry theory emerged in the 1980s and was based on the work of economists Paul Krugman and Kelvin Lancaster. Their theory focused on MNCs and their efforts to gain a competitive advantage against other global firms in their industry. Firms will encounter global competition in their industries and in order to prosper, they must develop competitive advantages. The critical ways that firms can obtain a sustainable competitive advantage are called the barriers to entry for that industry. The barriers to entry refer to the obstacles a new firm may face when trying to enter into an industry or new market. The barriers to entry that corporations may seek to **optimize** include:

- research and development,

- the ownership of intellectual property rights,
- economies of scale,
- unique business processes or methods as well as extensive experience in the industry, and
- the control of resources or favorable access to raw materials.

PORTER'S NATIONAL COMPETITIVE ADVANTAGE THEORY

In the continuing evolution of international trade theories, Michael Porter of Harvard Business School developed a new model to explain national competitive advantage in 1990. Porter's theory stated that a nation's competitiveness in an industry depends on the **capacity** of the industry to innovate and upgrade. His theory focused on explaining why some nations are more competitive in certain industries. To explain his theory, Porter identified four **determinants** that he linked together.

1. Local market resources and capabilities (factor conditions)

Porter recognized the value of the factor proportions theory, which considers a nation's resources (e.g., natural resources and available labor) as key factors in determining what products a country will import or export. Porter added to these basic factors a new list of advanced factors, which he defined as skilled labor, investments in education, technology, and infrastructure. He perceived these advanced factors as providing a country with a sustainable competitive advantage.

2. Local market demand conditions

Porter believed that a sophisticated home market is critical to ensuring ongoing innovation, thereby creating a sustainable competitive advantage. Companies whose domestic markets are sophisticated, trendsetting and demanding force continuous innovation and the development of new products and technologies. Many sources credit the demanding U.S. consumers with forcing U.S. software companies to continuously innovate, thus creating a sustainable competitive advantage in software products and services.

3. Local suppliers and complementary industries

To remain competitive, large global firms benefit from having strong, efficient supporting and related industries to provide the inputs required by the industry. Certain industries cluster geographically, which provides efficiencies and productivity.

4. Local firm characteristics

Local firm characteristics include firm strategy, industry structure, and industry rivalry. Local strategy affects a firm's competitiveness. A healthy level of rivalry between local firms will **spur** innovation and competitiveness.

In addition to the four determinants of the diamond, Porter also noted that government and chance play a part in the national competitiveness

Word Study

capacity /kəˈpæsɪti/ *n.*
能力
determinant
/dɪˈtɜːmɪnənt/ *n.*
决定因素
complementary
/ˌkɒmpləˈmentərɪ/
adj. 补足的，互补的
spur /spɜː/ *v.* 激励，
促进

of industries. Governments can, by their actions and policies, increase the competitiveness of firms and occasionally entire industries.

Porter's theory, along with the other modern, firm-based theories, offers an interesting interpretation of international trade trends. Nevertheless, they remain relatively new and minimally tested theories.

Which Trade Theory Is Dominant Today?

The theories covered in this chapter are simply that — theories. While they have helped economists, governments, and businesses better understand international trade and how to promote, regulate, and manage it, these theories are occasionally contradicted by real-world events. Countries don't have absolute advantages in many areas of production or services and, in fact, the factors of production aren't neatly distributed between countries. Some countries have a disproportionate benefit of some factors. The United States has ample arable land that can be used for a wide range of agricultural products. It also has extensive access to capital. While its labor pool may not be the cheapest, it is among the best educated in the world. These advantages in the factors of production have helped the United States become the largest economy in the world. Nevertheless, the United States also imports a vast amount of goods and services, as U.S. consumers use their wealth to purchase what they need and want — much of which is now manufactured in other countries that have sought to create their own comparative advantages through cheap labor, land, or production costs.

As a result, it's not clear that any one theory is dominant around the world. This section has sought to highlight the basics of international trade theory to enable you to understand the realities that face global businesses. In practice, governments and companies use a combination of these theories to both interpret trends and develop strategy. Just as these theories have evolved over the past five hundred years, they will continue to change and adapt as new factors impact international trade.

Key Terms
专业术语

trade pattern 贸易模式

trade deficit 贸易逆差

comparative advantage 比较优势

factor proportions theory 要素供给比例理论

Leontiff paradox 里昂惕夫悖论

country similarity theory 国家相似理论

product life cycle theory 产品生命周期理论

global strategic rivalry theory 全球战略竞争理论

national competitive advantage theory 国家竞争优势理论

trade surplus 贸易顺差

absolute advantage 绝对优势

barriers to entry 进入壁垒

亚当·斯密和《国富论》

亚当·斯密的《国富论》被后世经济学家认定为"古典经济学"的开端，被列为每位经济学专业学习者的必读本。斯密的经济自由主义涵盖国内贸易和国际贸易的各个方面。他的政策建议实际上成为英国乃至其他资本主义国家的实施准则。时至今日，斯密的自由主义经济学说仍然影响深远，成了各种观点的源泉和出发点。大卫·李嘉图(1772—1823)、让·巴蒂斯特·萨伊(1767—1832)、托马斯·罗伯特·马尔萨斯(1766—1834)都把斯密的理论作为自己的出发点，都从其著作中吸取了部分观点。斯密经济学说中科学的、合理的成分也被马克思批判继承，成为马克思主义的理论源泉之一。19世纪70年代出现的"边际革命"，斯密被视为主观效用学派的先驱。20世纪30年代经济大萧条出现之后，凯恩斯主义者把灾难归咎于经济学家过于信赖斯密的"看不见的手"的作用，主张用政府"看得见的手"取代"看不见的手"。

亚当·斯密的主要经济理论包括：

1. 经济增长理论

斯密关于经济增长问题的基本构思：经济增长是一个宏观问题，它表现在社会财富和国民财富的增长上，因此，国民财富的性质和来源必须得到说明。国民财富的增长决定于两个条件：劳动生产率和从事生产劳动的人数。影响劳动生产率的是分工，从事生产劳动的人数多寡和人口增减有关，更取决于资本的丰歉。国民财富的增长，在一个封闭的社会里，要受到本国资源和技术条件的限制，通过对外贸易则可以突破这种限制而利用外部条件促进增长，因此研究经济增长问题必然涉及对外贸易问题。经济增长既然是一个宏观问题，它与国家的决策就必然密切相关，因此，研究经济增长问题就应当研究经济政策。

2. 价值与货币理论

为了阐明支配商品交换的规律，斯密首先对价值的意义做了解释。他在著作中说道："价值一词有两个不同的意义。它有时表示特定物品的效用，有时又表示由于占有某物而取得的对他种货物的购买力。前者可以叫作使用价值，后者可以叫作交换价值。"明确区分了商品的使用价值与交换价值，是斯密的一个贡献。

斯密还认为，劳动是衡量一切商品交换价值的真实尺度。确认劳动是一切商品价值的源泉，是衡量一切商品交换价值的真实尺度，这是斯密在政治经济学上的重大贡献。他不仅证明生产商品耗费的劳动决定商品的价值，而且对价值的性质做了分析。

3. 工资与剩余价值理论

斯密在《国富论》中阐释了价值理论之后，立即转入分配理论的论述。这是因为按照他的逻辑，商品的价值是由三种收入(工资、利润、地租)决定的，而三种收入如何决定，必须在此之后做出理论回答。

斯密认为："一国土地和劳动的全部年产物，或者说，物的全部价格自然分解为土地地租、劳动工资和资本利润三部分。这三部分构成了三个阶级人民的收入，即以地租为生、以工资为生和以利润为生这三种人的收入。此三阶级构成了文明社会的三大主要和基本阶级。一切其他阶级的收入，归根结底，都来自这三大阶级的收入。"这样，斯密不仅解释了资本主义社会各种收入的源泉——土地和劳动的全部年产物，并且依据三种收入的归属解释了资本主义社会三大基本阶级的划分。这个理论为斯密分析资本主义生产方式和分配方式提供了前提。

4. 生产劳动与非生产劳动理论

斯密在《国富论》中指出，一国国民每年所拥有的生活必需品相对消费者人数的比例，决定一国供给情况的好坏。而这一比例受以下两种情况支配：第一、国民的素质，即劳动的熟练程度、技巧及其判断力；第二、从事有用劳动的人数和不从事这种劳动的人数的比例。

5. 经济自由与国际贸易理论

经济自由主义思想是亚当·斯密适应18世纪资本主义经济发展的时代要求，在《国富论》中论证和倡导的一种经济思想和政策主张。根据这种思想，资本主义经济要想发展，必须鼓励自由竞争，反对国家对经济活动的干预。但斯密的经济自由主义并不是绝对的、无限制的自由，他主张在国内政策中对自由竞争实行一些限制，因而提出了国家职能的问题。

资料来源：维基百科

Workbook
练一练

A. What are the firm-based trade theories covered in the text?

1. _____

2. _____

3. _____

4. _____

B. According to the text, fill in each of the following blanks with an appropriate word or phrase.

1) Mercantilists believed that a country should increase its holdings of _____ by promoting exports and discouraging imports.

2) Nearly every country, at one point or another, has implemented some form of _____ policy to guard key industries in its economy.

3) Adam Smith stated that trade should flow naturally according to _____.

4) In the early 1950s, Russian-born American economist Wassily W. Leontief analyzed the U.S. economy and his analysis became known as the _____.

5) The category of modern, firm-based theories emerged after _____ _____ and was developed in large part by business school _____ _____, not economists.

6) Linder's theory proposed that consumers in countries that are in the same or similar stage of development would have similar _____ _____.

7) Raymond Vernon developed _____ theory in the 1960s, which originated in the field of _____ .

8) The product life circle theory stated that a product life cycle has three distinct stages: new product, _____ , and standardized product.

9) _____ theory emerged in the 1980s and was based on the work of economists Paul Krugman and Kelvin Lancaster.

10) Porter's _____ theory focused on explaining why some nations are more competitive in certain industries.

C. Read the text and decide whether the following statements are True (T) or False (F).

1) Trade is the concept of exchanging goods and services between two people or entities. ( )

2) Thomas Friedman's flat-world approach segments history into four stages. ( )

3) By the mid-twentieth century, the theories began to shift to explain trade from a country perspective. ( )

4) Some countries still favor imports and discourage exports through a form of neo-mercantilism. ( )

5) The British colonial empire sought to increase its wealth by using raw materials from Americas and India. ( )

6) Adam Smith questioned the leading mercantile theory of the time in *The Wealth of Nations*. ( )

7) It's Marx who offered a new trade theory called absolute advantage. ( )

8) David Ricardo, an English economist, introduced the theory of comparative advantage in 1817. ( )

9) Absolute advantage occurs when a country cannot produce a product more efficiently than the other country. ( )

10) According to the factor proportions theory, America should have been exporting more labor-intensive goods. ( )

Discussion
讨论

1) What are the main opinions of mercantilism?

_____

_____

2) What are the differences between absolute advantage and comparative advantage?

_____

_____

3) Can you explain the determinants of the national competitive advantage?

_____

_____

4) Do you know some main international trade theories from our country?

_____

_____

5) What should governments and companies do with the variety of international trade theories to promote economic development in reality?

_____

_____

Case Story

Germany in World Trade: A Clear Winner of Globalization

Whenever a country is particularly good in one area, its products and services tend to seek their way to customers beyond national borders. It is the birth of a new export hit. The Swiss export their watches all over the world; China excels in trade in electronics; and the United States is particularly good in trade in services. Everyone does what they do best. That's how world trade works; that's how everyone benefits.

Today, value chains are strongly internationalized. Intermediate products, components, and industry-related services are traded across national borders in order to be further processed or finished by subsidiaries or industrial customers. In 2017, 46.5 percent of German merchandise exports and 51.6 percent of imported goods were intermediate products according to the World Trade Organization (WTO).

In addition, so-called intraindustry trade — trade in the same products — plays an important role in world trade, in particular in trade among industrialized countries. Germany, for example, produces cars and exports them to Sweden. Cars are also produced in Sweden and find their customers in Germany. The reasons for this include product differentiation and varying consumer preferences.

Cross-border trade makes it possible to utilize technological leadership. This benefits exporters as well as customers because they can choose the right products for them from a greater variety.

Furthermore, more trade makes production more cost-effective via specialization and economies of scale: Producing not only a few products of a certain type but larger quantities for a worldwide clientele reduces the share of fixed costs in overall costs. Because the manufacturer can standardize and prefabricate parts and automate work processes, costs decrease while the quality stays high.

Nevertheless, governments sometimes find it difficult to dismantle trade barriers due to the competition brought to their own markets by opening boarders. All in all, the aggregate welfare effects of trade are generally positive. Many academic studies show that trade liberalization and economic growth correlate positively. More competition essentially means more supply, pressure to innovate, and falling prices. However, trade can also have redistributional effects. Not all companies will be able to strive in the new environment. This makes it all the more important that states invest in training and education as well as research and development and that social systems are well-equipped to mitigate the adaptation costs.

Germany as Trading Power

Germany has long known how to take advantage of the benefits of globalization. Today, exports of goods and services account for around half of the country's value added. One in four jobs depends on exports; in industry, this is true for even more than every other job. Exports are not the only decisive factor here. As a manufacturing nation, Germany also heavily depends on inexpensive, high-quality imports. According to WTO data, around 25 percent of the value added in German exports in goods was directly attributable to foreign suppliers in 2015.

For years, Germany has ranked high on the list of top trading nations, placing third in 2018 (exports of goods and services taken together); only China and the United States sold more globally. The nation is also one of the top three importing countries after the United States and China. Germany could not maintain its position as a competitive exporter without German industry being deeply integrated in reliable, international value chains.

Trade Agreements: Free Trade, Strong Rules

Due to worldwide technological progress, transport costs are falling continuously. At the same time, however, customs duties and a large number of so-called non-tariff trade barriers continue to place a severe burden on global trade. Consumers pay the price in the form of higher prices and the unavailability of better products and services.

This certainly does not have to be the case. Countries have opened their markets under the General Agreement on Tariffs and Trade (GATT, 1947) and later under the WTO (founded in 1995). In addition, states have committed to liberalizing trade in more than 300 trade agreements (trade agreements notified to the WTO that are still in force today). In addition, there are numerous unilateral trade agreements in which industrialized and emerging countries grant developing countries preferential access.

However, free trade does not mean that trade takes place without rules. Quite the opposite, it means that countries commit to certain rules in trade agreements such as the non-discrimination principle. They also often sign up to rules on government procurement, competition, trade-related investment matters, and trade facilitation. Modern trade agreements also feature strong sustainability chapters on labor and environmental standards. Most trade agreements also feature dispute settlement procedures. Last but not least, countries can also re-implement trade barriers — for example, if a product or service poses a risk to the health of humans, animals or plants or are a threat to national security.

The content of trade agreements has changed over time: for example, the European Union (EU)'s free trade agreements with Mexico and Chile, negotiated in the late 1990s, focused mainly on dismantling tariffs. Newer trade agreements, such as those between the EU and South Korea, Vietnam, Singapore, Canada, and Japan, also cover the so-called WTO+ areas. These are issues that have not yet been discussed at the multilateral level, or only to a limited extent, including competition rules, the protection of intellectual property, government procurement, and investments.

In addition, EU member states have signed a multitude of investment treaties. They grant protection to foreign investors against political risks such as discrimination and expropriation. In the past, such agreements were usually signed by two states (some of them are also plurilateral) and negotiated separately from trade agreements. With the Lisbon Treaty in 2009, the EU gained competence to negotiate such treaties for the EU as a whole and made them part of free trade agreements (e.g. with Canada). Subsequently, the European Court of Justice clarified that investor-state arbitration proceedings do not fall within the exclusive competence of the EU and that corresponding agreements must therefore be ratified by all member states before they come into force. In order not to overburden free trade agreements with lengthy ratification processes of the chapters on investment protection, the EU has started to separate investment protection from free trade agreements wherever possible.

The dismantling of regulatory barriers to trade is another aim of free trade agreement. Of course, regulatory cooperation states should neither lead to lower standards, for example in consumer protection, nor should it restrict the scope for political action of the EU and its member states.

Case Discussion

1) What are the benefits of world trade to participants?

_____

_____

2) Which international trade theory do you think can be used to analyze Germany as a winner of globalization?

_____

_____

3) What roles do trade agreements play in world trade?

_____

_____

Case Summary

当一个国家在某个领域特别出色时,其产品和服务往往会寻求国外客户。比如,瑞士向世界各地出口手表;中国出口电子产品;美国则在服务贸易方面尤其出色。每个人都做自己最擅长的事,这就是世界贸易的运作方式。

德国作为国际贸易的受益者,其商品和服务出口占该国增加值的一半左右,四分之一的就业岗位取决于出口;而作为一个制造业大国,德国也严重依赖质优价廉的进口产品。根据WTO的数据,2015年德国商品出口增加值中约有25%直接归因于外国供应商。

多年来,德国在顶级贸易国名单上名列前茅,在2018年排名第三(商品和服务出口加起来)。该国也是仅次于美国和中国的前三大进口国之一。如果德国工业不能深入融入可靠的国际价值链,德国就无法保持其作为有竞争力的出口国的地位。

在国际贸易中,各国间签订大量贸易协定,以促进自由贸易,规范贸易行为、确保平等公正。德国国际贸易的发展也受益于自由贸易协定。

Reading I

Theory of Absolute Advantage of International Trade

Economist Adam Smith critically evaluated mercantilist trade policies in his seminal book *An Inquiry into the Nature and Causes of the Wealth of Nations*, first published in 1776. Smith posited that the wealth of a nation does not lie in building huge stockpiles of gold and silver in its treasury, but the real wealth of a nation is measured by the level of improvement in the quality of living of its citizens, as reflected by the per capita income.

Smith emphasized productivity and advocated free trade as a means of increasing global efficiency. As per his formulation, a country's standards of living can be enhanced by international trade with other countries either by importing goods not produced by it or by producing large quantities of goods through specialization and exporting the surplus.

An absolute advantage refers to the ability of a country to produce a good more efficiently and cost-effectively than any other country.

Smith elucidated the concept of "absolute advantage" leading to gains from specialization with the help of day-to-day illustrations as follows:

It is the maxim of every prudent master of a family, never to make at home what it will cost him more to make than to buy. The tailor does not attempt to make his own shoes, but buys them from the shoemaker. The shoemaker does not attempt to make his own clothes, but employs a tailor.

The farmer attempts to make neither one nor the other, but employs those different artificers. All of them find it for their interest to employ their whole industry in a way which they have some advantage over their neighbors.

What is prudence in the conduct of every private family can scarce be folly in that of a great kingdom. If a foreign country can supply us with a commodity cheaper than we ourselves can make it, better buy it with some part of the produce of our own industry. Thus, instead of producing all products, each country should specialize in producing those goods that it can produce more efficiently.

Such efficiency is gained through:

i. Repetitive production of a product, which increases the skills of the labor force.

ii. Switching production from one produce to another to save labor time.

iii. Long product runs to provide incentives to develop more effective work methods over a period of time.

Therefore, a country should use increased production to export and acquire more goods by way of imports, which would in turn improve the living standards of its people. A country's advantage may be either natural or acquired.

Natural Advantage

Natural factors, such as a country's geographical and agro-climatic conditions, mineral or other natural resources, or specialized manpower contribute to a country's natural advantage in certain products. For instance, the agro-climatic condition in India is an important factor for sizeable export of agro-produce, such as spices, cotton, tea, and mangoes.

The availability of relatively cheap labor contributes to India's edge in export of labor-intensive products. The production of wheat and maize in the U.S., petroleum in Saudi Arabia, citrus fruits in Israel, lumber in Canada, and aluminum ore in Jamaica are all illustrations of natural advantages.

Acquired Advantage

Today, international trade is shifting from traditional agro-products to industrial products and services, especially in developing countries like India. The acquired advantage in either a product or its process technology plays an important role in creating such a shift.

The ability to differentiate or produce a different product is termed as an advantage in product technology, while the ability to produce a homogeneous product more efficiently is termed as an advantage in process technology.

Production of consumer electronics and automobiles in Japan, software in India, watches in Switzerland, and shipbuilding in South Korea may be attributed to acquired advantage. Some of the exports centers in India for precious and semi-precious stones in Jaipur, Surat, Navsari, and Mumbai have come up not because of their raw material resources but the skills they have developed in processing imported raw stones.

To illustrate the concept of absolute advantage, an example of two countries may be taken, such as the UK and India. Let us assume that both the countries have the same amount of resources, say 100 units, such as land, labor, capital, etc., which can be employed either to produce tea or rice.

However, the production efficiency is assumed to vary between the countries because to produce a tonne of tea, the UK requires 10 units of resources whereas India requires only 5 units of resources. On the other hand, for producing one tonne of rice, the UK requires only 4 units of resources whereas India needs 10 units of resources.

Since India requires lower resources compared to the UK for producing tea, it is relatively more efficient in tea production. On the other hand, since the UK requires fewer resources compared to India for producing rice, it is relatively more efficient in producing rice.

Although each country is assumed to possess equal resources, the production possibilities for each country would vary, depending upon their production efficiency and utilization of available resources.

All of the possible combinations of the two products that can be produced with a country's limited resources may be graphically depicted by a production possibilities curve, assuming total resource availability of 100 units with each country.

The slope of the curve reflects the trade-off of producing one product over the other, representing opportunity cost. The value of a factor of production forgone for its alternate use is termed as opportunity cost.

For instance, if the UK wishes to produce one tonne of tea, it has to forgo the production of 2.5 tonnes of rice. Whereas in order to produce one unit of rice, it has to relinquish the production of only 0.4 tonne of tea.

Suppose no foreign trade takes place between the two countries and each employs its resources equally (i.e., 50:50) for production of tea and rice. The UK would produce 5 tonnes of tea and 12.5 tonnes of rice at point B whereas India would produce 10 tonnes of tea and 5 tonnes of rice at point A as shown in Fig. 4.1.

This would result in a total output of 15 tonnes of tea and 17.5 tonnes of rice. If both India and the UK employ their resources on production of only tea and rice, respectively, in which each of them has absolute advantage, the total output, as depicted in Fig. 4.1, of tea would increase from 15 tonnes to 20 tonnes (point C) whereas rice would increase from 17.5 tonnes to 25 tonnes (point D).

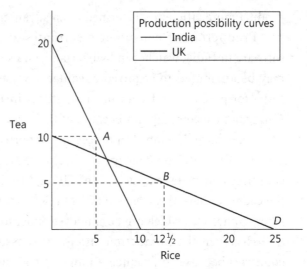

Fig. 4.1 *Production possibilities under absolute advantage*

Thus, both countries can mutually gain from trading, as the total output is enhanced as a result of specialization.

The theory of absolute advantage is based on Adam Smith's doctrine of *laissez faire* that means "let make freely". When specifically applied to international trade, it refers to "freedom of enterprise" and "freedom of commerce".

Therefore, according to Smith, the government should not intervene in the economic life of a nation or in its trade relations among nations, in the form of tariffs or other trade restrictions, which would be counterproductive.

A market would reach an efficient end by itself without any government intervention. Unlike as suggested by the mercantilist theory, trading is not a zero-sum game under the theory of absolute advantage, wherein a nation can gain only if a trading partner loses. Instead, the countries involved in free trade would mutually benefit as a result of efficient allocation of their resources.

Second Thoughts

For each of the following questions, choose the best answer.

1) Which of the following is the best method according to the absolute advantage theory?

   A. To produce products with the lowest labor cost.

   B. To produce products with the lowest price.

   C. To produce products with the highest efficiency.

   D. To produce products with the highest labor cost.

2) Which of the following do you think is NOT the best choice to import according to the absolute advantage theory?

   A. India's spice.   B. Arabia's petroleum.

   C. Russia's natural gas.   D. Kenya's water.

Reading II

Product Life Cycle Theory

International markets tend to follow a cyclical pattern due to a variety of factors over a period of time, which explains the shifting of markets as well as the location of production. The level of innovation and technology, resources, size of market, and competitive structure influence trade patterns.

In addition, the gap in technology and preference and the ability of the customers in international markets also determine the stage of international product life cycle (IPLC).

In case the innovating country has a large market size, as in case of the U.S., India, China, etc., it can support mass production for domestic sales. This mass market also facilitates the producers based in these countries to achieve cost-efficiency, which enables them to become internationally competitive.

However, in case the market size of a country is too small to achieve economies of scale from the domestic market, the companies from these countries can alternatively achieve economies of scale by setting up their marketing and production facilities in other cost-effective countries.

Thus, it is the economies of scope that assists in achieving the economies of scale by expanding into international markets. The theory explains the variations and reasons for change in production and consumption patterns among various markets over a time period.

The IPLC has four distinct identifiable stages that influence demand structure, production, marketing strategy, and international competition as follows.

Introduction

Generally, it is in high-income or developed countries that the majority of new product inventions take place, as product inventions require substantial resources to be expended on R&D activities and need speedy recovery of the initial cost incurred by way of market-skimming pricing strategies.

Since, in the initial stages, the price of a new product is relatively higher, buying the product is only within the means and capabilities of customers in high-income countries. Therefore, a firm finds a market for new products in other developed or high-income countries in the initial stages.

Growth

The demand in the international markets exhibits an increasing trend and the innovating firm gets better opportunities for exports. Moreover, as the market begins to develop in other developed countries, the innovating firm faces increased international competition in the target market.

In order to defend its position in international markets, the firm establishes its production locations in other developed or high-income countries.

Maturity

As the technical know-how of the innovative process becomes widely known, the firm begins to establish its operations in middle- and low-income countries in order to take advantage of resources available at competitive prices.

Decline

The major thrust of marketing strategy at this stage shifts to price and cost competitiveness, as the technical know-how and skills become widely available. Therefore, the emphasis of the firm is on most cost-effective locations rather than on producing themselves.

Besides other middle-income or developing countries, the production also intensifies in low-income or least-developed countries (LDCs). As a result, it has been observed that the innovating country begins to import such goods from other developing countries rather than manufacturing itself.

The UK, which was once the largest manufacturer and exporter of bicycles, now imports this product in large volumes. The bicycle is at the declining stage of its life cycle in industrialized countries whereas it is still at a growth or maturity stage in a number of developing countries.

The chemical and hazardous industries are also shifting from high-income countries to low-income countries as a part of their increasing concern about environmental issues, exhibiting a cyclical pattern in international markets.

Although the product life cycle explains the emerging pattern of international markets, it has got its own limitations in the present marketing era with the fast proliferation of market information, wherein products are launched more or less simultaneously in various markets.

Second Thoughts

1) What is product life cycle theory? Can you define it in your own words?

_____

_____

2) Which stage do you think is the most important? Why?

_____

_____

Foreign Direct Investment

外国直接投资

CHAPTER 5

本章概要

本章主要介绍外国直接投资的含义、方式、种类、收益、成本以及影响其波动的因素，介绍新加坡的全球投资战略，比较外国直接投资与外国证券投资的异同，并解释企业选择不同投资方式的考虑。

学习指南

外国直接投资亦称"外商直接投资"，指一国投资者为实现持久利益而对本国之外的企业进行投资，并对该国外企业的经营管理实施有效影响和控制的经济活动，既包括上述两个经济实体之间的初次交易，也包括它们之间以及所有附属企业之间的后续交易。由于企业的经营管理权通常受股权比例的影响，经济合作与发展组织建议以拥有国外企业 10% 的股权作为外国直接投资的最低标准。不过，有些国家以其他证据而非股权比例来认定对外国企业经营管理的有效影响。

通过本章学习，希望大家能够实现以下目标：

（1）基本目标（Text-based Goals）

● 掌握本章涉及话题的基本专业术语及词汇，如合资企业、国际收支、收购、东道国等。

● 掌握本章的主要知识点，即外国直接投资的含义、外国直接投资的方式和种类、外国直接投资的收益和成本，以及影响其波动的因素。

（2）拓展目标（Extended Goals）

● 思考本章引言，为什么"在过去的 25 年里，外国直接投资的增长速度比贸易快得多"？

● 通过学习背景知识、拓展阅读、案例分析进一步了解国际直接投资的结构、外国证券投资（也叫外国间接投资）。

In the past 25 years, FDI is growing at a much faster rate than trade and both of these have grown faster than world output.（在过去的25年里，国际直接投资的增长速度比贸易快得多，而且这两者的增长速度都快于世界产量。）

—Kozul-Wright and Rowthorn（柯睿智、罗森，于1998年）

What Is a Foreign Direct Investment (FDI)?

A foreign direct investment (FDI) is an investment made by a firm or individual in one country into business interests located in another country. Generally, FDI takes place when an investor establishes foreign business operations or acquires foreign business assets in a foreign company. However, FDIs are distinguished from portfolio investments in which an investor merely purchases **equities** of foreign-based companies.

How Does an FDI Work?

Foreign direct investments are commonly made in open economies that offer a skilled **workforce** and above-average growth prospects for the investor, as opposed to tightly regulated economies. Foreign direct investment frequently involves more than just a capital investment. It may include **provisions** of management or technology as well. The key feature of foreign direct investment is that it establishes either effective control of or at least substantial influence over the decision-making of a foreign business.

The Bureau of Economic Analysis (BEA), which tracks expenditures by foreign direct investors into U.S. businesses, reported total FDI into U.S. businesses of $253.6 billion in 2018. Chemicals represented the top industry, with $109 billion in FDI for 2018.

The **threshold** for a foreign direct investment that establishes a controlling interest, per guidelines established by the Organization of Economic Cooperation and Development (OECD), is a minimum 10% ownership stake in a foreign-based company. However, that definition is flexible, as there are instances where effective controlling interest in a firm can be established with less than 10% of the company's voting shares.

Methods of FDI

Foreign direct investments can be made in a variety of ways, including the opening of a **subsidiary** or associate company in a foreign country, acquiring a controlling interest in an existing foreign company, by means of merger or an acquisition of an unrelated enterprise and participating in an equity joint venture with another investor or enterprise.

Types of FDI

外国直接投资的种类
外国直接投资主要包括横向外国直接投资、纵向外国直接投资、企业型外国直接投资和平台型外国直接投资。

Foreign direct investments are commonly categorized as being horizontal and vertical FDI.

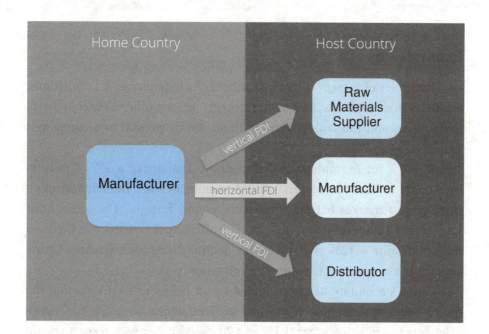

Horizontal: A horizontal direct investment refers to the investor establishing the same type of business operation in a foreign country as it operates in its home country, for example, a cell phone provider based in the United States opening stores in China.

Vertical: A vertical investment is one in which different but related business activities from the investor's main business are established or acquired in a foreign country, such as when a manufacturing company acquires an interest in a foreign company that supplies parts or raw materials required for the manufacturing company to make its products.

However, two other forms of FDI have also been observed: **conglomerate** and platform FDI.

Conglomerate: A conglomerate type of foreign direct investment is one where a company or individual makes a foreign investment in a business that is unrelated to its existing business in its home country.

Since this type of investment involves entering an industry in which the investor has no previous experience, it often takes the form of a joint venture with a foreign company already operating in the industry.

Platform: A business expands into a foreign country but the output from the foreign operations is exported to a third country. This is also

Word Study

conglomerate
/kənˈglɒmərət/ *n.*
企业集团

91

Word Study

retail /ˈriːteɪl/ *n.* 零售

logistic /ləʊˈdʒɪstɪk/ *n.* 物流

pivotal /ˈpɪvətəl/ *n.* 核心，枢纽

boost /buːst/ *v.* 使增长，促进

relay /ˈriːleɪ/ *v.* 使接替，传达

bullishness /ˈbʊlɪʃnəs/ *n.* 乐观，（行情）看涨

referred to as the export-platform FDI. Platform FDI commonly happens in low-cost locations inside free-trade areas. For example, Ford may purchase manufacturing plants in Ireland with the primary purpose of exporting cars to other countries in the EU.

Examples of FDI

Examples of foreign direct investments include mergers, acquisitions, **retail**, services, **logistics**, and manufacturing, among others. Foreign direct investments and the laws governing them can be **pivotal** to a company's growth strategy.

In 2017, for example, U.S.-based Apple announced a $507.1 million investment to **boost** its research and development work in China, Apple's third-largest market behind the Americas and Europe. The announced investment **relayed** CEO Tim Cook's **bullishness** toward the Chinese market despite a 12% year-over-year decline in Apple's Greater China revenue in the quarter preceding the announcement.

China's economy has been fueled by an influx of FDI targeting the nation's high-tech manufacturing and services, which according to China's Ministry of Commerce, grew 11.1% and 20.4% year over year, respectively, in the first half of 2017. Meanwhile, relaxed FDI regulations in India now allows 100% foreign direct investment in single-brand retail without government approval. The regulatory decision reportedly facilitates Apple's desire to open a physical store in the Indian market. Thus far, the firm's iPhones have only been available through third-party physical and online retailers.

Benefits of FDI for Host Country

It has been recognized that the maximizing benefits of FDI for the host country can be significant. In order to get more advantages from FDI, developing countries have started to make more suitable laws and policies related to FDI to attract investment. There are four main benefits for the host country: effects on resource transfer, effects on employment, effects on balance of payments, and effects on competition.

RESOURCE-TRANSFER EFFECTS

Foreign direct investment can add a great amount of value to a host economy by providing capital, innovative technology, and management resources that the host country might not have. Such resource transfer can contribute to **stimulating** the **fiscal** expanding of the host economy.

Capital

Multinational enterprises (MNEs) make investment on a long-term basis, taking risks and sending profits back to their home country only when the projects yield returns. The free flow of capital across nations is likely to be favored by many economists since it allows capital to seek out the highest rate of return. Many MNEs, by virtue of their large size and financial strength, have access to financial resources not available to host-country firms. These funds may be available from internal company sources, or, because of their reputation, large MNEs may find it easier to borrow money from capital markets than host-county firms would.

FDI can contribute to economic growth not only by providing foreign capital but also by crowding in additional domestic investment, so it increases the total growth effect of FDI.

Technology

If a company wants to grow stronger, it must be able to use and follow technology very well. Technology can create a movement and mobility in the economy which may be able to facilitate economic development and industrialization. It can take two forms, both of which are very valuable. Technology can be incorporated in a production process or it can be incorporated in a final product such as the smart phones. However, many countries lack the research and development resources and skills required to develop their own native product and process technology, especially the less developed countries. A vast majority of economic studies have found that technology transfer via FDI has contributed positively to productivity and economic growth in host countries.

Management

Foreign expertise for management which are gained by FDI is very helpful for the host country. The mentioned benefits can take different forms. First, local **personnel** who are trained to occupy managerial posts in a subsidiary of an MNE may leave the firm and help establish local firms. Secondly, a foreign MNE with superior management skills can stimulate local suppliers, distributors and competitors to improve their own management skills. Thirdly, workers get new skills through training in a foreign MNE and take these skills with them when they re-enter domestic labor market.

EMPLOYMENT EFFECTS

The effects on employment associated with FDI are both direct and indirect. In countries where capital is relatively scarce but labor is abundant, the creation of employment opportunities — either directly

Word Study

stimulate /'stɪmjʊleɪt/
  v. 刺激
fiscal /'fɪskəl/ adj. 财政的,财务的
personnel /ˌpɜːsəˈnel/
  n. 全体人员,职员

Word Study

offset /ˌɒfˈset/ *v.* 抵消，补偿

substitution /ˌsʌbstɪˈtjuːʃən/ *n.* 替代，代换

empirical /ɪmˈpɪrɪkəl/ *adj.* 凭经验的，实证的

edge /edʒ/ *n.* 优势

or indirectly — has been one of the most prominent impacts of FDI. The direct effect arises when a foreign MNE employs a number of host country citizens. Whereas, the indirect effect arises when jobs are created in local suppliers as a result of the investment and when jobs are created because of increased local spending by employees of the MNE.

However, some argue that not all the "new jobs" created by FDI represent net additions in employment. In the case of FDI by Japanese auto companies in the U.S., some argue that the jobs created by this investment have been more than **offset** by the jobs lost in U.S.- owned auto companies, which have lost market share to their Japanese competitors. As a consequence of such **substitution** effects, the net number of new jobs created by FDI may not be as great as initially claimed by an MNE.

BALANCE OF PAYMENTS EFFECTS

FDI's effect on a country's balance of payment accounts can be positive and negative. It is an important policy issue for most host governments. There are three potential balance of payments consequences of FDI. First, when an MNE establishes a foreign subsidiary, the capital account of the host country benefits from the initial capital inflow. However, this is a one-time only effect. Second, if the FDI is a substitute for imports of goods or services, it can improve the current account of the host country's balance of payment. A third potential benefit to the host country's balance of payment arises when the MNE uses a foreign subsidiary to export goods and services to other countries.

Evidence based on **empirical** research on the balance of payments effect of FDI, indicates that there is a difference between developed and developing countries, especially with respect to investment in the manufacturing industries.

EFFECTS ON COMPETITION

According to an OECD report (OECD 2002, p.16) the presence of foreign enterprises may greatly assist economic development by spurring domestic competition and thereby leading eventually to higher productivity, lower prices and more efficient resource allocation. Increased competition tends to stimulate capital investments by firms in plant, equipment and R&D as they struggle to gain an **edge** over their rivals. FDI's impact on competition in domestic markets may be particularly important in the case of services, such as telecommunication, retailing and many financial services, where exporting is often not an option because the service has to be produced where it is delivered.

Costs of FDI to Host Country

FDI is not always in the host county's best interest. There are adverse economic and political effects on the host country: adverse effects on

外国直接投资的成本
东道国在吸引外来投资方面主要面临三种成本：对东道国国内竞争的负面效应、对国际收支的负面影响，以及国家主权和独立性的丧失。

94

competition, adverse effects on the balance of payments, and the perceived loss of national sovereignty and autonomy.

ADVERSE EFFECTS ON COMPETITION

Although FDI can boost competition, host governments sometimes worry that the subsidiaries of foreign MNEs may have greater economic power than local competitors. If it is a part of large international organization, the foreign MNEs may be able to draw on funds generated elsewhere to **subsidize** its costs in the host market, which could drive local companies out of business and allow the firm to **monopolize** the market. This concern tends to be greater in countries that have few large firms of their own (i.e. less developed countries).

ADVERSE EFFECT ON BALANCE OF PAYMENTS

There are two main areas of concern with regard to the adverse effects of FDI on a host country's balance of payments. First, set against the initial capital inflow that comes with FDI must be the subsequent outflow of earnings from the foreign subsidiary to its parent company. Such outflows show up as a debit on the capital account. A second concern arises when a foreign subsidiary imports a substantial number of inputs from abroad, which results in a debit on the current account of the host country's balance of payments.

DOES FDI CAUSE LOSS OF NATIONAL SOVEREIGNTY?

Recognition of the economic benefits afforded by the freedom of capital movements sometimes **clashes** with concerns about loss of national sovereignty. Since FDI involves a controlling stake by often large MNEs over which domestic governments have little power. In small economies, large foreign companies can and often do, abuse their dominant market positions. For example, if an MNE is a monopoly natural gas provider in the host country, in a conflict situation between its home country and the host country, that MNE can cut out its supply of the natural gas.

The Volatility of FDI

Like domestic investment, FDI flows exhibit high levels of volatility. Investment requires a stable economic environment and changes in the economic cycle, currency fluctuations, and changes in business confidence create uncertainty, which is a general **deterrent** to international investment.

CHANGES IN THE ECONOMIC CYCLE

Sustained economic growth in an economy is likely to encourage FDI, while recession will deter it. The impact of the financial crisis on FDI flows

Word Study

subsidize /'sʌbsɪdaɪz/
 v. 资助, 补贴
monopolize
 /mə'nɒpəlaɪz/ v. 独
 占, 垄断
clash /klæʃ/ v. 与……
 迥然不同, 抵触
volatility /ˌvɒlə'tɪlɪti/
 n. 波动性
deterrent /dɪ'terənt/ n.
 威慑因素, 不利
 因素

外国直接投资的波
动性
　　与国内投资一
样, 外国直接投资也
表现出较高的波动
性。投资需要稳定
的经济环境作为支
撑。经济周期的变
化、汇率波动以及商
业信心的变化都会
给外国直接投资带
来不确定性, 造成负
面影响。

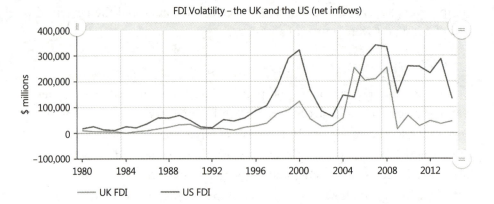

FDI Volatility – the UK and the US (net inflows)

—— UK FDI   —— US FDI

can clearly be seen in the above chart. When there is an economic recession, FDI net inflows fall correspondingly both in the US and in the UK.

FLUCTUATIONS IN MONETARY CONDITIONS

Changes in monetary conditions in an investor or recipient country can affect investment decisions. Tighter policy will tend to inhibit investment, while looser policy will encourage it. However, fears of **inflation** might act as a check against FDI if monetary expansion is seen as **reckless**.

EXPECTATIONS

Poor expectations can arise for a number of reasons, especially resulting from worries about the overall state of the economy in which the investment will take place. Rising budget deficits are also likely to be a cause for concern for the investing country.

CHANGES IN BUSINESS REGULATION

Tighter domestic regulations will deter FDI, while looser regulations will encourage it. The World Bank uses an index to rank countries in terms of the ease of doing business in each country. The index uses several criteria, including how long it takes to start up a business, the amount of documentation required, and how much time is taken up dealing with tax administration. In 2020, the top five countries or regions regarded as the easiest to do business in were New Zealand, Singapore, Hong Kong (China), Denmark and South Korea.

CHANGES IN THE LEVEL OF BUSINESS TAXES

Changes in business taxes, such as the UK's corporation tax, can attract or **repel** FDI. During the 2000s, low business taxes in Ireland encouraged inward investment from many large U.S. corporations, including Apple, Microsoft, and Adobe. In fact, U.S. investment in Ireland during 2009 stood at $166 billion — more than U.S. investment in China, India, Russia and Brazil combined.

Key Terms
专业术语

foreign direct investment 外国直接投资
portfolio investments 投资组合,间接投资
voting share 有表决权股票
associate company 联营公司(子公司)
equity joint venture 股份制合资经营企业
host country 东道国
balance of payments 国际收支
Organization of Economic Cooperation and Development (OECD)
经济合作与发展组织
national sovereignty and autonomy 国家主权与自主
budget deficit 财政预算赤字

Information Link
知识链接

重庆市外商直接投资的结构

改革开放的实践表明,合理利用外商直接投资是促进我国经济发展的重要因素。西部大开发将是一次大开放,西部地区如何充分利用外商直接投资将是新时期的重要课题。

重庆市不仅是西部地区唯一的直辖市,也是西部大开发的前沿阵地。2001年,重庆市新签利用外资协议191个,协议合同金额7.1884亿美元,分别比去年下降了19.4%和17.3%,显然受到了全球外商直接投资锐减的影响。其中新签外商直接投资协议172个,占利用外资协议合同总数的90.1%,协议合同金额4.4261亿美元,占外资合同金额的61.6%。全市实际利用外资并未受到影响。2001年实际利用外资总额为4.2442亿美元,其中外商直接投资2.5649亿美元,分别比去年增长了22.9个百分点和5.0个百分点。

重庆市是西部地区吸引外商直接投资的主要地区之一。

从地区分布来看,亚洲地区是重庆市外商直接投资的主要来源地,合同金额和实际利用金额都占外商直接在渝投资的七成以上,是重庆市相对稳定的投资来源地;其次是北美洲、拉丁美洲、欧洲和大洋洲。其中欧盟和美国、加拿大在渝投资的合同金额和实际利用金额占外商直接在渝投资的两成左右,而且所占比例逐渐增加。这也表明国际主流资本市场已经开始关注包括重庆在内的西部大开发,开始由观望或试探状态进入实际操作阶段。

2001年,分列重庆市外商直接投资合同金额前五位的国家或地区(以重庆市统计年鉴公布数据为准)是:中国香港、美国、泰国、中国台湾和瑞士,其合同金额占全市总额的80.6%。实际利用金额前五位的国家(地区)是:中国香港、美国、中国台湾、新加坡和日本,其到位资金总额占全市总额的77.0%。

目前,重庆市利用外商直接投资方式主要局限于中外合资、外商独资、中外合作三种基本形式。

另外,作为当今席卷全球的外商直接投资方式——跨国并购在重庆也已经展开。重庆铝业集团和腾辉地维水泥有限公司先后于2000年和2001年由外商通过并购形式控股收购而成外商投资企业。

对于中西部地区这样投资环境欠优的地区,努力改善投资环境固然是

吸引外商投资的基础，而一定期限内的激励性政策则是必要的保障。随着我国加入WTO，超国民待遇和非国民待遇将逐渐取消，外商投资政策应该从税收激励机制为主的优惠政策转向以公平竞争机制为主的激励政策，为外商投资企业和国内企业营造一个符合国际惯例、公平合理的商业竞争机制和环境。

文献来源：

陈俊华.重庆市外商直接投资的结构与对策分析［J］.西南师范大学学报，2003，（05）.53

A. Describe the methods of FDI.

Methods of FDI

1	2	3

B. According to the text, fill in each of the following blanks with an appropriate word or phrase.

1) A foreign direct investment is an investment made by a _____ in one country into business interests located in another country.

2) The key feature of foreign direct investment is that it establishes either _____ of or at least substantial influence over the decision-making of a foreign business.

3) A horizontal direct investment refers to the investor establishing the _____ type of business operation in a foreign country as it operates in its home country.

4) For the export-platform FDI, a business expands into a foreign country but the output from the foreign operations is exported to a _____ country.

5) A conglomerate type of foreign direct investment is one where a company or individual makes a foreign investment in a business that is _____ _____ to its existing business in its home country.

6) Foreign direct investment can add a great amount of value to a host economy by providing _____, innovative technology, and

management resources that the host country might not have.

7) Technology can create a movement and _____ in the economy which may be able to facilitate economic improvement and industrialization.

8) Investment requires a stable economic environment and changes in the economic cycle, _____, and changes in business confidence create uncertainty.

9) Sustained economic growth in an economy is likely to encourage FDI, while _____ will deter it.

10) In 2020, the top five countries or regions regarded as the easiest to do business in were _____, Singapore, Hong Kong (China), Denmark and South Korea.

C. Read the text and decide whether the following statements are True (T) or False (F).

1) Foreign direct investment frequently involves just a capital investment.

(　　)

2) A vertical direct investment refers to the investor establishing the same type of business operation in a foreign country as it operates in its home country.

(　　)

3) Platform FDI commonly happens in low-cost locations inside free-trade areas.

(　　)

4) According to China's Ministry of Commerce, China's economy has been fueled by an influx of FDI targeting the nation's high-tech manufacturing and services.

(　　)

5) FDI can have beneficial and negative effects on a country's balance of payments.

(　　)

6) Unlike domestic investment, FDI flows exhibit low levels of volatility.

(　　)

7) Changes in monetary conditions in an investor or recipient country can affect investment decisions.

(　　)

8) Rising budget deficits are also likely to be a cause for concern for the investing country.

(　　)

9) Looser domestic regulations will deter FDI, while tighter regulations will encourage it.

(　　)

10) Changes in business taxes, such as the UK's corporation tax, can attract or repel FDI.

(　　)

Discussion
讨论

1) Please summarize what is an FDI.

_____

_____

2) What are the four types of FDI?

_____

_____

3) What are the main benefits that FDI brings to the host country?

_____

_____

4) What are the adverse effects of FDI on the host country?

_____

_____

5) What may result in the volatility of FDI?

_____

_____

Case Story

Global Strategy Underpins Singapore's Foreign Investment Growth

For an island nation spreading over just 700 sq km, Singapore wields outsized economic clout. The city state has grown inordinately wealthy since its 1965 separation from neighboring Malaysia, recording gross domestic product per capita of nearly six times that of its former partner to the north.

Such wealth has been driven in part by Singapore's transformation from a sleepy trading post into a modern center for global finance.

As the economy developed, however, it soon became clear that a tiny domestic market presented limits to growth, while Singapore's position at the heart of Asian trade offered it the ideal location to seek opportunities abroad.

"It is critical for Singapore companies, especially small and medium-sized enterprises, to internationalize, given our small domestic market", says Kathy Lai, deputy chief executive of Enterprise Singapore, a government agency that supports business growth and foreign investment.

"Many companies already recognize internationalization as a necessary strategy for continued growth."

The strategy of looking outward, pioneered from the 1990s and actively encouraged by the government, has borne fruit. Singapore's total direct investments abroad have risen from S$672bn ($496bn) in 2011 to S$850bn in 2017, with more than 50% of that concentrated in Asia, according to the Singapore Department of Statistics.

Greenfield flows, which track new investment, show that foreign investment out of Singapore hit its highest figure yet in 2018, totaling $28.9bn, according to FDI Markets, an FT-owned database of cross-border investment. This represented a doubling from 2017.

China receives the lion's share from the Lion City, garnering more than $80bn in greenfield investment from Singapore since 2003. Other top greenfield investment destinations include India, which has received $27bn from Singapore, Vietnam with $22bn, Indonesia $19bn and Malaysia $10bn.

Trends in fast-growing neighbors continue to support these outflows, with infrastructure projects, strong consumer demand from young populations and emerging digital economies among the drivers, according to Ms. Lai.

"Asian countries are investing and building up their connectivity infrastructure, in turn lowering barriers to internationalization", she says.

Overseas investment by Singapore companies — which previously have focused on property, oil and gas, tourism and financial services — has broadened more recently to include communications and chemicals.

Government-linked companies have been among the foremost Singapore groups pushing into new markets. GLP, part-owned by sovereign wealth fund GIC, was one of the biggest investors in property out of Singapore in 2018, according to FDI Markets, investing in projects across Europe.

ST Telemedia (STT) is another case in point. An investor in media and communications, with revenues of S$3.9bn in 2018, the company comes under the umbrella of Temasek, another Singaporean sovereign wealth fund. Since the beginning of 2019, Temasek has invested $995m in new construction projects in India, Indonesia and Thailand. Last year, STT invested $227.5m in a Bangkok data center, due to open in 2020. Stephen Miller, group president and chief executive, says China, India and the UK are all important markets for STT.

"Despite the current economic and geopolitical volatility, [we] see sustained growth in countries where there is a strong government digitalization push supported by consistent policies to facilitate the rollout of digital infrastructure", he says.

State-linked companies are not the only big investors, however. Last year conglomerate Next Story Group put $180m into a city center development in Colombo, while Keppel Puravankara Development, a Singapore-India joint venture, invested $286m in an office tower development in Bangalore.

The Asian financial crisis of the late 1990s prompted the Singapore government to promote a policy of "regionalization" that encourages companies to look beyond Asia-Pacific to markets in Europe, Latin America and emerging Asia.

The goal, according to the ministry of trade and industry, is to "diversify risks from economic shocks in any one region".

"We stepped out into Asia in 2002, investing beyond Singapore into markets such as China and India. We also started to identify early opportunities in Brazil and Mexico, establishing offices in São Paulo and Mexico City about a decade ago", says Temasek, which over the past few years opened offices in New York, London, Washington DC and San Francisco.

That international spread might prove a prudent decision: China's economy is slowing, annual growth in Asia-Pacific is forecast to drop below 6 per cent for the first time since the Asian financial crisis, and the U.S.-China trade war is causing ripples across the region.

However, with much of Singapore's overseas investment centered in China, portfolios might start to feel one-dimensional. China's real estate market — a favorite sector for Singaporean investment — has slowed in 2019, as prices plateau in big cities and government regulations tighten.

Still, long-term investors believe they can weather slower growth. "We have been closely watching the global macroeconomic environment and how certain events might have an impact on our portfolio", Temasek says. "But as a long-term investor, we can ride out short-term market volatility."

Case Discussion

1) Why is it critical for Singapore companies, especially small and medium-sized enterprises, to internationalize?

_____

_____

2) What fields have Singapore companies invested abroad?

_____

_____

Case Summary

全球战略支撑新加坡的对外投资增长

新加坡的国土面积非常小,但是其经济影响力却很大。新加坡的国内市场很小,对于新加坡的公司,特别是中小型企业,会限制其经济的发展,所以实现国际化至关重要。新加坡政府从20世纪90年代开始鼓励对外投资。截至2017年,新加坡的海外直接投资总额已达8 500亿新元。其中超过50%集中在亚洲。新加坡公司的海外投资从以前一直专注的房地产、石油和天然气、旅游业和金融服务,已扩大到通信和化工领域。20世纪90年代后期的亚洲金融危机促使新加坡政府推行"区域化"政策,鼓励公司将目光投向亚太以外的地区,转向欧洲、拉丁美洲和新兴亚洲市场,以分散任何地区经济冲击带来的风险。

Reading I

Foreign Portfolio Investment

What Is Foreign Portfolio Investment?

Foreign portfolio investment (FPI) consists of securities and other financial assets held by investors in another country. It does not provide the investor with direct ownership of a company's assets and is relatively liquid depending on the volatility of the market. Along with foreign direct investment (FDI), FPI is one of the common ways to invest in an overseas economy. FDI and FPI are both important sources of funding for most economies.

Portfolio investment involves the making and holding of a hands-off — or passive — investment of securities, done with the expectation of earning a return. In foreign portfolio investment, these securities can include stocks, American depositary receipts (ADRs), or global depositary receipts of companies headquartered outside the investor's nation. Holding also includes bonds or other debt issued by these companies or foreign governments, mutual funds, or exchange traded funds (ETFs) that invest in assets abroad or overseas.

An individual investor interested in opportunities outside their own country is most likely to invest through an FPI. On a macro level, foreign portfolio investment is part of a country's capital account and shown on its balance of payments (BOP). The BOP measures the amount of money flowing from one country to other countries over one monetary year.

FPI vs. FDI

With FPI — as with portfolio investment in general — an investor does not actively manage the investments or the companies that issue the investments. They do not have direct control over the assets or the businesses.

In contrast, FDI lets an investor purchase a direct business interest in a foreign country. For example, say an investor based in New York City purchases a warehouse in Berlin to lease to a German company that needs space to expand its operations. The investor's goal is to create a long-term income stream while helping the company increase its profits.

This FDI investor controls their monetary investments and often actively manages the company into which they put money. The investor helps to build the business and waits to see their return on investment (ROI). However, because the investor's money is tied up in a company, they face less liquidity and more risk when trying to sell this interest. The investor also faces currency exchange risk, which may decrease the value of the investment when converted from the country's currency to the home currency or U.S. dollars. An additional risk is with political risk, which may make the foreign economy and his investment shaky.

Although some of these risks affect foreign portfolio investments as well, it is to a lesser degree than with foreign direct investments. Since the FPI investments are financial assets, not the property or a direct stake in a company, they are inherently more marketable.

So FPI is more liquid than FDI and offers the investor a chance for a quicker return on his money — or a quicker exit. However, as with most investments offering a short-term horizon, FPI assets can suffer from volatility. FPI money often departs the country of investment whenever there is uncertainty or negative news in a foreign land, which can further aggravate economic problems there.

Foreign portfolio investments are more suited to the average retail investor, while FDI is more the province of institutional investors, ultra-high-net-worth individuals, and companies. However, these large investors may also use foreign portfolio investments.

Example of FPI

The year 2018 was a good one for India in terms of FPI. More than 600 new investment funds registered with the Securities and Exchange Board of India (SEBI), bringing the total to 9,246. An easier regulatory climate and a strong performance by Indian equities over the last few years were among the factors sparking foreign investors' interest.

Second Thoughts

For each of the following statements or questions, choose the best answer.

1) Which of the following is NOT the pros of FPI?
   A. Feasible for retail investors.
   B. No direct control/management of investments.
   C. Quicker return on investment.
   D. More liquid.

2) The following statements about the FPI is true EXCEPT _____.
   A. FPI lets an investor purchase a direct business interest in a foreign country.
   B. An investor investing through an FPI doesn't manage the investments directly.
   C. An individual investor tends to invest through an FPI.
   D. Investing through FPI is relatively liquid depending on the volatility of the market.

Reading II

Why Would a Corporation Conduct Vertical Foreign Direct Investment?

Foreign direct investment is an investment made by a company (or individual) into a business located in another country. It can either be in the form of establishing business operations or acquiring business assets in a foreign country.

A horizontal direct investment occurs when a company establishes the same type of business operation in a foreign country as it operates in its home country. For example, Toyota assembles cars in both the United States and China.

Vertical foreign direct investment occurs when a multinational decides to acquire or build an operation that either fulfills the role of a supplier (backward vertical FDI) or the role of a distributor (forward vertical FDI). Companies that seek to enter into a backward vertical FDI typically seek to reduce the cost of raw materials or improve the supply of certain key components. For example, a Japanese car manufacturer acquires a tire manufacturer.

A third type of FDI is a conglomerate investment. This occurs when a company acquires an unrelated business in another country. There are two main challenges to this strategy, entering a foreign market and engaging in a new industry.

To better grasp the concept of vertical FDI, consider an American car manufacturer. One of the major materials used for car manufacturing is steel. An American car manufacturer would prefer that steel be as cheap as possible, but the price of steel can fluctuate dramatically depending on overall supply and demand. Furthermore, the foreign steel supplier would prefer to sell steel for as high a price as possible to please its owners or shareholders. If the car manufacturer acquires the foreign steel supplier, the car manufacturer would no longer need to transact with the steel supplier and its market-driven prices.

Most FDI is horizontal rather than vertical. As developed countries engage more heavily in FDI, it suggests that market access is more important than reducing production costs as a motive for FDI.

A company that engages in forward vertical FDI may experience a challenge finding distributors in a specific market. For example, assume that the earlier mentioned American car manufacturer wants to sell its cars in the Japanese auto market. Since many Japanese auto dealers do not wish to carry foreign brand vehicles, the American car manufacturer may lack sales channels. In this case, the manufacturer might engage in vertical FDI and build its own distribution network in Japan to fill this niche.

FDI is a way for countries and companies with limited capital to obtain financing beyond national borders from wealthier countries. China's rapid economic growth was aided by exports and FDI. The World Bank states that FDI is one way to develop the private sector in lower-income economies and reduce poverty.

Second Thoughts

1) When a multinational acquires an operation that acts as a supplier or distributor, is this a vertical FDI or a horizontal FDI?

_____

_____

2) How can FDI help reduce poverty in low-income economies?

_____

_____

Foreign Exchange Market

外汇市场

CHAPTER
6

本章概要

本章主要介绍外汇市场的含义、主要参与者、作用及其运作方式,并以沃尔玛、宝马等相关案例为例,说明了外汇对跨国公司的影响。

学习指南

外汇市场是决定全球货币汇率的场外交易全球市场,它决定着世界各地货币的汇率,起着转换货币、对冲风险等作用,主要由银行、跨国公司等参与。所有买卖外汇的商业银行、专营外汇业务的银行、外汇经纪人、进出口商以及其他外汇供求者都经营各种现汇交易及期汇交易。

通过本章学习,希望大家能够实现以下目标:

(1)基本目标(Text-based Goals)

- 掌握本章涉及话题的基本专业术语及词汇,如外汇市场、跨国公司、即期交易、远期交易等。
- 掌握本章的主要知识点,即外汇市场的含义、主要参与者、作用及其运作方式。

(2)拓展目标(Extended Goals)

- 思考本章引言,为什么"世界货币带来的好处将是巨大的"?
- 通过学习背景知识、拓展阅读、案例分析,进一步了解汇率的变动对跨国公司带来的影响以及跨国公司该如何做好风险规避。

What Is the Foreign Exchange Market?

什么是外汇市场？

外汇市场是指在国际间从事外汇买卖、调剂外汇供求的交易场所。它的职能是经营货币商品，即不同国家的货币。外汇市场是世界上最大的金融市场，甚至比股市还大。除了提供购买、出售、交换和投机货币的场所外，外汇市场还为国际贸易结算和投资进行货币转换。

The foreign exchange market (also known as forex, FX or the currency market) is a global decentralized or over-the-counter (OTC) market for the trading of currencies. Participants are able to buy, sell, exchange and **speculate** on currencies. It is one of the original financial markets formed to bring structure to the **burgeoning** global economy. In terms of trading volume, it is, by far, the largest financial market in the world. Aside from providing a **venue** for the buying, selling, exchanging and speculation of currencies, the forex market also enables currency **conversion** for international trade settlements and investments.

The foreign exchange or forex market is the largest financial market in the world — larger even than the stock market, with a daily volume of $5.1 trillion, vs. $84 billion for equities worldwide, according to the 2016 Triennial Central Bank Survey of FX and OTC derivatives markets.

An exchange rate is a price paid for one currency in exchange for another. It is this type of exchange that drives the forex market.

There are more than 100 different kinds of official currencies in the world. However, most international forex trades and payments are made using the U.S. dollar, British pound, Japanese yen, and the euro. Other popular currency trading instruments include the Australian dollar, Swiss franc, Canadian dollar, and New Zealand dollar.

Currency can be traded through spot transactions, forwards, **swaps** and option contracts where the underlying instrument is a currency. Currency trading occurs continuously around the world, 24 hours a day, five days a week.

Word Study

speculate /ˌspekjʊ'leɪt/ *v.* 投机

burgeon /'bɜːdʒən/ *v.* 激增，迅速发展

venue /'venjuː/ *n.* 场地

conversion /kən'vɜːʒən/ *n.* 转换

swap /swɒp/ *n.* 掉期交易

security /sɪ'kjʊərɪti/ *n.* 证券

spread /spred/ *n.* 价差，利差

Who Trades Forex?

外汇市场的主要参与者

外汇市场的主要参与者包括商业投资银行、中央银行、投资经理和对冲基金、跨国公司，以及个人投资者。

Unlike a stock market, the foreign exchange market is divided into levels of access. At the top is the interbank foreign exchange market, which is made up of the largest commercial banks and **securities** dealers. Within the interbank market, **spreads**, which are the difference between the bid and ask prices, are razor sharp and not known to players outside the inner circle. The forex market not only has many players but many types of players. Here we go through some of the major types of institutions and traders in forex markets.

COMMERCIAL & INVESTMENT BANKS

The greatest volume of currency is traded in the interbank market. This is where banks of all sizes trade currency with each other and through electronic networks. Big banks account for a large percentage of total currency volume trades. Banks facilitate forex transactions for clients and conduct speculative trades from their own trading desks.

CENTRAL BANKS

Central banks, which represent their nation's government, are extremely important players in the forex market. Open market operations and interest rate policies of central banks influence currency rates to a very large extent.

A central bank is responsible for fixing the price of its native currency on forex. This is the exchange rate **regime** by which its currency will trade in the open market. Exchange rate regimes are divided into floating, fixed and **pegged** types.

Any action taken by a central bank in the forex market is done to stabilize or increase the competitiveness of that nation's economy. Central banks (as well as speculators) may engage in currency interventions to make their currencies **appreciate** or **depreciate**. For example, a central bank may weaken its own currency by creating additional supply during periods of long **deflationary** trends, which is then used to purchase foreign currency. This effectively weakens the domestic currency, making exports more competitive in the global market.

Central banks also use such strategies to calm inflation. Their doing so also serves as a long-term indicator for forex traders.

Word Study

regime /reɪˈʒiːm/ n.
    制度,体制
peg /peg/ v. 钉住
appreciate /əˈpriːʃɪeɪt/
    v. 升值
depreciate /dɪˈpriːʃɪeɪt/
    v. 贬值
deflationary
    /dɪˈfleɪʃənəri/ adj.
    通货紧缩的
endowment
    /ɪnˈdaʊmənt/ n.
    捐赠,资助

INVESTMENT MANAGERS AND HEDGE FUNDS

Portfolio managers, pooled funds and hedge funds make up the second-biggest collection of players in the forex market next to banks and central banks. Investment managers trade currencies for large accounts such as pension funds, foundations, and **endowments**.

An investment manager with an international portfolio will have to purchase and sell currencies to trade foreign securities. Investment managers may also make speculative forex trades, while some hedge funds execute speculative currency trades as part of their investment strategies.

MULTINATIONAL CORPORATIONS

Firms engaged in importing and exporting conduct forex transactions to pay for goods and services. Consider the example of a German solar panel producer that imports American components and sells its finished products in China. After the final sale is made, the Chinese yuan the producer received

convert /'kɒnvɜːt/ v.
转换，兑换
hedge /hedʒ/ v. 对冲
draft /drɑːft/ n. 汇票

must be **converted** back to euros. The German firm must then exchange euros for dollars to purchase more American components.

Companies trade forex to **hedge** the risk associated with foreign currency translations. The same German firm might purchase American dollars in the spot market, or enter into a currency swap agreement to obtain dollars in advance of purchasing components from the American company in order to reduce foreign currency exposure risk.

Additionally, hedging against currency risk can add a level of safety to offshore investments.

INDIVIDUAL INVESTORS

The volume of forex trades made by retail investors is extremely low compared to financial institutions and companies. However, it is growing rapidly in popularity. Retail investors base currency trades on a combination of fundamentals (i.e., interest rate parity, inflation rates, and monetary policy expectations) and technical factors (i.e., support, resistance, technical indicators, price patterns).

Functions of Forex

外汇市场的作用
　　主要表现在三个方面：一是实现购买力的国际转移，将购买力从一个国家转移到另外一个国家；二是提供信贷功能，向进口商提供短期信贷，以促进货物和服务在不同国家之间的顺畅流动；三是对冲外汇风险，为外汇风险提供保障。

Foreign exchange market is a system, not a place. The transactions in this market are not confined to only one or few foreign currencies. In fact, there are a large number of foreign currencies which are treated, converted and exchanged in the foreign exchange market. The following are the main functions of foreign exchange market.

TRANSFER FUNCTION

The basic and the most visible function of foreign exchange market is the transfer of funds (foreign currency) from one country to another for the settlement of payments. It basically includes the conversion of one currency to another, wherein the role of Forex is to transfer the purchasing power from one country to another.

For example, if the importer of India import goods from the U.S. and the payment is to be made in dollars, then the conversion of the rupee to the dollar will be facilitated by Forex. The transfer function is performed through a use of credit instruments, such as bank **drafts**, bills of foreign exchange, and telephone transfers.

CREDIT FUNCTION

Forex provides a short-term credit to the importers so as to facilitate the smooth flow of goods and services from country to country. An importer can use credit to finance the foreign purchases. For example, if an Indian company wants to purchase the machinery from the U.S., it can pay for the purchase by issuing a bill of exchange in the foreign exchange market, essentially with a three-month **maturity**.

HEDGING FUNCTION

The third function of a foreign exchange market is to hedge foreign exchange risks. The parties to the foreign exchange are often afraid of the fluctuations in the exchange rates, i.e., the price of one currency in terms of another. The change in the exchange rate may result in a gain or loss to the party concerned.

Due to this reason, the Forex provides the services for hedging the anticipated or actual claims in exchange for the forward contracts. A forward contract is usually a three-month contract to buy or sell the foreign exchange for another currency at a fixed date in the future at a price agreed upon today. Thus, no money is exchanged at the time of the contract.

How Does Forex Work?

CURRENCY EXCHANGE

The currency exchange is to exchange the currency of one country into the currency of another on the international exchange rate. Currency exchange of physical money (coins and paper bills), is usually done over a counter at a teller station. Currency exchange businesses that operate such transactions can be found in a variety of forms and venues. It may be a stand-alone, small business operating out of a single office, or it may be a larger chain of small exchange-service booths at airports, or it may be a large international bank offering currency exchange services at its teller stations.

Currency exchange services can also be found through businesses that offer these services online. This may be offered as part of the services provided by a bank, forex **broker** or other financial institution. A currency exchange business profits from its services either through adjusting the exchange rate or charging fees or both.

Currency exchange businesses, both physical and online, allow you to exchange one country's currency for another by executing buy and sell transactions. For example, if you have U.S. Dollars and you want to exchange them for Australian Dollars, you would bring your U.S. Dollars (or bank card) to the currency exchange store and buy Australian Dollars with them. The amount you would be able to purchase would be dependent on the international spot rate, which is basically a daily changing value set by a network of banks that trade currencies.

The currency exchange store will modify the rate by a certain percentage to ensure that it makes a profit on the transaction. For example,

Word Study

maturity /məˈtjʊərɪti/
n. 到期（日）
broker /ˈbrəʊkə/ n. 经纪人，代理商

外汇市场如何运作？
　　外汇市场的交易方式有三种。一是货币兑换：按照一定汇率，把一种货币转换成另一种货币。这种交易可以在许多地方进行，包括银行、酒店、机场等地方，也可在线上进行。二是即期外汇交易：指的是外汇市场上买卖双方成交后，在当天或第二个营业日办理交割的外汇交易形式。三是远期外汇交易：指的是在外汇市场上进行远期外汇买卖的一种交易行为，与即期外汇交易的根本区别在于交割日不同。

suppose the spot rate for exchanging U.S. Dollars into Australian Dollars is listed as 1.2500 for the day. Which means that for each U.S. Dollar spent, you can buy 1.25 Australian dollars if traded at the spot rate. But the currency exchange store may modify this rate to 1.20, meaning you can buy 1.20 Australian Dollars for 1 U.S. Dollar. With this hypothetical rate change, their fee would effectively be 5 cents on the dollar.

SPOT TRANSACTIONS

A spot market deal is for immediate delivery, which is defined as two business days for most currency pairs. The major exception is the purchase or sale of USD/CAD, which is settled in one business day. The business day calculation excludes Saturdays, Sundays, and legal holidays in either currency of the traded pair. During the Christmas and Easter season, some spot trades can take as long as six days to settle. Funds are exchanged on the settlement date, not the transaction date. Market moves are driven by a combination of speculation, economic strength and growth, and interest rate **differentials**.

FORWARD TRANSACTIONS

Any forex transaction that settles for a date later than spot is considered a "forward". The price is **calculated** by adjusting the spot rate to account for the difference in interest rates between the two currencies. The amount of adjustment is called "forward points". The forward points reflect only the interest rate differential between two markets. They are not a **forecast** of how the spot market will trade at a date in the future.

A forward is a tailor-made contract: it can be for any amount of money and can settle on any date that's not a weekend or holiday. As in a spot transaction, funds are exchanged on the settlement date.

Example of Forex Transactions

Assume a trader believes that the EUR will appreciate against the USD. Another way of thinking of it is that the USD will fall relative to the EUR.

They buy the EUR/USD at 1.2500 and purchase $5,000 worth of currency. Later that day the price has increased to 1.2550. The trader is up $25 (5000 * 0.0050). If the price dropped to 1.2430, the trader would be losing $35 (5000 * 0.0070).

Currency prices are constantly moving, so the trader may decide to hold the position overnight. The broker will **rollover** the position, resulting in a credit or debit based on the interest rate differential between the **Eurozone** and the U.S. If the Eurozone has an interest rate of 4% and the U.S. has an interest rate of 3%, the trader owns the higher interest

Word Study

differential /ˌdɪfəˈrenʃəl/
 n. 差额，差价
calculate /ˈkælkjʊleɪt/
 v. 计算
forecast /ˈfɔːkɑːst/ n.
 预测
rollover /ˈrəʊlˌəʊvə/
 v. & n. 转期
Eurozone /ˈjʊərəʊzəʊn/
 n. 欧元区

rate currency because they bought EUR. Therefore, at rollover, the trader should receive a small credit. If the EUR interest rate was lower than the USD rate then the trader would be debited at rollover.

Word Study

unwind /ʌn'waɪnd/ v.
放松

How Does Forex Trading Shape Business?

The resulting collaboration of the different types of forex traders is a highly liquid, global market that impacts business around the world. Exchange rate movements are a factor in inflation, global corporate earnings and the balance of payments account for each country.

For instance, the popular currency carry trade strategy highlights how market participants influence exchange rates that, in turn, have spillover effects on the global economy. The carry trade, executed by banks, hedge funds, investment managers and individual investors, is designed to capture differences in yields across currencies by borrowing low-yielding currencies and selling them to purchase high-yielding currencies. For example, if the Japanese yen has a low yield, market participants would sell it and purchase a higher yield currency.

When interest rates in higher yielding countries begin to fall back toward lower yielding countries, the carry trade **unwinds** and investors sell their higher yielding investments. An unwinding of the yen carry trade may cause large Japanese financial institutions and investors with sizable foreign holdings to move money back into Japan as the spread between foreign yields and domestic yields narrows. This strategy, in turn, may result in a broad decrease in global equity prices.

There is a reason why forex is the largest market in the world: It empowers everyone from central banks to retail investors to potentially see profits from currency fluctuations related to the global economy. There are various strategies that can be used to trade and hedge currencies, such as the carry trade, which highlights how forex players impact the global economy.

The reasons for forex trading are varied. Speculative trades — executed by banks, financial institutions, hedge funds, and individual investors — are profit-motivated. Central banks move forex markets dramatically through monetary policy, exchange regime setting, and, in rare cases, currency intervention. Corporations trade currency for global business operations and to hedge risk.

foreign exchange market 外汇市场
over-the-counter (OTC) market 场外交易市场
international trade settlements 国际贸易结算

derivatives market 衍生品市场   spot transaction 即期交易

pension funds 养老金   currency intervention 货币干预

hedge funds 对冲基金   offshore investments 离岸投资

spot rate 现货汇率   forward transaction 远期交易

currency carry trade 货币利差交易   spillover effects 溢出效应

外汇风险

外汇风险,也叫汇率风险,是指在进出口经营贸易活动以及跨境股权交易及融资等相关活动中,由于外汇汇率的不确定性,导致可能引起企业或者经营活动的净现金价值发生变化的风险,通常指可能损失的风险。

(一)外汇风险种类

1. 结算风险

外汇结算风险是指用外汇进行的项目款结算因汇率变化而产生的风险。这类风险在国际项目中尤其是工程项目最常见。一般情况下,国际项目在招投标阶段就已确定回款结算货币及结算汇率,但因建设工期长,汇率的变化又不可预知,当项目回款以所在国家(地区)的货币计价时,其本身就包含一定的汇率风险,这种汇率风险的大小取决于计价货币币值的稳定程度。

2. 交易风险

交易风险是跨国公司在以非美货币计价跨国交易中,由于汇率变动而造成未结算外币交易发生的损益。我国跨国企业经常性的外币交易主要包括:以美元结算的材料采购应付款、尚未履行的远期外汇合约、其他以非美货币计价的资产和权益。

3. 汇兑风险

汇兑风险是因货币兑换及汇率的波动产生汇兑损益而带来的风险。跨国公司大量的外汇兑换业务经常会发生,项目前期启动资金需要用美元兑换成项目所在国货币,用以支付在当地的各项费用开支,项目回款到当地子公司后,需要将非美货币的项目供货款兑换成美元汇回给母公司等,在非美货币呈现单边贬值下这种兑换会产生汇兑风险。

4. 代理风险

代理风险是指在一定时间期限和特定市场范围内,由于中国公司没有注册子公司或子公司没有渠道进口、投标具备的相关资质等,必须通过联合代理组成联合投标体进行投标的项目。合作方式为中国跨国公司与代理签美元供货合同,代理与最终客户签东道国货币合同并从中赚取差价。但因美元强势崛起,东道国经济、金融、政治、政局等因素变化,导致东道国货币贬值带来汇率风险。具体表现为:东道国收到最终本币回款后,换汇后的美元头寸已经无法覆盖合同约定的美元金额。中国跨国公司的风险包括:一是合同直接被取消或项目不执行;二是渠道商在收到最终客户回款后,压住货款不对供货商进行背靠背支付。

（二）外汇风险特征

1.外汇风险大小由签约币种和支付条款决定

在对外招标文件中，一般都允许投标人按某一对外通用货币，选择一定的外汇比例进行投标报价。合同中规定的对外通用货币比例越大，外汇风险越小。我国跨国公司项目大多数在非洲、东南亚、南美洲等发展中国家，这些国家通常物价上涨较快，导致工程成本增加，当地货币贬值较快，易遭受汇兑损失。同时与项目的经营方式、施工组织与计划、工程进度等也密切相关。

2.双重汇兑风险

我国的跨国公司一般会在目的国成立子公司，一方面为承接DDP项目的需要，另一方面为中方员工的签证及本地用工风险进行考虑。

外汇风险既有所在国当地货币与美元的兑换，也有美元与人民币的兑换，跨国公司面临双重甚至多重外汇风险。跨国公司在签订合同时，供货部分可能是美元或欧元结算，服务部分则由本币支付。同时在项目前期，存在项目垫支，存在将美元换成本币进行本地采购、支付项目分包款、本地人员工资等，这些行为致使在实际的结算支付中，不可避免地产生汇兑风险。项目服务部分回款后，将本币换成美元后从本地子公司汇回国内母公司时，也会发生汇兑风险。这样跨国公司很可能会承受双重汇兑风险，最终影响到企业的利润。

3.外汇风险金额大、时间长、种类多

大部分国际项目尤其是国际EPC总包合同一般都有合同金额大、合同工期长的特点，EPC合同涉及的外汇风险更是复杂。

文献来源：

美元强势背景下非美货币外汇风险防范——基于F公司案例分析［J］.蒋辉清.新会计.2017（06）

A. Describe the three functions of the forex.

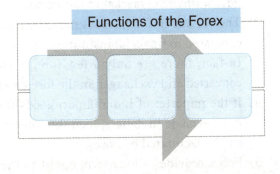

Functions of the Forex

B. According to the text, fill in each of the following blanks with an appropriate word or phrase.

1) The foreign exchange market is a global _____ or over-the-counter market for the trading of currencies.

2) Aside from providing a venue for the buying, selling, exchanging and

_____ of currencies, the forex market also enables currency conversion for international trade _____ and _____ _____.

3) An exchange rate is a _____ paid for one currency in exchange for another.

4) A central bank is responsible for _____ the price of its native currency on forex. This is the exchange rate regime by which its currency will trade in the open market.

5) Retail investors base currency trades on a combination of _____ _____ (i.e., interest rate parity, inflation rates, and monetary policy expectations) and _____ factors (i.e., support, resistance, technical indicators, price patterns).

6) The basic and the most visible function of foreign exchange market is the _____ of funds (foreign currency) from one country to another for the settlement of payments.

7) Currency exchange of physical money (coins and paper bills), is usually done over a _____ at a teller station.

8) If you exchange U.S. dollars for Australian dollars, the amount you would be able to purchase would be dependent on the international _____, which is basically a daily changing value set by a network of banks that trade currencies.

9) Market moves are driven by a combination of speculation, _____ _____ and growth, and interest rate differentials.

10) Any forex transaction that settles for a date later than spot is considered a "_____".

C. Read the text and decide whether the following statements are True (T) or False (F).

1) In terms of trading volume, the foreign exchange market is the second largest financial market in the world. ( )

2) The volume of forex trades made by retail investors is extremely high compared to financial institutions and companies. ( )

3) In fact, there are only a few foreign currencies which are treated, converted and exchanged in the foreign exchange market. ( )

4) If the importer of India import goods from the U.S. and the payment is to be made in dollars, then the conversion of the rupee to the dollar will be facilitated by Forex. ( )

5) Forex provides a long-term credit to the importers so as to facilitate the smooth flow of goods and services from country to country. ( )

6) A forward contract is usually a three-month contract to buy or sell the foreign exchange for another currency at a fixed date in the future at a price agreed upon today. ( )

7) The hedging against currency risk can add a level of safety to offshore investments. ( )

8) A currency exchange business profits from its services either through adjusting the exchange rate or charging fees or both. (   )

9) The currency exchange store has no right to modify the spot rate by a certain percentage. (   )

10) The forward points reflect only the interest rate differential between two markets, and they are a forecast of how the spot market will trade at a date in the future. (   )

1) What are the major types of institutions and traders in forex markets?

_____

_____

2) What are the functions of the foreign exchange market?

_____

_____

3) If a person wants to exchange the currency of one country into that of another, where can he/she go to complete the transaction?

_____

_____

4) What's the spot transaction?

_____

_____

5) Assume a trader believes that the EUR will appreciate against the USD. If someone buys the EUR/USD at 1.2500 and purchases $5,000 worth of currency. Later that day the price has increased to 1.2550. The trader is up $25 (5000 * 0.0050). But if the price drops to 1.2440, how much would the trader lose?

_____

_____

Case Story

Why Walmart Is Impacted by Foreign Exchange Fluctuations?

Most people in North America are familiar with the name Walmart. It conjures up an image of a gigantic, box-like store filled with a wide range of essential and nonessential products. What's less known is that Walmart is the world's largest company, in terms of revenues, as ranked by the Fortune 500 in 2010. With $408 billion in sales, it operates in fifteen global markets and has 4,343 stores outside of the United States, which amounts to about 50 percent of its total stores. More than 700,000 people work for Walmart internationally. With numbers like this, it's easy to see how important the global markets have become for this company.

Walmart's strength comes from the upper hand it has in its negotiations with suppliers around the world. Suppliers are motivated to negotiate with Walmart because of the huge sales volume the stores offer manufacturers. The business rationale for many suppliers is that while they may lose a certain percentage of profitability per product, the overall sales volume of an order from Walmart can make them far more money overall than orders from most other stores. Walmart's purchasing professionals are known for being aggressive negotiators on purchases and for extracting the best terms for the company.

In order to buy goods from around the world, Walmart has to deal extensively in different currencies. Small changes in the daily foreign currency market can significantly impact the costs for Walmart and in turn both its profitability and that of its global suppliers.

A company like Walmart needs foreign exchange and capital for different reasons, including the following common operational uses:

1. To build new stores, expand stores, or refurbish stores in a specific country

2. To purchase products locally by paying in local currencies or the U.S. dollar, whichever is cheaper and works to Walmart's advantage

3. To pay salaries and benefits for its local employees in each country as well as its expatriate and global workforce

4. To take profits out of a country and either reinvest the money in another country or market or save it and make profits from returns on investment

To illustrate this impact of foreign currency, let's look at the currency of China, the renminbi (RMB), and its impact on a global business like Walmart. Many global analysts argue that the Chinese government tries to keep the value of its currency low or cheap to help promote exports. When the local RMB is valued cheaply or low, Chinese importers that buy foreign goods find that the prices are more expensive and higher.

For Walmart, an American company, a cheap renminbi means that it takes fewer U.S. dollars to buy Chinese products. Walmart can then buy cheap Chinese products, add a small profit margin, and then sell the goods in the United States at a price lower than what its competitors can offer. If the Chinese RMB increased in value, then Walmart would have to spend more U.S. dollars to buy the same products, whether the products are clothing, electronics, or furniture. Any increase in cost for Walmart will mean an increase in cost for their customers in the United States, which could lead to a decrease in sales. So, we can see why Walmart would be opposed to an increase in the value of the RMB.

To manage this currency concern, Walmart often requires that the currency exchange rate be fixed in its purchasing contracts with Chinese suppliers. By fixing the currency exchange rate, Walmart locks in its product costs and therefore its profitability. Fixing the exchange rate means setting the price that one currency will convert into another. This is how a company like Walmart can avoid unexpected drops or increases in the value of the RMB and the U.S. dollar.

While global companies have to buy and sell in different currencies around the world, their primary goal is to avoid losses and to fix the price of the currency exchange so that they can manage their profitability with surety.

Global firms like Walmart often set up local operations that help them balance or manage their risk by doing business in local currencies. Walmart now has 304 stores in China. Each store generates sales in renminbi, earning the company local currency that it can use to manage its local operations and to purchase local goods for sale in its other global markets.

Case Discussion

1) A company like Walmart needs foreign exchange and capital for different reasons, please list at least two.

_____

_____

2) Why is Walmart concerned about foreign exchange rates?

_____

_____

Case Summary

沃尔玛，名列2010年《财富》杂志世界企业500强之列，是全球最大的跨国公司之一，其业务遍布全球15个国家和地区，员工多达70多万。作为一个大型跨国公司，沃尔玛需要从世界各地采购物资，必须以不同的货币进行大量交易。每日外汇市场上非常微小的变化，就会对沃尔玛的成本造成巨大的影响，进而影响其盈利能力及其全球供应商的盈利能力。

本文以人民币为例，描述了人民币的贬值和升值对沃尔玛全球业务的影响。对于美国公司沃尔玛来说，便宜的人民币意味着购买中国产品所需的美元更少。沃尔玛可以购买低价的中国产品，然后小幅加价以获取少量利润，最后以低于其竞争对手所能提供的价格在美国出售商品。如果人民币升值,那么沃尔玛将花费更多美元购买相同的产品,成本的增加意味着其美国客户的成本增加,这就可能导致其销售量下降。由此可见沃尔玛为什么会反对人民币升值。

为了解决汇率问题,沃尔玛常在与中国供应商的采购合同中确定汇率。通过固定货币汇率,固定其产品成本,从而稳定其盈利能力。这样,像沃尔玛这样的公司就可以规避因汇率的意外上升或者下跌而带来的风险。

Reading Expansion
拓展阅读

Reading I

Six Most Popular Currencies for Trading

Forex is the largest and most liquid market, with trillions of dollars traded between millions of parties around the globe each day. One of the first steps in understanding the market — which is also known as foreign exchange or currency trading — is to gain familiarity with some of the more commonly traded currencies. Here is a look at six major currencies, as well as the underlying traits and characteristics of each one.

1. The U.S. Dollar

The U.S. dollar, which is sometimes called the greenback, is first and foremost in the world of forex trading, as it is easily the most traded currency on the planet.

The U.S. dollar can be found in a currency pair with all of the other major currencies and often acts as the intermediary in triangular currency transactions. This is because the greenback acts as the unofficial global reserve currency, held by nearly every central bank and institutional investment entity in the world.

In addition, due to the U.S. dollar's global acceptance, it is used by some countries as an official currency, in lieu of a local currency, a practice known as dollarization. The U.S. dollar also may be widely accepted in other nations, acting as an informal alternative form of payment, while those nations maintain their official local currency.

The U.S. dollar is also an important factor in the foreign exchange rate market for other currencies, where it may act as a benchmark or target rate for countries that choose to fix or peg their currencies to the dollar's value. Quite often, countries will fix their currencies to the U.S. dollar to stabilize their exchange rates rather than allowing the free (forex) markets to drive the currency's relative value.

One other feature of the U.S. dollar is that it is used as the standard currency for most commodities, such as crude oil and precious metals. Thus, these commodities are subject not only to fluctuations in value due to the basic economic principals of supply and demand but also to the relative value of the U.S. dollar, with prices highly sensitive to inflation and U.S. interest rates, which can affect the dollar's value.

2. The Euro

The euro has become the second most traded currency behind the U.S. dollar. The official currency of the majority of the nations within the eurozone, the euro was introduced to the world markets on Jan. 1, 1999, with banknotes and coinage entering circulation three years later.

Along with being the official currency for most Eurozone countries, many nations within Europe and Africa peg their currencies to the euro, for much the same reason that currencies are pegged to the U.S. dollar — to stabilize the exchange rate. As a result, the euro is also the world's second-largest reserve currency.

With the euro being a widely used and trusted currency, it is prevalent in the forex market and adds liquidity to any currency pair it trades with. The euro is commonly traded by speculators as a play on the general health of the eurozone and its member nations. Political events within the eurozone can also lead to large trading volumes in the euro, especially in relation to nations that saw their local interest rates fall dramatically at the time of the euro's inception, notably Italy, Greece, Spain, and Portugal. The euro may be the most "politicized" currency actively traded in the forex market.

3. The Japanese Yen

The Japanese yen is easily the most traded of Asian currencies and viewed by many as a proxy for the underlying strength of Japan's manufacturing and export-driven economy. As Japan's economy goes, so goes the yen (in some respects). Forex traders also watch the yen to gauge the overall health of the Pan-Pacific region as well, taking economies such as South Korea, Singapore, and Thailand into consideration, as those currencies are traded far less in the global forex markets.

The yen is also well known in forex circles for its role in the carry trade (seeking to profit from the difference in interest rates between two currencies). The strategy involves borrowing the yen at next to no cost (due to low-interest rates) and using the borrowed money to invest in other higher-yielding currencies around the world, pocketing the rate differentials in the process.

With the carry trade being such a large part of the yen's presence on the international stage, the constant borrowing of the Japanese currency has made appreciation a difficult task. Though the yen still trades with the same fundamentals as any other currency, its relationship to international interest rates, especially with the more heavily traded currencies such as the U.S. dollar and the euro, is a large determinant of the yen's value.

4. The Great British Pound

The Great British pound, also known as the pound sterling, is the fourth most traded currency in the forex market. Although the U.K. was an official member of the European Union, the country never adopted the euro as its official currency for a variety of reasons, namely historic pride in the pound and maintaining control of domestic interest rates. As a result, the pound is sometimes viewed as a pure play on the United Kingdom.

Forex traders will often estimate the value of the British pound based on the overall strength of the British economy and political stability of its government. Due to its high value relative to its peers, the pound is also an important currency benchmark for many nations and represents a very liquid component in the forex market. The British pound also acts as a large reserve currency due to its historically high relative value compared to other global currencies.

5. The Canadian Dollar

Also known as the loonie, the Canadian dollar is probably the world's foremost commodity currency, meaning that it often moves in step with the commodities markets — notably crude oil, precious metals, and minerals. With Canada being such a large exporter of such commodities, the loonie often reacts to movements in underlying commodities prices, especially that of crude oil. Traders often trade the Canadian dollar to speculate on the movements of commodities or to hedge positions in the commodities market.

6. The Swiss Franc

Last is the Swiss franc, which, much like Switzerland, is viewed by many as a "neutral" currency. More accurately, the Swiss franc is considered a safe haven within the forex market, primarily due to the fact that the franc tends to move differently than more volatile commodity currencies, such as the Canadian and Australian dollars.

The Swiss National Bank has actually been known to be quite active in the forex market to ensure that the franc trades within a relatively tight range, to reduce volatility, and to keep interest rates in check.

Second Thoughts

For each of the following statements, choose one (or more than one) answer to fill in the blank.

1) _____ often acts as the intermediary in triangular currency transactions.

   A. The euro

   B. The U.S. dollar

   C. The Japanese yen

   D. The Canadian dollar

2) _____ has become the second most traded currency behind the U.S. dollar.

A. The Swiss franc

B. The Canadian dollar

C. The euro

D. The Japanese yen

Reading II

How BMW Dealt with Exchange Rate Risk

BMW Group, owner of the BMW, Mini and Rolls-Royce brands, has been based in Munich since its founding in 1916. But by 2011, only 17 percent of the cars it sold were bought in Germany.

In recent years, China has become BMW's fastest-growing market, accounting for 14 percent of BMW's global sales volume in 2011. India, Russia and eastern Europe have also become key markets.

The Challenge

Despite rising sales revenues, BMW was conscious that its profits were often severely eroded by changes in exchange rates. The company's own calculations in its annual reports suggest that the negative effect of exchange rates totaled €2.4bn between 2005 and 2009.

BMW did not want to pass on its exchange rate costs to consumers through price increases. Its rival Porsche had done this at the end of the 1980s in the U.S. and sales had plunged.

The Strategy

BMW took a two-pronged approach to managing its foreign exchange exposure.

One strategy was to use a "natural hedge" — meaning it would develop ways to spend money in the same currency as where sales were taking place, meaning revenues would also be in the local currency.

However, not all exposure could be offset in this way, so BMW decided it would also use formal financial hedges. To achieve this, BMW set up regional treasury centers in the U.S., the U.K. and Singapore.

How the Strategy Was Implemented

The natural hedge strategy was implemented in two ways. The first involved establishing factories in the markets where it sold its products; the second involved making more purchases denominated in the currencies of its main markets.

BMW now has production facilities for cars and components in 13 countries. In 2000, its overseas production volume accounted for 20 percent of the total. By 2011, it had risen to 44 percent.

In the 1990s, BMW had become one of the first premium carmakers from overseas to set up a plant in the U.S. — in Spartanburg, South Carolina. In 2008, BMW announced it was investing $750m to expand its Spartanburg plant. This would create 5,000 jobs in the U.S. while cutting 8,100 jobs in Germany.

This also had the effect of shortening the supply chain between Germany and the U.S. market. The company boosted its purchasing in U.S. dollars generally, especially in the North American Free Trade Agreement region.

Its office in Mexico City made $615m of purchases of Mexican auto parts in 2009, expected to rise significantly in following years.

A joint venture with Brilliance China Automotive was set up in Shenyang, China, where half the BMW cars for sale in the country are now manufactured. The carmaker also set up a local office to help its group purchasing department to select competitive suppliers in China. By the end of 2009, RMB6bn worth of purchases were from local suppliers. Again, this had the effect of shortening supply chains and improving customer service.

At the end of 2010, BMW announced it would invest 1.8bn rupees in its production plant in Chennai, India, and increase production capacity in India from 6,000 to 10,000 units. It also announced plans to increase production in Kaliningrad, Russia.

Meanwhile, the overseas regional treasury centers were instructed to review the exchange rate exposure in their regions on a weekly basis and report it to a group treasurer, part of the group finance operation, in Munich. The group treasurer team then consolidates risk figures globally and recommends actions to mitigate foreign exchange risk.

The Lessons

By moving production to foreign markets, the company not only reduces its foreign exchange exposure but also benefits from being close to its customers.

In addition, sourcing parts overseas, and therefore closer to its foreign markets, also helps to diversify supply chain risks.

Second Thoughts

1) What challenge did BMW face?

_____

_____

2) What strategy did BMW take to manage its foreign exchange exposure and how did the strategy work?

_____

_____

International Monetary System

国际货币体系

CHAPTER 7

本章概要

本章主要介绍国际货币体系，包括金本位制、布雷顿森林体系、国际货币基金组织、世界银行、固定汇率和浮动汇率。

学习指南

各国政府为了适应国际贸易和国际支付的需要，对货币在世界范围内发挥世界货币职能，做了一系列安排。包括为此所确定的原则、采取的措施和建立的组织机构，以确保世界经济的稳定和各国经济的发展。

通过本章学习，希望大家能够实现以下目标：

（1）基本目标（Text-based Goals）

- 掌握本章涉及话题的基本专业术语及词汇，如法定货币、金本位制、国际复兴开发银行等。
- 掌握本章的主要知识点，即金本位制度、布雷顿森林体系、国际货币基金组织、世界银行、固定汇率和浮动汇率的含义、基本要素及其特点。

（2）拓展目标（Extended Goals）

- 思考本章引言，为什么约翰·皮尔庞特·摩根会说"黄金才是钱。其他的都是信用"？
- 通过学习背景知识、拓展阅读、案例分析，进一步了解强势货币的优劣，并介绍人民币对稳定全球金融体系的作用及欧洲主权债务危机等。

国际货币体系的目的是促进经济交流，促进国际贸易的蓬勃发展，为全球的发展做贡献，同时促进价格和金融稳定。

The purpose of the international monetary system (IMS) is to facilitate international economic exchange since most countries have national currencies that are not typically accepted as legal payment beyond their borders. When the IMS is operating **mellifluously**, international trade/investment can flourish; however, when the IMS operates inefficiently or even completely fails (as in the Great Depression or the recent Credit Crisis), international trade/investment is **throttled**. The essential element of the IMS is to facilitate the exchange of goods, services, and capital among countries. The IMS seeks to contribute to stable and high global growth while currently fostering price and financial stability.

The Gold Standard

金本位制

金本位制是一种货币制度，在这种制度下，政府的货币是固定的，可以自由兑换为黄金。其中一国的货币或纸币的价值与黄金直接相关。根据金本位制度，各国同意将纸币转换为固定数量的黄金。使用金本位制度的国家设定了黄金的固定价格，并以该价格买卖黄金，该固定价格用于确定货币的价值。

WHAT IS THE GOLD STANDARD?

The gold standard is a fixed monetary regime under which the government's currency is fixed and may be freely converted into gold. It can also refer to a freely competitive monetary system in which gold or bank receipts for gold act as the principal medium of exchange; or to a standard of international trade, wherein some or all countries fix their exchange rate based on the relative gold parity values between individual currencies.

HOW DOES THE GOLD STANDARD WORK?

The gold standard is a monetary system where a country's currency or paper money has a value directly linked to gold. With the gold standard, countries agreed to convert paper money into a fixed amount of gold. A country that uses the gold standard sets a fixed price for gold and buys and sells gold at that price. That fixed price is used to determine the value of the currency. For example, if the U.S. sets the price of gold at $500 an ounce, the value of the dollar would be 1/500th of an ounce of gold.

The gold standard developed a **nebulous** definition over time, but is generally used to describe any commodity-based monetary regime that does not rely on un-backed **fiat** money, or money that is only valuable because the government forces people to use it. Beyond that, however, there are major differences.

Some gold standards only rely on the actual circulation of physical

Word Study

mellifluously
/mə'lɪfluəslɪ/ *adv.*
流畅地

throttle /'θrɒtəl/ *v.* 使
窒息

nebulous /'nebjuələs/
adj. 模糊的，不清
楚的

fiat /'fiːæt/ *n.* 法令，
命令

gold coins and bars, or **bullion**, but others allow other commodity or paper currencies. Recent historical systems only granted the ability to convert the national currency into gold, thereby limiting the inflationary and deflationary ability of banks or governments.

WHY GOLD?

Most commodity-money advocates choose gold as a medium of exchange because of its intrinsic properties. Gold has non-monetary uses, especially in jewelry, electronics and dentistry, so it should always retain a minimum level of real demand. It is perfectly and evenly divisible without losing value, unlike diamonds, and does not spoil over time. It is impossible to perfectly **counterfeit** and has a fixed stock — there is only so much gold on Earth, and inflation is limited to the speed of mining.

FEATURES OF GOLD STANDARD

There are many advantages to using the gold standard, including price stability. This is a long-term advantage that makes it harder for governments to inflate prices by expanding the money supply. Inflation is rare and hyperinflation doesn't happen because the money supply can only grow if the supply of gold reserves increases. Similarly, the gold standard can provide fixed international rates between countries that participate and can also reduce the uncertainty in international trade.

But it may cause an imbalance between countries that participate in the gold standard. Gold-producing nations may be at an advantage over those that don't produce the precious metal, thereby increasing their own reserves. The gold standard may also, according to some economists, prevent the **mitigation** of economic recessions because it **hinders** the ability of a government to increase its money supply — a tool many central banks have to help boost economic growth.

A BRIEF HISTORY OF THE GOLD STANDARD

Around 700 B.C., gold was made into coins for the first time, enhancing its usability as a monetary unit. Before this, gold had to be weighed and checked for purity when settling trades. Gold coins were not a perfect solution, since a common practice for centuries to come was to clip these slightly irregular coins to **accumulate** enough gold that could be **melted** down into bullion. In 1696, the Great Recoinage in England introduced a technology that automated the production of coins and put an end to clipping.

The U.S. Constitution in 1789 gave Congress the **sole** right to coin money and the power to regulate its value. Creating a united national currency enabled the standardization of a monetary system that had up until then consisted of **circulating** foreign coin, mostly silver. With silver

金本位的特点
金本位制度下的汇率非常稳定,不易发生通货膨胀,有助于国际贸易和金融的发展。金本位制也可能造成国家之间不平等,限制政府应对经济衰退的手段。

Word Study

bullion /ˈbʊlɪən/ n. 金（或银）条

counterfeit /ˈkaʊntəfɪt/ v. 伪造,造假

mitigation /ˌmɪtɪˈɡeɪʃən/ n. 减轻,缓解

hinder /ˈhɪndə/ v. 阻碍,妨碍

accumulate /əˈkjuːmjʊleɪt/ v. 积累,积聚

melt /melt/ v. 熔化;溶解

sole /səʊl/ adj. 唯一的

circulating /ˈsɜːkjuleɪtɪŋ/ adj. 流通的

Word Study

bimetallic /ˌbaɪmɪˈtælɪk/
　adj.（金银）两本位
　制的
erode /ɪˈrəʊd/ v. 逐渐
　毁坏，削弱
decree /dɪˈkriː/ n. 法令，
　政令
legal tender 法定货币

in greater abundance relative to gold, a **bimetallic** standard was adopted in 1792. While the officially adopted silver-to-gold parity ratio of 15 : 1 accurately reflected the market ratio at the time, after 1793 the value of silver steadily declined, pushing gold out of circulation, according to Gresham's law.

The so-called "classical gold standard era" began in England in 1819 and spread to France, Germany, Switzerland, Belgium and the United States. Each government pegged its national currency to a fixed weight in gold. For example, by 1879, U.S. dollars were convertible to gold at a rate of $20.67 per ounce. These parity rates were used to price international transactions. Other countries later joined to gain access to Western trade markets.

There were many interruptions in the gold standard, especially during wartime, and many countries experimented with bimetallic (gold and silver) standards. Governments frequently spent more than their gold reserves could back, and suspensions of national gold standards were extremely common. Moreover, governments struggled to correctly peg the relationship between their national currencies and gold without creating distortions.

As long as governments or central banks retained monopoly privileges over the supply of national currencies, the gold standard proved an ineffective or inconsistent restraint on fiscal policy. The gold standard slowly **eroded** during the 20th century. This began in the United States in 1933, when Franklin Delano Roosevelt signed an executive order criminalizing the private possession of monetary gold.

After WWII, the Bretton Woods Agreement forced allied countries to accept the U.S. dollar as a reserve rather than gold, and the U.S. government pledged to keep enough gold to back its dollars. In 1971, the Nixon administration terminated the convertibility of U.S. dollars to gold, creating a fiat currency regime.

GOLD STANDARD VS. FIAT MONEY

金本位和法定货币
对比

　　金本位是一种货
币体系，其中货币的
价值基于黄金。而
法定货币不代表任
何实质商品或货物，
它是依靠政府的法
令使其成为合法流
通的货币。

As its name suggests, the term gold standard refers to a monetary system in which the value of currency is based on gold. A fiat system, by contrast, is a monetary system in which the value of currency is not based on any physical commodity but is instead allowed to fluctuate dynamically against other currencies on the foreign-exchange markets. The term "fiat" is derived from the Latin "fieri", meaning an arbitrary act or **decree**. In keeping with this etymology, the value of fiat currencies is ultimately based on the fact that they are defined as **legal tender** by way of government decree.

In the decades prior to the First World War, international trade was conducted on the basis of what has come to be known as the classical gold standard. In this system, trade between nations was settled using physical gold. Nations with trade surpluses accumulated gold as payment for their exports. Conversely, nations with trade deficits saw their gold reserves decline, as gold flowed out of those nations as payment for their imports.

Bretton Woods System

The Bretton Woods Agreement was negotiated in July 1944 to establish a new international monetary system, the Bretton Woods System. The Agreement was developed by delegates from 44 countries at the United Nations Monetary and Financial Conference held in Bretton Woods, New Hampshire. Under the Bretton Woods System, gold was the basis for the U.S. dollar and other currencies were pegged to the U.S. dollar's value.

The principal goals are creating an efficient foreign exchange system, preventing competitive devaluations of currencies, and promoting international economic growth. The Bretton Woods Agreement and System were central to these goals. The Bretton Woods Agreement also created two important organizations, including the International Monetary Fund (IMF) and the World Bank. While the Bretton Woods System was dissolved in the 1970s, both the IMF and World Bank have remained strong pillars for the exchange of international currencies.

Though the Bretton Woods conference itself took place over just three weeks, the preparations for it had been going on for several years. The primary designers of the Bretton Woods System were the famous British economist John Maynard Keynes and American Chief International Economist of the U.S. Treasury Department Harry Dexter White. Keynes' hope was to establish a powerful global central bank to be called the Clearing Union and issue a new international reserve currency called the **bancor**. White's plan **envisioned** a more modest lending fund and a greater role for the U.S. dollar, rather than the creation of a new currency. In the end, the adopted plan took ideas from both, leaning more toward White's plan.

It wasn't until 1958 that the Bretton Woods System became fully functional. Once implemented, its provisions called for the U.S. dollar to be pegged to the value of gold. Moreover, all other currencies in the system were then pegged to the U.S. dollar's value. The exchange rate applied at the time set the price of gold at $35 an ounce.

THE BRETTON WOODS SYSTEM'S COLLAPSE

In 1971, concerned that the U.S. gold supply was no longer adequate to cover the number of dollars in circulation, President Richard M. Nixon declared a temporary suspension of the dollar's **convertibility** into gold. By

布雷顿森林体系

1944年7月，来自44个国家的代表出席了在美国新罕布什尔州布雷顿森林市举行的"联合国货币金融会议"，商讨建立有效的外汇体系。这次会议上形成的国际货币体系被称为"布雷顿森林体系"。

布雷顿森林体系创建了两个重要的组织，即国际货币基金组织（IMF）和世界银行。

布雷顿森林体系要求货币与美元挂钩，而美元又与黄金价格挂钩。

布雷顿森林体系在20世纪70年代崩溃，但通过国际货币基金组织和世界银行的发展，对国际货币交换和贸易产生了深远持久的影响。

Word Study

bancor /'bækɒ/ n. 班柯（一种国际货币单位）
envision /ɪn'vɪʒən/ v. 展望，想象
collapse /kə'læps/ n. &v. 崩溃，瓦解
convertibility /kən,vɜːtə'bɪlətɪ/ n. 可兑性

Word Study

surveillance /sɜ:ˈveɪləns/
    n. 监督, 监管
in aggregate 总计,
    合计
accompany /əˈkʌmpəni/
    v. 伴随, 陪同
economic distress 经
    济不景气
mitigate /ˈmɪtɪgeɪt/ v.
    使减轻, 使缓和

国际货币基金组织
　　国际货币基金组织(IMF)是一个旨在促进全球经济增长和金融稳定, 鼓励国际贸易并减少贫困的国际组织。国际货币基金组织总部设在华盛顿, 其职责是提供技术和资金协助, 监察货币汇率和各国贸易情况, 确保全球金融制度运作正常。

1973 the Bretton Woods System had collapsed. Countries were then free to choose any exchange arrangement for their currency, except pegging its value to the price of gold. They could, for example, link its value to another country's currency, or a basket of currencies, or simply let it float freely and allow market forces to determine its value relative to other countries' currencies.

The Bretton Woods Agreement remains a significant event in world financial history. The two Bretton Woods institutions it created in the International Monetary Fund and the World Bank played an important part in helping to rebuild Europe in the aftermath of World War II. Subsequently, both institutions have continued to maintain their founding goals while also transitioning to serve global government interests in the modern-day.

International Monetary Fund

WHAT IS THE IMF?

The International Monetary Fund (IMF) is an international organization that aims to promote global economic growth and financial stability, encourage international trade, and reduce poverty.

The International Monetary Fund is based in Washington, D.C., and currently consists of 189 member countries, each of which has representation on the IMF's executive board in proportion to its financial importance, so that the most powerful countries in the global economy have the most voting power.

IMF ACTIVITIES

Surveillance

The IMF collects massive amounts of data on national economies, international trade, and the global economy **in aggregate**, as well as providing regularly updated economic forecasts at the national and international levels. These forecasts, published in the *World Economic Outlook*, are **accompanied** by lengthy discussions of the effect of fiscal, monetary, and trade policies on growth prospects and financial stability.

Capacity building

The IMF provides technical assistance, training, and policy advice to member countries through its capacity building programs. These programs include training in data collection and analysis, which feed into the IMF's project of monitoring national and global economies.

Lending

The IMF makes loans to countries that are experiencing **economic distress** in order to prevent or **mitigate** financial crises. Members contribute the funds for this lending to a pool based on a quota system. These funds total around SDR 475 billion (U.S. $645 billion) as of September 2017. (IMF assets are denominated in special drawing rights or SDR, a kind of quasi-currency that is comprised of set proportions of the world's reserve currencies.)

HISTORY OF THE IMF

The IMF was originally created in 1945 as part of the Bretton Woods Agreement, which attempted to encourage international financial cooperation by introducing a system of convertible currencies at fixed exchange rates, with the dollar **redeemable** for gold at $35 per ounce. The IMF oversaw this system: for example, a country was free to readjust its exchange rate by up to 10% in either direction, but larger changes required the IMF's permission.

The IMF also acted as a gatekeeper: Countries were not **eligible** for membership in the International Bank for Reconstruction and Development (IBRD) — a World Bank forerunner that the Bretton Woods Agreement created in order to fund the reconstruction of Europe after World War II — unless they were members of the IMF.

Since the Bretton Woods System collapsed in the 1970s, the IMF has promoted the system of floating exchange rates, meaning that market forces determine the value of currencies relative to one another. This system continues to be in place today.

Word Study

redeemable /rɪˈdiːməbl/ *adj.* 可兑换的，可赎回的

eligible /ˈelɪdʒəbl/ *adj.* 有资格的，合格的

infusion /ɪnˈfjuːʒən/ *n.* 注入

World Bank

WHAT IS THE WORLD BANK?

The World Bank is an international organization dedicated to providing financing, advice, and research to developing nations to aid their economic advancement. The bank predominantly acts as an organization that attempts to fight poverty by offering developmental assistance to middle- and low-income countries.

Currently, the World Bank has two stated goals that it aims to achieve by 2030. The first is to end extreme poverty by decreasing the number of people living on less than $1.90 a day to below 3% of the world population. The second is to increase overall prosperity by increasing income growth in the bottom 40% of every country in the world.

The World Bank supplies qualifying governments with low-interest loans, zero-interest credits, and grants, all for the purpose of supporting the development of individual economies. Debt borrowings and cash **infusions** help with global education, healthcare, public administration, infrastructure, and private-sector development. The World Bank also shares information with various entities through policy advice, research

世界银行

世界银行是一个致力于向发展中国家提供融资、咨询和研究以帮助其经济发展的国际组织。

世界银行为符合条件的政府提供低息贷款、零息信贷、补助等金融援助产品和解决方案。

世界银行已经发展成为拥有五个合作组织的世界银行集团。

and analysis, and technical assistance. It offers advice and training for both the public and private sectors. **Headquartered** also in Washington, D.C., the World Bank currently has more than 10,000 employees in more than 120 offices worldwide.

HISTORY OF THE WORLD BANK

The World Bank was created in 1944 out of the Bretton Woods Agreement, which was secured under the auspices of the United Nations in the latter days of World War II.

Though titled as a bank, the World Bank, is not necessarily a bank in the traditional, chartered meanings of the word. The World Bank and its subsidiary groups operate within their own provisions and develop their own **proprietary** financial assistance products, all with the same goal of serving countries' capital needs internationally.

Through the years, the World Bank has expanded from a single institution to a group of five unique and cooperative institutional organizations, known as the World Banks or collectively as the World Bank Group. The first organization is the International Bank for Reconstruction and Development (IBRD), an institution that provides debt financing to governments that are considered middle income. The second organization within the World Bank Group is the International Development Association (IDA), a group that gives interest-free loans to the governments of poor countries. The International Finance Corporation (IFC), the third organization, focuses on the private sector and provides developing countries with investment financing and financial advisory services. The fourth part of the World Bank Group is the Multilateral Investment Guarantee Agency (MIGA), an organization that promotes foreign direct investments in developing countries. The fifth organization is the International Centre for Settlement of Investment **Disputes** (ICSID), an entity that provides arbitration on international investment disputes.

IMF VS. World Bank

The Bretton Woods Agreement included several components: a collective international monetary system, the formation of the World Bank, and the creation of the IMF. Since their founding the World Bank and the IMF, both based in Washington D.C., have worked together toward many of the same goals. The original goals of both the World Bank and the IMF were to support European and Asian countries needing financing to fund post-war reconstruction efforts.

The main difference between the IMF and the World Bank lies in their respective purposes and functions. The IMF oversees the world's

Word Study

headquarter /ˌhedˈkwɔːtə/ v. 设立总部
proprietary /prəˈpraɪətəri/ adj. 所有的,专有的
dispute /dɪsˈpjuːt/ n. 争端,纠纷

国际货币基金组织和世界银行对比
　　国际货币基金组织和世界银行都是《布雷顿森林协定》的一部分,总部都在华盛顿特区,两者的主要区别就在于各自的目的和功能不同。国际货币基金组织监督世界货币体系的稳定,而世界银行的目标则是通过向中等收入和低收入国家提供援助来减少贫困。

monetary system's stability, while the World Bank's goal is to reduce poverty by offering assistance to middle-income and low-income countries. The differing in the structuring of the two entities and their product offerings allows them to provide different types of financial lending and financing support. Each entity also has several of its own distinct responsibilities for serving the global economy.

Word Study

deprive /dɪ'praɪv/ v.
剥夺,使失去
outstrip /aut'strɪp/ v.
超过,胜过

Currency Exchange Rates

FIXED EXCHANGE RATE

A fixed exchange rate is a regime applied by a government or central bank that ties the country's currency official exchange rate to another country's currency or the price of gold. The purpose of a fixed exchange rate system is to keep a currency's value within a narrow band.

Proponents in favor of fixed exchange rates show that it ensures stability in the exchange rate that stimulates foreign trade, contributes to the coordination of macro policies of countries, and is more conducive to the expansion of world trade because it prevents risk and uncertainty in transactions involving speculation in foreign exchange markets. Some drawbacks of fixed exchange rates include the fear of devaluation, where a central bank may use its reserves to maintain the foreign exchange rate, and when reserves are exhausted that compels the government to devalue its domestic currency. Additionally, the benefits of free markets are **deprived** since everything is fixed and there is the possibility of undervaluation or overvaluation.

FLOATING EXCHANGE RATE

A floating exchange rate is a regime where the currency price of a nation is set by the forex market based on supply and demand relative to other currencies. This is in contrast to a fixed exchange rate, in which the government entirely or predominantly determines the rate.

Floating exchange rate systems mean long-term currency price changes that reflect relative economic strength and interest rate differentials between countries. Short-term moves in a floating exchange rate currency reflect speculation, rumors, disasters, and everyday supply and demand for the currency. If supply **outstrips** demand that currency will fall, and if demand outstrips supply that currency will rise. Extreme short-term moves can result in intervention by central banks, even in a floating rate environment. Because of this, while most major global currencies are considered floating, central banks and governments may step in if a nation's currency becomes too high or too low. A currency that is too high or too low could affect the nation's economy negatively,

货币汇率
固定汇率

固定汇率是政府或中央银行采用的一种将一国货币的官方汇率与另一国的货币或金价挂钩的制度。固定汇率制度的目的是将货币的价值保持在一定的范围内。

固定汇率能确保汇率的稳定,从而刺激对外贸易,有助于协调各国的宏观政策。固定汇率可能会导致货币贬值,并且使得自由市场的利益被降低。

浮动汇率

浮动汇率是指一国的货币价格由外汇市场根据相对于其他货币的供求确定的一种制度。浮动汇率是由公开市场上的供求决定的汇率。

浮动汇率并不意味着各国不会干预和操纵其货币价格,因为政府和中央银行经常试图保持其货币价格对国际贸易有利。

affecting trade and the ability to pay debts. The government or central bank will attempt to implement measures to move their currency to a more favorable price.

FIXED VS. FLOATING CURRENCIES

Today, there are two types of currency exchange rates that are still in existence — floating and fixed. Major currencies, such as the Japanese yen, euro, and the U.S. dollar, are floating currencies — their values change according to how the currency trades on foreign exchange or forex (FX) markets. This type of exchange rate is based on supply and demand. This rate is, therefore, determined by market forces compared to other currencies. Any changes in currency pricing point to strength in the economy, while short-term changes may point to weakness.

Fixed currencies, on the other hand, derive value by being fixed to another currency. Most developing or emerging market economies use fixed exchange rates for their currencies. This provides exporting and importing countries more stability, and also keeps interest rates low.

Key Terms
专业术语

gold standard 金本位制
bimetallic standard 复本位制
reserve currency 储备货币
World Economic Outlook《世界经济展望》
special drawing rights (SDR) 特别提款权
IBRD (International Bank for Reconstruction and Development)
国际复兴开发银行
IDA (International Development Association) 国际开发协会
IFC (International Finance Corporation) 国际金融公司
MIGA (Multilateral Investment Guarantee Agency) 多边投资担保机构
ICSID (International Centre for Settlement of Investment Disputes)
国际投资争端解决中心

fiat money 法定货币
fiscal policy 财政政策

Information
Link
知识链接

牙买加体系

继布雷顿森林体系以后,出现了以美元为中心的国际储备资产多元化和实行浮动汇率制的国际货币制度。根据1976年1月国际货币基金董事会达成的《牙买加协议》,增加成员国特别提款权份额,增幅达33.6%,并扩大其使用范围;建立信托基金,扩大对发展中国家的资金融通;废除黄金官价,降低黄金的作用;确认了浮动汇率制的合法化。同年4月通过《国际货币基金协定第二次修正案》,并于1978年4月1日正式生效,牙买加体系逐步形成。在该体系下，美元仍是国际货币，但日元和德国马克的地位在上升，一篮子货币计价的特别提款权、欧元等越来越引起人们关注，国际货币呈多极化趋势；出现以浮动汇率为主、固定汇率并存的混合体系，亦称"无体制的体制"，各国可自由安排汇率；通过汇率机制、利率机制、基金组织干预、国际金融市场、商业银行等联合进行国际收支调节。牙买加体系一定程度上解决了"特里芬难题"，摆脱了国际金融对一国通货（美元）的过分依赖，汇率制度和调节机制的功能也比以前健全，更能适应多变的国际金融。但这种体系也比较复杂，稳定性差，机制发育也不够成熟，仍有待于进一步改革。

文献来源：

戴相龙，黄达主编，《中华金融辞库》北京：中国金融出版社，1998年。

Workbook
练一练

A. Name the five organizations of the World Bank Group.

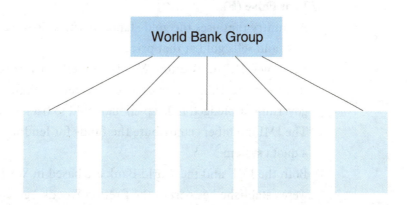

B. According to the text, fill in each of the following blanks with an appropriate word or phrase.

1) The gold standard is a monetary system where a country's currency or paper money has a value directly linked to _____.

2) The gold standard can provide _____ international rates between countries that participate and can also reduce the uncertainty in international trade.

3) Around _____, gold was made into coins for the first time, enhancing its usability as a monetary unit.

4) The Bretton Woods Agreement was negotiated in July _____ to establish a new international monetary system, the Bretton Woods System. The Agreement was developed by delegates from _____ countries at the United Nations Monetary and Financial Conference held in Bretton Woods, New Hampshire.

5) The Bretton Woods Agreement also created two important organizations — the _____ and the _____.

6) The International Monetary Fund is based in _____, and currently consists of 189 member countries.

7) The IMF makes loans to countries that are experiencing economic distress in order to prevent or mitigate _____.

8) The World Bank is an international organization dedicated to providing _____, _____, and _____ to developing nations to aid their economic advancement.

9) A floating exchange rate is a regime where the currency price of a nation is set by the _____ market based on supply and demand relative to other currencies.

10) Major currencies, such as the Japanese yen, the euro, and the U.S. dollar, are _____ currencies — their values change according to how the currency trades on foreign exchange or forex markets.

C. Read the text and decide whether the following statements are True (T) or False (F).

1) A country that uses the gold standard sets a floating price for gold and buys and sells gold at that price. ( )

2) After WWII, the Bretton Woods Agreement forced allied countries to accept the U.S. dollar as a reserve rather than gold, and the U.S. government pledged to keep enough gold to back its dollars. ( )

3) The IMF members contribute the funds for lending to a pool based on a quota system. ( )

4) Both the IMF and the World Bank are based in Washington, D.C., and were established as part of the Bretton Woods Agreement. ( )

5) The World Bank is indeed a bank in the traditional, chartered meanings of the word. ( )

6) In 1971, concerned that the U.S. gold supply was no longer adequate to cover the number of dollars in circulation, President John F. Kennedy declared a temporary suspension of the dollar's convertibility into gold. ( )

7) A fixed exchange rate is a regime applied by a government or central bank that ties the country's currency official exchange rate to another country's currency or the price of gold. ( )

8) According to the floating exchange rate, if supply outstrips demand that currency will rise, and if demand outstrips supply that currency will fall. ( )

9) Most developing or emerging market economies use fixed exchange rates for their currencies. This provides exporting and importing countries more stability, and also keeps interest rates low. ( )

10) The rate of floating currencies is determined by market forces compared to other currencies. ( )

1) Why do most commodity-money advocates choose gold as a medium of exchange?

_____

_____

2) What are the aims of the IMF?

_____

_____

3) What are the main activities of the IMF?

_____

_____

4) What are the two stated goals of the World Bank that it aims to achieve by 2030?

_____

_____

5) Please summarize the advantages and disadvantages of a fixed exchange rate.

_____

_____

Case Story

Strong Dollar: Advantages and Disadvantages

A strong U.S. dollar has several advantages and disadvantages to Americans holding dollars. It benefits some but negatively impacts others. The dollar is considered strong when it rises in value against other currencies in the foreign exchange market. A strengthening U.S. dollar means it can buy more of a foreign currency than before. For example, a strong dollar benefits Americans traveling overseas but puts foreign tourists visiting the U.S. at a disadvantage.

Advantages of a Strong Dollar

Traveling Abroad Is Cheaper

Americans holding U.S. dollars can see those dollars go further abroad, affording them a greater degree of buying power overseas. Because local prices in foreign countries are not influenced greatly by changes in the U.S. economy, a strong dollar can buy more goods when converted to the local currency. Expatriates, or U.S. citizens living and working overseas, will also see their cost of living decrease if they still own dollars or receive dollars as income.

Imports Are Cheaper

Goods produced abroad and imported to the United States will be cheaper if the manufacturer's currency falls in value compared to the dollar. Luxury cars from Europe, such as Audi, Mercedes, BMW, Porsche, and Ferrari, would all fall in dollar price. If a European luxury car costs €70,000 with an exchange rate of 1.35 dollars per euro, it will cost $94,500. The same car selling for the same amount of euros would now cost $78,400 if the exchange rate falls to 1.12 dollars per euro. Other lower-cost imports will also fall in price, leaving more disposable income in the pockets of American consumers. U.S. companies that import raw materials from abroad will have a lower total cost of production and enjoy larger profit margins as a result.

Multinationals That Do Business in the U.S. Benefit

Foreign companies that do a lot of business in the U.S. and their investors will benefit. Multinational corporations that have a large number of sales in the U.S., and therefore earn income in dollars, will see gains in the dollar translate to gains on their balance sheets. Investors in these companies should be rewarded, as well.

Status as World Reserve Currency Is Bolstered

The status of the dollar as a world reserve currency is bolstered with a strong dollar. While some countries, including Russia, Iran, and China, have questioned the status of the U.S. dollar as the de facto world reserve currency, a strong dollar helps keep its demand as a reserve high.

Disadvantages of a Strong Dollar

Tourism to the U.S. Is More Expensive

Visitors from abroad will find the prices of goods and services in America more expensive with a stronger dollar. Business travelers and foreigners living in the U.S. but holding on to foreign-denominated bank accounts, or who are paid incomes in their home currency, will be hurt and their cost of living increased.

Exporters Suffer

Just as imports become cheaper at home, domestically produced goods become relatively more expensive abroad. An American-made car that costs $30,000 would cost €22,222 in Europe, with an exchange rate of 1.35 dollars per euro; however, it increases to €26,786 when the dollar strengthens to 1.12 per euro. Some have argued that expensive exports can cost American jobs.

U.S. Companies Conducting Business Abroad Are Hurt

Companies based in the United States that conduct a large portion of their business around the globe will suffer as the income they earn from foreign sales will decrease in value on their balance sheets. Investors in such companies are also likely to see a negative impact. McDonalds Corp. (MCD) and Philip Morris International Inc. (PM) are well-known examples of U.S. companies with a large percentage of sales occurring overseas. While some of these companies use derivatives to hedge their currency exposures, not all do, and those that do hedge may only do so in part.

Emerging Market Economies Are Negatively Impacted

Foreign governments that require U.S. dollar reserves will end up paying relatively more to obtain those dollars. This is especially important in emerging market economies.

Special Considerations

Economic theory predicts that currency fluctuations will eventually revert to a mean since cheap foreign goods should increase the demand for them, raising their prices. At the same time, expensive domestic exports will have to fall in price as demand for those items declines worldwide until, ultimately, some equilibrium exchange level is found.

Case Discussion

1. What are the advantages of a strong dollar to Americans holding dollars?

_____

_____

2. What are the disadvantages of a strong dollar to Americans holding dollars?

_____

_____

3. How do you think a strong U.S. dollar will impact the emerging economies?

_____

_____

Case Summary

强势美元的利与弊

强势美元有利也有弊。

强势美元的优势包括以下几点：对于持有美元的人来说，出国旅行会更便宜，因为强势美元在转换为当地货币后，可以购买更多商品；进口更加便宜，对于从国外进口原材料的美国公司，生产成本将会更低，并因此享有更大的利润，在美国开展业务的跨国公司将从中受益；强势美元巩固了美元作为世界储备货币的地位。

美元的强势在许多方面使美国人受益，但同时也可能损害在国外开展业务的美国公司及其投资者的利益、出口商的利益，以及新兴经济市场的利益。

Reading I

The Rising RMB and the Stability of Global Financial System

Today, the Chinese currency renminbi (RMB), or the yuan, has become one of the most positively performing currencies in the world. RMB has gained a strong position in global foreign exchange reserves in which its share climbed to 2.79 percent in the last quarter of 2021, the IMF reported. At the same time, the Chinese currency soared more than 8 percent against major trading partners last year, a six-year-high record.

The rising value of the RMB in the global financial landscape is a result of the currency's internationalization and the support from China's robust economic growth.

China's gross domestic product grew 4.8 percent year on year to 27.02 trillion yuan (about $4.24 trillion) in the first quarter of 2022, picking up pace from a four-percent increase in the fourth quarter last year, data from the National Bureau of Statistics (NBS) showed on April 18.

The financial institutions in China are expecting a further rise in the value of RMB in the coming weeks and months due to regional and global economic and political situations. The consistent rise of the RMB also reflects strong fundamentals of the Chinese economy that can endure shocks and turbulences in the world market. Booming exports, growing trade surplus as well as capital inflow are a few of the additional supporting factors for a soaring RMB.

The ongoing tensions between the West and Russia have led to financial chaos. The major world currencies like the U.S. dollar and euro are under pressure amid stern sanctions against Russia. This is another factor transferring global attention towards the Chinese economy. This helps the RMB in growth get a stable position in the global market, shoring up confidence in the international currency market.

According to the data of the Currency Composition of Official Foreign Exchange Reserves (COFER) released by the IMF, the Chinese currency amassed $336.1 billion in the last quarter of 2021. By 2021, the RMB has become the world's fifth largest currency, following the U.S. dollar, euro, Japanese yen, and pounds sterling. The RMB's proportion in the global foreign exchange reserves witnessed an upward trajectory from the third quarter of the same year, recorded at 2.66 percent of the world total.

Along with the RMB reserves, China holds its 58.8 percent reserves in the U.S. dollars, but the country believes the attraction of dollars is declining by time. The international economists further believe that this trend is irreversible and that the growing influence of the RMB is deeply linked with the growing economy of China.

Over the past years, China has been applying multiple tools to promote its currency in the international market, such as currency swaps, investments through the Belt and Road Initiative (BRI), and global trade.

There is also an argument that the U.S. dollar-based international financial system led by the United States is crumbling, whereas many economies expect the RMB will become a stabilizing factor for the world economy in the future as the currency speeds up its internationalization.

This trend is further linked to the geopolitical situation. Some experts argue that the RMB's rise would have been rapid if the U.S.-led world order had not been pressed for protectionism and unilateralism. The Russia-Ukraine conflict will exert deep pressure on the stability of the euro and the U.S. dollar, but it is yet to be seen how these currencies will perform. Since China is easing the restrictions on capital flow, it is expected that the RMB will become the world's third largest reserve currency in the next decade.

The Chinese government has allowed international financial institutions to play their role in the Chinese economy and offer lucrative opportunities to foreign investors through relatively higher returns. The expected investment inflow worth $3 trillion would take precedence over foreign direct investment in the next decade to boost growth and currency valuation. With these investments, China will be able to hold more assets in the RMB, adding to global exchange reserves and ensuring the stability of the exchange pattern.

The Chinese realignment with its currency at the international level is reflective of its apprehensions of any global crisis, which may create more polarization in the world and negatively affect the currency exchange reserves.

The Western sanctions against Russia and Russia's demands for supporting the rouble in international trade would trim the use of the U.S. dollars and euros, but if the Ukraine crisis persists, it might have global implications. At this point, geopolitical conditions are generally favorable to China despite certain restrictions imposed by the United States on Chinese companies and products.

China is expanding its market in Africa, Europe, the Middle East,

South Asia, Southeast Asia, and Latin America, which gives China enough breathing space and capacity to push the RMB in the international market. It will be beneficial for China and the trading partners with fewer U.S. dollar reserves, including Pakistan. The stable RMB exchange reserves would be readily available to import goods from China or any other market in the world. All in all, the soaring RMB will strengthen the stability of the global financial system in the long run.

Second Thoughts

For each of the following statements, choose one answer to fill in the blank.

1) According to the IMF, RMB held a share of _____ in global foreign exchange reserves in the last quarter of 2021.
   A. 4.8 percent
   B. 58.8 percent
   C. 2.79 percent
   D. 4.24 percent
2) The following statements are true EXCEPT _____.
   A. The RMB will replace the U.S. dollar soon under the favorable geopolitical conditions.
   B. The RMB has become one of the most positively performing currencies in the world.
   C. The growing influence of the RMB is deeply linked with the growing economy of China.
   D. The rise of RMB will strengthen the stability of the global financial system in the long run.

Reading II

European Sovereign Debt Crisis

The European sovereign debt crisis was a period when several European countries experienced the collapse of financial institutions, high government debt, and rapidly rising bond yield spreads in government securities.

History of the Crisis

The debt crisis began in 2008 with the collapse of Iceland's banking system, then spread primarily to Portugal, Italy, Ireland, Greece, and Spain in 2009. It has led to a loss of confidence in European businesses and economies.

The crisis was eventually controlled by the financial guarantees of European countries, who feared the collapse of the euro and financial contagion, and by the International Monetary Fund (IMF). Rating agencies downgraded several Eurozone countries' debts.

Greece's debt was, at one point, moved to junk status. Countries receiving bailout funds were required to meet austerity measures designed to slow down the growth of public-sector debt as part of the loan agreements.

Contributing Causes of the Debt Crisis

Some of the contributing causes included the financial crisis of 2007 to 2008, the Great Recession of 2008 to 2012, the real estate market crisis, and property bubbles in several countries. The peripheral states' fiscal policies regarding government expenses and revenues also contributed.

By the end of 2009, the peripheral Eurozone member states of Greece, Spain, Ireland, Portugal, and Cyprus were unable to repay or refinance their government debt or bail out their beleaguered banks without the assistance of third-party financial institutions. These included the European Central Bank (ECB), the IMF, and, eventually, the European Financial Stability Facility (EFSF).

Also in 2009, Greece revealed that its previous government had grossly underreported its budget deficit, signifying a violation of EU policy and spurring fears of a euro collapse via political and financial contagion.

Seventeen Eurozone countries voted to create the EFSF in 2010, specifically to address and assist with the crisis. The European sovereign debt crisis peaked between 2010 and 2012.

With increasing fear of excessive sovereign debt, lenders demanded higher interest rates from Eurozone states in 2010, with high debt and deficit levels making it harder for these countries to finance their budget deficits when they were faced with overall low economic growth. Some affected countries raised taxes and slashed expenditures to combat the crisis, which contributed to social upset within their borders and a crisis of confidence in leadership, particularly in Greece. Several of these countries, including Greece, Portugal, and Ireland had their sovereign debt downgraded to junk status by international credit rating agencies during this crisis, worsening investor fears.

A 2012 report for the United States Congress stated, "The Eurozone debt crisis began in late 2009 when a new Greek government revealed that previous governments had been misreporting government budget data. Higher than expected deficit levels eroded investor confidence causing bond spreads to rise to unsustainable levels. Fears quickly spread that the fiscal positions and debt levels of a number of Eurozone countries were unsustainable."

Greek Example of European Crisis

In early 2010, the developments were reflected in rising spreads on sovereign bond yields between the affected peripheral member states of

Greece, Ireland, Portugal, Spain and, most notably, Germany.

The Greek yield diverged with Greece needing Eurozone assistance by May 2010. Greece received several bailouts from the EU and the IMF over the following years in exchange for the adoption of EU-mandated austerity measures to cut public spending and a significant increase in taxes. The country's economic recession continued. These measures, along with the economic situation, caused social unrest. With divided political and fiscal leadership, Greece faced sovereign default in June 2015.

The Greek citizens voted against a bailout and further EU austerity measures the following month. This decision raised the possibility that Greece might leave the European Monetary Union (EMU) entirely.

The withdrawal of a nation from the EMU would have been unprecedented, and if Greece had returned to using the Drachma, the speculated effects on its economy ranged from total economic collapse to a surprise recovery.

In the end, Greece remained part of the EMU and began to slowly show signs of recovery in subsequent years. Unemployment dropped from its high of over 27% to 16% in five years, while annual GDP when from negative numbers to a projected rate of over two percent in that same time.

Second Thoughts

1) What was Europe's sovereign debt crisis?

_____

_____

2) Please summarize the causes that contributed to the debt crisis.

_____

_____

Global Capital Market

全球资本市场

本章概要

本章主要介绍全球资本市场,包括资本市场的含义、一级市场和二级市场、股票市场、债券市场和欧洲货币市场。

学习指南

在经济学意义上,资本指的是用于生产的基本生产要素,即资金、厂房、设备、材料等物质资源。在金融学和会计领域,资本通常用来代表金融财富,特别是用于经商、兴办企业的金融资产。广义上,资本也可作为人类创造物质和精神财富的各种社会经济资源的总称。资本市场是市场形态之一,是金融市场的重要组成部分,市场由卖方和买方构成。

通过本章学习,希望大家能够实现以下目标:

(1)基本目标(Text-based Goals)

● 掌握本章涉及话题的基本专业术语及词汇,如欧元区、纳斯达克、首次公开募股、纽约证券交易所、欧洲货币等。

● 掌握本章的主要知识点,即资本市场的含义、股票市场及证券交易所、债券市场的含义及其种类和优缺点,以及欧洲货币市场的基本含义及其种类。

(2)拓展目标(Extended Goals)

● 思考本章引言,为什么巴菲特会说"当别人害怕时,你要贪婪;当别人贪婪时,你要害怕。"?

● 通过学习背景知识、拓展阅读、案例分析,进一步了解公司为何要发行债券,了解纽约证券交易所以及长期债券和短期债券之间的利率风险等。

Capital Markets

资本市场

资本市场是指资本提供者和资本需求方之间调拨储蓄和投资的场所。

资本市场包括一级市场和二级市场。一级市场将新股票和债券发行给投资者；二级市场对已经发行的证券进行交易，比如纽约证券交易所和纳斯达克市场就属于二级市场。

最常见的资本市场是股票市场和债券市场。一级市场的价格通常是事先确定的，而二级市场的价格则取决于供需能力。

Capital markets are venues where savings and investments are channeled between the suppliers who have capital and those who are in need of capital. The entities that have capital include retail and institutional investors while those who seek capital are businesses, governments, and people.

Capital markets are composed of primary and secondary markets. The most common capital markets are the stock market and the bond market.

Capital markets seek to improve **transactional** efficiencies. These markets bring those who hold capital and those seeking capital together and provide a place where entities can exchange securities.

UNDERSTANDING CAPITAL MARKETS

The term capital market broadly defines the place where various entities trade different financial instruments. These venues may include the stock market, the bond market, and the currency and foreign exchange markets. Most markets are concentrated in major financial centers including New York, London, Singapore, and Hong Kong.

Capital markets are composed of the suppliers and users of funds. Suppliers include households and the institutions serving them — pension funds, life **insurance** companies, charitable foundations, and non-financial companies — that generate cash beyond their needs for investment. Users of funds include home and motor vehicle purchasers, non-financial companies, and governments financing infrastructure investment and operating expenses.

Capital markets are used to sell financial products such as equities and debt securities. Equities are stocks, which are ownership shares in a company. Debt securities, such as bonds, are interest-bearing **IOUs**.

These markets are divided into two different categories: primary markets — where new equity stock and bond issues are sold to investors — and secondary markets, which trade existing securities. Capital markets are a crucial part of a functioning modern economy because they move money from the people who have it to those who need it for productive use.

Word Study

transational /træn'zækʃənəl/ adj. 交易的
insurance /ɪn'ʃʊərəns/ n. 保险
IOU /ˌaɪəʊ'juː/ n. 借据，欠条（表示 I owe you）

Capital markets are composed of primary and secondary markets. The majority of modern primary and secondary markets are computer-based electronic platforms.

Primary markets are open to specific investors who buy securities directly from the issuing company. These securities are considered primary offerings or initial public offerings (IPO). When a company goes public, it sells its stocks and bonds to large-scale and institutional investors such as hedge funds and mutual funds.

The secondary market, on the other hand, includes venues overseen by a regulatory body like the Securities and Exchange Commission (SEC) where existing or already-issued securities are traded between investors. Issuing companies do not have a part in the secondary market. The New York Stock Exchange (NYSE) and NASDAQ are examples of the secondary market.

Primary market prices are often set beforehand, while prices in the secondary market are determined by the basic forces of supply and demand. If the majority of investors believe a stock will increase in value and rush to buy it, the stock's price will typically rise. If a company loses favor with investors or fails to post sufficient earnings, its stock price declines as demand for that security **dwindles**.

Major Components of the Global Capital Markets

Stock Market

WHAT IS THE STOCK MARKET?

A stock market is also called the equity market. It is a market in which shares are issued and traded, either through **exchanges** or over-the-counter markets. It is one of the most vital areas of a market economy because it gives companies access to capital and investors a slice of ownership in a company with the potential to realize gains based on its future performance.

TRADING IN THE STOCK MARKET

In the stock market, investors bid for stocks by offering a certain price, and sellers ask for a specific price. When these two prices match, a sale occurs. Often, there are many investors bidding on the same stock. When this occurs, the first investor to place the bid is the first to get the stock. When a buyer will pay any price for the stock, he or she is buying at market value; similarly, when a seller will take any price for the stock, he or she is selling at market value.

Companies sell stocks in order to get capital to grow their businesses. When a company offers stocks on the market, it means the company is

资本市场的主要组成要素
股票市场
　　股票市场是已经发行的股票转让、买卖和流通的场所，包括交易所市场和场外交易市场两大类别。股份公司通过面向社会发行股票进行集资，实现生产的规模经营。

Word Study

dwindle /'dwɪndl/ *v.*
（逐渐）减少，变小
exchange /ɪks'tʃeɪndʒ/
n. 交易所

publicly traded, and each stock represents a piece of ownership. This appeals to investors, and when a company does well, its investors are rewarded as the value of their stocks rise. The risk comes when a company is not doing well, and its stock value may fall. Stocks can be bought and sold easily and quickly, and the activity surrounding a certain stock impacts its value. For example, when there is a high demand to invest in the company, the price of the stock tends to rise, and when many investors want to sell their stocks, the value goes down.

STOCK EXCHANGES

证券交易所
证券交易场所是供已发行的证券进行流通转让的地方，比如纽约证券交易所。

The place where stocks in the equity market are traded is the stock exchange. There are many stock exchanges around the world, and they can be either physical places or virtual gathering spots. NASDAQ is an example of a virtual trading post, in which stocks are traded electronically through a network of computers. Electronic stock exchanges often include a market maker, which is a broker-dealer company that both buys and sells stocks in order to facilitate trading for a particular stock. This comes at a risk to the company, but it makes the exchange process for a given stock operate smoothly. Electronic trading posts are becoming more common and a preferred method of trading over physical exchanges.

The New York Stock Exchange (NYSE) on Wall Street is a famous example of a physical stock exchange; however, there is also the option to trade in online exchanges from that location, so it is technically a **hybrid** market. In a physical exchange, orders are made in open outcry format, which is **reminiscent** of depictions of Wall Street in the movies: traders shout and display hand signals across the floor in order to place trades. Physical exchanges are made on the trading floor through a floor broker, who finds the trading post specialist for that stock to put through the order. Physical exchanges are still very much human environments, although there are a lot of functions performed by computers. Brokers are paid **commissions** on the stocks they work.

Word Study

hybrid /ˈhaɪbrɪd/ *adj.*
混合的
reminiscent
/ˌremɪˈnɪsənt/ *adj.*
使回忆起（人或事）的，怀旧的
commission
/kəˈmɪʃən/ *n.* 佣金，手续费

The first stock market in the world was the London Stock Exchange. It was started in a coffeehouse, where traders used to meet to exchange shares, in 1773. The first stock exchange in the United States of America was started in Philadelphia in 1790. The Buttonwood Agreement, so named because it was signed under a buttonwood tree, marked the beginnings of New York's Wall Street in 1792. The agreement was signed by 24 traders and was the first American organization of its kind to trade in securities. The traders renamed their venture as New York Stock and Exchange Board in 1817.

SIGNIFICANCE OF THE STOCK MARKET

The equity market is one of the most vital components of a free-market economy. It allows companies to raise money by offering stock shares and corporate bonds. It lets common investors participate in the financial achievements of the companies, make profits through capital gains, and earn money through **dividends**, although losses are also possible. While institutional investors and professional money managers do enjoy some privileges owing to their deep pockets, better knowledge and higher risk taking abilities, the stock market attempts to offer a level playing field to common individuals.

The stock market works as a platform through which savings and investments of individuals are channelized into the productive investment proposals. In the long term, it helps in capital formation and economic growth for the country.

Bond Market

WHAT IS THE BOND MARKET?

The bond market — often called the debt market, fixed-income market, or credit market — is the collective name given to all trades and issues of debt securities. Governments typically issue bonds in order to raise capital to pay down debts or fund infrastructural improvements. Publicly-traded companies issue bonds when they need to finance business expansion projects or maintain ongoing operations.

UNDERSTANDING BOND MARKETS

The bond market is broadly segmented into two different **silos**: the primary market and the secondary market. The primary market is frequently referred to as the "new issues" market in which transactions strictly occur directly between the bond issuers and the bond buyers. In essence, the primary market yields the creation of brand-new debt securities that have not previously been offered to the public.

In the secondary market, securities that have already been sold in the primary market are then bought and sold at later dates. Investors can purchase these bonds from a broker, who acts as an **intermediary** between the buying and selling parties. These secondary market issues may be packaged in the form of pension funds, mutual funds, and life insurance policies — among many other product structures.

TYPES OF BOND MARKETS

The general bond market can be segmented into the following bond classifications, each with its own set of **attributes**.

Corporate Bonds

Companies issue corporate bonds to raise money for a **sundry** of reasons, such as financing current operations, expanding product lines, or

Word Study

dividend /ˈdɪvɪdend/
    n. 股息,分红
silo /ˈsaɪləʊ/ *n.* 独立
    运行的系统
intermediary
    /ˌɪntəˈmiːdɪəri/ *n.*
    中介,媒介
attribute /ˈætrɪˌbjut/ *n.*
    属性,特征
sundry /ˈsʌndri/ *n.* 杂
    项,各种各样

债券市场
　　债券市场是发行和买卖债券的场所。投资者在债券市场购买由政府或者上市公司发行的债券。各国政府通常将债券收益用于改善基础设施和偿还债务,公司通过发行债券筹集资金,维持运营。债券可以在发行新债的一级市场上发行,也可以在二级市场上发行。在二级市场,投资者可以通过经纪人或其他第三方购买现有债券。

债券市场的种类
　　债券种类包括公司债券、政府债券、市政债券、抵押支付债券和新兴市场债券。

entice /ɪn'taɪs/ v. 吸引

conservative
/kən'sɜ:vətɪv/ adj.
传统的，老派的

municipal /mjuː'nɪsɪpəl/
adj. 市政的

mortgage /'mɔːgɪdʒ/
n. 抵押贷款

collateralize
/kə'lætərəlaɪz/ v.
以…做抵押

eurocurrency
/'jʊərəʊˌkʌrənsi/ n.
欧洲货币

deposit /dɪ'pɒzɪt/ v.&n.
存储，存款

circumvent
/ˌsɜ:kəm'vent/ v.
规避

eurodollar /jʊərəʊ'dɒlə/
n. 欧洲美元

opening up new manufacturing facilities. Corporate bonds usually describe longer-term debt instruments that provide a maturity of at least one year.

Government Bonds

National-issued government bonds (or Treasuries) **entice** buyers by paying out the face value listed on the bond certificate, on the agreed maturity date, while also issuing periodic interest payments along the way. This characteristic makes government bonds attractive to **conservative** investors.

Municipal Bonds

Municipal bonds — commonly abbreviated as "muni" bonds — are locally issued by states, cities, special-purpose districts, public utility districts, school districts, publicly-owned airports and seaports, and other government-owned entities who seek to raise cash to fund various projects.

Mortgage-Backed Bonds

These issues, which consist of pooled mortgages on real estate properties, are locked in by the pledge of particular **collateralized** assets. They pay monthly, quarterly, or semi-annual interest.

Emerging Market Bonds

Issued by governments and companies located in emerging market economies, these bonds provide much greater growth opportunities, but also greater risks, than domestic or developed bond markets.

Eurocurrency Market

欧洲货币市场

欧洲货币，也称"境外货币"，是在货币发行国境外被存储和借贷的各种货币的总称。欧洲货币市场是法定货币国家境外的货币市场。欧洲货币市场并不局限于欧洲境内的金融中心，而是超出了欧洲的范围。"欧洲"一词失去了地理上的意义，实际等同于"境外"或"离岸"的意思。欧洲货币市场包括欧洲美元、欧洲日元和欧洲债券。

WHAT IS THE EUROCURRENCY MARKET?

Eurocurrency is currency **deposited** by national governments or corporations, outside of its home market. Commonly it is currency held in banks located outside of the country which issues the currency. The eurocurrency market is the money market for currency outside of the country where it is the legal tender. The eurocurrency market is utilized by banks, multinational corporations, mutual funds, and hedge funds. They wish to **circumvent** regulatory requirements, tax laws, and interest rate caps often present in domestic banking, particularly in the United States.

The term eurocurrency is a generalization of **eurodollar** and should not be confused with the EU currency, the euro. The eurocurrency market functions in many financial centers around the world, not just Europe.

UNDERSTANDING THE EUROCURRENCY MARKET

The eurocurrency market originated in the aftermath of World War II when the Marshall Plan to rebuild Europe sent a flood of dollars overseas. The market developed first in London, as banks needed a market for dollar deposits outside the United States. Dollars held outside the United States are called eurodollars, even if they are held in markets outside Europe, such as Singapore or the Cayman Islands.

The eurocurrency market has expanded to include other currencies, such as the Japanese yen and the British pound, whenever they trade outside of their home markets. However, the eurodollar market remains the largest.

Interest rates paid on deposits in the eurocurrency market are typically higher than in the domestic market. That is because the depositor is not protected by the same national banking laws and does not have governmental deposit insurance. Rates on eurocurrency loans are typically lower than those in the domestic market for essentially the same reasons. Eurocurrency bank accounts are also not subject to the same reserve requirements as domestic accounts.

TYPES OF EUROCURRENCY MARKETS

Eurodollar

Eurodollars were the first eurocurrency, and they still have the most influence. It is worth noting that U.S. banks can have overseas operations dealing in eurodollars. These subsidiaries are often registered in the Caribbean. However, the majority of actual trading takes place in the United States.

The eurodollar trades mostly overnight, although deposits and loans out to 12 months are possible. A 2016 study by the Federal Reserve Bank indicated that the average daily **turnover** in the eurodollar market was $140 billion. Transactions are usually for a minimum of $25 million and can top $1 billion in a single deposit.

Word Study

turnover /ˈtɜːn.əʊvə/ *n.*
成交量

Euroyen

The offshore euroyen market was established in the 1980s and expanded with Japan's economic influence. As interest rates declined in Japan during the 1990s, the higher rates paid by euroyen accounts became more attractive.

Eurobond

There is an active bond market for countries, companies, and financial institutions to borrow in currencies outside of their domestic markets. The first such eurobond was issued by the Italian company Autostrade in 1963. It borrowed $15 million for 15 years in a deal arranged in London and listed on the Luxembourg Stock Exchange. Issuing eurobonds remained popular in Italy, and the Italian government sold seven billion U.S. dollars in eurobonds in October 2019. It is essential to avoid confusing eurobonds with euro bonds, which are simply bonds denominated in euros issued by countries or firms in the eurozone.

PROS & CONS OF EUROCURRENCY MARKETS

The main benefit of eurocurrency markets is that they are more competitive. They can simultaneously offer lower interest rates for borrowers and higher interest rates for lenders. That is mostly because eurocurrency markets are less regulated. On the downside, eurocurrency markets face higher risks, particularly during a **run** on the banks.

Key Terms
专业术语

primary market 一级市场   secondary market 二级市场
financial instruments 金融工具   initial public offerings (IPO) 首次公开募股
mutual funds 互惠基金   interest rate caps 利率上限
Marshall Plan 马歇尔计划   deposit insurance 存款保险（制度）
NASDAQ 纳斯达克；美国全国证券交易商协会自动报价系统
New York Stock Exchange (NYSE) 纽约证券交易所

Information Link
知识链接

国际绿色债券市场发展现状和趋势

绿色债券（green bonds），泛指融资资金投资于气候或环境保护项目和计划的债券产品（ICMA, 2014），直接或间接为绿色项目融资是绿色债券区别于传统债券的最突出特征。狭义的绿色债券仅指那些经由独立的中介机构（second party）对投资项目或所涉及资产的绿色特性进行评估，并通过第三方如气候债券标准委员会（Climate Bond Standard Board）获得绿色债券资质认证的债券。这类债券具有更高的市场透明度和认知度，目前市场规模约为659亿美元。

绿色债券市场规模快速增长，为各国的可持续发展项目提供了中长期低成本的资金支持。2007年以来，绿色债券的数量从无到有，经历了爆发式增长。2007年发行规模不到10亿美元，2013年发行量超过100亿美元，2014年全年发行366亿美元，增长了30多倍，全球累计未清偿面额达562亿美元，截至2015年6月全球未清偿规模达到659亿美元。广义的绿色债券规模更为庞大，截至2014年年底，400多家发行人发行了接近2800只债券，未清偿规模约5977亿美元。与此同时，绿色债券的认证率不断提升，2014年约32%的新发行债券获得了绿色认证。当然，在全球债券市场每年数以万亿美元的庞大发行量面前，绿色债券市场占比仍不足5%，存量更是微不足道，意味着债券市场具有巨大的"绿化"潜力。

绿色债券市场的参与者日益多元化，市场专业化程度增强。绿色债券发行人包括多边开发银行、地方政府和市政机构、公司企业以及金融机构（商业银行）。绿色债券具有期限长、信用高的特点，普遍受到资本市场青睐。从债券的期限看，绿色债券主要是中长期债券，3年期以上的债券约6000亿美元，其中超过六成是10年期以上债券。3年期以内的债券不到200亿美元，债券普遍期限较长，为融资者提供了中长期稳定的资金来源。

展望未来国际绿色债券市场的发展，随着各国绿色可持续发展政策的逐步推进和绿色金融体系的建立,绿色债券发行主体和债券品种多样化的态势将持续,在传统的国际开发机构之外,越来越多的银行、企业和市政部门将加入发行者行列,而广大的发展中国家也将越来越积极地利用绿色债券市场推动自身的可持续发展进程,一些同绿色指数挂钩的衍生债券也将不断出现,广义绿色债券市场的外延和规模将不断扩张。另一方面,全球范围内绿色债券的标准化和评估体系正在建立和完善,相关的评估、监测、发行等流程日益标准化,高标准、透明的绿色标准债券的市场吸引力将日益提高,有助于建立规范的市场秩序。

文献来源:

万志宏,曾刚.国际绿色债券市场:现状、经验与启示[J].金融论坛,2015(09),02.

A. Name the types of bond markets.

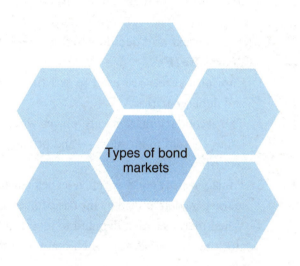

B. According to the text, fill in each of the following blanks with an appropriate word or phrase.

1) Capital markets are venues where _____ and _____ _____ are channeled between the suppliers who have capital and those who are in need of capital.

2) Capital markets seek to improve transactional efficiencies. These markets bring those who _____ and those seeking capital together and provide a place where entities can exchange securities.

3) The secondary market includes venues overseen by a regulatory body like the Securities and Exchange Commission (SEC) where _____ _____ securities are traded between investors.

4) A stock market is also called the equity market. It is a market in which shares are issued and traded, either through exchanges or _____ markets.

5) The first stock market in the world was the _____ Stock Exchange.

6) The bond market — often called the debt market, fixed-income market, or credit market — is the collective name given to all trades and issues of _____ .

7) Companies issue corporate bonds to _____ for a sundry of reasons, such as financing current operations, expanding product lines, or opening up new manufacturing facilities.

8) Eurocurrency is currency deposited by national governments or corporations, _____ of its home market.

9) The term eurocurrency is a generalization of _____ and should not be confused with the EU currency, the euro.

10) The eurocurrency market has expanded to include other currencies, such as the _____ and the British pound, whenever they trade outside of their home markets.

C. Read the text and decide whether the following statements are True (T) or False (F).

1) Capital markets are used to sell financial products such as equities and debt securities. ( )

2) The secondary markets are places where new equity stock and bond issues are sold to investors — and primary markets, which trade existing securities. ( )

3) Primary market prices are often set beforehand, while prices in the secondary market are determined by the basic forces of supply and demand. ( )

4) When there is a high demand to invest in the company, the price of the stock tends to rise, and when many investors want to sell their stocks, the value goes down. ( )

5) There are many stock exchanges around the world, and they can be either physical places or virtual gathering spots. NASDAQ is an example of a physical place. ( )

6) Electronic trading posts are becoming more common and a preferred method of trading over physical exchanges. ( )

7) Issued by governments and companies located in emerging market economies, emerging market bonds provide much greater growth opportunities, but less risks, than domestic or developed bond markets. ( )

8) The eurocurrency market is the money market for currency outside of the country where it is the legal tender. ( )

9) The eurocurrency market functions just in Europe. ( )

10) The main benefit of eurocurrency markets is that they are more competitive. They can simultaneously offer lower interest rates for borrowers and higher interest rates for lenders. ( )

1) According to the text, what are initial public offerings (IPOs)?

_____

_____

2) For companies, what's the purpose of selling stocks?

_____

_____

3) Please summarize the significance of the stock market.

_____

_____

4) What are the purposes of issuing bonds for governments and publicly-traded companies?

_____

_____

5) What is eurocurrency?

_____

_____

Case Story

Why Companies Issue Bonds

Issuing bonds is one way for companies to raise money. A bond functions as a loan between an investor and a corporation. The investor agrees to give the corporation a certain amount of money for a specific period of time. In exchange, the investor receives periodic interest payments. When the bond reaches its maturity date, the company repays the investor.

The decision to issue bonds instead of selecting other methods of raising money can be driven by many factors. Comparing the features and benefits of bonds versus other common methods of raising cash provides some insight. It helps to explain why companies often issue bonds when they need to finance corporate activities.

Bonds vs. Banks

Borrowing from a bank is perhaps the approach that comes to mind first for many people who need money. That leads to the question, "Why would a corporation issue bonds instead of just borrowing from a bank?"

Like people, companies can borrow from banks, but issuing bonds is often a more attractive proposition. The interest rate that companies pay bond investors is usually less than the interest rate available from banks. Companies are in business to generate corporate profits, so minimizing the interest is an important consideration. That is one of the reasons why healthy companies that don't seem to need the money often issue bonds. The ability to borrow large sums at low interest rates gives corporations the ability to invest in growth and other projects.

Issuing bonds also gives companies significantly greater freedom to operate as they see fit. Bonds release firms from the restrictions that are often attached to bank loans. For example, banks often make companies agree not to issue more debt or make corporate acquisitions until their loans are repaid in full.

Such restrictions can hamper a company's ability to do business and limit its operational options. Issuing bonds enables companies to raise money with no such strings attached.

Bonds vs. Stocks

Issuing shares of stock grants proportional ownership in the firm to investors in exchange for money. That is another popular way for corporations to raise money. From a corporate perspective, perhaps the most attractive feature of stock issuance is that the money does not need to be repaid. There are, however, downsides to issuing new shares that may make bonds the more attractive proposition.

Companies that need to raise money can continue to issue new bonds as long as they can find willing investors. The issuance of new bonds does not affect ownership of the company or how the company operates. Stock issuance, on the other hand, puts additional stock shares in circulation. That means future earnings must be shared among a larger pool of investors. More shares can cause a decrease in earnings per share (EPS), putting less money in owners' pockets. EPS is also one of the metrics that investors look at when evaluating a firm's health. A declining EPS number is generally viewed as an unfavorable development.

Issuing more shares also means that ownership is now spread across a larger number of investors. That often reduces the value of each owner's shares. Since investors buy stocks to make money, diluting the value of their investments is highly undesirable. By issuing bonds, companies can avoid this outcome.

Why Companies Issue Callable Bonds

Companies issue callable bonds to allow them to take advantage of a possible drop in interest rates in the future. The issuing company can redeem callable bonds before the maturity date according to a schedule in the bond's terms. If interest rates decrease, the company can redeem the outstanding bonds and reissue the debt at a lower rate. That reduces the cost of capital.

Calling a bond is similar to a mortgage borrower refinancing at a lower rate. The prior mortgage with the higher interest rate is paid off, and the borrower obtains a new mortgage at the lower rate.

The bond terms often define the amount that must be paid to call the bond. The defined amount may be greater than the par value. The price of bonds has an inverse relationship with interest rates. Bond prices go up as interest rates fall. Thus, it can be advantageous for a company to pay off debt by recalling the bond at above par value.

Case Discussion

1) Why would a corporation issue bonds instead of just borrowing from a bank?

_____

_____

2) Why do companies issue callable bonds?

_____

_____

3) If companies want to raise capital, what can they do?

_____

_____

Case Summary

公司为何发行债券

发行债券是公司筹集资金的一种方式。债券融资通常比股权融资便宜，并且不需要放弃对公司的任何控制权。公司可以以贷款形式从银行获得债务融资，也可以向投资者发行债券。债券比银行贷款具有更多的优势，并且可以以不同的方式、不同的期限进行结构化。相比从银行贷款，公司发行债券并支付给债券投资者的利率通常低于银行贷款利率，债券使公司摆脱了通常与银行贷款有关的限制，获得了更多的经营自由。而相比发行股票，新债券的发行不会影响公司的所有权或公司的运作方式。公司发行可赎回债券，以使他们能够利用未来可能降低的利率。如果利率降低，公司可以赎回未偿还的债券并以较低的利率重新发行债券，从而降低成本。

Reading I

New York Stock Exchange

What Is the New York Stock Exchange?

The New York Stock Exchange (NYSE) is a stock exchange located in New York City that is the largest equities-based exchange in the world, based on the total market capitalization of its listed securities. Formerly run as a private organization, the NYSE became a public entity in 2005 following the acquisition of electronic trading exchange Archipelago. In 2007 a merger with Euronext, the largest stock exchange in Europe, led to the creation of NYSE Euronext, which was later acquired by Intercontinental Exchange, the current parent of the New York Stock Exchange.

How the New York Stock Exchange Works

Located on Wall Street in New York City, the NYSE — also known as the "Big Board" — is made up of 21 rooms that are used to facilitate trading. The main building, located at 18 Broad Street, and the one at 11 Wall Street, were both designated historical landmarks in 1978. The NYSE is the world's largest stock exchange by market cap, estimated to be $28.5 trillion as of June 30, 2018.

The NYSE relied for many years on floor trading only, using the open outcry system. Many NYSE trades have transitioned to electronic systems, but floor traders are still used to set pricing and deal in high-volume institutional trading.

Currently, the NYSE is open for trading Monday through Friday from 9:30 AM to 4:00 PM ET. The stock exchange is closed on all federal holidays. When federal holidays fall on a Saturday, the NYSE is sometimes closed the preceding Friday. When the federal holiday falls on a Sunday, the NYSE may be closed the following Monday.

The NYSE's Opening and Closing Bells

The opening and closing bells of the exchange mark the beginning and end of the trading day. The opening bell is rung at 9:30 AM ET and at 4:00 PM ET the closing bell is rung — closing trading for the day. Each of the four main sections of the NYSE has bells that ring simultaneously when a button is pressed. But trading days did not always begin and end with a bell — the original signal was actually a gavel. During the late 1800s, the NYSE changed the gavel to a gong. The bell became the official signal for the exchange in 1903 when the NYSE moved to 18 Broad Street.

Prior to 1995, the bells were rung by the exchange's floor managers. But the NYSE began inviting company executives to ring the opening and closing bells on a regular basis, which later became a daily event. The executives are from companies listed on the exchange, who sometimes coordinate their appearances with marketing events, such as the launch of a new product or innovation, or a merger or acquisition. Sometimes, the bells are rung by other public figures, including athletes and celebrities. Some of the more notable figures include singer/actor Liza Minnelli, Olympic medalist Michael Phelps, and the New York Yankees' Joe DiMaggio. In July 2013, United Nations Secretary Ban Ki-moon rang the closing bell to mark the NYSE joining the U.N. Sustainable Stock Exchanges Initiative.

History of the New York Stock Exchange

The New York Stock Exchange dates back to May 17, 1792. On that day, 24 stockbrokers from New York City signed the Buttonwood Agreement at 68 Wall Street. The New York Stock Exchange kicked off with five securities, which included three government bonds and two bank stocks.

Thanks to the NYSE's head start as the major U.S. stock exchange, many of the oldest publicly traded companies are on the exchange. Con Edison is the longest listed NYSE stock, tracing its roots back to 1824 as New York Gas Light Company. Along with American stocks, foreign-based corporations can also list their shares on the NYSE if they adhere to certain Securities and Exchange Commission (SEC) rules, known as listing standards.

The New York Stock Exchange passed the milestone of 1 million shares traded in a day in 1886. In 1987, 500 million shares were trading hands on the NYSE during a normal business day. By 1997, 1 billion shares were traded daily on the NYSE.

A series of mergers has given the New York Stock Exchange its massive size and global presence. The company started as NYSE before adding the American Stock Exchange and merging with the Euronext. NYSE Euronext was purchased in an $11 billion deal by the Intercontinental Exchange (ICE) in 2013. The following year, Euronext emerged from ICE via an initial public offering (IPO), but ICE retained ownership of the NYSE.

Notable Dates in the NYSE's History

- Oct. 24, 1929: The most devastating stock market crash in the history of the U.S. began on Black Thursday and continued into a sell-off panic on Black Tuesday, Oct. 29.

It followed the crash of the London Stock Exchange that took place in September and signaled the onset of the Great Depression, which affected all of the industrialized countries in the West.

- Oct. 1, 1934: The NYSE registered as a national securities exchange with the SEC.
- Oct. 19, 1987: The Dow Jones Industrial Average (DJIA) dropped 508 points or a loss of 22.6% in a single day.
- Sept. 11, 2001: Trading was shut down for four days at the NYSE

following the 9/11 attacks, and resumed on Sept. 17. About $1.4 trillion was lost in the five days of trading following the reopening — the biggest losses in NYSE history.

- Oct. 2008: NYSE Euronext completes the acquisition of the American Stock Exchange for $260 million in stock.
- May 6, 2010: The DJIA suffers its largest intraday drop since the Oct. 19, 1987, crash. It dropped 998 points, called the 2010 Flash Crash.
- Dec. 2012: ICE proposed to buy NYSE Euronext in a stock swap worth $8 billion.
- May 1, 2014: The NYSE was fined $4.5 million by the SEC in order to settle charges of market rule violations.
- May 25, 2018: Stacey Cunningham became the first female president of the NYSE.

Second Thoughts

For each of the following statements, choose one answer to fill in the blank.

1. The New York Stock Exchange (NYSE) now relies on _____.
   A. floor trading only
   B. electronic systems only
   C. mostly floor trading
   D. both floor trading and electronic systems
2. On _____, the DJIA suffers its largest intraday drop since the Oct. 19, 1987, crash.
   A. Sep. 11, 2001
   B. May 6, 2010
   C. May 1, 2014
   D. May 25, 2018

Reading II

Interest Rate Risk Between Long-Term and Short-Term Bonds

Long-term bonds are most sensitive to interest rate changes. The reason lies in the fixed-income nature of bonds: when investors purchase a corporate bond, for instance, they are actually purchasing a portion of a company's debt. This debt is issued with specific details regarding periodic coupon payments, the principal amount of the debt and the time period until the bond's maturity.

Interest Rates and Duration

A concept that is important for understanding interest rate risk in bonds is that bond prices are inversely related to interest rates. When interest rates go up, bond prices go down, and vice versa.

There are two primary reasons why long-term bonds are subject to greater interest rate risk than short-term bonds:

There is a greater probability that interest rates will rise (and thus negatively affect a bond's market price) within a longer time period than within a shorter period. As a result, investors who buy long-term bonds but then attempt to sell them before maturity may be faced with a deeply discounted market price when they want to sell their bonds. With short-term bonds, this risk is not as significant because interest rates are less likely to substantially change in the short term. Short-term bonds are also easier to hold until maturity, thereby alleviating an investor's concern about the effect of interest rate-driven changes in the price of bonds.

Long-term bonds have a greater duration than short-term bonds. Duration measures the sensitivity of a bond's price to changes in interest rates. For instance, a bond with a duration of 2 years will lose 2% for every 1% increase in rates. Because of this, a given interest rate change will have a greater effect on long-term bonds than on short-term bonds. This concept of duration can be difficult to conceptualize but just think of it as the length of time that your bond will be affected by an interest rate change. For example, suppose interest rates rise today by 0.25%. A bond with only one coupon payment left until maturity will be underpaying the investor by 0.25% for only one coupon payment. On the other hand, a bond with 20 coupon payments left will be underpaying the investor for a much longer period. This difference in remaining payments will cause a greater drop in a long-term bond's price than it will in a short-term bond's price when interest rates rise.

How Interest Rate Risk Impacts Bonds

Interest rate risk arises when the absolute level of interest rates fluctuates. Interest rate risk directly affects the values of fixed-income securities. Since interest rates and bond prices are inversely related, the risk associated with a rise in interest rates causes bond prices to fall and vice versa.

Interest rate risk affects the prices of bonds, and all bondholders face this type of risk. As mentioned above, it's important to remember that as interest rates rise, bond prices fall. When interest rates rise and new bonds with higher yields than older securities are issued in the market, investors tend to purchase the new bond issues to take advantage of the higher yields.

For this reason, the older bonds based on the previous level of interest rate have less value, and so investors and traders sell their old bonds and the prices of those decrease.

Conversely, when interest rates fall, bond prices tend to rise. When interest rates fall and new bonds with lower yields than older fixed-income securities are issued in the market, investors are less likely to purchase new issues. Hence, the older bonds that have higher yields tend to increase in price.

For example, assume the Federal Open Market Committee (FOMC) meeting is next Wednesday and many traders and investors fear interest rates will rise within the next year. After the FOMC meeting, the committee decides to raise interest rates in three months. Therefore, the prices of bonds decrease because new bonds are issued at higher yields in three months.

How Investors Can Reduce Interest Rate Risk

Investors can reduce, or hedge, interest rate risk with forward contracts, interest rate swaps and futures. Investors may desire reduced interest rate risk to reduce uncertainty of changing rates affecting the value of their investments. This risk is greater for investors in bonds, real estate investment trusts (REITs) and other stocks in which dividends make up a healthy portion of cash flows.

Primarily, investors are concerned about interest rate risk when they are worried about inflationary pressures, excessive government spending or an unstable currency. All of these factors have the ability to lead to higher inflation, which results in higher interest rates. Higher interest rates are particularly deleterious for fixed income, as the cash flows erode in value.

Forward contracts are agreements between two parties with one party paying the other to lock in an interest rate for an extended period of time. This is a prudent move when interest rates are favorable. Of course, an adverse effect is the company cannot take advantage of further declines in interest rates. An example of this is homeowners taking advantage of low-interest rates by refinancing their mortgages. Others may switch from adjustable-rate mortgages to fixed-rate mortgages as well.

Futures are similar to forward contracts, except they are standardized and listed on regulated exchanges. This makes the arrangement more expensive, though there's less of a chance of one party failing to meet obligations. This is the most liquid option for investors.

Interest rate swaps are another common agreement between two parties in which they agree to pay each other the difference between fixed interest rates and floating interest rates. Basically, one party takes on the interest rate risk and is compensated for doing so. Other interest rate derivatives that are employed are options and forward rate agreements (FRAs). All of these contracts provide interest rate risk protection by gaining in value when bond prices fall.

Investors holding long-term bonds are subject to a greater degree of interest rate risk than those holding shorter-term bonds. This means that if interest rates change by, say 1%, long-term bonds will see a greater change to their price — rising when rates fall, and falling when rates rise. Explained by their greater duration measure, interest rate risk is often not a big deal for those holding bonds until maturity. For those who are more active traders, however, hedging strategies may be employed to reduce the effect of changing interest rates on bond portfolios.

Second Thoughts

1) Why are long-term bonds subject to greater interest rate risk than short-term bonds? Please summarize the reasons.

_____

_____

2) How can investors reduce the interest rate risk? Please make a summary.

_____

_____

Strategy of International Business

CHAPTER 9

国际企业战略

本章概要

本章主要介绍国际企业战略的含义、要素、类型、重要性、益处以及代价，以及以跨国企业海尔的战略为案例，介绍不同的企业如何选择自己的战略。

学习指南

"战略"指在不确定条件下实现一个或多个目标的高级计划。当我们把战略和跨国企业放在一起时，这意味着管理者对战略决策采取一系列方法组合，通过观察企业的所有业务来确定如何创造最大的价值和实现企业的目标。

管理者们制定企业战略，首先分析他们所处的行业或环境条件，然后评估他们所面对的对手的强弱。在行业和竞争分析的基础上，确定一个独特的战略地位，建立竞争优势，从而超越对手。

通过本章学习，希望大家能够实现以下目标：

（1）基本目标（Text-based Goals）

- 掌握本章涉及话题的基本专业术语及词汇，如全球战略、竞争优势、多国化战略等；
- 掌握本章的主要知识点，即国际企业战略的含义、要素、类型、重要性、益处以及相关的代价。

（2）拓展目标（Extended Goals）

- 思考本章引言，为什么李·博尔曼认为"没有战略的愿景仍然是幻觉"？
- 通过学习背景知识、拓展阅读、案例分析进一步了解国际企业战略的应用，以及如何制定适合本企业的战略。

What Is Strategy?

The term of "strategy" was initially used in military field when leading an army facing the enemy with the purpose of attaining the victory; with the passing of time it was also used in governing a region or for global governing and planning, being afterwards transferred to the business environment. At the same time, strategy is also one of the key disciplines of management, complete with its own vocabulary, tools, and no shortage of expert opinions on what it means and how to best develop it. And like everything else in management in this era of accelerating change and increased volatility, our understanding and our approaches to developing and executing on firm's strategy must evolve as well.

Strategy (from Greek στρατηγία stratēgia, "art of troop leader; office of general, command, generalship") is a high level plan to achieve one or more goals under conditions of uncertainty. When we put the strategy and the multinational enterprise abreast, it means that the managers take a portfolio approach to strategic decisions by looking across all of a firm's businesses to determine how to create the most value and attain the goals of the firms. In order to develop a successful strategy and maximize the value of an enterprise, managers ought to pursue strategies which can increase the profits. Commonly speaking, the growth of profit can be measured by the percentage increase in net profits over time, and meanwhile, the value of the firms will increase as their profits increase.

When executives develop corporate strategy, they nearly always begin by analyzing the industry or environmental conditions in which they operate. They then assess the strengths and weaknesses of the players they are up against. With these industry and competitive analyses in mind, they set out to carve a distinctive strategic position where they can outperform their rivals by building a competitive advantage. To obtain such an advantage, a company generally chooses either to differentiate itself from the competition for a **premium** price or to pursue lower costs. The organization aligns its value chain accordingly, creating manufacturing, marketing, and human resource strategies in the process. On the basis of these strategies, financial targets and budget allocations are set.

Key Elements of Strategy

战略的要素

战略是一个综合的、以外部为导向的概念，即一个公司如何实现其目标，如何与竞争对手竞争。良好的战略制定意味着要细化战略要素。管理层在决策时必须考虑的五个要素：(1) 活动场所；(2) 差异要素；(3) 工具；(4) 节奏；(5) 经济逻辑

A strategy is an integrated and externally oriented concept of how a firm will achieve its objectives — how it will compete against its rivals. Good strategy formulation means refining the elements of the strategy. A strategy consists of an integrated set of choices. These choices relate to five elements managers must consider when making decisions: (1) **arenas**, (2) **differentiators**, (3) vehicles, (4) staging and pacing, and (5) economic logic.

ARENAS

Arenas are areas in which a firm will be active. Decisions about a firm's arenas may encompass its products, services, distribution channels, market segments, geographic areas, technologies, and even stages of the value-creation process. Unlike vision statements, which tend to be fairly general, the identification of arenas must be very specific. It clearly tells managers what the firm should and should not do. For example, as the largest U.S. bicycle distributor, Pacific Cycle owns the Schwinn, Mongoose, and GT brands and sells its bikes through **big-box** retail outlets and independent dealers, as well as through independent agents in foreign markets. In addition to these arena choices, Pacific Cycle has entirely outsourced the production of its products to Asian manufacturers, because Asia happens to be a low-cost source of high-quality manufactured goods. The arenas help you answer questions about business strategy — that is, it helps you determine which particular industry or geographic segments are the firm's prime competitive arenas. The arenas **facet** also allows you to summarize corporate strategy — that is, it allows you to summarize which group of industry and geographic segments the firm competes in.

DIFFERENTIATORS

Differentiators are features and attributes of a company's product or service that help it beat its competitors in the marketplace. Firms can be successful in the marketplace along a number of common dimensions, including image, reliability, customization, technical superiority, price, and quality.

Japanese automakers Toyota and Honda have done very well by providing effective combinations of differentiators. They sell both inexpensive cars and high-end cars with high-quality features, and many consumers find the value that they provide hard to match. There are two critical factors in selecting differentiators:

- Decisions must be made early. Key differentiators rarely materialize without significant **up-front** decisions, and without valuable differentiators firms tend to lose marketplace battles.

Word Study

arena /əˈriːnə/ n. 场所，竞争舞台

differentiator /dɪfəˈrenʃɪeɪtə/ n. 区分因素

big-box /bɪɡˈbɒks/ n. 大卖场

facet /ˈfæsɪt/ n. 部分，方面

up-front /ʌpˈfrʌnt/ adj. 预先的

- Identifying and executing successful differentiators mean making tough choices — **trade-offs**. Managers who can't make tough decisions about trade-offs often end up trying to satisfy too broad a **spectrum** of customer needs; as a result, they execute poorly on most dimensions.

Differentiators are what drive potential customers to choose one firm's offerings over those of competitors. The earlier and more consistent the firm is at driving these differentiators, the greater the likelihood that customers will recognize them.

Word Study

trade-off /treɪd'ɒf/ *n.*
　权衡, 协调
spectrum /'spektrəm/
　n. 范围, 幅度
credibility /ˌkredə'bɪləti/
　n. 可信性, 可靠性

VEHICLES

Vehicles are the means for participating in targeted arenas. For instance, a firm that wants to go international can do so in different ways. In a recent drive to enter certain international markets (e.g., Argentina), Walmart has opened new stores and grown organically — meaning that it developed all the stores internally as opposed to acquiring stores already based in the countries it wanted to enter. Elsewhere (namely, in England and Germany), Walmart has purchased existing retailers and is in the process of transferring its unique way of doing business to the acquired companies. Likewise, a firm that requires a new technology could develop it through investments in research and development (R&D). Or it could opt to form an alliance with a competitor or a supplier that already possesses the technology, accelerating the integration of the missing piece into its set of resources and capabilities. Finally, it could simply buy another firm that owns the technology. In this case, the possible vehicles for entering a new arena include acquisitions, alliances, and organic investment and growth.

STAGING AND PACING

Staging and pacing refer to the timing and speed, or pace, of strategic moves. Staging choices typically reflect available resources, including cash, human capital, and knowledge. At what point, for example, should Walmart have added international markets to its strategy? Perhaps if the company had pursued global opportunities earlier, it would have been able to develop a better sense of foreign market conditions and even spread the cost of entry over a longer period of time. However, by delaying its international moves, the company was able to focus on dominating the U.S. market, which is — after all — the largest retail market in the world. Despite mixed results overseas, Walmart is the undisputed leader in global retailing and has recently increased its emphasis on international markets as the basis for future growth.

Staging decisions should be driven by several factors — resources, urgency, **credibility**, and the need for early wins. Because few firms have the resources to do everything they'd like to do immediately, they usually have to match opportunities with available resources. In addition, not all

window /'wɪndəʊ/ n.
机会，时机
fulcrum /'fʌlkrəm/ n.
支柱，支点
variable /'veəriəbəl/
    adj. 可变的，多变的
reside /rɪ'zaɪd/ v. 在于，
    归于
revitalized
    /riː'vaɪtəlaɪzd/ adj.
    使新生的，使有新
    活力的
maneuver /mə'nuːvə/
    n. 策略，手段

opportunities to enter new arenas are permanent; some have only brief **windows**. In such cases, early wins and the credibility of certain key stakeholders may be necessary to implement a strategy.

ECONOMIC LOGIC

Economic logic refers to how the firm will earn a profit — that is, how the firm will generate positive returns over and above its cost of capital. Economic logic is the "**fulcrum**" for profit creation. Earning normal profits, of course, requires a firm to meet all fixed, **variable**, and financing costs. Achieving desired returns over the firm's cost of capital is a tall order for any organization. In analyzing a firm's economic logic, think of both costs and revenues. Sometimes economic logic **resides** primarily on the cost side of the equation. Irish airline Ryanair, for example, can fly passengers for significantly lower costs per passenger mile than any major competitor. At other times, economic logic may rest on the firm's ability to increase the customer's willingness to pay premium prices for products (in other words, prices that significantly exceed the costs of providing enhanced products).

When the five elements of strategy are aligned and mutually reinforcing, the firm is generally in a position to perform well. High performance levels, however, ultimately mean that a strategy is also being executed well. This leads to strategy implementation.

Firms and International Strategies

New markets, fresh revenue streams, high returns on the reinvestment, **revitalized** product development. "Going global" is a strategic **maneuver** opening the next chapter for many organizations seizing the moment to expand their global footprint. Foreign expansion strategies make growth more structured and sustainable. When composed properly, these plans mitigate expansion risk and encourage efficient use of resources, timelines, and capital for global expansion.

For most companies, international growth is a value accelerator. On median, the high international revenue growth group derived notable benefits from their expansion.

Types of International Strategies

A firm that has operations in more than one country is known as a multinational corporation (MNC). The largest MNCs are major players within the international arena. Walmart's annual worldwide sales, for example, are larger than the dollar value of the entire economies of Austria, Norway, and Saudi Arabia. Although Walmart tends to be viewed as an American retailer, the firm earns more than one-quarter of its revenues outside the United States. Walmart owns significant numbers of stores in Mexico (1,730 as of mid-2011), Central America (549), Brazil (479), Japan (414), the United Kingdom (385), Canada (325), Chile (279), and Argentina (63). Walmart also participates in joint ventures in China (328 stores) and India (5). Even more modestly sized MNCs are still very powerful. If Kia were a country, its current sales level of approximately $21 billion would place it in the top 100 among the more than 180 nations in the world.

Multinationals such as Kia and Walmart must choose an international strategy to guide their efforts in various countries. There are three main international strategies available: (1) multidomestic, (2) global, and (3) transnational. Each strategy involves a different approach to trying to build efficiency across nations and trying to be responsive to variations in customer preferences and market conditions across nations.

MULTIDOMESTIC STRATEGY

A firm using a multidomestic strategy sacrifices efficiency in favor of emphasizing responsiveness to local requirements within each of its markets. Rather than trying to force all of its American-made shows on viewers around the globe, MTV customizes the programming that is shown on its channels within dozens of countries, including New Zealand, Portugal, Pakistan, and India. Similarly, food company H. J. Heinz adapts its products to match local Indians who will not eat garlic and onion, for example. Heinz offers them a version of its signature ketchup that does not include these two ingredients.

GLOBAL STRATEGY

A firm using a global strategy sacrifices responsiveness to local requirements within each of its markets in favor of emphasizing efficiency. This strategy is the complete opposite of a multidomestic strategy. Some minor modifications to products and services may be made in various markets, but a global strategy stresses the need to gain economies of scale by offering essentially the same products or services in each market.

Microsoft, for example, offers the same software programs around the world but adjusts the programs to match local languages. Similarly, consumer goods maker Procter & Gamble attempts to gain efficiency by creating global brands whenever possible. Global strategies also can be very effective for firms whose product or service is largely hidden from the customer's view, such as **silicon** chip maker Intel. For such firms, **variance** in local preferences is not very important.

TRANSNATIONAL STRATEGY

A firm using a transnational strategy seeks a middle ground between a multidomestic strategy and a global strategy. Such a firm tries to balance

现有的国际战略主要有三种：（1）多国化战略；（2）全球战略；（3）跨国战略。不同的战略代表企业为了提高在各国业务的效率，并努力对各国客户偏好和市场状况的变化做出反应而采取的不同方法。

Word Study

silicon /'sɪlɪkən/ n. 硅
variance /'veərɪəns/ n. 变化幅度，差额

the desire for efficiency with the need to adjust to local preferences within various countries. For example, large fast-food chains such as McDonald's and Kentucky Fried Chicken (KFC) rely on the same brand names and the same core menu items around the world. These firms make some **concessions** to local tastes too. In France, for example, wine can be purchased at McDonald's. This approach makes sense for McDonald's because wine is a central element of French diets.

The Importance of an International Strategy

国际战略的重要性
从企业的角度看，国际扩张为新的销售和利润提供了机会；从客户的角度看，国际贸易至少在理论上会使商品和服务的价格下降；从国际政府组织的角度看，降低世界贸易壁垒、给予一些国家和行业一定程度的保护等国际谈判少不了国际战略；但从国际非政府组织的角度看，部分跨国企业的国际战略存在剥削发展中国家的嫌疑。

FROM A COMPANY'S PERSPECTIVE, international expansion provides the opportunity for new sales and profits. In some cases, it may even be the situation that profitability is so poor in the home market that international expansion may be the only opportunity for profits. For example, poor profitability in the Chinese domestic market was one of the reasons that the Chinese consumer electronics company, TCL decided on a strategy of international expansion. It has then pursued this with new overseas offices, new factories and acquisitions to develop its market position in the two main consumer electronics market: the U.S. and the European Union. In addition to new sales opportunities, there may be other reasons for expansion beyond the home market. For example, oil companies expand in order to secure resources — called resource seeking. Clothing companies expand in order to take advantage of low labor costs in some countries — called efficiency seeking. Some companies acquire foreign companies to enhance their market position versus competitors — called strategic asset seeking.

FROM A CUSTOMER'S PERSPECTIVE, international trade should — in theory at least — lead to lower prices for goods and services because of the economies of scale and scope that will derive from a larger global base. For example, Nike sources its sports shoes from low labor cost countries like the Philippines and Vietnam. In addition, some customers like to purchase products and services that have a global image, such as Disney cartoon characters or "Manchester United" branded soccer shirts.

FROM THE PERSPECTIVE OF INTERNATIONAL GOVERNMENTAL ORGANIZATIONS — like the World Bank — the recent dominant thinking has been to bring down barriers to world trade while giving some degree of protection to some countries and industries. Thus global strategy is an important aspect of such international negotiations.

FROM THE PERSPECTIVE OF SOME INTERNATIONAL NON-GOVERNMENTAL ORGANIZATIONS like Oxfam and Medicin sans Frontières, the global strategies of some — but not necessarily all — multinational companies are regarded with some suspicion. Such companies have been accused of exploiting developing countries — for example in terms of their natural mineral resources — in ways that are **detrimental** to those countries.

Word Study

detrimental /ˌdetrɪˈmentəl/ *adj.* 有害的，不利的

Benefits of an International Strategy

实施国际战略的好处
　实施国际战略的好处主要体现以下五个方面：范围经济效应、全球品牌认知度、全球客户满意度、最低的劳动力和其他投入成本、在尽可能多的国家回收研发成本和其他开发成本。

ECONOMIES OF SCOPE: the cost savings developed by a group when it shares activities or transfers capabilities and competencies from one part of the group to another — for example, a biotechnology sales team sells more than one product from the total range.

GLOBAL BRAND RECOGNITION: the benefit that derives from having a brand that is recognized throughout the world — for example, Disney.

GLOBAL CUSTOMER SATISFACTION: multinational customers who demand the same product, service and quality at various locations around the world — for example, customers of the Sheraton Hotel chain expect and receive the same level of service at all its hotels around the world.

LOWEST LABOUR AND OTHER INPUT COSTS: these arise by choosing and switching manufacturers with low(er) labor costs — for example, computer assembly from imported parts in Thailand and Malaysia where labor wages are lower than in countries making some sophisticated computer parts (such as high-end computer chips) in countries like the U.S.

RECOVERY OF R&D COSTS AND OTHER DEVELOPMENT COSTS ACROSS THE MAXIMUM NUMBER OF COUNTRIES — new models, new drugs and other forms of research often amounting to billions of U.S. dollars. The more countries of the world where the goods can be sold means the greater number of countries that can contribute to such costs. For example, the Airbus Jumbo A380 launched in 2008 where development costs have exceeded US$ 10 billion.

Business case for globalization is strengthened by competitive pressures: the fear of some companies that they will be left behind other companies if they fail to globalize. The Japanese car company, Toyota, has built itself into the world's largest car company. It has developed this through a global strategy that includes economies of scope, branding, customer recognition and the recovery of its extensive research and development costs in many markets around the world. Yet it has also been cautious in its global strategy. For example, its strategy in China has been through joint ventures with the local car companies FAW and Guangzhou Auto. Whereas, its main strategies in Europe have been partly through wholly-owned ventures and partly through cooperation with other European car companies on some joint production. For other models like the Lexus, Toyota still exports directly from its major production plant in Japan. The reason is that it is able to gain the economies of scale for the up-market low-volume, Lexus brand that would not be present if it was to produce in smaller quantities in each world region, like the U.S. and the European Union.

Costs of an International Strategy

实施国际战略经济代价

实施全球战略的成本可能大于收益，与收益相比，至少有五项经济成本：

（1）对当地需求缺乏敏感性；（2）运输和物流成本；（3）规模效益在实践中可能难以获得；（4）沟通成本更高；（5）管理协调成本。

The costs of operating a global strategy may be greater than the benefits, setting against these benefits, there are at least five economic costs of international strategies.

LACK OF SENSITIVITY TO LOCAL DEMAND

Leavitt argued that people would be prepared to compromise on their individual tastes if the product was cheap enough deriving from economies of scale and scope. Is this really correct? Others argued that there could be costs in adapting products to match local tastes, local conditions like the climate and other local factors like special laws on environmental issues.

TRANSPORT AND LOGISTICS COSTS

Manufacturing takes place in one country, then it will be necessary to transport the finished products to other countries. The costs for some heavy products, like steel bars, may be greater than the economies of scale from centralized production in one country.

ECONOMIES OF SCALE BENEFITS MAY BE DIFFICULT TO OBTAIN IN PRACTICE

Plant takes time to commission, so local competitors still using old plant and cheap labor may still be competitive.

COMMUNICATIONS COSTS WILL BE HIGHER

Standardization of products and services needs to be communicated to every country. In virtually every case, it will also be necessary to monitor and control the result. All this is time consuming, expensive and at the mercy of local managers who may have their own agendas and interests.

MANAGEMENT COORDINATION COSTS

In practice, managers and workers in different countries often need to be consulted, issues need to be explored and discussed, local variations in tax and legal issues need to be addressed. This means that senior managers operating a global strategy need to spend time visiting countries. It cannot all be done on the telephone and worldwide web. This takes a tremendous toll of people personally.

industry and competitive analysis 行业与竞争分析

economic logic 经济逻辑   vision statement 愿景陈述

multidomestic strategy 多国化战略   global strategy 全球战略

transnational strategy 跨国战略   economies of scale 规模经济

economies of scope 范围经济

global brand recognition 全球品牌认知

蓝海战略

随着经济的进一步增长，企业面对的市场竞争越来越激烈。为了获得即时的利益，争夺有限的市场，企业不惜一切代价保护自己的市场份额，在这种情况下，企业的利润空间日趋缩小。另一方面，企业为了获取更大的市场份额，将更多的精力用于对市场进行细分和关注竞争对手的竞争策略，并没有真正站在消费者的角度去考虑。企业感到生存环境越来越恶劣，而消费者的需求却亟待满足。通过多年的研究，W·钱·金和勒妮·莫博涅教授逐步构建了价值创新战略理论体系，将其命名为"蓝海战略"。

其研究以战略行动为分析单位。战略行动包含开辟市场的主要业务项目所涉及的一整套管理动作和决定。在研究1880年～2000年30多个产业150次战略行动的基础上，W·钱·金和勒妮·莫博涅教授指出，价值创新是蓝海战略的基石。价值创新挑战了基于竞争的传统教条，即价值和成本的权衡取舍关系，让企业将创新与效用、价格与成本整合一体，不是比照现有产业最佳实践去赶超对手，而是改变产业景框重新设定游戏规则；不是瞄准现有市场"高端"或"低端"顾客，而是面向潜在需求的买方大众；不是一味细分市场满足顾客偏好，而是合并细分市场整合需求。

它主要包括四项行动架构：一、消除。思考产业内哪些竞争因素应该消除，这些存在已久的因素，往往被视为理所当然，但实际上其价值日渐流失，甚至减损其现有价值。二、降低。让设计者正视其产品及服务是否设计过度，只为超越对手；企业若是对顾客过度周到，往往使成本增加，却得不到好处。三、提升。找出产业有哪些盲点，是顾客必须"将就的"，必须解决。四、创造。创造新需求，并改变产业战略定价。

蓝海战略可发挥众多功能，其中最主要包括以下三点：首先，促进企业同时追求差异化和低成本，破除了价值成本抵换的常规。其次，促使企业管理者主动检讨每个竞争因素，以便了解在竞争过程中企业在不知不觉中形成的假设。最后，有助于提升买方价值及创造新需求，促使企业去超越当前竞争标准所设定的价值极大化，及激励企业改变这些因素，使现有的竞争规则失去着力点。

文献来源：

庞玥.对企业蓝海战略的有效应用的探析［J］.现代经济信息，2005（08），136.

A. Name the key elements of a strategy.

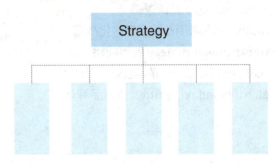

B. According to the text, fill in each of the following blanks with an appropriate word or phrase.

1) In order to develop a successful strategy and _____ the value of an enterprise, managers ought to pursue strategies which can increase the profits.

2) The _____ facet allows you to summarize corporate strategy — that is, it allows you to summarize which group of industry and geographic segments the firm competes in.

3) A firm that has operations in more than one country is known as a _____.

4) _____ are features and attributes of a company's product or service that help it beat its competitors in the marketplace.

5) When composed properly, these plans mitigate _____ and encourage efficient use of resources, timelines, and capital for global expansion.

6) A firm using a _____ strategy sacrifices efficiency in favor of emphasizing responsiveness to local requirements within each of its markets.

7) Some companies acquire foreign companies to enhance their market position versus competitors — called _____.

8) _____ is the complete opposite of a multidomestic strategy.

9) In some cases, it may even be the situation that profitability is so poor in the home market that _____ expansion may be the only opportunity for profits.

10) Leavitt argued that people would be prepared to compromise on their individual tastes if the product was cheap enough deriving from economies of _____.

C. Read the text and decide whether the following statements are True (T) or False (F).

1) Strategy is a high-level plan to achieve one or more goals under conditions of certainty.   (   )

2) Commonly speaking, the value of the firms will decrease as their profits increase. ( )

3) Strategy is one of the key disciplines of management, complete with its own vocabulary, tools, and there are many expert opinions on what it means and how to best develop it. ( )

4) Pacific Cycle has partly outsourced the production of its products to Asian manufacturers, because Asia happens to be a low-cost source of high-quality manufactured goods. ( )

5) Differentiators are what drive potential customers to choose one firm's offerings over those of competitors. ( )

6) Early wins and the credibility of certain key stakeholders means little to implementing a strategy. ( )

7) For most companies, international growth is a value accelerator. ( )

8) Each strategy involves a different approach to trying to build efficiency across nations and trying to limit variations in customer preferences and market conditions across nations. ( )

9) Poor profitability in the Chinese domestic market was one of the reasons that the Chinese consumer electronics company, TCL decided on a strategy of international expansion. ( )

10) Toyota's main strategies in China have been partly through wholly-owned ventures and partly through cooperation with other Chinese car companies on some joint production. ( )

Discussion
讨论

1) What is a firm's strategy?

_____

_____

2) Can you give some examples about a specific strategy that a famous international business has adopted?

_____

_____

3) Why do firms adopt international strategies?

_____

_____

4) What's the difference between the multidomestic strategy and the global strategy?

_____

_____

5) What's your opinion on the benefits and costs of an international strategy?

_____

_____

Case Story

Haier's Road to Growth

Haier is now the fastest-growing provider of appliances in the world. Since 2011, it has held the largest worldwide market share in white goods. With its upscale brands in China, such as Casarte, and its growing presence in the United States, Europe, and Japan, this US$38 billion company has moved out of the value-priced and niche appliance domain to compete directly with top-of-the-line appliances from more established companies. It has accomplished this by being a consistently coherent and capable company: staying true to its core identity as a company dedicated to solving problems for consumers, while continually reinventing itself with imagination and verve.

Brand Building Strategy

It was at the beginning of the reform and opening-up in the 1980s, and many companies including Haier imported from abroad advanced refrigerator technologies and equipment. At the time, household appliances were in short supply, which led to many companies striving to expand in scale. Focus was put on quantity at the expense of quality. Instead of following this trend blindly Haier made quality a priority, putting into place a comprehensive quality management system. "Either not in it or in it for the win", as it was put. When finally there was an oversupply in the household appliance market, Haier was already well positioned to win with its differentiated quality. During this period Haier was dedicated to making refrigerators, developing successful portable models in management, technologies, personnel, capital and corporate culture.

Diversification Strategy

It was during the 1990s and state policies encouraged business mergers and acquisitions. However, some companies either failed after annexation and reorganization, or decided that it was in their interest to get specialized rather than diversified. In the innovation spirit of Haier Culture Revitalizing the "Stunned Fish", Haier over time acquired altogether eighteen domestic businesses, ushering in a broader development dimension in terms of diversified operation and expansion in scale. Competition in the home appliance market was stiff and quality had become users' basic demand. Haier was the first to launch the "Star Service" system. While other home appliance manufacturers were engaged in a price war Haier was already well positioned to win with its differentiated services.

At this stage Haier began to implement OEC (Overall Every Control and Clear) management, i.e. overall control and sort-out of everything that every employee finishes on his or her job every day, with the aim to "accomplish what's planned each day and improve on what's accomplished the previous day". This management approach also became the cornerstone of Haier's innovation.

Internationalization Strategy

China acceded into the WTO at the end of the 1990s. In answering the call of the state many Chinese companies went abroad only to retreat later to the old way of licensing agreements due to frustrating challenges. Haier decided that going abroad was not just for earning foreign exchange. More importantly, it was for creating China's own brands. Therefore, Haier came up with the "three-step strategy" of "going out, going in and going up". Acting on the idea of "taking on the more difficult ones first" Haier started by entering developed countries first to build a brand. Having done that, Haier took to the markets of developing countries with a much more advantageous position. In time, it created the localization mode of "three in one", combining design, manufacture and sales.

In this phase, Haier implemented a "Market Chain" management which was based on computer information system and centered around order information flow, to drive logistics and capital flows and realize reengineering of business processes. This innovation on management system facilitated information flows within the enterprise, and encouraged employees to align their value orientation with the needs of users.

Global Brand Strategy

The Internet Age brings with it segmentation of marketing. The production-inventory-sales model of traditional businesses can no longer meet personalized demands of users, and a firm has to transform from the self-centered product selling to a user-centric sale of services, i.e. a user-driven "on-demand manufacturing and delivery" mode. The Internet also gives rise to integration of global economies. And the relationship between internationalization and globalization is one of logical progression. "Internationalization" means creating international brands with an enterprise's own resources, while "globalization" refers to making use of global resources to create localized mainstream brands, which are different in essence. Therefore, Haier consolidated global resources in R&D, manufacturing, and marketing to create a global brand.

In this phase, the business model Haier explored in order to create customers in the Internet Age was the Win-win Model of Individual-Goal Combination.

Networking Strategy

In the networking strategy stage, Haier transforms from a traditional enterprise manufacturing household appliances to a platform oriented to incubator makers in the whole society, and strives to become an internet company, aiming to break the self-closed system of traditional enterprises, turn itself into a node of network interconnection, interlink all kinds of resources, build a new co-creation and win-win platform, and achieve win-win and added value of interested parties.

To this end, Haier has conducted subversive explorations in strategy, organization, employees, users, compensation, and management, creating a dynamic cycle system and accelerating the transformation of the Internet. In terms of strategy, Haier builds a co-creation and win-win ecosphere centered on users to achieve win-win and added value of interested parties in the ecosphere. In terms of organization, Haier turns itself from a traditional self-closed enterprise to an open internet node and reforms the bureaucracy structure to a network structure. During this process, the staffs change from employees and executors to entrepreneurs and dynamic partners, thus forming a social ecosphere with best experience to meet the individual demands of users. In compensation mechanism, it shifts from "paid by enterprise" to "paid by user", encouraging the employees to become real entrepreneurs and to realize their own value while creating value for users. In terms of management innovation, Haier endeavors to achieve self-evolution towards its goal eventually through exploration on non-linearity management.

Case Discussion

1) Retell the different strategies that Haier has adopted in its road to success in your own words.

_____

_____

2) What's your opinion on these five strategies? Discuss with your partner.

_____

_____

3) Do you know other important strategies that Haier has adopted? Discuss with your partner.

_____

_____

Case Summary

　　海尔现在是世界上增长最快的家电供应商。自2011年以来,它在全球家电产品市场占有率最高。凭借其在中国的高端品牌,如卡萨帝,以及在美国、欧洲和日本的日益增长的业务,这家价值380亿美元的公司已经走出了价值定价的老牌家电领域,直接与更成熟的顶级家电公司竞争。

　　本文主要介绍了海尔在其成功之路上所实行的五项重要的战略。第一,品牌塑造战略。海尔把质量放在首位,建立了全面的质量管理体系。当家电市场最终出现供过于求的局面时,海尔已经具备了以差异化质量取胜的良好条件。第二,多样化战略。海尔率先推出"星级服务"体系。当其他家电制造商陷入价格战时,海尔已经做好了赢得差异化服务的准备。第三,国际化战略。海尔首先进入发达国家市场,然后以更为有利的地位进入发展中国家市场,及时开创了设计、制造、销售"三位一体"的国产化模式。第四,全球品牌战略。海尔利用企业自身资源打造国际品牌。第五,网络战略。海尔从传统的家电制造企业转型为面向全社会的孵化器制造商平台,力争成为互联网公司,打破传统企业的自我封闭体系。

Reading Expansion 拓展阅读

Reading I

The Different Approaches Firms Use to Set Strategy

What is your strategy? Most senior executives can confidently answer this question. How has that strategy changed over time? This one usually gets a quick answer too. How do you make decisions about changing that strategy? Now it gets much more difficult. The fact is, many senior executives struggle to describe how they make strategic decisions. That's a serious problem, since the process for making strategic decisions can shape the strategy itself. Making a strategy without knowing your process is like sailing without a compass. You are setting yourself up for a long, stressful journey. Even worse, if you eventually reach your destination, you may not realize that you're in the right place.

To better understand how companies really make strategic choices, we recently interviewed 92 current CEOs, founders, and senior executives. We asked each to answer detailed questions about their approach to strategic decision making. Their replies revealed both striking variety and underlying patterns. Here, we offer a typology of four approaches. Our results can't say that any single approach to strategy is always the best, but we do offer some evidence that one of the approaches is often flawed.

Four Approaches to Strategic Decision Making

Companies' processes differed from each other in two ways. The first was whether a firm uses a high or low level of process to make strategic decisions. That is, does it have recurring routines for discussing strategy, triggering strategic changes, and reviewing those changes? The second was the amount of input from other employees that the leader considers while making a strategic decision. This factor focuses on employee involvement in decision making, not simply attendance at meetings or post-decision communication. These two factors can exist in any pairing, and based on our interviews, firms populate all boxes, which gives us four distinct archetypes of strategic decision making.

Unilateral firms are both low process and low input. They tend to have a top-down leader who makes decisions alone. During our interviews, these individuals often had difficulty explaining their decision-making process and the role other employees played. Interestingly, these interviewees had two different types of attitudes: Some disliked their process and admitted that they should do things differently, while others seemed very confident with how they made decisions. A potential benefit for unilateral firms is that leaders can make decisions quickly, without the constraints of process complexity and debate. However, the bad news is that, lacking checks and balances, unilateral firms can make bad decisions fast. Moreover, speed is not a sure thing in a unilateral firm: If the top-down leader chooses to procrastinate on a tough decision, no process is there to force timely action.

Ad hoc firms are low process and high input. These firms do not have a codified, recurring process that they follow every time they make a strategic change. But when a change needs to be made, the leader pulls their team together to take action. The exact steps the firm follows and the exact people in the room change from one decision to the next. The benefit of an ad hoc system is that rigid rules don't constrain the firm. Leaders can tailor the process to each decision by adjusting the length of deliberations, the involved parties, and other factors. The main risk is that the firm may not learn over time how to get better at making strategic decisions. The top leader of an ad hoc firm might also use the process flexibility to exclude stakeholders who disagree with the leader's position. This will eliminate the debate that fuels ad hoc decision making and, in essence, shift the firm down to the unilateral box.

Administrative firms are high process but low input. These firms follow rigorous processes and well-defined routines to make strategic decisions without actually eliciting debate from other employees. One benefit is the detailed data collection and documentation that accompanies this extensive process. If administrative firms are smart, they can leverage this information to improve future decision making. But, similar to unilateral firms, the low level of input can result in bad decisions if leaders do not consider key information or opinions. In fact, this risk can be especially grave in administrative firms because the detailed process and the sheer quantity of information gathered can act as theater, masking the lack of broad input from internal and external stakeholders.

Collaborative firms are both high process and high input. These firms have the rigorous process of an administrative firm, but also the engaged employees of an ad hoc firm. During interviews, these leaders showed strong consistency across different types of decisions and could clearly articulate how employees added value during the process. The detailed process ensures that the leaders don't miss any steps. The frequent input ensures that they don't miss any information. However, the inflexible system can potentially slow down decision making and prevent firms from acting on time-sensitive opportunities. For example, collaborative firms may inadvertently include irrelevant parties in strategy discussions or spend too much time achieving consensus among the participants in order to maintain engagement.

Which Approach Should a Firm Use?

Each of these archetypes has benefits and risks, which invites a question: Where should a firm sit in the matrix? Our interview data shows tremendous variation in archetype within each industry and across firms of similar size, which suggests that the right archetype for a given firm depends on subtle features of the company and its context. Our current research does not include enough data on context and firm performance to pinpoint the conditions in which one archetype would be the winner.

That said, our early data does make us skeptical about the unilateral archetype. In our interviews, we asked managers to give us a sense of where their approach stood in terms of five attributes that are generally associated with good strategic decision-making processes, namely:

Alternatives. Does the firm consider alternative options when making strategic decisions?

Information. How much information does the firm use to spark debate about decisions?

Implementation. Is a detailed implementation plan available when a decision is made?

Learning. Does the firm study successes and failures to learn for future decisions?

Communication. Does the firm have a clear plan to communicate changes to employees?

We then scored executives' responses based on a quantitative rubric. Unilateral firms scored lower on all criteria, to the point of statistical significance, than collaborative firms; on four of the five than administrative firms; and on three of the five than ad hoc firms. The low scores of unilateral firms raise a red flag about this approach. If you are using the unilateral archetype, you should pressure-test it and consider whether it is the best option for your firm. In contrast, the other three archetypes do not differ much in terms of the five attributes. For example, the chances of establishing learning routines appear very similar across ad hoc, collaborative, and administrative archetypes.

Ultimately, the wide variation in strategy-making approaches, even within similar industries and across organizations of similar sizes, was a real eye opener for our research team. An optimistic interpretation of this finding is that managers have considerable leeway to choose the archetype that best fits their specific context. A less rosy interpretation is that managers may inadvertently be stuck with less-than-optimal approaches. Our future research will aim to shed more light on this important question.

Second Thoughts

For each of the following statements, choose one (or more than one) answer to fill in the blank.

1) Ad hoc firms do not have a _____ process that they follow every time they make a strategic change.
   A. repeating
   B. warranting
   C. wanting
   D. unbefitting

2) Good strategic decision-making processes involve the following attributes except _____.
   A. Information.
   B. Implementation.
   C. Learning.
   D. Orientation.

Reading II

The Leader's Role in Strategy

Leadership is critical to forming and implementing strategy and without it, good strategy does not happen.

Developing a Strategic Vision and Mission

Vision is the core of leadership and is at the heart of strategy. The leader's job is to create the vision for the enterprise in a way that will engage both the imagination and the energies of its people. The vision must be tied to what the firm values, and the leader must make this connection in a way that the organization can understand, grasp, and support. Vision moves the enterprise; values stabilize the enterprise. Vision looks to the future, values to the past.

The vision and value statements need not be complicated. Howard Schultz earns high marks for bringing Starbucks to where it is today: a vibrant, growing, hugely profitable company with global brand recognition. He has developed and promoted a strategic vision from the beginning: to make Starbucks "the most respected brand name in coffee and for the company to be admired for its corporate responsibility." Two key values that supported this vision were "to build a company with a soul" and to pursue "the perfect cup of coffee." Simple phrases, but they have given direction to a highly successful enterprise!

Setting Goals and Objectives

Good visions do not become reality by magic. The process of realizing the vision — strategy — is just as important to the firm as having the foresight and the commitment to achieve the vision. Somewhere just beyond the horizon of vision and before the hard edge of strategy kicks in begins the leader's work of setting strategic goals and objectives for the organization. This activity calls for disciplined thinking to narrow the organization's focus.

Jim Collins, who presented the traits of eleven outstanding companies in his book *Good to Great*, maintains that focused, disciplined thought is a common element of good-to-great leaders and their companies. Great leaders focus their firms on a single, organizing idea that unifies and guides all decisions. They boil down complexities into simple ideas that answer three questions: (1) What can we do best? (2) What is the economic denominator that drives our business? (3) What do our core people care passionately about? It is the leader's job to ask these questions, even if others produce the answers.

The leader sets measurable goals and objectives for the organization. A goal or objective for which attainment cannot be measured is worthless. The leader makes measurable goals effective by building in incentives for attainment, what Jim Collins describes as "catalytic mechanisms." These incentives reward goal-attaining behavior, discourage the opposite, and thus make strategy "happen" by virtue of their self-enforcement power, but they must be created to fit the organization. Consider Granite Rock's short pay policy: every invoice that the gravel company issues includes a statement that if the customer is not satisfied for any reason, they simply do not pay for the line item and they do not need to return it. It is easy to imagine how a "short paid" invoice provides enormous incentive to fix quality or delivery problems immediately, thus moving Granite Rock toward its goal of customer satisfaction. Granite Rock's short pay policy, 3M's 15 percent discretionary time, and Nucor Steel's production bonus system, all mechanisms designed to incentivize desired behavior, were developed to work within their respective organizations. When the leaders establish goals and build in incentives that reward attainment, the organization moves to achieve them.

Crafting a Strategy

The leader must now ask the question, "How are we as a firm going to employ our resources to achieve our goals?" Taking a strategic position means accepting that there will be trade-offs with other positions. It also means choosing what not to do, as well as what to do, because no company can compete successfully in every business segment featuring every variation of product or service. "The essence of strategy is choosing what not to do", says Michael Porter, groundbreaking author of *Competitive Strategy* and creator of the "five forces" model of competition. Tough choices must be made, and the leader must be the one to force the issue.

But crafting strategy is not all top-down. Gary Hamel asserts that "revolutionary" strategy-making involves getting to the "revolutionaries" who are embedded in every organization and involving them in the strategy-making process. He advocates taking a "diagonal slice" through the organization to pick up these revolutionaries who exist at every level and across every function. Furthermore, the leader should make sure that three kinds of people participate in strategy-making: the young, those who are new to the firm, and those on the "periphery", that is, the geographic boundaries of the business. Why these people? Because they are the ones — together with those picked up in the diagonal slice — who are certain to have the most revolutionary ideas for the company. They are the ones most likely to challenge the assumptions that the senior managers have all been taught to share. They are the most likely to redefine the industry by challenging its accepted beliefs. Such challenges require an attitude of humility and openness from the leader who crafts strategy for the firm.

In the end, it is the leader's job to define the company's strategic position and make the trade-offs. Instead of broadening into every segment in which profits may be earned, the leader focuses the company on deepening its strategic position and communicates the strategy externally to customers who value it, as well as internally to the firm. Taking a strategic position that delivers value and communicating that value inside and out are the core leadership tasks in crafting strategy.

Executing the Strategy

Leaders have primary responsibility for implementing the chosen strategy. While an action plan involves many discrete tasks, at the core the leader must build an organization that can carry out the strategy. The leader builds both an organizational culture and an organizational capability for executing strategy.

The "Southwest Spirit" is a positive, fun-loving, can-do approach to the job of flying passengers to their destinations. The company promotes two core values: LUV (love) and fun. LUV, the company's ticker symbol, has to do with treating employees and customers with courtesy, caring, and respect. Former CEO Herb Kelleher took a different tack than most company executives do by insisting that the employees come first, the customer second. He reasoned that by treating employees well, they would be happier in their jobs and would in turn treat customers well.

However, it would be naïve to think that Southwest Airlines is successful solely because of a good company culture. Kelleher and his management team drove the company hard to squeeze cost out of every activity, from ticketing through baggage handling, and achieved distinctive capabilities that rivals have not been able to imitate. The Southwest Spirit undergirds this competitive capability with a company culture that, taken together, has made the airline consistently profitable.

Concepts that provide a simple framework for the leader who would implement good strategy are: (1) embed strategy in the organization's culture while focusing the organization on a few key strategic capabilities; (2) build a good team, and (3) remember that any strategy is temporary at best, so watch the environment and make adjustments in the organization as needed.

Evaluating Performance

How does the firm keep its strategy fresh? By keeping both the organization and its leadership agile. Gary Hamel and Liisa Vlikangas coined the term "strategic resilience" to describe the firm's ability to continuously anticipate and adjust to trends that can permanently impair the earning power of the company. The goal is a resilient organization that is "constantly making its future rather than defending its past."

In the face of rapid change, the firm must conquer denial, nostalgia, and arrogance by cultivating good habits, such as visiting the places where change is taking place and getting to the real ideas and opinions of those who make change. The leader recognizes that even the best strategy decays with time and has to be renewed or altogether reinvented. Competitors, market forces, and technology changes cause such decay. Astute leaders must keep their eyes open in order to accurately and honestly appraise strategy decay as it occurs.

At the same time, the leader must see that there is an adequate supply of options that can be cultivated into full-fledged strategies to replace the decaying ones. These may start out as small stakes bets; the most promising ones are then selected and funded to full development. The more strategy options that are created in this fashion, the more resilient the firm will be in the face of change. The agile leader must nurture this process of renewal that replaces decay.

Can active inertia be prevented? Yes! When a company finds itself challenged in the marketplace, instead of asking, "What should we do?" the leader should pause and ask, "What hinders us?" By reframing the question, the leader shifts focus to the strategic framework, activities, and patterns of behavior that by force of habit can channel energy in the wrong direction.

However, the leader should not try to change everything at once, since everything is probably not all bad. In trying to uproot everything, managers often destroy more than they create in crucial competencies and social relationships, thereby disorienting employees and alienating customers in the process. A company's strategic vision can shift in subtle ways over time, so the wise leader must consciously re-ask the questions, "What are we all about and where are we going?" and then, "Are we going where we need to go?"

Second Thoughts

1) Can you retell the five important roles leaders play in forming and implementing strategy in your own words?

_____

_____

2) Do you have any other ideas about the roles that leaders play in strategy? Write down your ideas.

_____

_____

3) Do you know any famous leaders? Discuss his/her role in the related field with your partner.

_____

_____

Organization of International Business

国际企业的组织结构

本章概要

本章主要介绍国际企业的组织结构的含义、要素、类型,以及建立有效组织结构的关键,介绍联合利华的组织结构特点,以谷歌为例说明企业文化的重要性,并介绍有效组织变革管理的原因和六大步骤。

学习指南

　　组织结构是一个系统,它概述如何通过执行某些特定的活动去实现组织目标。这些活动可以包括规则、角色和职责。组织结构也决定了信息在公司各层级之间如何流转。例如,在集中化的组织结构中,决策从上到下进行传达;而在一个非集中化的组织结构中,决策权分散在各个层级。适当的组织结构可使企业高效运转、目标明确。

　　通过本章学习,希望大家能够实现以下目标:

（1）基本目标（Text-based Goals）

- 掌握本章涉及话题的基本专业术语及词汇,如组织结构、空心组织、模块化组织、虚拟组织、矩阵结构等;
- 掌握本章的主要知识点,即国际企业的组织结构的含义、要素、类型,以及建立有效组织结构的关键等。

（2）拓展目标（Extended Goals）

- 思考本章引言,为什么李卡多·赛姆勒认为"一个公司必须有一个以变革为基本前提的组织结构,让公司文化蓬勃发展,并培养一种源于尊重而非规则的力量"?
- 通过学习背景知识、拓展阅读、案例分析,进一步了解国际企业的企业文化,思考如何做好组织变革管理。

> To survive in modern times, a company must have an organizational structure that accepts change as its basic premise, lets tribal customs thrive, and fosters a power that is derived from respect, not rules.（为了在现代社会生存，一个公司必须有一个以变革为基本前提的组织结构，让公司文化蓬勃发展，并培养一种源于尊重而非规则的力量。）
>
> —Ricardo Semler（李卡多·赛姆勒）

What Is an Organizational Structure?

什么是组织结构?

组织结构是一个系统，它规定如何通过执行某些特定的活动去实现组织目标。这些活动可以包括规则、角色和职责。

吉尔·考金达尔认为"糟糕的组织设计和结构导致了令人困惑的矛盾泥潭：角色内部的混乱、职能之间缺乏协调、无法分享想法、决策制定缓慢等，给管理者带来了不必要的麻烦、压力和冲突。"

An organizational structure is a system that outlines how certain activities are directed in order to achieve the goals of an organization. These activities can include rules, roles, and responsibilities. The organizational structure also determines how information flows between levels within the company. For example, in a centralized structure, decisions flow from the top down, while in a decentralized structure, decision-making power is distributed among various levels of the organization. Having an organizational structure in place allows companies to remain efficient and focused.

"Poor organizational design and structure results in a bewildering morass of contradictions: confusion within roles, a lack of coordination among functions, failure to share ideas, and slow decision making bring managers unnecessary complexity, stress and conflict", wrote Gill Corkindale in the *Harvard Business Review*.

Key Elements of an Organizational Structure

组织结构的关键要素
① 部门化
② 指挥链
③ 控制幅度
④ 集权与分权
⑤ 工作分工
⑥ 正规化

An ineffective structure can cause significant problems for a company, including lost profits, rapid employee turnover and loss in productivity. Management experts use the six basic elements of the organizational structure to devise the right plan for a specific company. These elements are: departmentalization, chain of command, span of control, centralization or decentralization, work specialization and the degree of formalization. Each of these elements affects how workers engage with each other, management and their jobs in order to achieve the employer's goals.

DEPARTMENTALIZATION

Departmentalization refers to how the organizational structure groups the company's functions, offices and teams.

Those individual groups are typically referred to as departments. Departments are usually sorted on the basis of the kinds of tasks that workers in each department perform, but this is not the only way to create a company's departmental breakdown. You could also divide the business into groups based on product or brand lines, geographic locations or even customer needs.

CHAIN OF COMMAND

Most organizations, from businesses to nonprofits to the military, utilize a chain of command. This helps eliminate inefficiencies by having each employee report to a single manager, instead of to several bosses. In the corporate context, this type of chain of command is reflected in the organizational structure and affects job descriptions as well as office **hierarchies**. Managers assign tasks, communicate expectations and deadlines to employees, and provide motivation on a one-to-many basis.

When employees encounter obstacles or problems, they report back to the appropriate manager. When necessary, the manager is then responsible for taking the concern or issue up the chain of command to the next level, and so forth. This chain of authority or command **streamlines** corporate operations and communications for a more efficient and productive business.

SPAN OF CONTROL

An organization's span of control defines how many employees each manager is responsible for within the company. There is no single type of span of control that's ideal for all companies or even for all businesses in a specific industry. The optimal span will depend on a number of factors, including the size of the workforce, how the company is divided into departments and even the company's specific business goals and strategies.

CENTRALIZATION AND DECENTRALIZATION

Organizational structures also rest somewhere on a spectrum of centralization. Generally, more conservative corporate entities adopt a centralized structure. In this design, C-level managers make all the decisions, management designs a plan for execution and front-line employees carry out that plan. C-level officers are generally those at the uppermost level of the organizational chart, such as the chief executive officer, chief operating officer and chief marketing officer.

Centralizing authority in a business means that middle management typically is left with little to no input about the goals the company sets. This system is typical in larger corporate organizations, as well as at companies in more conservative industries. On the other hand, a company could adopt a more decentralized approach. A decentralized system allows all levels of management the opportunity to give input on **big-vision** goals and objectives. Larger, company-wide decisions are still generally reserved to C-level officers, but departmental managers enjoy a greater degree of latitude in how their teams operate.

Word Study

hierarchy /ˈhaɪərɑːki/ n. 等级，分类
streamline /ˈstriːmlaɪn/ v. 使（企业、组织等）简化并更有效率
big-vision /bɪɡˈvɪʒən/ adj. 远大前景的

WORK SPECIALIZATION

In any business, employees at all levels typically are given a description of their duties and the expectations that come with their positions. In larger companies, job descriptions are generally formally adopted **in writing**. This approach helps ensure that the company's specific workforce needs are met, without any unnecessary duplication of effort. Work specialization ensures that all employees have specific duties that they are expected to perform based on each employee's work experience, education and skills. This prevents an expectation that employees will perform tasks for which they have no previous experience or training and to keep them from performing beneath their capacities.

FORMALIZATION

Finally, organizational structures implement some degree of formalization. This element outlines interorganizational relationships. Formalization is the element that determines the company's procedures, rules and guidelines as adopted by management. Formalization also determines company culture aspects, such as whether employees have to sign in and out upon arriving and exiting the office, how many breaks workers can take and how long those breaks can be, how and when employees can use company computers and how workers at all levels are expected to dress for work.

Types of Organizational Structures

Organizational structures can be tall, in the sense that there are a number of **tiers** between entry-level employees and the leaders of the company. Organizational structures can also be fairly flat, in the sense that there are only a couple of levels separating the bottom from the top. Depending on your goals, pay structure, and division of work, you may relate more to one structure than another. While you don't necessarily have to use an organizational structure that currently exists, it helps to be aware of what other companies are using. Here are a few of the most common structures in modern businesses.

VERTICAL STRUCTURES (FUNCTIONAL AND DIVISIONAL)

Two main types of vertical structures exist, functional and divisional. The functional structure divides work and employees by specialization. It is a hierarchical, usually vertically integrated structure. It emphasizes standardization in organization and processes for specialized employees in relatively narrow jobs.

A *functional* organizational chart might look something like this:

Word Study

in writing 以书面形式
（作为凭证）
tier /tɪə/ *n.* 层，级

组织结构的类型
　　组织结构既可以层级很多，也可以相对扁平。企业的组织结构主要从以下三大层面分类：（1）垂直式结构；（2）矩阵式结构；（3）开放边界结构。每种分类都有其各自的优缺点。

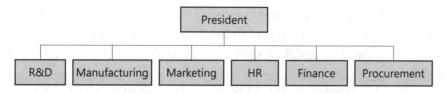

Fig. 10.1 Functional structure

This traditional type of organization forms departments such as production, sales, research and development, accounting, HR, and marketing. Each department has a separate function and specializes in that area. For example, all HR are part of the same function and report to a senior leader of HR. The same reporting process would be true for other functions, such as finance or operations. In functional structures, employees report directly to managers within their functional areas who in turn report to a chief officer of the organization. Management from above must centrally coordinate the specialized departments.

Advantages of a functional structure include the following: The organization develops experts in its respective areas; Individuals perform only tasks in which they are most proficient.

Disadvantages center on coordination or lack thereof: People are in specialized "silos" and often fail to coordinate or communicate with other departments; Cross-functional activity is more difficult to promote; The structure tends to be resistant to change.

This structure works best for organizations that remain centralized (i.e., a majority of the decision-making occurs at higher levels of the organization) because there are few shared concerns or objectives between functional areas (e.g., marketing, production, purchasing, IT). Given the centralized decision-making, the organization can take advantage of economies of scale in that there are likely centralized purchasing functions. An appropriate management system to coordinate the departments is essential. The management system may be a special leader, like a vice president, a computer system or some other format.

A *divisional* organizational chart might look something like this:

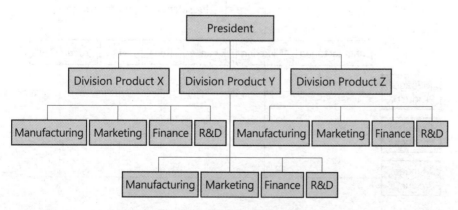

Fig. 10.2 Divisional structure

Word Study

variable /'veərɪəbl/ *n.*
变量
catalog /'kætəlɒg/ *n.*
（商品）目录
duplication
/ˌdjuːplɪ'keɪʃən/ *n.*
（不必要的）重复
matrix /'meɪtrɪks/ *n.*
矩阵

Also a vertical arrangement, a divisional structure most often divides work and employees by output, although a divisional structure could be divided by another **variable** such as market or region. For example, a business that sells men', women' and children' clothing through retail, e-commerce and **catalog** sales in the Northeast, Southeast and Southwest could be using a divisional structure in one of three ways:

Product — men' wear, women' wear and children' clothing.

Market — retail store, e-commerce and catalog.

Region — Northeast, Southeast and Southwest.

The advantages of this type of structure are the following: It provides more focus and flexibility on each division's core competency; It allows the divisions to focus on producing specialized products while also using knowledge gained from related divisions; It allows for more coordination than the functional structure; Decision-making authority pushed to lower levels of the organization enables faster, customized decisions.

The disadvantages of this structure include the following:

It can result in a loss of efficiency and a **duplication** of effort because each division needs to acquire the same resources; Each division often has its own research and development, marketing, and other units that could otherwise be helping each other; Employees with similar technical career paths have less interaction; Divisions may be competing for the same customers; Each division often buys similar supplies in smaller quantities and may pay more per item.

This type of structure is helpful when the product base expands in quantity or complexity. But when competition among divisions becomes significant, the organization is not adapting quickly enough, or when economies of scale are lacking, the organization may require a more sophisticated **matrix** structure.

MATRIX ORGANIZATIONAL STRUCTURES

A typical *matrix* organizational structure might look like this:

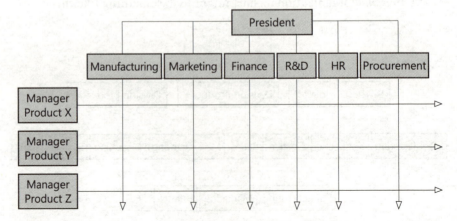

Fig. 10.3 Matrix organizational structure

A matrix structure combines the functional and divisional structures to create a dual-command situation. In a matrix structure, an employee reports to two managers who are jointly responsible for the employee's performance. Typically, one manager works in an administrative function, such as finance, HR, information technology, sales or marketing, and the other works in a business unit related to a product, service, customer or geography.

Advantages of the matrix structure include the following: It creates a functional and divisional partnership and focuses on the work more than on the people; It minimizes costs by sharing key people; It creates a better balance between time of completion and cost; It provides a better overview of a product that is manufactured in several areas or sold by various subsidiaries in different markets.

Disadvantages of matrix organizations include the following: Responsibilities may be unclear, thus complicating governance and control; Reporting to more than one manager at a time can be confusing for the employee and supervisors; The dual chain of command requires cooperation between two direct supervisors to determine an employee's work priorities, work assignments and performance standards.

Matrix structures are common in heavily project-driven organizations, such as construction companies. These structures have grown out of project structures in which employees from different functions formed teams until completing a project, and then **reverted** to their own functions. In a matrix organization, each project manager reports directly to the vice president and the general manager. Each project is, in essence, a mini profit center, and therefore, general managers usually make business decisions.

OPEN BOUNDARY STRUCTURES (**HOLLOW**, **MODULAR** AND VIRTUAL)

More recent trends in structural forms remove the traditional boundaries of an organization. Typical internal and external barriers and organizational boxes are eliminated, and all organizational units are effectively and flexibly connected. Teams replace departments, and the organization and suppliers work as closely together as parts of one company. The hierarchy is flat; status and rank are minimal. Everyone — including top management, managers and employees — participates in the decision-making process.

Advantages of boundary-less organizations include the following: Ability to **leverage** all employees' talents; Faster response to market changes; Enhanced cooperation and information sharing among functions, divisions and staff.

Disadvantages include the following: Difficulty in overcoming silos inside the organization; Lack of strong leadership and common vision; Time-consuming processes; The possibility of employees being adversely affected by efficient efforts; The possibility of organizations abandoning change if restructuring does not improve effectiveness quickly.

Boundary-less organizational structures can be created in varied

Word Study

revert /rɪˈvɜːt/ v. 恢复，回到
hollow /ˈhɒləʊ/ adj. 空心的
modular /ˈmɒdjʊlə/ adj. 模块化的
leverage /ˈlevərɪdʒ/ v. 充分利用

payroll /'peɪrəʊl/ *n.*
工资名单
subtract /səb'trækt/ *v.*
扣除，减去
exceptional /ɪk'sepʃənl/
adj. 罕见的，特别的
autocratic /ˌɔːtə'krætɪk/
adj. 专制的，专横的
misaligned /ˌmɪsə'laɪnd/
adj. 方向偏离的，
未对准的

forms, including hollow, modular and virtual organizations.

Hollow organizations

Hollow structures divide work and employees by core and non-core competencies. Hollow structures are an outsourcing model in which the organization maintains its core processes internally but outsources non-core processes. Hollow structures are most effective when the industry is price competitive and choices for outsourcing exist. An example of a hollow structure is a sports organization that has its HR functions (e.g., **payroll** and benefits) handled by outside organizations.

Modular organizations

Modular structures differ from hollow organizations in that components of a product are outsourced. Modular structures may keep a core part of the product in-house and outsource non-core portions of the product. Networks are added or **subtracted** as needs change. For a modular structure to be an option, the product must be able to be broken into chunks. For example, computer manufacturer Dell buys parts from various suppliers and assembles them at one central location. Suppliers at one end and customers at the other become part of the organization; the organization shares information and innovations with all. Customization of products and services results from flexibility, creativity, teamwork and responsiveness. Business decisions are made at corporate, divisional, project and individual team member levels.

Virtual organizations

A virtual organization is cooperation among companies, institutions or individuals delivering a product or service under a common business understanding. Organizations form partnerships with others — often competitors — that complement each other. The collaborating units present themselves as a unified organization.

Virtual structures are collaborative and created to respond to an **exceptional** and often temporary marketing opportunity. The key to effective boundary-less organizations is placing adaptable employees at all levels. Management must give up traditional **autocratic** control to coach employees toward creativity and the achievement of organizational goals. Employees must apply initiative and creativity to benefit the organization, and reward systems should recognize such employees.

Problems Created by a Misaligned Organizational Structure

**组织结构失调会造成
的问题**
　　业务单位、部门
或职能的快速重组
可能导致无效、错位
的组织结构，不利于
企业发展。构思欠
佳的重组可能会产
生四项重大问题。

Rapid reorganization of business units, divisions or functions can lead to ineffective, misaligned organizational structures that do not support the business. Poorly conceived reorganizations may create significant problems, including the following:

- Structural gaps in roles, work processes, accountabilities and critical information flows can occur when companies eliminate middle management levels without eliminating the work, forcing employees to take on additional responsibilities.

- Diminished capacity, capability and **agility** issues can arise when a) lower-level employees who step in when middle management is eliminated are ill-equipped to perform the required duties b) when higher-level executives must take on more **tactical** responsibilities, minimizing the value of their leadership skills.

- Disorganization and improper staffing can affect a company's cost structure, cash flow and ability to deliver goods or services. Agile organizations can rapidly **deploy** people to address shifting business needs. With resources cut to the bone, however, most organizations' staff members can focus only on their immediate responsibilities, leaving little time, energy or desire to work outside their current job scope. Ultimately, diminished capacity and **lagging** response times affect an organization's ability to remain competitive.

- Declining workforce engagement can reduce **retention**, decrease customer loyalty and limit organizational performance and stakeholder value.

The Importance of Aligning the Structure with the Business Strategy

The key to profitable performance is the extent to which four business elements are aligned:

- Leadership. The individuals responsible for developing and deploying the strategy and monitoring results.
- Organization. The structure, processes and operations by which the strategy is deployed.
- Jobs. The necessary roles and responsibilities.
- People. The experience, skills and competencies needed to execute the strategy.

An understanding of the inter-dependencies of these business elements and the need for them to adapt to change quickly and strategically are essential for success in the high-performance organization. When these four elements are **in sync**, outstanding performance is more likely.

The organizational design process is the pivotal connector between the business of the organization (e.g., top-level leadership and organizational strategy and goals) and forms of HR support (e.g., workflow process design, selection, development and compensation). Strategy must continually drive structure and people decisions, and the structure and design must reflect and enable effective leadership.

Achieving alignment and sustaining organizational capacity requires

Word Study

agility /əˈdʒɪləti/ n.
灵敏性,敏捷
tactical /ˈtæktɪkəl/
adj. 战术上的,策略上的
deploy /dɪˈplɔɪ/ v. 部署,调动
lag /læg/ v. 滞后,发展缓慢
retention /rɪˈtenʃən/ n.
(员工)保留,(员工)留任
in sync 同步,一致

结构与业务战略保持一致的重要性
　　盈利绩效的关键在于四个业务要素的协调程度,分别是领导力、组织、职位、人员。了解这些业务要素之间的相互依赖性,以及它们快速、战略性地适应变化的必要性,对于高绩效组织的成功至关重要。

Word Study

recalibrate /rɪˈkælɪˌbreɪt/
v. 重新校准,再调整
scale back 相应缩减
metric /ˈmetrɪk/ n. 标
准,指标
subordinate /səˈbɔːdɪnət/
n. 下级,部属

time and critical thinking. Organizations must identify outcomes the new structure or process is intended to produce. This typically requires **recalibrating** the following:

- Which work is mission-critical, can be **scaled back** or should be eliminated
- Existing role requirements, while identifying necessary new or modified roles
- Key **metrics** and accountabilities
- Critical information flows
- Decision-making authority by organization level

Keys to Erecting an Effective Organizational Structure

All sorts of different organizational structures have been proven effective in contributing to business success. Some firms choose highly centralized, rigidly maintained structures, while others — perhaps even in the same industrial sector — develop decentralized, loose arrangements. Both of these organizational types can survive and even thrive. There is no best way to design an organization or type of structure. Each depends upon the company involved, its needs and goals, and even the personalities of the individuals involved in the case of small businesses. The type of business in which an organization is involved is also a factor in designing an effective organizational structure. Organizations operate in different environments with different products, strategies, constraints, and opportunities, each of which may influence the design of an ideal organizational structure. But despite the wide variety of organizational structures that can be found in the business world, the successful ones tend to share certain characteristics. Indeed, business experts cite a number of characteristics that separate effective organizational structures from ineffective designs. Recognition of these factors is especially important for entrepreneurs and established small business owners, since these individuals play such a pivotal role in determining the final layout of their enterprises.

As business owners weigh their various options in this realm, they should make sure that the following factors are taken into consideration:

- Relative strengths and weaknesses of various organizational forms
- Legal advantages and disadvantages of organizational structure options
- Advantages and drawbacks of departmentalization options
- Likely growth patterns of the company
- Reporting relationships that are currently in place
- Reporting and authority relationships that you hope will be implemented in the future
- Optimum ratios of supervisors/managers to **subordinates**
- Suitable level of autonomy/empowerment to be granted to employees at various levels of the organization (while still recognizing individual capacities for independent work)
- Structures that will produce greatest worker satisfaction
- Structures that will produce optimum operational efficiency

centralized structure 集权结构　　decentralized structure 分权结构
chain of command 指挥链　　　　span of control 控制幅度
work specialization 工作分工　　departmental breakdown 部门划分
functional structure 职能型结构　divisional structure 事业部型结构
matrix structure 矩阵型结构　　open boundany structure 开放边界型结构
hollow organization 空心组织　　modular organization 模块化组织
virtual organization 虚拟组织

虚拟经济与跨国公司组织结构

　　20世纪90年代，在企业竞争环境改变与组织能力发展的推动下，越来越多的跨国公司开始注重组织结构的调整和优化，各种类型的跨国组织形式被提及和应用。比如，大量跨国公司从塔形层级结构中解放出来，向着扁平化与网络化的方向行进，其内部资源与能力也发生了变化，而这必然要求跨国公司的组织模式对其海外企业的治理与控制做出相应改变，以适应企业跨国发展的需要。

　　在全球化视野下，跨国公司的生产经营活动范围越来越广泛，原始的实体经济模式中已经越来越多地渗入虚拟经济的成本。

　　在这种情况下，虚拟组织作为介于市场与企业之间的全新交易模式，在组织结构设计方面放弃了以实体结构为主的形态，就连法人实体也不再是唯一的。因此，为了达到更有效的全球化运营，越来越多的跨国公司开始在经济实体的基础上，基于特定的目标临时组建起大量联盟结构。

　　在这一组织形态下，跨国公司能够借助计算机网络、生产运作软件和虚拟现实技术等，把更多的跨国公司、供应商、经销商乃至客户等联系在一起。这样一来，跨国公司能够在资源共享的前提下，更好地选择适合自己的联盟伙伴，继而形成更具有竞争优势的产业链条与价值链，让跨国公司实现更健康、更经济的发展。

　　而之所以如此，是因为随着世界经济一体化与科学技术扩散化的影响，不断有跨国公司对其产业链和供应链进行重组，原有的实体经济因为固有的缺陷难以在链条上扮演重要角色，其组织结构模式也就逐渐呈现出虚拟化的趋势。这样一来，出于成本和收益的考虑，很多跨国公司放弃了技术创新组织及其相关的实体形态，转而按照市场机会和全球资源重新组建起虚拟的创新公司或者生产联合体，以达到共担风险、共享利益的目的。而一旦之前设定的目标得以实现，跨国公司的联盟和虚拟组织也就随之解散。

文献来源：

马晓瑜，汪占熬.当前跨国公司组织模式与结构演化研究[J].河南社会科学，2019（03）：87-92.

A. Describe the key elements of an organizational structure.

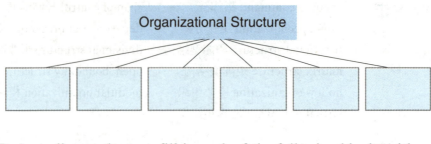

B. According to the text, fill in each of the following blanks with an appropriate word or phrase.

1) An _____ is a system that outlines how certain activities are directed in order to achieve the goals of an organization.

2) In a _____ structure, decisions flow from the top down, while in a decentralized structure, decision-making power is distributed among various levels of the organization.

3) An _____ structure can cause significant problems for a company, including lost profits, rapid employee turnover and loss in productivity.

4) An organizational structure includes six key elements: _____ _____, chain of command, span of control, centralization or decentralization, work specialization and the degree of _____.

5) Managers assign tasks, communicate expectations and deadlines to employees, and provide motivation on a _____ basis.

6) An organization's _____ defines how many employees each manager is responsible for within the company.

7) Generally, more _____ corporate entities adopt a centralized structure.

8) A _____ system allows all levels of management the opportunity to give input on big-vision goals and objectives.

9) In any business, employees are given a _____ of their jobs and the _____ that come with their positions.

10) Formalization is the element that determines the company's procedures, rules and _____ as adopted by management.

C. Read the text and decide whether the following statements are True (T) or False (F).

1) A divisional structure emphasizes standardization in organization and processes for specialized employees in relatively narrow jobs. (   )

2) In functional structures, employees report directly to managers within their functional areas who in turn report to a chief officer of the organization.
(   )

3) In a functional organization, an appropriate management system to coordinate the departments is not necessary. (   )

4) Employees with similar technical career paths have less interaction and this is one of the disadvantages of a functional structure.   (   )
5) When economies of scale are lacking, an organization may require a more sophisticated matrix structure.   (   )
6) In a matrix organization, each project manager reports directly to the general manager who reports to the vice president.   (   )
7) Boundaryless organizational structures can be created in varied forms, including hollow, modular and virtual organizations.   (   )
8) An example of a virtual structure is a sports organization that has its HR functions handled by outside organizations.   (   )
9) The fact that components of a product are outsourced is the main difference between modular structures and hollow organizations.   (   )
10) A virtual organization is cooperation among companies, institutions or individuals delivering a product or service under a common business understanding.   (   )

1) What's your understanding of an organizational structure?

_____

_____

2) How many types of organizational structures are illustrated in the text? Please retell them with your own words.

_____

_____

3) What are the advantages and disadvantages of each type of the organizational structures? Please give a brief summery.

_____

_____

4) What problems would be created by a misaligned organizational structure?

_____

_____

5) Can you give some examples of multinational enterprises with a successful or failed organizational structure respectively? Share with your partner.

_____

_____

Case Story

Unilever's Organizational Structure for Product Innovation

These days, Unilever is often described as one of the foremost transnational companies. When Unilever was founded in 1930 as a Dutch-British company, it produced soap, processed foods, and a wide array of other consumer goods in many countries. Ever since then, the company has evolved mainly through a Darwinian system of retaining what was useful and rejecting what no longer worked — in other words, through actual practice as a business responding to the marketplace. In essence, Unilever's story, idiosyncratic though it may be, is one example of how a single company has come to manage far-flung units that share a common culture. Over the course of its particular lifetime, the company has successfully weathered numerous changes.

Unilever's corporate structure is responsible for ensuring adequate support for product innovation in the firm's global business. A company's organizational structure or corporate structure is the design that defines the arrangement and systems used to build and interconnect various organizational components, such as offices and teams. Unilever's organizational structure adapts to changes in the consumer goods industry and global market. At present, the company maintains a structure that addresses corporate needs in terms of managing product types across the world. As a leading consumer goods firm, Unilever has an organizational structure that suitably supports diversified global operations.

Features of Unilever's Organizational Structure

The following are the main characteristics of Unilever's organizational structure:
- Product type divisions
- A matrix of managers
- Geographic divisions

Product Type Divisions

A product type division functions as a unit that enables Unilever to manage the development, manufacturing, distribution and sale of its consumer goods. For example, corporate managers use this feature of the organizational structure to match markets needs with appropriate products. An advantage of this structural characteristic is its facilitation of the company's efforts to apply product differentiation, which is Unilever's generic strategy for competitive advantage. This corporate structure is beneficial, especially because the company already has a diverse portfolio of products. Unilever maintains the following product type divisions in its organizational structure: Foods; Refreshment; Personal Care; Home Care.

A Matrix of Managers

Since the 1950s, Unilever has pioneered new managerial selection systems in western Europe. And in many developing countries, it used advanced methods to recruit the best university graduates. For instance, teams of Unilever managers are charged with spotting talent in local universities at an early stage; or prizes were given for work done by young scientists to make contact with them. The company also sponsored an extensive program of business courses for university students in many countries, from Turkey to the United Kingdom. Through these courses, Unilever instructors and students got to know each other, determining what they had in common. Every candidate who survived this initial screening was then reviewed by a panel of senior managers, which often included board members from the parent company.

The greatest challenge of recruiting, of course, was to find the best and brightest who would fit into the company. They certainly did not want a homo unileverensis; but for international careers in their current operating companies, they looked for people who could work in teams and understand the value of cooperation and consensus. For managerial trainees, preparation included both on-the-job experience and courses at Four Acres. In fact, many have joked that Unilever is really a management education institute financed by soap and margarine. The courses go beyond teaching specific subjects like "Edible Oil Refining" or "Developments in the Retail Trade." They also offered the "International Management Seminar" and the "Senior Management Course." These general courses were often taught by visiting professors from well-known business schools, with Unilever instructors participating occasionally.

In a company with a product portfolio of fast-moving consumer goods, it's also useful for young managers to work in more than one product group. Clearly, not all of the creative ideas used to market skin cream were applicable to instant soups, but a surprising number of good ideas resulted from cross-fertilization between product groups. Of course, they did not design their extensive system of recruitment, training, and attachments with the idea of forming a "transnational network." However, in practice, this network — as represented by both the company's formal structure and the informal exchanges between managers — might well be one of the ingredients in the glue that held Unilever together.

Geographic Divisions

Geographic divisions are another feature of Unilever's organizational structure. The company uses this structural characteristic to support regional strategies. For example, Unilever's marketing strategies for Europe are different from strategies applied for Asian consumer goods markets. Also, this corporate structure feature is used to analyze the company's financial performance. The following geographic divisions are maintained in Unilever's organizational structure: Asia/AMET/RUB (Africa, Middle East, Turkey; Russia, Ukraine, Belarus); The Americas; Europe.

Unilever's Corporate Structure — Advantages, Disadvantages and Implications

An advantage of Unilever's organizational structure is its support for product development and innovation. For example, each product type division has its semi-autonomous capabilities to develop products that directly suit the needs in consumer goods market segments. This corporate structure is also advantageous because it enables Unilever to differentiate its products despite the large size of its global operations.

A disadvantage of Unilever's organizational structure is its minimal support for regional strategic implementation. Even though geographic divisions are one of its structural features, the company focuses more on product type divisions. As a result, there is limited support for market-specific or regional strategic reforms. Thus, to improve this organizational structure, a recommendation is that Unilever must increase its emphasis on geographic divisions to empower regional managerial teams. Such structural change improves strategic effectiveness in regional consumer goods markets.

Case Discussion

1) Why is Unilever often described as one of the foremost transnational companies?

   _____

   _____

2) How a matrix of managers help Unilever succeed?

   _____

   _____

3) Are there any other advantages or disadvantages of Unilever's corporate structure? Discuss with your partner.

   _____

   _____

Case Summary

如今,联合利华常被称为最重要的跨国公司之一。

联合利华的组织结构负责确保为公司全球业务中的产品创新提供足够的支持。作为一家领先的消费品公司,联合利华的组织结构适合多元化的全球业务。

　　本文主要介绍了联合利华的组织结构的特点以及其优缺点。第一，联合利华有一个根据产品类型进行划分的部门组织结构。一个产品类型部门负责该产品的开发、制造、分销和销售，方便联合利华管理。第二，联合利华在招募、培养经理层方面，比较重视跨国家、跨文化、跨产品类型，培养了具备多样化背景的经理团队。第三，地域划分是联合利华组织结构的另一个特点。该公司利用这一结构特征来支持区域战略。

　　联合利华的组织结构有其优缺点。优点主要包括支持产品开发和创新，使联合利华能够在全球业务规模庞大的情况下，使其产品与众不同。缺点体现在对区域战略实施的支持很少，对特定市场或区域战略改革的支持有限。

Reading
Expansion
拓展阅读

Reading I

What Is Organizational Culture?
And Why Should We Care? — Taking Google

If you want to provoke a vigorous debate, start a conversation on organizational culture. While there is universal agreement that (1) it exists, and (2) that it plays a crucial role in shaping behavior in organizations, there is little consensus on what organizational culture actually is, never mind how it influences behavior and whether it is something leaders can change.

This is a problem, because without a reasonable definition (or definitions) of culture, we cannot hope to understand its connections to other key elements of the organization, such as structure and incentive systems. Nor can we develop good approaches to analyzing, preserving and transforming cultures. If we can define what organizational culture is, it gives us a handle on how to diagnose problems and even to design and develop better cultures.

"Organizational culture is civilization in the workplace." — Alan Adler

Culture is a social control system. Here the focus is the role of culture in promoting and reinforcing the "right" thinking and behavior, and sanctioning the "wrong" thinking and behavior. Key in this definition of culture is the idea of behavioral "norms" that must be upheld, and associated social sanctions that are imposed on those who don't "stay within the lines". This view also focuses attention on how the evolution of the organization shaped the culture. That is, how have the existing norms promoted the survival of the organization in the past?

"Culture is the organization's immune system." — Michael Watkins

Culture is a form of protection that has evolved from situational pressures. It prevents "wrong thinking" and "wrong people" from entering the organization in the first place. It says that organizational culture functions much like the human immune system in preventing viruses and bacteria from taking hold and damaging the body. The problem, of course, is that organizational immune systems also can attack agents of needed change, and this has important implications for on-boarding and integrating people into organizations.

"Organizational culture [is shaped by] the main culture of the society we live in, albeit with greater emphasis on particular parts of it." — *Elizabeth Skringar*

Organizational culture is shaped by and overlaps with other cultures — especially the broader culture of the societies in which it operates. This observation highlights the challenges that global organizations face in establishing and maintaining a unified culture when operating in the context of multiple national, regional and local cultures. How should leaders strike the right balance between promoting "one culture" in the organization, while still allowing for influences of local cultures?

Google's Organizational Culture & Its Characteristics

Google's organizational culture is a driving force that pushes the company to continue its leadership in the information technology and online advertising industries. Google's corporate culture motivates employees to share information for the purpose of supporting innovation. Innovation is a factor that enables the company to maintain its competitiveness against other technology businesses. Through its corporate culture, Google LLC ensures that its workforce is competent in addressing business needs linked to the external forces generated by the competitors. The corporation actively develops its cultural strengths through institutional measures, like training, and through informal approaches, such as personalized leadership and management support. Efforts to continuously improve the characteristics of Google's organizational culture are applied to maintain creativity and innovation.

The following characteristics define Google's corporate culture:
- Openness
- Innovation
- Excellence that comes with smartness
- Hands-on approach
- Small-company-family rapport

Openness. This cultural characteristic refers to the sharing of information among Google's employees. The company's objective in promoting openness is to encourage the dissemination of valuable knowledge that can support further innovation. For example, the corporate culture motivates individual employees to interact with each other at various times of their typical workday, as a way of improving the knowledge they use in their jobs. In relation, Google's operations management strategy supports this cultural trait through appropriate workplace layouts that facilitate such interaction. Also, the design of Google's organizational structure enhances the organizational culture by encouraging workers to communicate and share their ideas.

Innovation. Innovation is a critical success factor in Google's business. The company's organizational culture motivates employees to contribute to the overall innovation of the business and its products. For example, this cultural characteristic promotes employees' out-of-the-box thinking to discover or invent new solutions to current and emerging needs in the multinational market. Innovation contributes to business effectiveness in addressing the trends enumerated in the PESTEL/PESTLE analysis of Google LLC. This condition also means that the company's types and level of innovation changes according to the relevant needs identified in the information technology and services market.

Excellence. This cultural characteristic focuses on achieving excellent results from all areas of Google's business. This characteristic of the organizational culture is integrated in human resource development programs to inculcate an appreciation for excellence among employees. For example, training programs are designed to motivate workers to continually improve their output, and to not settle for mediocre results. In this regard, Google's corporate culture promotes smartness in the workforce, and pushes employees to strive for excellent work.

Hands-on Approach. Through its corporate culture, Google applies a hands-on approach to human resource development. This cultural characteristic focuses on using experiential learning as an effective way of improving employees' knowledge, skills, and abilities. Theoretical knowledge is not enough at Google LLC. Workers are expected to learn as they continue in their journey as part of the company's organization. In practice, this feature of the organizational culture is implemented through policies that support employees' involvement in projects and experiments. Such experiments test new ideas in support of innovation in product development that affect Google's marketing mix or 4P. In this way, the company's corporate culture enhances employees' experience, including on-the-job learning and training that contribute to human resource competencies.

Small-Company-Family Rapport. Google LLC is known for its support for small-company-family rapport in its workspaces. This cultural characteristic focuses on the social interactions among workers. For example, Google maintains a warm work environment where employees can easily talk and share ideas with each other. The objective in this case is to use the corporate culture as a way of optimizing internal communications and idea generation. This characteristic of the organizational culture also helps Google in optimizing employee morale. In theory, warm social relations in the workplace contribute to employee satisfaction in their jobs.

Second Thoughts

For each of the following statements, choose one (or more than one) answer to fill in the blank.

1) We try to define what organizational culture is, because it gives us a handle on _____.
   A. how to diagnose problems
   B. how to find out the methods
   C. how to know about the results
   D. how to foster and develop better cultures

2) Google's corporate culture motivates employees to share information so as to _____.
   A. make profits
   B. support innovation
   C. retain human resource
   D. cater for customers

Reading II

Effective Organizational Change Management

A change management plan can support a smooth transition and ensure your employees are guided through the change journey. The harsh fact is that approximately 70 percent of change initiatives fail due to negative employee attitudes and unproductive management behavior. Using the services of a professional change management consultant could ensure you are in the winning 30 percent.

Why Do Organizations Change?

An organizational change is the movement of an organization from one state of affairs to another. A change in the environment often requires change within the organization operating within that environment. A change in almost any aspect of a company's operation can be met with resistance, and different cultures can have different reactions to both the change and the means to promote the change. To better facilitate necessary changes, several steps can be taken that have been proved to lower the anxiety of employees and ease the transformation process. Often, the simple act of including employees in the change process can drastically reduce opposition to new methods. In some organizations, this level of inclusion is not possible, and instead organizations can recruit a small number of opinion leaders to promote the benefits of coming changes.

Organizational change can take many forms. It may involve a change in a company's structure, strategy, policies, procedures, technology, or culture. The change may be planned years in advance or may be forced on an organization because of a shift in the environment.

Workplace Demographics

Organizational change is often a response to changes to the environment. What does this mean for companies? Organizations may realize that as the workforce gets older, the types of benefits workers prefer may change. Work arrangements such as flexible work hours and job sharing may become more popular as employees remain in the workforce even after retirement.

Technology

Sometimes change is motivated by rapid developments in technology. Moore's law (a prediction by Gordon Moore, cofounder of Intel) dictates that the overall complexity of computers will double every 18 months with no increase in cost. Such change is motivating corporations to change their technology rapidly. Sometimes technology produces such profound developments that companies struggle to adapt.

Globalization

Globalization is another threat and opportunity for organizations, depending on their ability to adapt to it. Because of differences in national economies and standards of living from one country to another, organizations in developed countries are finding that it is often cheaper to produce goods and deliver services in less developed countries. This has led many companies to outsource (or "offshore") their manufacturing operations to countries such as Mexico.

Changes in the Market Conditions

Market changes may also create internal changes as companies struggle to adjust. For example, as of this writing, the airline industry in the United States is undergoing serious changes. At the same time, the widespread use of the Internet to book plane travels made it possible to compare airline prices much more efficiently and easily, encouraging airlines to compete primarily based on cost.

Steps to Effective Organizational Change Management

1. Clearly define the change and align it to business goals

It might seem obvious but many organizations miss this first vital step. It's one thing to articulate the change required and entirely another to conduct a critical review against organizational objectives and performance goals to ensure the change will carry your business in the right direction strategically, financially, and ethically. This step can also assist you to determine the value of the change, which will quantify the effort and inputs you should invest.

Key questions:

- What do we need to change?
- Why is this change required?

2. Determine impacts and those affected

Once you know exactly what you wish to achieve and why, you should then determine the impacts of the change at various organizational levels. Review the effect on each business unit and how it cascades through the organizational structure to the individual. This information will start to form the blueprint for where training and support is needed the most to mitigate the impacts.

Key questions:

- What are the impacts of the change?
- Who will the change affect the most?
- How will the change be received?

3. Develop a communication strategy

Although all employees should be taken on the change journey, the first two steps will have highlighted those employees you absolutely must communicate the change to. Determine the most effective means of communication for the group or individual that will bring them on board. The communication strategy should include a timeline for how the change will be incrementally communicated, key messages, and the communication channels and mediums you plan to use.

Key questions:

- How will the change be communicated?
- How will feedback be managed?

4. Provide effective training

With the change message out in the open, it's important that your people know they will receive training, structured or informal, to teach the skills and knowledge required to operate efficiently as the change is rolled out. Training could include a suite of micro-learning online modules, or a blended learning approach incorporating face-to-face training sessions or on-the-job coaching and mentoring.

Key questions:

- What behaviors and skills are required to achieve business results?
- What training delivery methods will be most effective?

5. Implement a support structure

Providing a support structure is essential to assist employees to emotionally and practically adjust to the change and to build proficiency of behaviors and technical skills needed to achieve desired business results. Some change can result in redundancies or restructures, so you could consider providing support such as counseling services to help people navigate the situation. To help employees adjust to changes to how a role is performed, a mentorship or an open-door policy with management to ask questions as they arise could be set up.

Key questions:
- Where is support most required?
- What types of support will be most effective?

6. Measure the change process

Throughout the change management process, a structure should be put in place to measure the business impact of the changes and ensure that continued reinforcement opportunities exist to build proficiencies. You should also evaluate your change management plan to determine its effectiveness and document any lessons learned.

Key questions:
- Did the change assist in achieving business goals?
- Was the change management process successful?
- What could have been done differently?

Second Thoughts

1) What is an organizational change? And what are the reasons for organizational changes?

_____

_____

2) Can you retell the steps to effective organizational change management? Summarize them with your own words.

_____

_____

Entry Strategy and Strategic Alliances

进入战略和战略联盟

本章概要

本章主要介绍国际企业的进入战略和战略联盟的含义、模式、类型、原因,以传音科技为例,分析海外市场进入战略、影响进入战略的因素、确保有效战略联盟的措施。

学习指南

从国内企业过渡到国际企业可能会很复杂,不了解相关细节的企业在进入国际市场时可能会举步维艰。

尽管投资另一个市场可能会有风险,需要大量资本,但回报也可能是巨大的。通过在另一个国家销售产品或服务,可以将其公司引入巨大的市场,增加销售和利润,获得品牌认可,降低仅在一个市场运营的风险(例如,经济或季节性衰退),并延长产品的生命周期。

通过本章学习,希望大家能够实现以下目标:

(1)基本目标(Text-based Goals)

- 掌握本章涉及话题的基本专业术语及词汇,如进入战略、战略联盟、竞争联盟等;
- 掌握本章的主要知识点,即进入战略和战略联盟的含义、模式、类型、原因。

(2)拓展目标(Extended Goals)

- 思考本章引言,为什么理查德·布兰森鼓励人们"去寻求战略联盟"?
- 通过学习背景知识、拓展阅读、案例分析进一步了解影响进入战略的因素、确保有效战略联盟的措施。

As a company's business grows and expands, it can reach a point where the executive board has to decide whether or not to enter new markets. Once a company is well established in its domestic market, it makes sense to start looking at foreign markets and considering market entry overseas. However, transitioning from a domestic business to an international one can be complicated, and companies that don't understand the details involved are likely to struggle when entering the international market.

Although investing in another market can be risky and require a lot of capital, the rewards can be huge. By selling your product or service in another country, you can introduce your company to huge markets, increase your sales and profits, gain brand recognition, reduce the risk of only operating in one market (e.g., due to economic or seasonal **downturns**) and extend your product's life cycle.

从国内企业过渡到国际企业可能会很复杂，不了解相关细节的企业在进入国际市场时可能会举步维艰。

尽管投资另一个市场可能会有风险，需要大量资本，但回报也可能是巨大的。通过在另一个国家销售产品或服务，可以将其公司引入巨大的市场，增加销售和利润，获得品牌认可，降低仅在一个市场运营的风险（例如，经济或季节性衰退），并延长产品的生命周期。

Basic Foreign Market Entry Decisions

A company looking to expand into foreign markets needs to consider three things as part of its entry strategy.

拓展海外市场的基本决策

一家公司想要拓展海外市场，需要考虑三件事：市场、时机、规模。

WHICH COUNTRY?

You may already have a country in mind, or you may simply have the idea of exporting but no idea where to. Start by making a list of countries you are interested in.

When you have a list, consider more carefully your product — is it suitable for any of the countries on your list? The culture, religion and law of each country are extremely important to consider here. Some countries are very conservative in comparison to the UK, so trying to export items such as clothes or alcohol may be **tricky.** The majority of the population in other countries may have certain dietary requirements — for examples, **Hindus** do not eat beef.

When you have narrowed down your list, consider international business laws in each country. You may need to consult locals to research regional laws and customs to ensure that you are able to take your product or service into that country.

You will also need to undertake the usual market research, to ensure that

Word Study

downturn /'daʊntɜːn/ n.（商业经济的）衰退

tricky /'trɪki/ adj. 难办的，难对付的

Hindu /hɪnˈduː/ n. 印度教徒

211

people in your target market will definitely want to buy your product or service.

WHEN TO ENTER?

If you know that your competitors are considering entering the same market as you, there are two options: aim to be "first to market" or wait and see how successful your competitors are and follow them into the market.

By aiming to be "first to market", you will be taking several risks. Firstly, regardless of how thorough your market research is, you cannot guarantee that people will buy what you are selling. Secondly, depending on your market entry method, you may have to invest high capital or meet resistance from potential local partners who are unsure that the product will succeed.

By following your competitors should they succeed, you will know that there is a market for your business and it is much more likely that local companies will be willing to partner with you. However, you run the risk that local customers will have become loyal to your competitors' brand and will not want to buy from another company.

SCALE OF ENTRY

The obvious issue here is cost. Entering a market on a large scale will require significant resources. Although this is more likely to make an impression on a new market as it will attract the attention of customers and local businesses alike, it may be risky financially if your company does not take off.

Entering on a smaller scale can offer business owners the chance to learn about the new market and limit risks — however, you are much less likely to gain significant amounts of attention.

Foreign Market Entry Modes

海外市场进入模式
① 出口
② 授权经营
③ 特许经营
④ 联合运营
⑤ 国际直接投资
⑥ 全资子公司
⑦ 搭顺风车

When you know the scale of entry, you will need to work out how to take your business abroad. This will require careful consideration as your decision could significantly impact your results. There are several market entry methods that can be used.

EXPORTING

Exporting is the direct sale of goods and/or services in another country. It is possibly the best-known method of entering a foreign market, as well as the lowest risk. It may also be cost-effective as you will not need to invest in production facilities in your chosen country — all goods are still produced in your home country then sent to foreign countries for sale. However, rising transportation costs are likely to increase the cost of exporting in the near future.

The majority of costs involved with exporting come from marketing expenses. Usually, you will need the involvement of four parties: your business, an importer, a transport provider and the government of the country of which you wish to export to.

LICENSING

Licensing is somewhat similar to **piggybacking**, except instead of talking to domestic firms and asking them to carry the product, you talk to foreign firms and ask them to temporarily own the product. It allows another company in your target country to use your property. The property in question is normally **intangible** — for example, trademarks, production techniques or **patents**. The licensee will pay a fee in order to be allowed the right to use the property.

Licensing requires very little investment and can provide a high return on investment. The licensee will also take care of any manufacturing and marketing costs in the foreign market.

FRANCHISING

Franchising is somewhat similar to licensing in that intellectual property rights are sold to a franchisee. However, the rules for how the franchisee carries out business are usually very strict — for example, any processes must be followed, or specific components must be used in manufacturing.

The good thing about franchising is that it's one of the easier ways to break into new markets. All you have to do is to take your existing, successful business model, find a franchisee in your target market, build out the franchise, and open your doors. The bad thing about franchising is that there is almost always a compromise.

JOINT VENTURE

A joint venture consists of two companies establishing a jointly-owned business. One of the owners will be a local business (local to the foreign market). The two companies would then provide the new business with a management team and share control of the joint venture.

There are several benefits to this type of venture. It allows you the benefit of local knowledge of a foreign market and allows you to share costs. However, there are some issues — there can be problems with deciding who invests what and how to split profits.

FOREIGN DIRECT INVESTMENT

Foreign direct investment (FDI) is when you directly invest in facilities in a foreign market. It requires a lot of capital to cover costs such as **premises**, technology and staff. FDI can be done either by establishing a

Word Study

piggyback /ˈpɪɡɪˌbæk/ v.
捎带，代售
intangible /ɪnˈtændʒəbl/
adj. 无形的
patent /ˈpætənt/ n. 专利
franchise /ˈfræntʃaɪz/ v.
给……特许经销权
premise /ˈpremɪs/ n.
企业或机构使用
的）房屋及土地

hurdle /ˈhɜːdl/ *n.* 难关，
障碍
baguette /bæˈget/ *n.*
长条形法式面包，
法棍
propel /prəˈpel/ *v.* 推
动，驱动

new venture or acquiring an existing company.

WHOLLY OWNED SUBSIDARY

A wholly owned subsidiary (WOS) is somewhat similar to foreign direct investment in that money goes into a foreign company but instead of money being invested into another company, with a WOS the foreign business is bought outright. It is then up to the owners whether it continues to run as before or they take more control of the WOS.

Wholly owned subsidiaries incur more risks than all the entry modes previously mentioned, however if implemented correctly and in the right circumstances, it generally results in high rewards (profits). An organization that enters a market as a wholly owned subsidiary has: high control, high commitment, high presence and high risk/reward.

PIGGYBACKING

In order to piggyback, you need to already be selling product to other domestic companies.

Piggybacking involves two non-competing companies working together to cross-sell the other's products or services in their home country. Although it is a low-risk method involving little capital, some companies may not be comfortable with this method as it involves a high degree of trust as well as allowing the partner company to take a large degree of control over how your product is marketed abroad.

Familiar Examples of International Business Entry

Starbucks faced a major **hurdle** when entering China's markets, as Chinese culture distinctly favors tea over any other beverage. Starbucks focused on marketing its stores as a comfortable place to come and be social, unrelated to work or home. This concept resonated with the Chinese market, and Starbucks has expanded successfully into this tea-soaked market.

McDonald's offers franchising options in many countries and has learned that making small changes that appeal to new international customers can have a large effect on success. For example, in France, McDonald's incorporated **baguettes** on its menu and marketed itself as a coffee-shop-type venue, where the French could continue to have multiple small meals and socialize. This **propelled** McDonald's from being a middling market player to big success.

Citgo formed a strategic alliance with Fujitsu (a Japanese company) to help grow its Japanese market share. It decided to co-brand certain products in order to leverage Fujitsu's excellent reputation in IT services with Citgo's broader resource pool and global reputation. This type of agreement benefits both parties and gave Citgo an opportunity to build brand recognition in Japan for other products it might introduce at a later date.

Strategic Alliance

战略联盟

A strategic alliance can be defined as an agreement between two or more companies to achieve common business goals by sharing their strengths and resources. However, the parties involved in a strategic alliance remain independent in their business operations.

A strategic alliance is a popular way of doing business in the modern business world. This is happening because of globalization, rapid change in technology, etc., as a result of which the business environment has become complex and sheer competitive.

The **duration** of the strategic alliance is decided based on the goals of the alliance and the gains and needs of the strategic partners. With the help of a strategic alliance, companies grow their business at a much faster pace than they would not have grown working alone.

战略联盟可以定义为两个或多个公司之间通过共享其优势和资源来实现共同业务目标的协议。然而，战略联盟中的各方在其业务运作中仍然是独立的。

战略联盟是现代企业界普遍采用的一种经营方式。

Common Reasons for a Strategic Alliance

战略联盟的原因
主要体现在缓慢业务周期、标准业务周期、快速业务周期三个阶段。

SLOW CYCLE OF THE BUSINESS

When the business cycle is slow in nature owing to the various external and internal factors, the company's competitive advantage is relatively **shielded** for a relatively long time period. Even the company doesn't come up with the new and latest offerings for the target market.

In this case, strategic alliances can be formed to explore the new and restricted markets and gain stability in the market by sharing and competencies through the alliance.

STANDARD CYCLE OF THE BUSINESS

During the standard cycle of the business, the company launches the new line of products every few years and in regular intervals but may or may not be able to maintain its leading and top as a market leader.

In this case **scenario**, strategic alliances as formulated to gain higher market share, gain access to the complementary resources, generate economies of scale, beat other competitive companies, and pool resources for the projects that require a large number of funds and capital investments.

FAST CYCLE OF THE BUSINESS

In the fast cycle of the business, the company needs to come up with an offer of the new range of products on a constant and continuous basis

Word Study

duration /djʊəˈreɪʃən/
n. 持续时间
shield /ʃiːld/ v. 保护，防护
scenario /sɪˈnɑːrɪəʊ/
n. 设想，方案

215

to survive in the market. The company's competitive advantages are not protected.

In this case scenario, strategic alliances are formed in order to speed up with the development of new products, overcome the factor of uncertainty, share the expenses of research and development, and align the process of market **penetration**.

Types of Strategic Alliances

There are four types of strategic alliances. Let us learn about them one by one.

PROCOMPETITIVE ALLIANCE

This type of strategic alliance works based on low interaction and low conflicts. In this type of strategic alliance, companies involved in the alliance have minimal involvement, and they don't merge their capital.

An example of a procompetitive strategic alliance can be seen in businesses between the distributors or suppliers and manufacturers. These companies work with each other without merging their capital in the business. This type of strategic alliance takes advantage of vertical integration.

NONCOMPETITIVE ALLIANCE

This type of strategic alliance results in high interaction and low conflicts. This type of strategic alliance takes place among the companies which are part of the same industry but does not consider themselves direct competitors.

This is because the operations of these companies are quite distinctive from one another. This type of alliance takes place between companies whose businesses are the same but operate in different geographical areas.

COMPETITIVE ALLIANCE

This type of strategic alliance works on the principle of high interaction and high conflicts. Companies which are direct competitors of each other come together to form a competitive strategic alliance.

Being direct competitors to each other, and because of the high interaction, there is a high risk of conflicts between the companies involved.

This type of strategic alliance takes place between the companies dealing in the same industry but in different countries. Usually, companies get in a competitive alliance with the local companies to establish their business in a new country.

PRECOMPETITIVE ALLIANCE

This type of strategic alliance results in low interaction and high conflicts. This type of strategic alliance is common between two companies from two completely different industries.

Precompetitive alliance takes place when two companies work together to develop a new product or a new technology.

The best example to explain precompetitive strategic alliance is the alliance between an advertising company and a company using its services to develop its products.

Advantages of a Strategic Alliance

战略联盟的优势
实行战略联盟主要有以下八个优势。

• Speed up the entry into a new market

A strategic alliance is an effective way to enter a new market. Companies can easily reach the customers and can avoid initial hardships of new business by getting into alliance with already existing companies in the market.

• Enhance sales

Companies can increase their sales and expand their business by getting into alliance with other companies which otherwise is very difficult for companies.

• Learn new skills and technology

Companies can learn and obtain skills and technology of other companies to enhance their own business.

• Divided fixed costs and resources

When companies get into an alliance, they work for a common goal by dividing fixed costs and resources required for the business.

• Innovative products and services

When two companies from completely two industries come together, they develop innovative products which are beneficial for both companies and help them to enhance their profits.

• Enhanced distribution channels

Companies share their resources when they get into business alliance. This allows companies to establish business relationships with new distribution channels and in this way, they can increase the **reachability** and availability of their products and services.

• Easy to get into the international market

Usually, it is a complex and difficult process for a company to enter into the international market. A strategic alliance between two international companies make it easy for foreign companies to establish their business.

Word Study

reachability
/ˌriːtʃəˈbɪlɪti/ *n.*
可达性,可及性

With such an alliance, both companies take advantage of and boost their business.

- Build the image of the brand

Strategic alliance with leading companies improves the image of a company in the market. Customers trust the brand if they know about the association of a brand with the brand that they already know.

Risks Involved in a Strategic Alliance

- There can be differences between both the parties on the processes and operations of the business activities even after the arrangement is clear and **crisp** for both the organizations.
- If there is a term in the agreement of the strategic alliance that the parties need to inform each other of their proprietary information that it requires a high level of trust between both the entities.
- The parties may become mutually dependent on each other in case of the long-term strategic alliances.
- Partners may misrepresent or lie about their competencies or other crucial factors.
- One party may be able to stand to the commitment of resources and capabilities to the other party involved.
- In the alliance, one of the parties may commit heavily whilst the other may not be that serious about the accomplishment of the common goals and objectives.
- It can be the case that the partners may fail to utilize their complementary resources in an effective manner.

Examples of Strategic Alliance

Strategic Alliance between Spotify and Uber: The alliance between Spotify and Uber is an example of a strategic alliance between two companies. These two companies, through this alliance, increase their customer bases when they offer Uber riders to take control of the stereo.

In this way, both companies are getting an edge over their competitors. Customers of Spotify can play their favorite playlist while riding in the Uber ride by getting the premium package of Spotify.

Apple Pay and Master Card: When Apple Inc. decided to get into digital payment business, it became a big competitor to all existing companies in this field.

Rather than getting into the competition, the second-largest digital payment company "Master Card" decided to get into an alliance with the Apple Inc. In this way, both companies get the benefit of the alliance.

Master Card become the first company to provide Apple Pay's services, and Apple Pay got the benefit of the Master Card's reputation.

Google and Luxottica: Luxottica is a leading luxury and sports eyewear company, and Google is an international company which provides internet-based services and products. There is no way that one can think of two such different companies getting into a business alliance with each other.

But these two companies get into an alliance to set an example in the market. With each other's alliance both companies expanded their business by combining technology with luxury.

Information Link
知识链接

市场进入壁垒

在不完全竞争市场中,进入壁垒是必然存在的,也是导致垄断的重要原因。垄断的存在是其他厂商认为此市场已经饱和,也就是认为这一市场无利可图或者十分难以进入。因此,进入壁垒是垄断的根本来源。市场的进入壁垒大体可分为两类:技术壁垒与法律壁垒。

技术壁垒也可以用规模经济的概念来解释,是指商品的生产在一个很大的范围内表现为边际成本递减的趋势,也就是满足函数的拟凹性——随着生产规模的增加,技术成本会变得越来越低,工人的熟练度会越来越高。所以生产规模比较大的厂商,其生产成本会很低,在这种情况下,就形成了自然垄断。已经存在的厂商通过降价等手段可以把其他厂商挤出该行业,对于规模较小的新厂商,生产的成本比较高,因此进入市场就比较困难,这是进入壁垒的第一类表现形式。

第二类进入壁垒是法律壁垒,它是由于政府的管制或者法律的保护形成的壁垒。比如政府对通过专利形成的生产技术进行法律上的保护,这是一个由政府给予企业的垄断地位,人们通过创新可以获得更多的利润,从而达到鼓励创新的目的。但是,这种措施导致的收益与成本的权衡问题也引发了社会的讨论。另一种法律保护在于企业可能会说服政府立法限制新的进入者,以此来维持市场的均衡和秩序。如果进入者与现有企业获得相同的成本曲线,那么规模经济性就不构成我们所说的进入壁垒。新进入的厂商能够进入市场生产,拥有与现有企业相同的最大产量,而且享受与现有企业同样高的成本,在这个时候就不存在规模经济对进入壁垒的促进作用了,所以说,规模经济未必一定导致进入壁垒。

进入壁垒的影响因素有规模经济、产品差异化、进入的沉没成本、先动者对后动者的进入阻止等诸多因素。进入壁垒是现实经济中一个十分重要而且确实存在的重要问题,进入壁垒的高低决定了市场的垄断程度和社会福利的损失程度。

文献来源:

缪轩永.关于市场进入壁垒的若干思考[J].现代商业.2018(07): 43-44.

A. Describe and write down the foreign market entry modes.

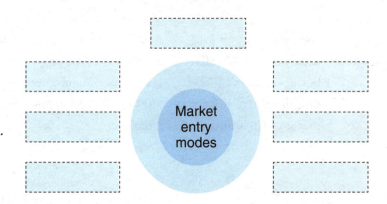

B. According to the text, fill in each of the following blanks with an appropriate word or phrase.

1) Once a company is well established in its domestic market, it makes sense to start looking at _____ markets and considering market entry _____.

2) Some countries are very _____ in comparison to the UK, so trying to export items such as clothes or alcohol may be tricky.

3) _____ is possibly the best-known method of entering a foreign market, as well as the lowest risk.

4) Licensing is somewhat similar to _____, except instead of talking to domestic firms and asking them to carry the product, you talk to foreign firms and ask them to temporarily own the product.

5) _____ allows you the benefit of local knowledge of a foreign market and allows you to share costs.

6) A _____ is somewhat similar to foreign direct investment in that money goes into a foreign company but instead of money being invested into another company.

7) A _____ can be defined as an agreement between two or more companies to achieve common business goals by sharing their strengths and resources.

8) The duration of the strategic alliance is decided based on the _____ _____ of the alliance and the gains and needs of the strategic partners.

9) An example of a _____ strategic alliance can be seen in businesses between the distributors or suppliers and manufacturers.

10) _____ takes place between companies dealing in the same industry but in different countries.

C. Read the text and decide whether the following statements are True (T) or False (F).

1) Although investing in another market can be risky and require a lot of capital, the rewards can be huge. ( )

2) When companies form a procompetitive strategic alliance, they have maximal involvement, and they don't merge their capital. ( )

3) Noncompetitive alliance takes place between companies whose businesses are the same but operate in different geographical areas. ( )

4) Precompetitive alliance takes place between the companies dealing in the same industry but in different countries. ( )

5) Competitive alliance takes place when two companies from different industries work together to develop a new product or a new technology. ( )

6) Companies can easily reach the customers and can avoid initial hardships of new business by getting into alliance with already existing companies in the market. ( )

7) A strategic alliance between two international companies makes it easier for them to establish their business. ( )

8) In a strategic alliance, one of the parties must commit heavily whilst the other may not be that serious about the accomplishment of the common goals and objectives. ( )

9) Customers of Spotify can play their favorite playlist while riding in the Uber ride by getting the premium package of Spotify. ( )

10) Master Card is not the first company to provide Apple Pay's services, and Apple Pay does not get the benefit of the Master Card's reputation. ( )

Discussion
讨论

1) What are "entry strategy" and "strategic alliance"? Can you explain them in your own words?

_____

_____

2) What are the three important things for a company looking to expand into foreign markets?

3) Can you give more examples of international business entry? Discuss with your partner.

_____

_____

4) Can you retell the common reasons for a strategic alliance? Give your example to make it clear.

_____

_____

5) Do you know any cases with an unsuccessful strategic alliance? Discuss with your partner about the reasons for such a failure.

_____

_____

Case Story

The Chinese Phone Giant That Beat Apple to Africa

One of China's biggest smartphone makers has never sold a handset in the country. Yet thousands of miles away, it dominates markets across Africa. Unknown in the West, Transsion has left global players like Samsung and Apple trailing in its wake in a continent that's home to more than a billion people.

In cities like Lagos, Nairobi and Addis Ababa, busy streets are awash with the bright blue shopfronts of Transsion's flagship brand, Tecno. In China, the company doesn't have a single store, and its towering headquarters in the southern megacity of Shenzhen goes largely unnoticed among skyscrapers bearing the names of more famous Chinese tech firms.

The company took a different path to success from other top Chinese smartphone makers such as Huawei and Xiaomi, which started out in China before eventually expanding overseas. Transsion built its business in Africa. And it has no plans to come home.

The Perfect Selfie

In Edna Mall on the bustling Bole Road in Addis Ababa, the capital of Ethiopia, Mesert Baru poses for her Tecno Camon i. "This phone is seriously nice for selfies", says the 35-year-old shop assistant, admiring the picture she just took.

Mesert's satisfaction is no accident. Tecno cameras have been optimized for African complexions, explains Arif Chowdhury, vice president of Transsion. "Our cameras adjust more light for darker skin, so the photograph is more beautiful", he says. "That's one of the reasons we've become successful."

Transsion founder George Zhu had spent nearly a decade traveling Africa as head of sales for another mobile phone company when he realized that selling Africans handsets made for developed markets was the wrong approach.

His timing could hardly have been better. By the mid-2000s, the Chinese government, under its "Going Out" strategy, was encouraging entrepreneurs to look abroad and forge stronger ties with African nations in particular. Cell phones were spreading rapidly in China, but in Africa — which has a roughly similar population — they were still a very rare luxury.

Africa, in other words, could be the new China.

Giving Consumers What They Want

In 2006, Zhu launched Tecno in Nigeria, targeting Africa's most populous nation first. From the start, the company's motto was "think global, act local", which meant making phones that met Africans' specific needs.

"When we started doing business in Africa, we noticed people had multiple SIM cards in their wallet", Chowdhury says. They would awkwardly swap the cards throughout the day to avoid the steep charges operators would levy for calling different networks, says Nabila Popal, who tracks the use of devices in Africa for research firm IDC. "They can't afford two phones", says Chowdhury, "so we brought a solution to them." Zhu made all Tecno handsets dual SIM.

More innovations followed. Transsion opened research and development centers in China, Nigeria and Kenya to work out how to better appeal to African users. Local languages such as Amharic, Hausa and Swahili were added to keyboards and phones were given a longer battery life.

Extra juice was important. In Nigeria, South Africa and Ethiopia, for example, the government frequently shuts off electricity to conserve power, leaving people unable to charge their phones for hours. In less developed markets, such as the Democratic Republic of Congo, Chowdhury says, consumers might have to walk 30 kilometers to charge their phone at the local market — and have to pay to do so. "For those kind of consumers, longer battery life is a blessing", he adds.

Sewedo Nupowaku, the Lagos-based CEO of entertainment company Revolution Media, says he switched from a Samsung S3 to a Tecno L8 for this reason. "I can spend 24 hours constantly talking, browsing on this phone, no problem. With a Samsung, no way."

But perhaps Transsion's smartest move was its pricing. It has three main brands: Tecno, Infinix and Itel. Most of their feature and smartphones sell for between $15 and $200.

Mesert says she bought her Tecno smartphone for 2,000 birr ($72). At a shop near her workplace, an iPhone 7 costs the equivalent of $906, and a Samsung Galaxy J7 around $360. Average monthly wages in Ethiopia range from 1,500 birr ($54) to 3,000 ($108) birr, and most vendors across Africa don't allow customers to pay in installments.

"About 95% of Transsion smartphones cost under $200", says Mo Jia, an analyst at technology research firm Canalys. "They are the king of the budget smartphone."

Tecno: "We Are African"

Less than a decade ago, Chinese phones were barely on the radar in Africa. In 2010, Nokia and Samsung (SSNLF) dominated sales across the continent. By the first half of this year, Nokia's share of the market had collapsed and Samsung was selling only one in 10 phones. Transsion had come from nowhere to take more than 50% of the market, according to Canalys. For smartphones alone, it accounts for nearly a third of all sales in Africa, according to IDC.

Apple (AAPL) has been complacent about African markets, Jia says, because it deemed the slim profit margins on low-cost phones not worth fighting for. Transsion, on the other hand, is happy to work with tight margins, he adds. Apple didn't respond to requests for comment.

Transsion's rise reflects the wider role Chinese firms now play in providing the technology people across Africa use to communicate, including the high-speed internet networks on which smartphones rely. Despite the so-called "security concerns" in countries such as the United States and Australia about Huawei and ZTE, Jia expects demand for Chinese products to remain strong in Africa, where governments and consumers are so price sensitive.

In its marketing, Transsion plays down its Chinese roots. "In Africa, we say that we are African."

Chowdhury says, explaining why Tecno's stores carry no Chinese characters or signs of being a Chinese brand. In the 2017–2018 Brand Africa 100 report, published by African Business magazine, Tecno ranked as the 7th most admired brand in Africa. That was up from 14th the previous year, but it still lagged Samsung (2nd) and Apple (5th). The iPhone is still considered a luxury product that many Africans aspire to own.

In Ethiopia, Transsion went a step further to assimilate. Since 2011, every phone it sells in Africa's second most populous nation has been assembled at its facilities in the suburbs of Addis Ababa. About 700 workers piece together Shenzhen-manufactured screens, circuit boards and batteries to churn out 2,000 smartphones and 4,000 feature phones a day.

Transsion says it has a total of 10,000 local employees in Africa, and 6,000 in China. Its low-cost African workforce helps it keep down prices, according to Jia. It also adds appeal for some consumers. "I like that my phone is made in Ethiopia", Mesert says.

A Homegrown Rival to Spotify

Nigeria, with its population of 186 million, is Transsion's biggest market. It has connected with consumers there through one of their biggest passions: music.

Oye Akideinde, an amateur rapper turned software developer, was recruited by Tecno in 2015 to launch a music app called Boomplay, a homegrown rival to iTunes or Spotify. Most Nigerian internet users grew up illegally downloading music or streaming it for free on YouTube, according to Akideinde, a 40-year-old Lagos resident.

Tecno's vision was to attract music lovers by uniting African and international artists on a single platform offering affordable downloads and streaming with advertising. It preloaded the app onto every Tecno smartphone and made it the default music player. The app now has 32 million users.

Tecno spun off Boomplay and its apps division into a new company, TranssNet, last year. Backed by NetEase, a $30 billion Chinese internet company, TranssNet plans to introduce a suite of financial apps on smartphones made by Transsion.

Chinese companies have been eager to use technology to tap into Africans' spending habits. In 2015, Kenyan mobile payments operator M-Pesa migrated all of its 12.8 million subscribers to Huawei's Mobile Money platform as it expanded across East Africa and beyond. The move increased the number of transactions M-Pesa could process, and the app's user base has more than doubled since then.

Expanding in India and Beyond

For Transsion, future growth is set to come from building its business outside Africa in other developing markets, such as Russia, Indonesia and Bangladesh. In 2017, it launched Tecno in India and within a year had claimed 5% of the huge market, according to IDC.

How did Tecno make such rapid progress? Transsion's Chowdhury says another innovation tailored to local customs has helped.

"Indian people use their hands to eat food," he says, "so their fingers get oily. What if you're having lunch and your boss calls? You try to take the call but your fingerprint won't work."

The fix: screens that can read greasy fingers.

Case Discussion

1) What are the external conditions for Transsion to enter foreign markets?

_____

_____

2) What are Transsion's measures to attract foreign customers in the part of "Giving consumers what they want"?

_____

_____

3) What can you learn from Transsion's foreign market entry strategy? Discuss with your partner.

_____

_____

Case Summary

中国最大的智能手机制造商之一从未在中国销售过手机。然而在数千英里之外,它主宰着整个非洲的市场。传音在西方不为人知,但在拥有10亿多人口的非洲大陆,它甩开了三星和苹果等全球厂商。与华为和小米等其他中国智能手机顶级制造商相比,传音的成功之路与众不同。

本文重点介绍了传音在世界其他地区的市场进入策略,主要从以下五个方面进行了论述:第一,完美自拍。传音创始人竺兆江把其旗下品牌Tecno的相机针对非洲肤色进行了优化。第二,给消费者想要的。公司的座右铭就是"思考全球,行动本地",这意味着生产满足非洲人特定需求的手机。第三,"我们是非洲手机"。传音乐于在利润率较低的情况下深耕非洲市场,为非洲人民提供沟通技术,弱化其中国企业形象,雇佣本地员工进行组装,打造本地化生产的智能手机品牌形象。第四,作为Spotify的本土竞争对手,传音研发了Boomplay的音乐播放器,并试图利用技术来挖掘非洲人的消费习惯。第五,在印度及其他地区扩张。传音负责人认为未来的业务增长将来自非洲以外的其他发展中市场(如俄罗斯、印度尼西亚和孟加拉国)。

Reading I

Factors Affecting the Choice of Entry Mode by MNCs

When the multinational enterprises (MNEs) decide to enter a foreign market, the most crucial decision they face is the choice of entry mode, i.e., selecting an institutional arrangement for organizing and conducting international business transactions. The choice of entry mode has a major impact on the firm's performance as well as survival.

Firms can choose from a variety of entry modes. The various types of entry modes can be classified into two categories, namely equity and non-equity modes. Equity modes involve higher resource commitment, provide a higher degree of control on operations and higher returns on investment. But at the same time, they have higher exit costs and carry a higher level of risk exposure. On the other hand, the non-equity modes involve lower resource commitment, provide lower degree of control over the operations and lower returns on investment. But they have lower exit costs and carry a lower level of risk exposure.

There are various factors that can influence the entry mode choice of an MNC. These factors can be clubbed into two groups, namely, internal factors and external factors. Internal factors relate to the company's internal environment, whereas external factors pertain to the conditions that are external to the company.

Internal Factors

- Firm size: One of the most important factors that influence the entry mode choice is the size of the firm. Smaller firms have limited financial and human resources at their disposal and are therefore exposed to more risks as chances of failure of foreign investment can lead to insolvency of the entire firm. On the other hand, larger firms possess greater productive resources, greater market power, greater knowledge and economies of scale. They are better placed than smaller firms to bear the risks associated with foreign market entry. Therefore, firm size (larger firms) is positively related to the adoption of an equity entry mode.

- International experience: As a firm ventures into foreign markets, it gains the knowledge of dealing with local economic and environmental conditions. As the experience increases, the firm's potential to project the costs and returns, to gauge the market demand, to assess the customer's needs and to evaluate the true economic worth of the foreign market also increases. It becomes more confident of its ability to manage foreign operations and consequently willing to invest greater resources. On the other hand, firms with less experience tend to perceive greater uncertainty, and are more likely to wrongly estimate the risks and returns. They, therefore hesitate to commit greater resources in the foreign market. Thus, the greater the international experience, the more likely it is that the firm will go for an equity entry mode.

- Technological capability: Firms which possess high R&D capability face greater risk of leaking proprietary technology to their rivals if they opt for lower control modes or non-equity modes. With non-equity modes, there is a risk of the firm losing the control of its technology to the local partner. So in order to prevent the dissemination of technological know-how, firms with greater technological capability will prefer equity modes over non-equity modes.

- Product characteristics: The product characteristics provide the firm with the ability to differentiate its product offering from its rivals. It includes the attributes like degree of product uniqueness, extent of product establishment, training needs of sales force, and the degree of maintenance and service requirement for the product. Products that are service-intensive are hard to serve from a distant market. The company needs to be close to the customer and therefore local production is appropriate in such cases. Thus, in case of service-intensive products, the equity mode will be preferred. Similarly, innovative products possess highly intangible components in terms of technological and marketing know-how. For such products, specialized training programs for the employees must be put in place. Therefore, a high level of product differentiation in product characteristics is associated with the adoption of an equity entry mode.

External Factors

- Cultural distance: Perhaps one of the most often talked about external factors affecting the choice of an entry mode is the cultural distance between the host country and the home country. Culturally close countries ought to have similar languages, similar sets of norms governing business and industry and also similar cultural characteristics. The greater the cultural distance between the home country and the host country, the greater the uncertainty and the cost of collecting information and communication will be. Therefore, when the cultural distance is large, the company will avoid using equity entry modes and will use entry modes which require lower resource commitment.

- Market size and growth potential: Market size and growth potential are important host country parameters affecting the entry mode choice. The larger the size of the market, the greater the potential for growth and the more likely the firm to commit greater resources for its development. In smaller markets, firms tend to reduce their commitment and will go for non-equity entry modes. Root (1987) observed that in markets characterized by low sales potential, entry modes such as indirect exporting and licensing are favored. Similarly, in declining markets firms tend to prefer lower commitment or non-equity modes.

- Country risk: Country risk emanates from political and economic factors both of which can significantly influence the potential attractiveness of a country. Unstable and unpredictable political and economic environment increases the risk of doing business in a particular country and discourages the firm to adopt entry modes which require greater resource commitment. On the other hand, politically stable countries which have free market mechanisms and where the macro-economic indicators are relatively stable will induce the firms to adopt equity entry modes.

- **Legal barriers:** Imposition of tariffs and quotas on the import of foreign products and excessive trade regulations encourages local production and will lead the firm to go for an equity entry mode like a wholly owned subsidiary or a joint venture. Similarly, excessive restrictions on foreign ownership by host country governments will push the firm to go for non-equity entry modes.

Firms choose an entry mode in response to a variety of internal and external factors so as to maximize profit and optimize their market position.

Second Thoughts

For each of the following statements, choose one (or more than one) answer to fill in the blank.

1) Equity entry modes involve higher resource commitment, provide a higher degree of control on operations and _____.
   A. lower risks of operations
   B. higher gains on investment
   C. higher returns on publicity
   D. lower costs of borrowing

2) Product characteristics including the following EXCEPT _____ can affect a firm's choice of an entry mode.
   A. degree of product uniqueness
   B. training needs of sales force
   C. extent of product establishment
   D. degree of cultural distance

Reading II

10 Ways to Ensure Successful Strategic Alliances

"Alliances can be tricky", Nina Kaufman, an attorney, entrepreneur and professional speaker, sighs. Alliances must foster mutual benefits and can exist only as long as they are advantageous to both parties. The concept of gaining a marketplace advantage by teaming up with another company whose products or services fit well with your own is not only seductive, but it's also critical for an increasing number of businesses.

Perhaps you met at an industry event, worked together at a previous company, or someone made a referral. You think, "let's partner on a project". "That's premature", said Kaufman. "You need to date and get to know each other." Here are some rules of the road.

Identify the Need

"First, determine why you would work together", Kaufman points out. Do your companies have complementary skills or are you adding extra capacity to each other? Understand the strengths and weaknesses of each firm.

Determine how the alliance fits into your business plan. Be clear with yourself about why you're entering into the partnership and what you expect to gain.

Evaluate Partners

Even when you know someone or get a referral from a trusted advisor, researching a prospective partner is crucial. It's not just the capabilities the other company brings to the table. You must feel comfortable with the work style of the potential alliance. Once you've determined the other firm has complementary skills, it's critical that you look objectively at management styles, work ethics and values, and identify where potential clashes could occur.

Key questions to ask:

- How are decisions made? Who owns the relationship with the client?
- Who is paying whom? If you're not in charge of payment, how fast will they pay you and other vendors?
- What is the company's work ethic? At what pace is work done? Is it similar to yours?
- How competitive or aggressive is the company? How does that compare to you?

Establish Joint Objectives and Goals

Developing key objectives and goals that reflect what both parties expect to gain is critical. Be sure that expectations are realistic in light of the resources both parties are willing to put forth, and make adjustments as needed. Nothing sours an alliance faster than the notion that one party is giving everything while the other is getting a free ride. Strategic partnerships have to foster an environment in which both parties gain something; otherwise, they're not partnerships.

Define Roles and Responsibilities

"Many problems can be avoided by setting expectations upfront", Kaufman advises. Assess each company's strengths, and define responsibilities accordingly — especially in the area of management. Many alliances fail because of poor management relationships, so document clearly what's expected. Be specific:

Decide how many people from each company will be involved in the alliance and what their particular roles will be. Each party has to dedicate resources to the relationship, and both parties need someone within their organization who will champion the cause.

Develop a Good Communication Process

Clear communication is key to creating an enduring partnership. "This is one of the key pieces that often gets overlooked", said Kaufman. Disappointments and misunderstandings can be avoided by establishing an effective process for working with your partner. The relationship must be developed to the point where both parties can be honest when

evaluating progress and offering recommendations for improvement —
both of which should be done on a regular basis. For example, you might
want to exchange weekly sales reports.

Develop Conflict-Resolution Systems

An alliance is rarely a match made in heaven. Misunderstandings,
compromises, and disagreements are natural. "Determine how you will
voice them when you feel your partner isn't responsive", said Kaufman.
When misalignments arise, resolve them as quickly as possible. It's best to
meet in neutral territory where both parties can speak openly and honestly.
Then, focus on creating solutions rather than placing blame. Be prepared
for the possible break-up of the relationship. "Have an exit process worked
out in advance."

Demonstrate Commitment

The alliance needs to assume a position of status and importance.
Both partners must be willing to nurture and care for it. This means that
the top people in both organizations must be supportive. The point of
any strategic alliance should be to make an impact, and you can't do that
without active engagement at the top. It also means giving extra effort to
making the venture work, even if that means a willingness to go beyond
contractual obligations. Committed partners dedicate resources and
energy, and face risks to make the venture work.

Be Patient

Strategic alliances take time to develop and maintain. When you're
starting, don't make judgments about potential partners if they seem
reluctant. Figure out how to stand out from the crowd.

Formalize with an Agreement

A written document formalizes what you have agreed to. It is an
outline of expectations and protects you and your alliance if those
expectations aren't met. If a disagreement arises, there is a document you
can refer back to in order to get the relationship back on track.

Second Thoughts

1) According to Nina Kaufman, why can alliances be tricky?

_____

_____

2) Can you retell the ten rules to ensure a successful strategic alliance? Do
you have any other ideas?

_____

_____

Exporting, Importing, and Countertrade

出口、进口和对等贸易

CHAPTER 12

本章概要

本章主要介绍进出口和对等贸易的含义、重要性、风险性，以全球回收行业为例，说明进出口贸易的相互影响，介绍开始进出口贸易的步骤，以及对等贸易的作用、形式、挑战及应对策略等。

学习指南

贸易是保持经济和国家活力的因素。贸易需求创造了国内生产和海外资金的流入，全球出口量每年都在增长。

除了出口，各国还可能进口其国内工业无法像出口国那样高效或廉价生产的货物或服务。自由贸易提高了从较廉价的生产区进口货物和材料的能力，并减少了对国内货物的依赖。

有时，标准的商品现金支付结构不起作用，呈现出繁琐、昂贵或不可能的特点。在这些情况下，公司可以采用对等贸易。

通过本章学习，希望大家能够实现以下目标：

（1）基本目标（Text-based Goals）

- 掌握本章涉及话题的基本专业术语及词汇，如对等贸易、补偿贸易、出口管理公司等；
- 掌握本章的主要知识点，即进出口和对等贸易的含义、重要性、风险性等。

（2）拓展目标（Extended Goals）

- 思考本章引言，为什么乔·凯瑟尔认为"我们所有的财富和我们所有的出口能力也来自其他国家愿意看到我们"？
- 通过学习背景知识、拓展阅读、案例分析，进一步了解国际贸易的相互影响、进出口贸易的步骤。

> All our wealth and all our export power has also come by the fact that other nations were willing to see us. This is very important.（我们所有的财富和我们所有的出口能力也来自其他国家愿意看到我们，这很重要。）
>
> —Joe Kaeser（乔·凯瑟尔）

Trade is what keeps economies and nations alive. Trade demands create domestic production and the inflows of funds from overseas. Exporting is increasing yearly, globally. This is due to various factors. First, both large and small firms export — not just large firms. Also, under the World Trade Organization (WTO) there has been a decline in trade barriers. This holds true for other regional trade agreements such as the European Union (EU) and the North American Free Trade Agreement (NAFTA).

Countries are also likely to import goods or services that their domestic industries cannot produce as efficiently or cheaply as the exporting country. Free trade opens the ability to import goods and materials from cheaper production zones and reduces reliance on domestic goods.

At times, standard goods-for-cash payment structures do not work, are **cumbersome**, expensive, or simply impossible. In these cases, companies can adopt countertrade. Countertrade involves the exchange of goods in **barters** or other ways in place of money. For example, if a nation's currency is not exchangeable or no good overseas, they may offer a commodity or other product in place of cash.

Why Is Importing and Exporting Important?

As soon as a business starts operating internationally, there are many additional factors which can have a huge impact on its success. Exporting and importing goods is not just the core of any large, successful business; it also helps national economies grow and expand.

Each country is endowed with some specific resources. At the same time, a country may lack other resources in order to develop and improve its overall economy. For example, while some countries are rich in minerals and precious metals or fossil fuels, others are experiencing a shortage of these resources. Some countries have highly developed educational systems or infrastructures, while others do not.

Once countries start exporting whatever they are rich in, as well as importing goods they lack, their economies begin developing. Importing and exporting goods is not only important for businesses; it is important for individual consumers, too. Consumers can benefit from certain

贸易是保持经济和国家活力的因素。贸易需求创造了国内生产和海外资金的流入。出口在全球每年都在增长。

除了出口，各国还可能进口其国内工业无法像出口国那样高效或廉价生产的货物或服务。自由贸易提高了从较廉价的生产区进口货物和材料的能力，并减少了对国内货物的依赖。

当标准的商品现金支付结构不可行时，公司可采用对等贸易。

为什么进出口很重要？

出口和进口商品不仅是任何大型成功企业的核心，而且有助于国民经济的增长和扩张。进口和出口可以带来一系列的好处。

products or components that are not produced locally, but are available to purchase online from a business abroad.

BENEFITS OF IMPORTING

When people talk about importing in terms of trade, they refer to purchasing products or services from another country. These products or services are then offered to customers by the importing business or individual, broadening their choice of purchase. However, this is not the only benefit of importing; there are many more to consider. Here are some of them.

1. Introducing new products to the market

Many businesses in India and China produce goods for the European and American markets. This is mostly due to the size of these markets and the purchasing power of the population there. But once a new product is introduced to these two markets, it may take a year or more before the product is introduced to other, smaller markets.

If a product produced in China seems attractive/useful to entrepreneurs in Australia, they can import it and introduce it to their potential consumers. Thanks to the internet expansion, entrepreneurs can conduct market research prior to importing a certain product. This will help them determine if there is an actual need on the market for such an imported product, so they can develop an effective marketing strategy in advance.

2. Reducing costs

Another major benefit of importing is the reduction in manufacturing costs. Many businesses today find importing products, parts of products and resources more affordable than producing them locally.

There are numerous cases when entrepreneurs find products of good quality that are inexpensive even when the overall import expenses are included. So instead of investing in modern, expensive machinery, entrepreneurs choose to import goods and reduce their costs. In most cases, they end up ordering large quantities in order to get a better price and minimize the costs.

3. Becoming a leader in the industry

One of the key benefits of importing products is the opportunity to become a market leader in the industry of interest. Since manufacturing new and improved products is a never-ending process, many businesses worldwide use the chance to import new and unique products before their competitors do. Being the first to import a fresh product can easily lead you to becoming a leader in a certain industry.

4. Providing high quality products

Another benefit of importing is related to the ability to market products of high quality. Lots of successful entrepreneurs travel abroad, visit factories and other highly professional sellers in order to find high quality products and import them into their own country. Moreover, manufacturers may provide **informative** courses and training, as well as introduce standards and practices to ensure the company abroad is well prepared to sell their products.

If you choose to base your business on importing products, chances are you are going to get high quality products. This is due to the fact that manufacturing businesses are very aware that their reputation largely depends on the quality of the items they produce. This is a reason more to consider importing the essence of your new business.

BENEFITS OF EXPORTING

Just as there is a variety of benefits of importing products and services, there are numerous reasons for exporting, too. Here are the two key benefits of exporting products to other countries.

1. Increasing your sales potential

While importing products can help businesses reduce costs, exporting products can ensure increasing sales and sales potential in general. Businesses that focus on exporting expand their vision and markets regionally, internationally or even globally. Instead of earning money by selling their offerings on the local market, these businesses are focused on discovering new opportunities to present their work abroad.

Exporting products is especially good for medium and large businesses — the ones that have already expanded within the local market. Once they have **saturated** the market in their country, exporting products abroad can be a great opportunity for these businesses to increase the sales potential. Additionally, exporting can be one way of **scanning** opportunities for overseas franchising or even production.

2. Increasing profits

Exporting products can largely contribute to increasing your profits. This is mainly due to the foreign orders, as they are usually larger than those placed by the local buyers. While local customers buy a few products or a **pallet**, businesses abroad oftentimes order a container of products which inevitably leads to increased profits. Moreover, if your products are considered unique or innovative abroad, your profits can increase rapidly in no time.

Common Pitfalls in Importing and Exporting

International trade is not easy. If it were, more people would be doing it. Focus on these trouble spots and you will put yourself on the path to what we all crave — a **glitch-free** international trade experience.

Word Study

informative /ɪnˈfɔːmətɪv/ adj. 提供信息的，给予知识的

saturate /ˈsætʃəreɪt/ v. 渗透，浸透

scan /skæn/ v. 扫描，浏览

pallet /ˈpælət/ n. 托盘，运货板

glitch-free /ɡlɪtʃfriː/ n. 毫无故障的，顺畅的

进出口常见陷阱
　　国际贸易并不容易，注意以下几点可以帮助避免国际贸易中的各种问题。

LACK OF KNOWLEDGE ON EXCHANGE RATES

If you don't know the exchange rates when trading internationally, you are exposed to potential currency fluctuations and are restricted when planning ahead or trying to get the best price. The **workaround**? Consult with your banker on how best to lock in your profit on a transaction and protect yourself from exposure to risk. That way you hedge against the roller coaster ride of currency fluctuations.

LOUSY RELATIONSHIP WITH CUSTOMS OFFICIALS

Don't underestimate the importance of a good relationship with customs officials, transportation folks and customs brokers. And never assume you know more than they do! You are responsible for compliance with all import and export laws, so get along with everyone and listen to what they have to say. Even if you hire a firm to carry out import-export procedures on your behalf, the **buck** still stops with you.

MAKING A BRIBE

If you are conducting business in a foreign market, you must be familiar with and comply with laws about bribery and corruption, such as the Foreign Corrupt Practices Act (FCPA) of the U.S. You should learn about the laws and regulations and discover how to avoid or handle bribery disputes.

BEING CLUELESS ABOUT IMPORT RESTRICTIONS OR CONTROL ON A PRODUCT

Import restrictions comprise of quotas, import licensing requirements and so forth. Importing goods that violate quota restrictions or are unsafe could end up costing you money in fines and penalties, and that will erode your profits. Are you complying with both state and federal government import regulations?

FAILURE TO CONFORM TO PACKAGING, MARKING, AND LANGUAGE (LOCALIZATION) LAWS

What are the laws of the country you are entering? Consult with your transportation specialist and your customer and then compare notes. For example, do labels on your product have to be in the local language? How sturdy must the carton be? What markings need to be on the outside of the cartons to comply with the law? Is there any **taboo** to the number of products packed in the box — eight chocolate bars versus 13, for instance? The point is to leave no stone unturned when it comes to **honing** in on the details of your product movement.

Word Study

workaround /'wɜːkəˌraʊnd/ n. 变通方法
buck /bʌk/ n. （美）钱，元
taboo /təˈbuː/ n. 禁忌，忌讳
hone /həʊn/ v. 磨练，训练

UNFAMILIARITY OF INCOTERMS AND HOW THEY AFFECT A SALE

Incoterms are considered essential to use in contracts for the sale of goods internationally. For example, here I discuss preparing a **pro forma invoice** using one of the common terms, CNF, which means cost and **freight** — you are responsible for paying the freight costs and collecting from your customer later. You must understand the costs and responsibilities that come with using a specific Incoterm. If you don't, it can lead to underpayment to you, for instance, on an export sale or overpayment to your supplier on an import.

It can also lead to customs problems, including documentation that might be prepared incorrectly. You can reduce the risk of the sale of goods internationally by negotiating effective trade terms.

NEVER VERIFYING THE REPUTATION AND LEGITIMACY OF A SUPPLIER OR CUSTOMER

Have you done your due diligence on who you are about to conduct business with? Verify prospective manufacturers. If you find them on a global sourcing site such as Global Sources or Alibaba, check to see whether they have a website on their own. If not, why not? What does that tell you? Conduct a search on the Internet to see what pops up.

On verifying customers, conduct an online search and see what turns up on search engines. Also, contact government officials to see what they know about the customer. If you are exporting from the United States to a customer in Brazil, for instance, contact one of the international trade specialists based on your sector of activity to find out more on the customer. You might also reach out to the U.S. Embassy in Brazil to see what they know.

Measures to Improve Import and Export Performance

DO YOUR MARKET RESEARCH

To maximize success, it's important to examine the target country's growth rates, internal market practices and pricing structures. Assess and re-assess the competition and whether the product makes sense in the target market. By collecting the necessary information, companies can overcome the lack of knowledge of foreign markets that often prevents firms from exporting.

By using different information sources, firms can gain better knowledge through foreign market research as well as guidance in how to attack a specific foreign market. These information sources can also provide valuable information about marketing and distribution channels

Word Study

Incoterm /ɪnˈkɒtɜːm/
  n. 国际贸易条规
pro forma invoice 形
  式发票
freight /freɪt/ n. 货运，
  货物

提高出口绩效的措施
① 进行市场调查
② 管好现金流
③ 寻找服务公司

as well as trade events and special assistance.

MANAGE YOUR CASHFLOW

International trade often results in working capital gaps between supplier terms and customer payments. Ensuring your ability to pay your suppliers promptly will mean you can develop a robust supply chain while offering favorable terms to the customers. This increase the potential for successful import and export trade.

FIND YOUR SERVICE PROVIDERS

There are several companies that specialize in providing services for firms wanting to start exporting. An EMC, export management company, offers all kinds of options from conducting the full export from production to retailer or distributor, or just one step in the exporting process.

Furthermore, there are plenty of different companies that provide similar services.

Hiring an EMC or at least someone to help navigate all the paperwork and regulations is useful in the beginning as well as focusing on one market or just a handful of markets. It can be a good idea to enter a market on a small scale to reduce costs of failure and allow more time and opportunity to learn about the market. Recognize the time and managerial commitment involved in building export sales.

Countertrade and Its Forms

对等贸易及其形式

对等贸易为流动资金渠道有限的国家提供了一种与其他国家交换商品和服务的机制，也为出口国提供了更大的国际市场。其主要形式包括：以货换货、反向购买、抵销贸易等。

In any form, countertrade provides a mechanism for countries with limited access to liquid funds to exchange goods and services with other nations. Countertrade is part of an overall import and export strategy that ensures a country with limited domestic resources having access to needed items and raw materials. Additionally, it provides the exporting nation with an opportunity to offer goods and services in a larger international market, promoting growth within its industries.

There are three primary reasons for countertrade: (1) it provides a trade financing alternative to those countries that have international debt and liquidity problems, (2) countertrade relationships may provide LDCs and MNCs with access to new markets, and (3) countertrade fits well conceptually with the resurgence of **bilateral** trade agreements between governments.

BARTER

Bartering is the oldest countertrade arrangement. It is the direct exchange of goods and services with an equivalent value but with no cash settlement. The bartering transaction is referred to as a trade. For example,

Word Study

bilateral /baɪˈlætərəl/ *adj.* 双边的

a bag of nuts might be exchanged for coffee beans or meat.

COUNTERPURCHASE

Under a counterpurchase arrangement, the exporter sells goods or services to an importer and agrees to also purchase other goods from the importer within a specified period. Unlike bartering, exporters entering into a counter purchase arrangement must use a trading firm to sell the goods they purchase and will not use the goods themselves.

OFFSET

In an offset arrangement, the seller assists in marketing products manufactured by the buying country or allows part of the exported product's assembly to be carried out by manufacturers in the buying country. This practice is common in aerospace, defense and certain infrastructure industries.

Offsetting is also more common for larger, more expensive items. An offset arrangement may also be referred to as industrial participation or industrial cooperation.

OTHER EXAMPLES OF A COUNTERTRADE

- A buyback is a countertrade occurs when a firm builds a manufacturing facility in a country — or supplies technology, equipment, training, or other services to the country and agrees to take a certain percentage of the plant's output as partial payment for the contract.
- Compensation trade is a form of barter in which one of the flows is partly in goods and partly in hard currency.
- A switch trade involves a triangular rather than bilateral trade agreement. When goods, all or part, from the buying country are not easily usable or salable, it may be necessary to bring in a third party to **dispose of** the merchandise.
- A clearing agreement is clearing account barter with no currency transation required. With a line of credit being established in the central banks of the two countries, the trade in this case is continuous, and the exchange of products between two governments is designed to achieve an agreed-on value or volume of trade **tabulated** or calculated in nonconvertible "clearing account units".

Benefits and Drawbacks

A major benefit of countertrade is that it facilitates the conservation of foreign currency, which is a prime consideration for cash-strapped nations and provides an alternative to traditional financing that may not be available in developing nations. Other benefits include lower

Word Study

dispose of 处理,处置
tabulate /'tæbjʊleɪt/ v.
列成表格,列表显示

实行对等贸易的益处
和缺点
　　对等贸易有助于
保存外汇,这是资金
短缺国家的首要考
虑因素,并为发展中

239

unemployment, higher sales, better capacity utilization, and ease of entry into challenging markets.

A major drawback of countertrade is that the value proposition may be uncertain, particularly in cases where the goods being exchanged have significant price volatility. Other disadvantages of countertrade include complex negotiations, potentially higher costs and logistical issues.

Additionally, how the activities interact with various trade policies can also be a point of concern for open-market operations. Opportunities for trade advancement, shifting terms, and conditions instituted by developing nations could lead to discrimination in the marketplace.

Key Terms 专业术语

countertrade 对等贸易
export management company 出口管理公司
bilateral trade agreements 双边贸易协定
hard currency 硬通货
clearing agreement 清算协定

sales potential 销售潜力
currency fluctuations 币值波动
compensation trade 补偿贸易
switch trade 转换贸易

Information Link 知识链接

国际贸易发展面临的挑战

（一）世界经济增长速度放缓

近年来，在众多因素的共同影响下，国际贸易整体发展速度趋缓。尤其是自2008年世界金融危机爆发以来，全球经济逐渐进入休眠、调整时期，国际贸易活动明显减弱。虽然近年来在科技创新、政治互动的作用下，世界国际贸易发展内在、外在动力充足，实现了快速增长，但随着日益频发的国际贸易纠纷、地缘政治风险、英国脱欧、全球金融波动等事件的发生，又在很大程度上加大了世界经济下行压力，使主要经济体增速逐渐触顶，新兴经济体增速回落。

（二）全球贸易保护主义抬头

一般而言，经济危机爆发后总是伴随着贸易保护主义的发生。2008年随着全球经济危机影响力的逐渐显现，世界经济增长速度放缓，贸易保护主义在全球范围内不断蔓延开来。2019年世界各国面对全球经济下行压力增大的现实情况，逐渐开启了贸易保护主义，并在贸易政策的制定上向内倾斜。国际货币基金组织在《世界经济展望》中也对各国贸易摩擦的不良影响进行了分析，将其视为拖累全球经济发展的"主要威胁"。

（三）全球贸易规则面临重构

在全球经济一体化不断发展的背景下，国际贸易发展外部影响因素逐渐增多，这对于企业家投资决策的制定、信心的树立以及对市场的敏锐性等都将造成一定的干扰。各国为最大程度上确保本国企业家利益，实现国际贸易的顺畅发展，不断就国际贸易问题展开博弈。尤其是在各国国际贸易发展政策差异化的情况下，更是增加了博弈的不确定性，造成了各国贸易关系的紧张化。

文献来源：

李达.新时代国际贸易发展面临的挑战分析［J］.商讯，2020（08）：130-131.

A. Describe the benefits of importing and exporting respectively.

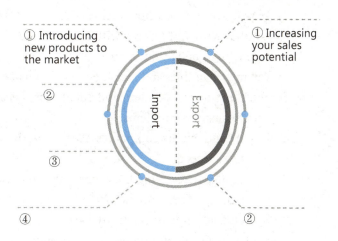

B. According to the text, fill in each of the following blanks with an appropriate word or phrase.

1) Free trade opens the ability to import goods and materials from cheaper production zones and reduces reliance on _____ goods.

2) If a nation's currency is not _____ or no good overseas, they may offer a commodity or other product in place of cash.

3) Importing and exporting goods is not only important for businesses; it is important for _____, too.

4) Thanks to internet expansion, entrepreneurs can conduct _____ _____ prior to importing a certain product.

5) Instead of investing in modern, expensive machinery, entrepreneurs may choose to import goods and reduce their _____.

6) One of the key benefits of importing products is the opportunity to become a _____ in the industry of interest.

7) Manufacturing businesses are very aware that their _____ largely depends on the quality of the items they produce.

8) While importing products can help businesses reduce costs, _____ _____ products can ensure increasing sales and sales potential in general.

9) Exporting products is especially good for _____ and _____ businesses — the ones that have already expanded within the local market.

10) If your products are considered unique or _____ abroad, your profits can increase rapidly in no time.

C. Read the text and decide whether the following statements are True (T) or False (F).

1) You have to know the exchange rates when trading internationally, or you will be exposed to potential currency fluctuations. ( )

2) It is unnecessary for businessmen to build a good relationship with customs officials, transportation folks and customs brokers. ( )

3) If you are conducting business in a foreign market, you must be familiar with and comply with the laws and regulations there. ( )

4) Importing goods that violate quota restrictions could end up costing you money in fines and penalties, and that will erode your profits. ( )

5) You don't have to understand Incoterms, because they are unlikely to lead to customs problems. ( )

6) Import and export companies need to do thorough market research in order to succeed. ( )

7) The customer receiving the goods (importer) and the lending institution that's financing the operation constitute the trade flow process. ( )

8) Switch trade involves a third party to take care of the goods that are not easily usable or salable in the receiving country. ( )

9) By collecting the necessary information, companies is still not able to overcome the lack of knowledge of foreign markets that often prevents firms from exporting. ( )

10) Bartering is the direct exchange of goods and services with an equivalent value but with no cash settlement. ( )

Discussion
讨论

1) What's exporting, importing, and countertrade respectively? Why are they important in international trade?

_____

_____

2) Can you explain the common pitfalls involved in importing and exporting?

_____

_____

3) What's the measures to improve import and export performance? Retell them with you own words.

_____

_____

4) Besides the three primary reasons for countertrade, can you give more reasons? Discuss with your partner.

_____

_____

5) Can you give some examples of goods that are exported to or imported from China? Discuss with your partner.

_____

_____

Analyzing
the Case
案例分析

Case Story

A Chinese Ban on Rubbish Imports Is Shaking up the Global Junk Trade

On the first day of 2018, a huge shock hit the global recycling industry. China, which is the world's biggest scrap importer, stopped accepting virtually any recycled plastic and unsorted scrap paper from abroad, and severely curbed imports of cardboard. The amount of recovered material that America, the world's biggest exporter of scrap, sent to China was 3m tonnes less than in the first half of 2018 than a year earlier, a drop of 38%. China plans to phase in bans on most other rubbish, of which it imports $24bn-worth a year. At recycling plants across the Western world, bales of mixed paper and polymers now languish in forecourts awaiting offers.

China used to import a significant portion of the world's scrap. Suddenly, revenues from selling mixed waste to China which waste-management companies used to cross-subsidise collection, dried up, hitting margins for American waste-management companies.

The Chinese ban removed the third leg of the "collect, sort, export" system on which the West had long relied. Improvements to automation could in time sort some of the surplus rubbish no longer sailing to China, but they have been incremental. High labor costs make hiring enough human sorters to deal with Western waste volumes prohibitively expensive. Because they, too, cannot rely on cheap labor, Western reprocessing firms need cleaner inputs than their Chinese counterparts, so shun a lot of what MRFs currently spit out. Even if they did not, their capacity is insufficient to deal with the glut. Incinerators and landfill will take some of the surplus waste. But the capacity of both is limited. Building a new incinerator costs upwards of $200m. Landfills are being gradually regulated out of existence, with many places, including California and the European

Union, mandating cuts to the volume of waste being landfilled.

The ban is likely to prove more of a long-term headache than the trade spat. It is part of a broader clampdown on polluting industries in China. It aims to banish "solid waste with major environmental hazards" and thus protect the public. That will deprive many countries of the destination of choice for their waste. But many experts are already seeing a silver lining. Activists and advocates of "circularity" say that it is forcing rich countries to rethink what they do with their waste now that a chunk of it can no longer be swept away overseas. It is in that way forcing a longer-term change.

Slow Boat or Junk?

China came to dominate the global rubbish trade in much the same way it has come to dominate all areas of trade. It has desire for resources, including second-hand ones, to feed its booming economy. China's $24bn-worth of recycled-materials imports are a quarter of the total traded globally, and up from $12bn a decade earlier. On the eve of the ban, more than half of the world's used plastic, paper and cardboard — around 32m tonnes each year in all — sailed to China, chiefly from the rich world. Plenty of metal scrap went there too, especially copper to wire cities or manufacture electronics.

It was also helped by the nature of its trade flows. Bulky scrap shipments to Chinese ports were only affordable thanks to "backhauling". Container vessels had crossed the Pacific laden with Chinese products for North American markets. Rather than let them sail back empty, shipping companies ferried scrap for the return leg at rock-bottom prices. Around half of all westbound trans-Pacific container traffic was rubbish for recycling.

Because of the ban, shipping companies, whose low margins were offset by massive volumes, now risk losing the backhaul trade. Drewry, a shipping consultancy, estimates that the ban could jeopardise 4m-5m containers sailing west across the Pacific annually. That is equivalent to 3% of worldwide container traffic. Port authorities from New York to California are rewriting their long-term strategies to take account of the change.

China is not immune from the impact. Its operation, dubbed "National Sword", looks double-edged too, striking at its domestic reprocessing industry — and manufacturing more broadly. Western scrap-industry veterans express astonishment at the Chinese authorities' willingness to sacrifice the needs of its industrial base, parts of which rely heavily on reprocessed materials, in order to protect the environment. China recycled 85% of the 7m tonnes of plastic it imported in 2016 (the rest went to landfills or was incinerated). Many Chinese reprocessing firms are now worried about the future.

Some also see the benefits. Liu Jianguo, an expert on waste management at Tsinghua University in Beijing, calls the ban "good news for domestic waste recycling", for the same reason that it will help Western countries. It will force the Chinese industry to change, adapt and be less reliant on imported foreign trash (though there is a danger in the short run that some Chinese reprocessors, starved suddenly of imported inputs, could fold, resulting in the dumping or burning of even more rubbish than it does already).

The ban has, however, given a boost to one group of Western entrepreneurs. In 2017 Rashad Abbasov co-founded Scrapo. It is an online marketplace that matches buyers and sellers of second-hand polymers in different countries. Since its inauguration in November, suppliers have posted offers to sell 1.5m tonnes of recovered plastic on Scrapo. It now has more than 10,000 users, 70% outside America. Just 6% are from traditional plastic-waste importers like China, Indonesia or Vietnam.

Other parts of the trade are also moving online. Scrap Monster, a platform for trading recovered metal, has 50,000 registered users. MerQbiz is a digital platform to streamline the $30bn annual reused-paper market. Another forum, the Materials Marketplace, allows American manufacturers to exchange factory by-products and leftovers more easily. State-level versions exist in Ohio and Tennessee. Two years ago the project spawned an offshoot in Turkey. Another is under development in Vietnam. Advocates of "circularity" welcome such initiatives, which aim to wring the most out of available resources. The Chinese ban has done them all a favour by enabling recovered materials to flow to the highest bidder — and so the highest-value use. But it has also exposed the shortcomings of the recycling industry.

Case Discussion

1) Why does the author say that "this ban on rubbish imports is shaking up the global junk trade"?

   _____

   _____

2) What does Liu Jianguo mean by calling the ban "good news for domestic waste recycling"?

   _____

   _____

3) How has the ban given a boost to Western entrepreneurs?

   _____

   _____

Case Summary

2018年的第一天，全球回收业受到巨大冲击。作为世界上最大的废品进口国，中国几乎不再接受任何来自国外的回收塑料和未分类废纸，并严格限制纸板进口。中国计划逐步禁止大多数其他垃圾，价值240亿美元/每年。

本文主要讲述中国禁止进口垃圾的禁令对全球垃圾贸易的冲击，体现出全球贸易环环相扣、相互影响的特点。由于这项禁令，西方废品管理公司利润大打折扣，废品回收行业受到巨大冲击。利润率较低的航运公司现在面临着失去回程贸易的风险，同时中国国内后处理工业和更广泛的制造业也不能免受冲击。但这项举措也让一些人看到了好处。它可促使西方发达国家改变现有依赖出口处理废品的模式，也促使中国工业改变、适应和减少对进口外国垃圾的依赖。同时，它也激励了一批企业家，部分贸易向网上转移。

Reading I

How to Start an Import / Export Business?

International trade is one of the hot industries of the new millennium. But it's not new. Think Marco Polo. Think the great caravans of the biblical age with their cargoes of silks and spices. Think even further back to prehistoric man trading shells and salt with distant tribes. Trade exists because one group or country has a supply of some commodity or merchandise that is in demand by another. And as the world becomes more and more technologically advanced, as we shift in subtle and not so subtle ways toward one-world modes of thought, international trade becomes more and more rewarding, both in terms of profit and personal satisfaction.

Importing is not just for those lone footloose adventurer types who survive by their wits and the skin of their teeth. Everything from beverages to commodes — and a staggering list of other products you might never imagine as global merchandise — are fair game for the savvy trader. And these products are bought, sold, represented and distributed somewhere in the world on a daily basis. But the import/export field is not the sole purview of the conglomerate corporate trader, according to the U.S. Department of Commerce, the big guys make up only about 4 percent of all exporters, which means that the other 96 percent of exporters — the lion's share are small outfits.

Types of Import / Export Businesses

• Export management company (EMC): An EMC handles export operations for a domestic company that wants to sell its product overseas but doesn't know how (and perhaps doesn't want to know how). The

EMC does it all — hiring dealers, invoicing customers, distributors and representatives; handling advertising, marketing and promotions; overseeing marking and packaging; arranging shipping; and sometimes arranging financing or contracting out for developing a credit card app.

- **Export trading company (ETC):** While an EMC has merchandise to sell and is using its energies to seek out buyers, an ETC attacks the other side of the trading coin. It identifies what foreign buyers want to spend their money on and then hunts down domestic sources willing to export. An ETC sometimes takes title to the goods and sometimes works on a commission basis.

- **Import/export merchant:** This international entrepreneur is a sort of free agent. He has no specific client base, and he doesn't specialize in any one industry or line of products. Instead, he purchases goods directly from a domestic or foreign manufacturer and then packs, ships and resells the goods on his own. This means, of course, that unlike the EMC, he assumes all the risks (as well as all the profits).

Swimming the Trade Channel

Now that you're familiar with the players, you'll need to take a swim in the trade channel, the means by which the merchandise travels from the manufacturer to the end user. Who your fellow swimmers are will depend on how you configure your trade channel, but they could include any of the following:

- **Manufacturer's representative:** a salesperson who specializes in a type of product or line of complementary products.

- **Distributor or wholesale distributor:** a company that buys the product you've imported and sells it to a retailer or other agent for further distribution until it gets to the end user.

- **Representative:** a savvy salesperson who pitches your product to wholesale or retail buyers, then passes the sale on to you.

- **Retailer:** the tail end of the trade channel where the merchandise smacks into the consumer.

Target Market

Every business needs consumers for its products and services to, as the Vulcans so eloquently put it, live long and prosper. Now that you know what running an import/export business entails, you need to plan, or target, your market, and determine who your potential clients will be, which geographic areas you'll draw from, and what specific products or services you'll offer to draw them in.

Who Are Your Customers?

Any manufacturer, supplier, crafter, artisan, importer, exporter or retailer is fair game. You can go after companies that deal in gourmet goodies or pet food, telecommunications or toys. The only essential requirement is that they want to sell their merchandise or buy someone else's.

What's My Niche?

You've narrowed the list of products you'll target. Now you'll want to find your niche, the unique angle that will set your business apart from — and above — the competition. This is where you can really let your creativity shine through. You may decide to start as an export management company (EMC), seeking out buyers for domestic manufacturing firms, or as an export trading company (ETC), finding domestic sources willing to export.

Market Research

Here's a rapid-fire overview of your market research tasks. You'll want to do some in-depth investigation into each of these areas:

The product or service you'll sell;

The end user you'll aim for (mass-market consumer, heavy industry, light industry, medical or hospital use, government, business or professional);

The country or countries you'll export to or import from;

The trade channel you'll use (direct sales, representative, distributor or commission representative).

Startup Costs

One of the catch-22s of being in business for yourself is that you need money to make money — in other words, you need startup funds. These costs range from less than $5,000 to more than $25,000 for the import/export business. One of the many nifty things about an import/export business is that its startup costs are comparatively low.

Your basic necessities will be a computer, printer, fax machine and modem. If you already have these items, then you're off and running.

Income & Billing

What can you expect to make as an international trader? The amount's entirely up to you, depending only on how serious you are and how willing you are to expand. As an international trader, you're an intermediary in the buying and selling, or importing and exporting, transaction. Therefore, you have to determine not just the price of the product, but the price of your services as well.

Operations

What you will be doing during your peak hours and beyond will depend upon how you've structured your services. Some traders act only as sales representatives, finding buyers and taking commissions, but steer clear of the shipping, documentation and financing aspects of the deal. No matter how exotic you want to get, your most basic tasks will be obtaining merchandise, selling it, transporting it and getting paid for it.

The Export Path

Exporter — you've found a buyer for your merchandise. Follow the export path:

Generate the pro forma invoice — give the importer a quote on your merchandise; negotiate if necessary.

Receive the letter of credit from your bank.

Fulfill terms of the letter of credit: Have the merchandise manufactured if necessary; make shipping and insurance arrangements; pack the merchandise; and have the merchandise transported.

Collect shipping documents.

Present shipping documents to your bank.

The Import Path

Importer — you've found the merchandise you want to buy and then resell. Follow the import path:

Receive the proforma invoice, the exporter's quote on the merchandise; negotiate if necessary.

Open a letter of credit at your bank.

Verify that the merchandise has been shipped.

Receive documents from the exporter.

See merchandise through customs.

Collect your merchandise.

Marketing

As an international trader, your mission is sales — in two different but overlapping arenas: a) selling yourself and your company to clients as an import/export manager for their products, and b) selling the products themselves to representatives and distributors. Success in one of these arenas will contribute to your success in another. Once you've established a favorable sales record with one client's goods, you'll have a track record with which to entice other clients. And, of course, each success will contribute to your own self-confidence, which will, in turn, lend that air of confidence to your negotiations with new prospects.

Second Thoughts

For each of the following statements, choose one (or more than one) answer to fill in the blank.

1) An EMC handles _____ for a _____ that wants to sell its product overseas but doesn't know how.
   A. export operations
   B. import operations
   C. foreign company
   D. domestic company

2) In the part of "Target Market", you need to find your *niche* because
_____.

    A. it is the sole purview of the conglomerate corporate trader

    B. it has no specific client base and cheap mechanism

    C. it is the unique angle that will make you stand out in competition

    D. it is a track record with which to entice other clients

Reading II

Countertrade and International Marketing: Take a Proactive Approach!

In setting prices for products marketed and sold internationally, a company faces a dilemma: In what currency should price be quoted?

Three choices are possible: the price may be quoted in the seller's currency, the buyer's currency, or the currency of a third country.

For a number of reasons, importers and exporters both prefer that their own currency be used. There are, however, options other than currencies.

Using Countertrade in International Commerce

As markets become more global, companies are realizing that selling a widget does not necessarily bring in a currency of choice. It may bring in a case of vodka, a voucher for a Caribbean tour package, or advertising space.

Here are a few examples:

A multinational marketer in the soft drink industry such as CocaCola, Pepsi or Schweppes might agree to operate a tomato factory in one country, market the host country's beer in its home country, and find a market for vodka in yet another country. In order to make a sale, the soft drink company may agree to accept fruit and vegetables, greeting cards, carpet backings, or pig skins.

Under foreign direct investment schemes, an automobile manufacturer may build an auto plant in a foreign country and agree to purchase the finished product back. They would then agree to market the product in its home country or in other countries of the world. In other instances, it may sign an agreement to purchase sheepskin, potatoes, toilet seats, cranes, coffee or any other product that the host government or the prospective buyer might wish to dispose of.

An aircraft manufacturer might accept responsibility for finding markets for a variety of consumer goods produced in a host country in return for the sale of its aircraft. In order to sell its products in a particular country, a steel manufacturer might be required to take back products ranging from palm oil to coffee to timber.

These are all examples of countertrades — transactions that link exports and imports of goods or services in addition to, or in place of, financial settlements.

New World Order

In the global economy of the 21st Century, countertrade is being increasingly viewed by firms and nations as an excellent mechanism to gain entry into new markets. Studies by the U.S. government, United Nations, and other independent organizations estimate that countertrade represents somewhere between 10% and 20% of all world trade.

Many countries of the world lack a fully elastic currency capable of expanding with the growth of production to meet the demands of product and service markets. The money supply in these countries is often controlled by monetary authorities targeting specific economic objects like curbing inflation, ensuring full employment, and protecting the value of its currency in foreign exchange markets. Countertrade and financing terms in these country markets are becoming as important as the quality and availability of desirable product.

Countertrade as Marketing Tool

To the uninitiated, countertrade is a generic term for parallel business transactions that link a sales contract with an agreement to purchase goods or services as a means of reducing the flow of convertible currency. For marketers suffering from marketing myopia, it is a last ditch sales strategy.

For proactive marketers, it is viewed as a respectable, almost essential global strategy tool. Countertrade is a resourceful way to arrange for the sale of a product from an exporter to a company in a country that does not have the resources to pay for it in hard currency.

The main reason that American firms engage in countertrade is to meet requirements set forth by foreign governments or customers. Countertrade, however, can be an effective and excellent mechanism to gain entry into new markets.

The party receiving the goods as a mode of full or partial payment of exported goods or services may be instrumental in opening up new international marketing channels and ultimately expanding the market for mutual benefit of both exporter and importer. Yet, countertrade remains essentially a reactionary trade practice for many companies.

Forms of Countertrade

All countertrade transactions explicitly link import and export transactions between two traders, but they can differ from each other in terms of whether they involve foreign exchange in the transaction, whether the two trade flows are temporarily separated, and where the trade flows stand in technical relation to each other.

The Global Offset and Countertrade Association (GOCA) identifies five categories of countertrade based on the degree of complexity of the trading arrangement. These include:

Barter/swap,

Counterpurchase,

Compensation/buyback,

Clearing arrangements/switch trading, and

Offsets.

Counterpurchase is the most frequently used form of countertrade, followed by offsets, buy back/compensation, barter/swaps, and switch trading.

Challenges of Countertrade

One of the unique challenges of countertrade transactions is that companies often find themselves handling products with which they are not familiar. In addition, they may receive products that vary in quality from shipment to shipment.

Since many countertrade transactions are longer-term contracts, the price of a countertrade product may vary substantially on the world market over the term of the contract. If a company has a fixed price for a product in a countertrade, they may end up with substantial losses or an inability to sell the product.

Marketers accepting goods in countertrade must also be concerned with many of the following issues:

- Quality and consistency of products accepted as part of the agreement, and unavailability of preferred items offered on a compensation account shopping list.
- Determining the value and potential demand for the goods offered in countertrade.
- Unavailability of a ready market for goods bartered.
- Extended and complex negotiation processes and increased transaction costs.
- Lack of time to conduct a market analysis; it is not unusual to have sales negotiations almost completed before countertrade is introduced as a requirement for the transaction.
- Added overall complexity and time commitment due to the risks associated with the political, legal, cultural and economic environment in the importing country.

Developing a Proactive Strategy

It is important that global marketers develop appropriate market entry and countertrade strategies to take advantage of new opportunities. These strategies involve decisions in areas including, but not limited to: which markets to enter, which products to accept, and when to walk away from a countertrade offer.

Exporters generally have three options for disposing of countertraded goods: They may (1) use the products in-house as part of their own production process, (2) use in-house marketing resources to find a market for the goods, or (3) hire intermediaries/barter houses to find markets for the countertraded goods.

Retaining a reliable trading company or barter house familiar with either the country or the product reduces strategic risks involved in countertrade agreements. Large commodity traders, barter houses, export trading companies, banks, and independent agents are well trained and experienced in arranging countertrade transactions for global marketers.

Second Thoughts

1) How many examples did the author give that use countertrade in international commerce? Please give more examples.

   _____

   _____

2) What are the three options for disposing of countertraded goods? Summarize it with your own words.

   _____

   _____

Global Production, Outsourcing and Logistics

全球化生产、业务外包及物流

CHAPTER 13

本章概要

本章主要介绍全球化生产的含义、特点及机制、全球供应链、物流业务外包,以及以中国、印度等国家为代表的全球化生产参与者。

学习指南

当公司准备走向全球时,掌握全球化生产的定义并了解相关成功案例会大有裨益。全球化生产是指企业用来生产产品或服务的一个全球化系统。虽然听起来简单,但全球化生产涉及多个领域,有许多方面需要保持同步。例如,企业员工、系统运行所需信息、所使用的资源,甚至企业用来遵守政府规定所使用的工具等等,都可以被认为是全球化生产的一部分。

通过本章学习,希望大家能够实现以下目标:

(1)基本目标(Text-based Goals)

- 掌握本章涉及话题的基本专业术语及词汇,如全球化生产、供应链管理、物流外包等。
- 掌握本章的主要知识点,即全球化生产的含义、特点及机制、全球化物流及业务外包等。

(2)拓展目标(Extended Goals)

- 思考本章引言,为什么奥巴马认为"全球化进程不会走回头路"?
- 通过学习背景知识、拓展阅读、案例分析进一步了解全球化生产的主要背景、内涵及影响。

Learning the definition of and best practices for global production now can help when your company is ready to go global. The definition of global production is pretty straightforward: it is the worldwide system that a business uses to produce products or services. That sounds simple enough. Global production can be anything, but there are so many facets that need to be in sync. Employees, the information they need to keep the system running, the resources that they use, and even the tools businesses use to stay compliant with government regulations can be considered part of global production.

Global Production and Supply Chain Management

BENEFITS OF A GLOBAL SUPPLY CHAIN

One of the benefits of a global supply chain is lowered costs for businesses. Granted, at first glance, you wouldn't think extending a supply chain around the planet would help a business bring down the price of their final product or service. (Freight and transportation obviously will always add numbers to the bottom line.) But many countries have lower production costs that make it attractive to expand a supply chain to other parts of the world. You also may be able to bring down expenses by purchasing goods and services from a supplier when the dollar is stronger against the national currency of the country that you're doing business with.

Another benefit is that a global supply chain can make it easier to sell to customers around the world. If your company has outposts in the supply chain throughout, say, Asia and Europe, your business may find it easier to start selling to those parts of the world as well.

You're also potentially spreading your risk by having a global supply chain. Let's say you didn't have a global supply chain, and your supply chain was **relegated** to one particular region. If that area had a severe natural disaster, you could see your entire business come to a halt for a few days, weeks or even longer, depending on how bad of a disaster we're talking. Of course, you could argue that you're increasing your risks by having a global supply chain. Odds are, something will go wrong somewhere along the chain. But the better the supply chain management, the lower those risks can be.

全球化生产和供应
链管理
　　全球供应链的优
势主要有三点：降低
企业生产成本；使企
业更容易把产品或
服务销售给世界各
地的客户；分散企业
承担的风险。

Word Study

relegate /'relɪgeɪt/ v.
使降级，降低……
的地位

Word Study

pinpoint /ˈpɪnˌpɔɪnt/ v.
准确指出
imperative /ɪmˈperətɪv/
adj. 至关重要的
robust /rəʊˈbʌst/ adj.
强劲的

WHAT DOES A GLOBAL SUPPLY CHAIN NEED TO SUCCEED?

There are a lot of factors that come together to make a global supply chain successful, and it's almost impossible to **pinpoint** one as the most important.

Cash flow and a good financial steward is obviously vital. If your business doesn't have enough working capital and can't pay for its own infrastructure, it probably won't stay in business very long. It's important to run the supply chain well so that you don't lose money on it. Daren Samuels is practice director of operations at Patina Solutions, which offers on-demand executives in all industries and is headquartered in Brookfield, Wisconsin. According to Samuels, a supply chain can consume up to 85 percent of a company's revenue. "So getting it right is really important", he says.

Things such as managing waste and avoiding employee theft are also very important. You need to have policies that prevent loss, says Mark Struss, practice director of manufacturing operations at Patina Solutions. For instance, if you have valuable components being made or stored in warehouses, your manufacturing plants may require using "only clear trash bags and, depending on the size and value of the components, lunch box inspections at clock out may make sense." That may sound extreme, but hire the wrong people, and you could lose a lot of money over the years.

A clear plan for your logistics is also **imperative**, especially if you're dealing in e-commerce. "It's critical for businesses to be able to reach as many customers as quickly — and cheaply — as possible", says Jake Rheude, vice president of marketing at Red Stag Fulfillment, a third-party logistics (3PL) company headquartered in Knoxville, Tennessee. "We're in a very competitive industry, as there are lots of warehouses all over the country, placed strategically near urban centers to minimize delivery distance", Rheude says. "Just because you, the customer, got free shipping on that order from a department store doesn't mean shipping was actually free. So a major component of supply chains is to use 3PLs to help fill that cost gap by minimizing the resources sunk into moving orders from point A to point B."

Again, it all comes down to cost. A global supply chain needs to be as efficient as possible, so costs don't go out of control. For instance, say you produce too many goods, and they end up sitting in a warehouse for an extended period of time.

WHAT TYPES OF BUSINESS SEE THE MOST SUCCESS FROM GLOBAL SUPPLY CHAINS?

Many manufacturing companies can benefit from a global supply chain, and certainly any business that wants to be an international force and sell to countries around the world is going to need a **robust** system for getting its products or services from Point A to Point B. Food and beverage, mining, oil and gas, electronics and the textile industries are just a few of the many that thrive with global supply chains. If your business produces a product to sell to the public on large scale, you may do well to have a global supply chain, if you don't have one already.

HOW IS A GLOBAL SUPPLY CHAIN RELATED TO GLOBAL VALUE CHAINS?

The term global value chain refers to an international supply chain of people and activities that go into creating and offering goods or services when the supply chain needs to be managed across different countries.

This, of course, sounds like the definition of a global supply chain. The subtle difference is that a global supply chain generally is referred to when discussing the manufacturing and distribution steps. For example, you probably wouldn't include your research and development or marketing team when talking about your global supply chain. They add a lot of value, but you could probably produce or distribute your goods without them.

A global value chain, however, describes it all, and when you have a global supply chain, you need to be thinking about it all. Even your **custodial** service might be considered part of your global value chain, especially if your product or service is in the food or medical industries.

Basically, if a partner, vendor or supplier adds value to your business, and could hurt your supply chain if something broke down, then that's an important part of your global value chain — even if it's only indirectly part of the supply chain. And if you don't have the working capital or resources to quickly fix a problem that suddenly surfaces, you could quickly have a problem that doesn't go away any time soon.

But that's why it can be smart to think about a global value chain along with your global supply chain. If you place importance on every piece of the system that produces your goods or services, your business is less likely to be inefficient and run into trouble in the future. There's a lot of value in thinking about a global value chain.

Outsourcing Logistics: Does It Make Sense for Everyone?

The benefits of outsourcing logistics processes to a third-party logistics provider are well documented. As the world's economy has become increasingly complex, it has become impossible for a single entity to control all of the warehousing, transportation and administrative tasks that come with shipping and managing inventory. For this reason, more companies are turning to 3PLs to help with cost reductions and overall management of supply chain processes. However, organizations must be careful to ensure they do not overstep their bounds before, during and after selecting a 3PL.

全球供应链与全球价值链的关系

全球价值链指的是当需要跨国管理供应链时，由创造提供商品或服务的人员和活动组成的国际供应链。全球供应链通常只涉及制造和销售，而全球价值链则包含了所有的一切。

Word Study

custodial /kʌˈstəʊdɪəl/
adj. 照管的

物流业务外包：真的对所有人都适用吗？

有大量证据证明，将物流业务外包给第三方物流供应商大有裨益。随着世界经济变得越来越复杂，一个单一实体已经不可能控制所有的仓储、运输以及管理任务，因此更多的企业转向第三方物流，以降低成本，方便供应链的整体管理。

For example, a complete legacy warehouse management system may need to be significantly updated in terms of technology and physical space before integrating with a newer, more comprehensive system. Ultimately, the decision to outsource should not be taken lightly, and company executives need to understand a few facts before outsourcing and a few considerations when selecting a provider. This is the only way to make sure outsourcing benefits a company.

BASIC FACTS TO UNDERSTAND BEFORE OUTSOURCING LOGISTICS

Know what services you need to outsource

Many 3PLs have extensive offerings, and you need to know what services will and will not improve your existing operation. In other words, you must understand what needs to be improved before considering outsourcing. Create a list of services you offer, and define what services you would like to have. This may include the following:

- Better inventory management
- Auditing services
- Small package processing and shipping
- Labeling
- Tracking of packages via the Internet of Things (IoT)
- Advanced order and payment processing
- Defined roles of Importer and Exporter of Record
- Preventative maintenance initiatives
- **Holistic** transportation management system (TMS)

Omni-channel globalization of the supply chain requires more contacts and options

Small to medium businesses routinely operate in local or regional spaces, but as the world grows more interconnected, you need to look beyond your optimal service area. This helps you grow your business, and a 3PL can provide you access to resources that you may have never even considered as needing improvement. Essentially, a 3PL expands your access to other service providers, and the third-party nature of operations helps all partnered businesses gain a competitive advantage and other benefits.

Don't expect more than reasonable

The third core concept involves how a 3PL can reasonably improve your operations. This seems **redundant**, but many companies fail to realize the limitations of a 3PL. 3PLs have limits, and while some may be able to provide access to fast-track programs for customs processing, there will still be some delays. The key to truly taking advantage of a 3PL is knowing what is and is not reasonable, and if you can make this distinction, you can be ready to start the process of looking for and selecting a 3PL to outsource logistics.

Word Study

holistic /həʊˈlɪstɪk/
adj. 全盘的，全方位的
omni- /ɒmnɪ/ suf. 全方位的
redundant /rɪˈdʌndənt/
adj. 多余的，过剩的

CRITICAL THINGS TO KNOW WHEN CONSIDERING OUTSOURCING LOGISTICS

Once you've made the decision to outsource, it can feel like a turn-key operation. However, your input is still greatly needed and helpful, and you should look to a 3PL as a new employee, not just a service provider. As a result, you need to consider four aspects of 3PL practices before making a final selection.

3PLs aren't designed for short-term benefits

The best 3PLs in the world cannot help a financially bankrupt or consumer-**ousted** organization. As explained by Leslie Hansen Harps of inbound logistics, there is no guarantee that outsourcing will be successful, but you will never know if you only stick to outsourcing for short-term gains. Your company needs to understand the benefits of a 3PL are seen in long-term execution. You may not save money in the first few weeks, or even months, but the savings will start to roll in when your inefficiencies have been addressed and your opportunities have been widened.

3PLs focus on long-term, mutually beneficial business strategy

Although it may appear holistic and thorough, outsourcing is not a business strategy. It only makes up a portion of your business strategy, and you need to define your own business strategy to be successful. The key to making this work is aligning your business strategy with the long-term strategy of your 3PL. Moreover, you should look for a 3PL that has similar values and strengths that you listed as services you want to offer.

There are many different types of 3PL services

There're hundreds, if not thousands, of logistics outsourcing providers. They come in all shapes and sizes, and you must not be willing to ignore any of them. You need to give all 3PLs an equal opportunity to work with your company. This does not mean you have to sign contracts with each, but you do need to pay attention to what services each provider may offer. Look at the whole picture, and select a 3PL that goes just beyond what you actually need. In addition, make sure your partnered 3PL offers one-stop solutions. In other words, you should be able to complete all of your outsourcing requirements with one company that can connect you to other partners if needed.

3PLs are ineffective without collaboration

Outsourcing can take much of your burden of work off your shoulders. But, this is not an excuse to stop working for your organization. The 3PL may be effective at managing processes and identifying ways to save, but you have the most power to leverage. You can define what is and is not working for your employees' sense of direction and ability. For example, a 3PL can

Word Study

oust /aust/ *v.* 驱逐, 罢免

259

provide you with plenty of **metrics**, but if your employees hate a specific process, you need to let the provider know what is happening. Ultimately, you become a more important part of the supply chain's chain of command by acting as the bridge between your company and the 3PL. As a result, you must collaborate on both sides of the bridge to ensure all parties gain a positive return on investment for the creation of the business relationship.

Outsourcing logistics is a great opportunity for your company, and it can provide you with a way to grow your business beyond your expectations. However, not all businesses are ready for the expansion and capability granted by outsourcing. Fortunately, you can help prepare your business for outsourcing by understanding where you stand now and how to be realistic in your expectations when outsourcing logistics. Outsourcing logistics makes sense for many businesses, but it would not make sense if your business is incapable of considering what is and is not likely to occur.

Key Terms 专业术语

global production 全球化生产
financial steward 财务管家
third-party logistics (3PL) 第三方物流
global value chain 全球价值链
Importer and Exporter of Record 注册进出口商
Internet of Things (IoT) 物联网

supply chain management 供应链管理
working capital 营运资本
global supply chain 全球供应链
logistics outsourcing 物流外包

Information Link 知识链接

全球生产网络治理模式

全球生产网络是跨国公司在组织上的重要创新,它是以互补性分工为基础,通过相互依存的关系来并以一定正式的规制或契约相互联系在一起的一种组织模式。

全球生产网络作为一种复杂的生产组织方式,弥补和充实了除市场与企业这两个极端的协调方式之外的大量中间产品的交易和中间状态的交易组织。市场是组织经济活动最为简单和有效的一种模式,市场上各个经济行为主体通过货币买卖各种商品和服务,其运行的核心机制是价格机制。企业制运行的核心是管理控制。全球生产网络治理模式与其他两种方式相比呈现出以下特点。

第一,生产网络方式的主体关系。从各个主体关系看,生产网络中的领导厂商与其他厂商之间不是上下等级关系。它是以互补性分工为基础,以互惠互利为原则,通过相互依存的关系往来以一定正式的规则或契约相互联系在一起的一种生产组织治理模式。这种模式是一种稳定的双边交易契约,能将不确定性降至最低。

第二,实现资源共享的治理模式。传统的治理结构安排以企业内部资源配置效率为核心,强调企业的内部治理,而全球生产网络中的企业则更注重外部治理、共同治理模式。在全球生产网络中,供应商作为领导厂商内部生产系统的延伸和领导厂商有着共同的利益基础,二者在一定程度上实现资源共享,从而实现共同决策和共同治理。

第三,领导厂商成为生产网络的核心者。在一个全球生产网络中总是存在着一个核心治理者即领导厂商,它占据了生产网络上的高附加值的生产环节,抓住了整个生产网络,成为生产网络的核心者。领导厂商凭借自己拥有的特质资本,处于优势地位,吸附全球生产网络其他合作伙伴。

第四,领导厂商的治理模式呈多元化特征。一个参与到全球生产网络中的企业与其面对的不同关系的交易伙伴往往采取互不相同的治理模式。从购买协议到组建战略联盟再到股权的合资等方式,生产网络的联系程度逐渐加强,领导厂商就要根据交易类型、交易环境变化确定合适的网络联系程度,选择恰当的协作和治理方式。

文献来源:

杨继红,沈红霞.全球生产网络下的企业集群发展策略研究[J].沿海企业与科技,2006,(1): 1-2.

A. Write down the factors that a global supply chain needs to succeed.

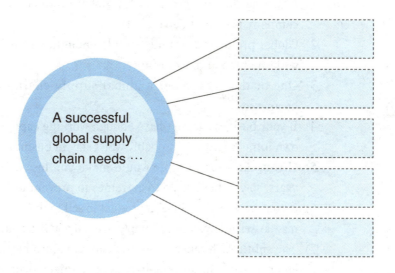

B. According to the text, fill in each of the following blanks with an appropriate word or phrase.

1) The global production is a _____ that a business uses to produce products or services.

2) If your supply chain was relegated to one region and that area had a severe natural disaster, you could see your entire business come to a _____ for a few days, weeks or even longer.

3) If your company has _____ in the supply chain throughout Asia and Europe, your business may find it easier to start selling to those parts of the world as well.

4) Things such as managing _____ and avoiding employee _____ are also very important for a global supply chain to succeed.

5) A global supply chain needs to be as _____ as possible, so costs don't go out of control.

6) Food and beverage, mining, oil and gas, electronics and the textile industries are just a few of the many that _____ with global supply chains.

7) It is smart to think about a _____ along with your global supply chain.

8) The benefits of _____ logistics processes to a third-party logistics provider are well documented.

9) 3PLs have limits, and while some may be able to provide access to fast-track programs for customs processing, there will still be some _____.

10) The 3PL may be effective at _____ processes and _____ ways to save, but you have the most power to leverage.

C. Read the text and decide whether the following statements are True (T) or False (F).

1) Learning the best practices for global production can help when your company is ready to go global. ( )

2) Global production sounds simple enough, and it is simple to do, too, with the help of outsourcing. ( )

3) One of the benefits of a global supply chain is lowered costs for businesses. ( )

4) If your business doesn't have enough working capital and can't pay for its own infrastructure, it probably won't stay in business very long. ( )

5) Hiring the wrong people would make you lose a lot of money over the years, so you have to go to extremes to prevent loss. ( )

6) If your business produces a product to sell to the public on large scale, you may do well to have a global supply chain, if you don't have one already. ( )

7) The subtle difference between a global value chain and a global supply chain is that the former is generally referred to when discussing the manufacturing and distribution steps. ( )

8) As the world's economy has become increasingly complex, it has become impossible for a single entity to control all of the warehousing, transportation and administrative tasks that come with shipping and managing inventory. ( )

9) Large businesses routinely operate in local or regional spaces, but as the world grows more interconnected, you need to look beyond your optimal service area. ( )

10) Outsourcing can take much of your burden of work off your shoulders, but this is not an excuse to stop working for your organization. ( )

1) What are the major benefits of a global supply chain?

_____

_____

2) What does a global supply chain need to succeed?

_____

_____

3) What are some of the benefits of outsourcing logistics?

_____

_____

4) What should be understood before outsourcing logistics?

_____

_____

5) How can a company select a 3PL to outsource logistics?

_____

_____

Case Story

Logistics Is Booming in China
— But Not Where You Think

Inland cities serve as land bridges between China and Europe, making them ripe for warehouse and transportation development.

China's coastal cities are booming with shipping and manufacturing, but there's a problem — they're running low on space, pushing some manufacturing and logistics hubs to nearby satellite cities and to that big land mass with people and plenty of area for development: The interior.

These inland cities serve as land bridges between eastern and western China, and between western China and Europe or Russia. But mostly, their growth serves their own population, as China consumes more goods domestically.

"The development of Grade A warehouses and modern transport infrastructure is dramatically upgrading inland cities' role in China's overall logistics system and positioning them to grow as major distribution hubs going forward", Joe Zhou, regional director and head of research for China at JLL, a commercial real estate advisory company focusing on warehouses and their supply chains customers, said so.

Top 3 Emerging Inland Logistics Hubs

Zhengzhou

The capital city of the Henan province is closely associated with Foxconn, which has manufactured and exported about half the world's Apple iPhones since 2010. It was China's first economic zone built around an airport and thought to be one of China's fastest growing airports for cargo and passengers. The Henan province is expected to increase the number of international air freight lines to 40 by 2020, up from 29 in 2016.

In 2017, four cargo trains began weekly service between Zhengzhou and Hamburg, Germany, though trains have been running between the cities less frequently since 2013, shuttling $2.82 billion in goods to Germany in that time. The Zhengzhou to Europe rail route accounts for about 30% of total rail volume for all Chinese rail routes to Europe, with cargo including electronics, industrial robotics and automobile parts.

Chengdu

This large city in southwestern China's Sichuan province is increasing rail and air service as well, while trying to attract high growth tech companies. In May, DHL Global Forwarding, along with the Rail Cargo Group, announced they were extending Vienna to China rail connections to Chengdu. DHL will offer door-to-door services for high value exports.

Lufthansa Cargo also started a new freighter operation there in May, with two round trip freighter flights weekly between Chengdu and Frankfurt. DHL's goal is to serve western China, and this is their first foray into a Chinese inland city with no port access. These rail containers are part of a multimodal network with remotely monitored temperature control and tracking, and fully managed customs clearance and consolidation.

Xi'an

Xi'an, in the middle of central China, opened a logistics park in 2008, with a free trade zone dry port and a rail link to western Europe.

"Xi'an is/has been one of the most attractive national center cities in China for traditional manufacturing and logistics industries", Jiang Wu, Xi'an general manager of GLP, a logistics property developer, said so. "To be the next big logistics center, it has a long way to go, because the industrial base is not yet mature enough, meaning high-tech industries have not yet set up shop in Xi'an on a larger scale."

However, it is an extremely attractive location for R&D centers, with increasing numbers of manufacturers, e-commerce companies and their logistics suppliers planning to invest there, he said, and that's generating more demand for Grade A warehouses.

In the past five years, GLP saw prime warehouse space demand double to 2.6 million square meters due to warehouse reorganization. The company currently has five logistics parks and is planning to develop two more in the greater Xi'an area.

Growing Pains in Inland Logistics Hubs

While higher real estate and labor costs on the coasts make inland growth attractive, the interior cities suffer from trained talent shortages, inconsistent infrastructure, regulatory limitations across geographies, fragmented distribution systems and underusage of technology in some regions, according to a PwC Hong Kong report.

China has more than 700,000 registered logistics companies, but they don't provide comprehensive service domestically because of localized regulations. Logistics providers don't usually serve coastal Chinese cities and the interior Chinese cities, making visibility difficult as cargo moves from area to area.

Part of the growth process is building up transportation infrastructure. Ocean freight is the cheapest way to move cargo (and most manufacturing is done in the coastal Chinese areas). The midrange alternative is rail, which doesn't hold as many goods, and air freight, with higher cost but faster delivery.

Transportation	Trade by volume	Trade by value
Ocean	94%	64%
Air	1.8%	28%
Rail	0.9%	2%
Road	3%	6%

Center for Strategic & International Studies

Currently government rail subsidies are helping to promote that growth, but some are concerned about what will happen should the government decrease or cut the subsidies completely. Compared to ocean and air freight data, access to basic rail lines information like rates, volume and even route frequency is difficult, making rail use more complex.

E-commerce Is Taking over Warehouse Space

While road transportation makes up a much smaller volume of trade, inland cities sit at the center of strong highway networks connecting dozens of small and medium size cities. "All of these cities are focal points of economic development in central and western China", Zhou said. They're drawing developers and tenants looking to build out regional warehouse and distribution networks.

As China's largest prime warehouse developer, GLP's data of leased area by tenant type is considered representative of the Chinese market as a whole. In its 2016 annual report, GLP indicated 90% of their warehouses were stocked by businesses serving the domestic market. E-commerce is growing in China as well, with such orders taking up 26% of GLP's warehouse space in 2016, compared to 3% in 2009.

GLP plans to remove more than half of their lower quality warehouses in the outskirts of Xi'an, in the West Third Ring Expressway area, to make room for commercial and residential developments. With the city expanding, "We believe that demand for high-end warehouse facilities will continue to grow", said Wu.

As demand for high quality warehousing grows, however, much of the older, less functional warehouses sit empty. "Experience shows that these cases of vacancy are resolved over time as demand for modern warehouse space continues to expand", Zhou said.

Case Discussion

1) Why are some manufacturing and logistics hubs of coastal cities now moving to nearby satellite cities or inland cities in China?

_____

_____

2) What are the growing pains that inland logistics hubs are facing?

_____

_____

3) If you were the mayor of Chengdu, what strategies would you take to boost the development of logistics industry in your city?

_____

_____

Case Summary

中国沿海城市的航运和制造业欣欣向荣，但却受到一个问题的困扰——沿海城市空间不足，迫使一些制造业和物流中心转移到附近的卫星城，以及人口众多、发展空间大的内陆地区。内陆城市拥有广阔的土地和大量的消费人口，是连接中国东部和西部，连接中国和欧洲的陆上桥梁。同时，不断兴修的现代化仓库以及不断发展的现代交通基础设施，也极大地提升了内陆城市在中国整体物流体系中的地位。

本文重点列举了三个蓬勃发展的中国内陆物流城市：与富士康关系紧密的郑州市、吸引高科技企业合作的成都市、传统制造业和物流业发达的西安市。尽管发展势头良好，但中国内陆物流业也面临着成长的烦恼与挑战。相较于发达的东部沿海城市，内陆地区仍然受到高素质劳动力短缺、基础设施建设落后、政策监管漏洞等不利因素的制约。此外，内陆城市还应该把握住如今电子商务发展崛起的时代机遇，顺势而为，在仓储设施、交通运输等方面做出及时转变。

Reading I

9 Major Companies Tied to the Apple Supply Chain

Apple (AAPL) is one of the most valuable companies in the U.S. with a market cap of over $1.3 trillion as of April 2020. A big part of its success has come from its ability to be a true innovator in personal technology. Millions of customers are willing to pay top dollar for the quality, design, and features of Apple devices, making products like the iPhone, iPad, Mac, iPod, and Apple Watch top sellers. To achieve this greatness though, Apple doesn't depend on its own manufacturing alone. It has over 200 suppliers that it relies on for procuring components for assembly.

Apple puts a great deal of effort into the monitoring of its supplier relationships that help to make the tech giant a manager of one of the most efficient supply-chain management systems on the market right now. Each year it releases a progress report outlining its supplier relationship efforts as well as a list of its top 200 suppliers — which account for 98% of its procurement. Below discusses nine of the most prominent.

In general, China is a very important global region for Apple. The 2019 suppliers list shows Chinese mainland and Hong Kong-based suppliers growing to account for a larger share than America and Japan, second only to the region of Taiwan, China. By physical location, China accounts for 380 of the total 809 production facilities.

1. Hon Hai Precision Industry — Foxconn (HNHPF)

Hon Hai Foxconn is one of the major reasons that Taiwan, China is on the map for Apple. Foxconn is one of Apple's oldest and largest suppliers. The company has its headquarters in Tucheng, New Taipei City.

Foxconn is often thought of as Apple's largest China supplier because of its vast number of Chinese supplier locations. In 2018, Foxconn had 35 supplier locations servicing Apple from China, India, Brazil, Vietnam, and the United States. 29 of its 35 locations are in Chinese mainland. Foxconn has also helped Apple to branch out to India with one location there.

2. Wistron

Wistron is another Taiwan-based company that's also helping Apple expand into India. Wistron has five supplier locations with three in Chinese mainland and two in India. A focus for Wistron in India is printed circuit boards for iPhones.

3. Pegatron

Pegatron has its headquarters in Taiwan, China with only one local supplier location in Taoyuan. Pegatron's other 17 locations include 12 sites in Chinese mainland along with sites in the Czech Republic, Singapore, Korea, Japan, and the United States. Pegatron is similar to Foxconn in that it provides iPhone assembly.

4. Goertek

Goertek and Luxshare are two Chinese companies that have been in the Apple supplier spotlight. Both companies agreed to setup productions in Vietnam to improve the manufacturing cost efficiency of the Airpod. Goertek has three supplier locations, two in China and one in Vietnam. The company has its headquarters in Weifang, China.

5. Luxshare

Luxshare is also in partnership with Apple for production of the Airpods. It has eight supplier locations with seven in China and one in Vietnam.

Despite reliance on an international supply chain, Apple is also still very dependent on many companies in the U.S., including 3M (MMM), Broadcom (AVGO), Qualcomm (QCOM), Intel (INTC), Jabil (JBL), On (ON), Micron (MU), and Texas Instruments (TXN). Other U.S. companies also include Finisar (FNSR), Qorvo (QRVO), Skyworks (SWKS), and Corning (GLW).

6. Qualcomm (QCOMM)

Qualcomm and Intel have made U.S. headlines over fierce legal actions. NASDAQ-listed Qualcomm is a world leader in semiconductor, mobile, and telecom products and services. It is known to supply multiple electronic components to Apple, including envelope power trackers, baseband processors, power management modules, and GSM/CDMA receivers and transceivers. These are various instruments used in device power management systems and in mobile signaling.

Qualcomm has also come through for Apple devices, offering necessary modem technology.

Modem technology is however at the core of the Apple, Intel, and Qualcomm disputes. Apple announced it was buying Intel's smartphone modem business. This led to a lawsuit by Qualcomm which resulted in maintenance of the modem manufacturing relationship for Qualcomm even after the Intel acquisition.

7. Intel (INTC)

In July of 2019 Apple announced its agreement with Intel to acquire the majority of its smartphone modem business. With the acquisition Apple broadened its patent ownership and setup a strong plan for 5G development. Moreover, after the acquisition, the Mac now uses Intel processors. On the 2019 supplier list, Intel reports nine supplier locations, with three locations in the U.S. and others in China, Israel, Vietnam, Ireland, and Malaysia.

8. Murata Manufacturing Ltd. (MRAAY)

Murata is based in Kyoto, Japan. It supplies to Apple from 26 manufacturing facilities spread across Malaysia, Japan, Thailand, Vietnam, China, and Singapore. It has 16 supplier sites in Japan.

Apple and Samsung are Murata's top two clients, procuring ceramic capacitors from the company. These electronic parts are used to control the flow of electricity in electronic devices.

9. Samsung

Samsung has its headquarters in South Korea. It supplies multiple components, including flash memory used for storing data content, the mobile DRAM used for multi-tasking various applications in devices, and the application processors responsible for controlling and keeping devices running.

Despite being a competitor to Apple in the mobile phones market, Samsung uses its supplier status to reduce its own component manufacturing costs via bulk production.

Apple needs suppliers and suppliers need Apple — it's a streamlined relationship that is often mutually beneficial, but at times can create tension. Suppliers have major exposure to Apple and its overall market performance. Financial reports of supplier companies are frequently used by market analysts to project sales for Apple products. Investors also often look to Apple's underlying suppliers for insights on Apple's performance as well as more granular investment opportunities independently.

Second Thoughts

For each of the following statements, choose one answer to fill in the blank.

1. _____ is Apple's number one supplier.
   A. Foxconn
   B. Intel
   C. Wistron
   D. Qualcomm
2. Apple is still very dependent on the following companies in the U.S. EXCEPT _____.
   A. Qualcomm
   B. Samsung
   C. Intel
   D. Jabil

Reading II

Outsourcing Works, So India Is Exporting Jobs

Thousands of Indians report to Infosys Technologies' campus here to learn the finer points of programming. Lately, though, packs of foreigners have been roaming the manicured lawns, too. Many of them are recent American college graduates, and some have even turned down job offers from coveted employers like Google. Instead, they accepted a novel assignment from Infosys, the Indian technology giant: fly here for six months of training, then return home to work in the company's American back offices.

India is outsourcing outsourcing. One of the constants of the global economy has been companies moving their tasks — and jobs — to India. But rising wages and a stronger currency here, demands for workers who speak languages other than English, and competition from countries looking to emulate India's success as a back office — including China, Morocco and Mexico — are challenging that model.

Many executives here acknowledge that outsourcing, having rained most heavily on India, will increasingly sprinkle tasks around the globe. Or, as Ashok Vemuri, an Infosys senior vice president, put it, the future of outsourcing is "to take the work from any part of the world and do it in any part of the world."

To fight on the shifting terrain, and to beat back emerging rivals, Indian companies are hiring workers and opening offices in developing countries themselves, before their clients do. In May, Tata Consultancy Service, Infosys's Indian rival, announced a new back office in Guadalajara, Mexico; Tata already has 5,000 workers in Brazil, Chile and Uruguay. Cognizant Technology Solutions, with most of its operations in India, has now opened back offices in Phoenix and Shanghai.

Wipro, another Indian technology services company, has outsourcing offices in Canada, China, Portugal, Romania and Saudi Arabia, among other locations. And last month, Wipro said it was opening a software development center in Atlanta that would hire 500 programmers in three years. In a poetic reflection of outsourcing's new face, Wipro's chairman, Azim Premji, told Wall Street analysts this year that he was considering hubs in Idaho and Virginia, in addition to Georgia, to take advantage of American "states which are less developed." (India's per capita income is less than $1,000 a year.)

For its part, Infosys is building a whole archipelago of back offices — in Mexico, the Czech Republic, Thailand and China, as well as low-cost regions of the United States. The company seeks to become a global matchmaker for outsourcing: any time a company wants work done somewhere else, even just down the street, Infosys wants to get the call. It is a peculiar ambition for a company that symbolizes the flow of tasks from the West to India.

Most of Infosys's 75,000 employees are Indians, in India. They account for most of the company's $3.1 billion in sales in the year that ended March 31, from work for clients like Bank of America and Goldman Sachs. "India continues to be the No. 1 location for outsourcing", S. Gopalakrishnan, the company's chief executive, said in a telephone interview. And yet the company opened a Philippines office in August and, a month earlier, bought back offices in Thailand and Poland from Royal Philips Electronics, the Dutch company. In each outsourcing hub, local employees work with little help from Indian managers.

Infosys says its outsourcing experience in India has taught it to carve up a project, apportion each slice to suitable workers, double-check quality and then export a final, reassembled product to clients. The company argues it can clone its Indian back offices in other nations and groom Chinese, Mexican or Czech employees to be more productive than local outsourcing companies could make them. "We have pioneered this movement of work", Mr. Gopalakrishnan said. "These new countries don't have experience and maturity in doing that, and that's what we're taking to these countries." Some analysts compare the strategy to Japanese penetration of auto manufacturing in the United States in the 1970s. Just as the Japanese learned to make cars in America without Japanese workers, Indian vendors are learning to outsource without Indians, said Dennis McGuire, chairman of TPI, a Texas-based outsourcing consultancy.

Though work that bypasses India remains a small part of the Infosys business, it is growing. The company can be highly secretive, but executives agreed to describe some of the new projects on the condition that clients not be identified. In one project, an American bank wanted a computer system to handle a loan program for Hispanic customers. The system had to work in Spanish. It also had to take into account variables particular to Hispanic clients: many, for instance, remit money to families abroad, which can affect their bank balances. The bank thought a Mexican team would have the right language skills and grasp of cultural nuances.

But instead of going to a Mexican vendor, or to an American vendor with Mexican operations, the bank retained three dozen engineers at Infosys, which had recently opened shop in Monterrey, Mexico. Such is the new outsourcing: A company in the United States pays 7,000 miles away to supply it with Mexican engineers working 150 miles south of the United States border.

In Europe, too, companies now hire Infosys to manage back offices in their own backyards. When an American manufacturer, for instance, needed a system to handle bills from multiple vendors supplying its factories in different European countries, it turned to the Indian company. The manufacturer's different locations scan the invoices and send them to an office of Infosys, where each bill is passed to the right language team. The teams verify the orders and send the payment to the suppliers while logged in to the client's computer system.

More than a dozen languages are spoken at the Infosys office, which is in Brno, Czech Republic. The American program here in Mysore is meant to keep open that pipeline of diversity. Most trainees here have no software knowledge. By teaching novices, Infosys saves money and hopes to attract workers who will turn down better-known companies for the chance to learn a new skill. "It's the equivalent of a bachelor's in computer science in six months", said Melissa Adams, a 22-year-old trainee. Ms. Adams graduated last spring from the University of Washington with a business degree, and rejected Google for Infosys.

And yet, even as outsourcing takes on new directions, old perceptions linger. For instance, when Jeff Rand, a 23-year-old American trainee, told his grandmother he was moving to India to work as a software engineer for six months, "she said, 'Maybe I'll get to talk to you when I have a problem with my credit card.'" Said Mr. Rand with a rueful chuckle, "It took me about two or three weeks to explain to my grandma that I was not going to be working in a call center."

Second Thoughts

1) What is Infosys? Can you briefly introduce Infosys after reading this passage?

_____

_____

2) Think about the example in the last paragraph, would you like to work in an outsourcing company like Infosys? Write down your own ideas.

_____

_____

Global Marketing

全球营销

CHAPTER 14

本章概要

本章主要介绍全球营销的含义、益处、战略影响因素、常见错误,以及以字节跳动等为代表的全球营销案例。

学习指南

全球营销可以定义为"在全球范围内,在不同国家,协调或利用全球运营的商业优势,以实现全球目标的营销"。随着经济全球化的发展,世界各国、各地区的资源配置不再受到国界和地域的约束,它们在全球范围内寻求最优化的配置方式和高水平的配置效率,呈现出世界经济总量不断扩大的局面。所以,越来越多的企业逐渐走向国际舞台,参与全球营销竞争。

通过本章学习,希望大家能够实现以下目标:

(1) 基本目标(Text-based Goals)

- 掌握本章涉及话题的基本专业术语及词汇,如全球营销、营销组合等;
- 掌握本章的主要知识点,即全球营销的含义、特点及常用战略等。

(2) 拓展目标(Extended Goals)

- 思考本章引言,为什么阿尔·里斯认为"市场营销是在预期顾客的心中构建一个品牌形象"? 这对于全球营销有何启示?
- 通过学习背景知识、拓展阅读、案例分析进一步了解全球营销的主要背景、内涵及影响。

全球营销可以定义为"在全球范围内，在不同国家，协调或利用全球运营的商业优势，以实现全球目标的营销"。它也是一种通过向国际市场推销和做广告来增加销售量的产品战略。因此可以说，当一家公司向全球市场销售相同的产品时，它就被称为全球营销。

Global marketing can be defined as "marketing on a worldwide scale, in different countries, **reconciling** or taking commercial advantage of global operational differences, similarities, and opportunities in order to meet global objectives". It can also be considered as a product strategy to increase sales through promotion and advertisements to the international market. Nearly every business has a global presence. Even companies doing business within their homes can market and attract business internationally. Thus basically, when a firm sells the same products to the global market, then it is known as global marketing.

Marketing of products is done regularly by companies locally. But since ages, foreign products have constantly been introduced in other markets and the sellers or marketers in a modern-day term, have **tweaked**, changed or **revamped** their strategies in order to appeal and gain acceptance from local market.

Many multinationals have offices abroad in various countries they cater to. Currently, with the expansion of the internet, even small organizations can reach a global audience in a small amount of time and little investment.

Benefits of Global Marketing

全球营销的益处包括：1）提高产品或服务效率；2）增强竞争优势；3）提高品牌知名度；4）降低成本。

First, it can improve the effectiveness of the products or services. This is because the more the marketers grow, the more they learn, and the faster they learn, they become more effective at producing new product or service offerings.

Second, they are able to have a strong competitive advantage. It is easy enough for companies to be competing in the local market. But there are very few companies who can do so on the worldwide arena. Hence, if a company can compete in the worldwide market and the competitors cannot, it means the company has become a strong force in the industry.

Third, it helps increase consumer awareness of the brand and product or service. Through the internet, consumers can keep track of your progress in the world.

Finally, global marketing can reduce costs and increase savings. In focusing on other markets, companies can attain economies of scale and range by standardizing their processes-not to mention the savings that they get when they leverage the internet!

Word Study

reconcile /ˈrekənsaɪl/
 v. 调合，使配合
tweak /twiːk/ v. 拧，
 扯，调整
revamp /riːˈvæmp/ v.
 修改

Four Dimensions of Global Marketing

BUSINESS FUNCTIONS

A company's approach to global marketing depends, first, on its overall business strategy. In many multinationals, some functional areas have greater program standardization than others. Headquarters often controls manufacturing, finance, and R&D, while the local managers make the marketing decisions. Marketing is usually one of the last functions to be centrally directed. Partly because product quality and accounting data are easier to measure than marketing effectiveness, standardization can be greater in production and finance.

PRODUCTS

Products that favor economies of scale or high efficiencies and are not highly culture-bound are easier to market globally than others.

1. Economies of scale. Manufacturing and R&D in a large scale can result in a price spread between the global and the local product that is too great for even the most culture-bound consumers to resist. In addition, management often has neither the time nor the R&D resources to adapt products to each country. The markets for high-tech products like computers are not only very competitive but also affected by rapid technological change.

Most packaged consumer goods are less **susceptible** than durable goods like televisions and cars to manufacturing or even R&D in a large scale. Coca-Cola's global policy and Nestlé's interest in tighter marketing coordination are driven largely by a desire to capitalize on the marketing ideas that their managers around the world generate rather than by potential economies of scale. Nestlé, for example, manufactures its packaged soups in dozens of locally managed plants around the world, with some transference of engineering know-how through a headquarters staff. Products and marketing programs are also locally managed, but new ideas are aggressively transferred, with local managers encouraged — or even **prodded** — to adapt and use them in their own markets. For Nestlé, global marketing does not help it yield so much as using scarce new ideas.

2. Cultural grounding. Consumer products used in the home — like Nestlé's soups and frozen foods — are often more culture-bound than products used outside the home such as automobiles and credit cards, and industrial products are inherently less culture-bound than consumer products. Experience also suggests that products will be less culture-bound if they are used by young people whose cultural norms are not ingrained, people who travel in different countries, and ego-driven consumers who can be appealed to through myths and fantasies shared across cultures.

影响全球营销的因素包括四个方面：企业功能、产品、营销组合要素、国家。

Word Study

susceptible /sə'septəbl/ *adj.* 易受影响的
prod /prɒd/ *v.* 催促，督促

275

Managers shouldn't be bound by any matrix, however; they should find creative ways to prepare a product for global marketing. If a manufacturer develops a new version of a seemingly culture-bound product that is based on new capital-intensive technology and generates superior performance benefits, it may well be possible to introduce it on a standard basis worldwide. Procter & Gamble developed Pampers **disposable** diapers as a global brand in a product category that intuition would say was culture-bound.

MARKETING MIX ELEMENTS

Few consumer goods companies go so far as to market the same products using the same marketing program worldwide. And those that do, like Lego, the Danish manufacturer of construction toys, often distribute their products through sales companies rather than full-fledged marketing subsidiaries.

For most products, the appropriate degree of standardization varies from one element of the marketing mix to another. Strategic elements like product positioning are more easily standardized than execution-sensitive elements like sales promotion. In addition, when headquarters believes it has identified a superior marketing idea, whether it be a package design, a brand name, or an advertising copy concept, the pressure to standardize increases.

Marketing can usually contribute to economies of scale most significantly by creating a standard product design that will sell worldwide, permitting savings through globalized production. In addition, economies of scale in marketing programming can be achieved through standard commercial executions and copy concepts. McCann-Erickson claims to have saved $90 million in production costs over 20 years by producing worldwide Coca-Cola commercials. To ensure that they have enough attention-getting power to overcome their foreign origins, however, marketers often have to make worldwide commercials expensive productions.

To **compensate** local management for having to accept a standard product and to fit the core product to each local market, some companies allow local managers to adapt those marketing mix elements that aren't subject to significant economies of scale. On the other hand, local managers are more likely to accept a standard concept for those elements of the marketing mix that are less important and, ironically, often not susceptible to economies of scale. Overall, then, the driving factor in moving toward global marketing should be the efficient worldwide use of good marketing ideas rather than any economies of scale from standardization.

In judging how far to go in standardizing elements of the marketing mix, managers must also be mindful of the interactions among them. For example, when a product with the same brand name is sold in different countries, it can be difficult and sometimes impossible to sell them at different prices.

How far a decentralized multinational wishes to pursue global marketing will often vary from one country to another. Naturally, headquarters is likely to become more involved in marketing decisions in countries where performance is poor. But performance aside, small markets depend more on headquarters assistance than large markets. Because a standard marketing program is superior in quality to what local executives, even with the benefit of local market knowledge, could develop themselves, they may welcome it.

Large markets with strong local managements are less willing to accept global programs. Yet these are the markets that often account for most of the company's investment. To secure their acceptance, headquarters should make standard marketing programs reflect the needs of large rather than small markets. Small markets, being more **tolerant** of **deviations** from what would be locally appropriate, are less likely to resist a standard program.

Word Study

tolerant /ˈtɒlərənt/ *adj.*
容忍的
deviation /ˌdiːvɪˈeɪʃən/
n. 偏离
synchronize
/ˈsɪŋkrənaɪz/ *v.* 使同
步,同步化

Global Marketing Strategies

全球营销战略
制定全球营销战略首先需要回答以下几个问题: 我在全球市场上意在达成的目标是什么? 我的公司在该市场的优劣势是什么? 我该如何应对该市场上的挑战? 我在该市场上有何发展潜力?

Global marketing strategies are actually important parts of a global strategy. In order to create a good global marketing strategy, you must be able to answer: "What I am trying to achieve in an international market?" "What are my company's strengths and weaknesses for that market?" "How can I counter challenges in the market?" "What potential will I have in this market?"

Moreover, a good global marketing strategy incorporates all the countries from all regions of the world and coordinates their marketing efforts accordingly. Of course, this strategy does not always cover all the countries but should be applied for particular regions. For example, you can break down regions like North America, Latin America, Europe and the Middle East, Asia and the Pacific, and Africa.

Beyond its breakdown per country or region, a global marketing strategy almost always consists of several things: (1) uniform brand names; (2) identical packaging; (3) similar products; (4) standardized advertising messages; (5) **synchronized** pricing; (6) coordinated product launches; and (7) harmonious sales campaigns.

As a whole, these two are the most well-known global marketing strategies used by companies expanding internationally:

Create a consistent and strong brand culture. Creating a strong and consistent brand that always seems familiar to customers is a priority for companies growing internationally. With the ever-more rising and expanding internet, brand structure has become more of a brand culture. To be more specific, it has become more prevalent nowadays that the brand you support reflects your culture. It can be damaging if you compromise your brand culture.

Market as if there were no borders. Due to the **proliferation** of digital platforms, brands cannot always adopt different strategies per country. In a way, due to the internet, companies have to adopt a marketing approach that is more or less unified.

Global Marketing Campaign Development

开展全球营销活动

开展全球营销活动需要注意以下事项:1)了解市场;2)制定营销计划;3)采用定制方法;4)沟通方式本地化

In order to develop a successful global marketing campaign, there are a few things to keep in mind. You have to know the market, create a marketing plan, tailor your approach to marketing, and localize your communications.

KNOW YOUR MARKET

As soon as your company decides to extend your marketing worldwide, you have to understand the context of where you will be working. Every region has various behaviors and norms as it deals with marketing messages, such as how people would like to be contacted, and what is appropriate for that place, etc.

You have to make sure that you research how the market will respond to the marketing strategy you have, so you can get much leverage from your new market.

CREATE A MARKETING PLAN

Becoming successful worldwide is not merely altering the language. You have to make your global marketing plan consistent with your local efforts. Yet it still needs to be customized, according to your regional knowledge. Once you have an insight of the global environment, draft a marketing plan that details your actions.

The first thing is to identify your objectives and goals. As soon as that has been established, draw a map that covers the overall strategy and techniques to attain those objectives.

TAILOR YOUR APPROACH

Keep in mind that what may have worked for your local audience may not translate as well to your foreign audience. Try to adapt your initiatives to your audience, giving them a tailor fit experience. Definitely, what works for one country may not work for another.

LOCALIZE YOUR COMMUNICATIONS

It is not only relevant to know the language and cultural hurdles and adjusting your communications for every market, it is also critical to know all the cultural **references** and relevant holidays and events. You need to create a more personalized experience.

But make sure not to make international marketing mistakes when translating your brand message.

The Most Common Mistakes Companies Make with Global Marketing

企业在全球营销中最常犯的错误

一些常见的营销错误可能会阻挡全球营销的成功：1）不明确具体的国家；2）不够重视内部数据；3）不调整销售和营销渠道；4）不调整产品；5）不允许本地团队做决策；6）不从全球视角考虑问题。

Marketers often find themselves at the forefront of a company's global expansion. The marketing team is usually responsible for carrying out the market research that will determine where a company should expand, and it's usually charged with creating a plan for attracting customers.

As a former business consultant to marketing executives at companies trying to expand globally, I've noticed some common marketing roadblocks that can stand in the way of international success.

NOT SPECIFYING COUNTRIES

Executives tend to think about overseas markets in vague regional terms (e.g., "We're shifting our focus to Asia" or "We'd like to double our growth in Europe"), but this oversimplification is problematic. Ask people what they mean by "Europe" and you'll get widely varying answers — Western Europe, the European Union, the euro zone, and so on. Customers identify at the national level, and marketers need to remember that every country has its own local laws, cultural norms, forms of currency and payment, and unique business practices.

It's essential to break up broader geographic "markets" into individual countries with distinct revenue and lead generation goals — and to conduct adequate local research. Being more specific from the beginning helps tremendously with market. **Prioritizing** one market over another, creating a staffing plan, and budget allocation — all of which are necessary for helping a company achieve its desired global goals. Research into local markets has to be aimed at understanding the market size, the challenges customers face, the solutions they currently have, and where your product can fit in. Many companies fail to think about these basics of product positioning at the country level and overlook things like strong local competitors.

NOT PAYING ENOUGH ATTENTION TO INTERNAL DATA

Developing a global marketing strategy requires more complex and specialized market research. In the vast universe of data that can help you figure out which markets are best for you, the most important data points are: 1) how much estimated opportunity is available in that market, 2) how easy it will be for your company to do business in that market, and 3) how much success you've already had with that market.

Word Study

reference /'refərəns/
    n. 参考，指引
prioritize /praɪˈɒrɪtaɪz/
    v. 优先

Many companies rely heavily on external data sources to guide this decision-making. However, analyzing your own data will help you answer the latter two questions and determine whether you have a strong product-market fit. Are you seeing a **surge** in leads from a particular market, in spite of not investing heavily there? Do you see a shorter sales cycle or a higher win rate in some countries? Is the average purchase price higher in a given market? Third-party data sources don't know your customer or understand your brand — only you can answer these types of questions. Marketers can do a better job of utilizing their own data to prioritize their global marketing decisions.

NOT ADAPTING THEIR SALES AND MARKETING CHANNELS

Many companies (especially Western ones) believe they can enter new markets by following the same playbook that brought them domestic success. While brand consistency is important, different markets favor different sales and marketing approaches. For example, in countries where relationships have a higher cultural value, such as Japan, selling products and services through local partners, such as resellers or channel partners, achieve faster success than direct sales models. Conversely, **SaaS**, online, and "touchless" sales models are often popular in markets where the cost of living is higher and automation is prized, such as the Nordic market.

Similarly, marketers need to change up their own channels according to the behaviors of each market, and this can vary across countries within the same region. For example, in Brazil, a marketing campaign might find more success with promoted messages on Facebook due to the popularity of this social network there, while in other Latin American countries, Twitter might attract a larger audience more quickly, and thus be a more effective marketing tool. While some channels work across a large number of markets, you want to explore what delivers the best result in each market by conducting detailed market research that relies heavily on local, in-country experts in advance.

NOT ADAPTING THE PRODUCT OFFERING

Companies achieve "product-market fit" one country at a time. Yet all too often, companies try to launch identical products in different markets, ignoring the fact that they're dealing with very different customers. For example, a software company won't succeed abroad if it sells the same product that it sells at home if users in the new market aren't as familiar with certain advanced features. Instead, they should start with a more basic version of the product to get people accustomed to it. Likewise, a more advanced market might require more features than a product currently has available.

Pricing is a similar issue. Because the value proposition varies from one market to the next, pricing will vary. While it's not always essential for companies to change their pricing structure for international markets, many companies find that they are able to grow much more quickly by making adjustments at the local level. Forms of payment vary widely from one country to another. Marketers need to consider different pricing strategies for markets that are predominantly cash-based versus credit card-oriented, for example.

NOT LETTING LOCAL TEAMS LEAD THE WAY

One of the most disappointing mistakes that I've seen companies make is that they hire highly competent, intelligent local people to serve their overseas markets, but then fail to consider their input when making strategic decisions.

In my global consulting engagements, marketing executives would often ask me, "What do you think our best way forward is in France? Why aren't we succeeding there? What should we do differently?" My answer was often, "Ask your local teams." They would frequently admit that they hadn't tapped resources like the salespeople who sold there, and their local partners, vendors, consultants, and customers.

This is extremely important, because these individuals not only know the country in question, they know your business.

The biggest challenge companies face with incorporating local insight tends to be communication. The marketing team must therefore put a system in place to help ensure that local views are captured and **disseminated** frequently enough. Don't bring your company into a country the hard way. Leverage your existing relationships, and make sure to give their feedback extra weight. They are by far your most credible advisors.

NOT THINKING THROUGH THE GLOBAL LOGISTICS

Marketers use software that enables them to publish content on their website, send out email communications, publish social media updates, and carry out other key marketing tasks. But the same tools don't support every market. For example, perhaps the software you use to conduct **webinars** only supports five languages, while your marketing automation software allows you to market in dozens of languages. Maybe your payment solutions only work for a few countries, but yet your CRM is filled with contacts from more than 100 countries.

Marketers need to ensure that they can actually market to people in the countries they're looking to enter, which means considering details like how to display local currency, being able to email customers in their time zone, and supporting the languages customers speak.

As business continues to become more global, companies can gain

Word Study

disseminate /dɪˈsemɪneɪt/
  v. 散布, 传播
webinar /ˈwebɑːnɑː/ n.
  在线研讨会

competitive advantage by focusing their marketing efforts on targeting the right international markets and adapting their products and strategies to appeal to local customers. They'd be wise to avoid these pitfalls.

global marketing 全球营销

culture-bound 文化局限

product positioning 产品定位

product-market fit 产品市场匹配

marketing tool 营销手段

product strategy 产品战略

marketing mix 营销组合

brand culture 品牌文化

brand consistency 品牌一致性

value proposition 价值主张

全球营销的概念解读

随着经济全球化的发展,世界各国、各地区的资源配置不再受到国界和地域的约束,它们在全球范围内寻求着最优化的配置方式和高水平的配置效率,呈现出世界经济总量不断扩大的局面。所以,我们看到越来越多的企业逐渐走向国际舞台,参与全球竞争。

全球营销的概念最早由哈佛大学莱维特教授(Theodore Levitt)提出,即在不同的国家以相同的价格水平和促销方式,通过相同的分销渠道,销售相同的产品。莱维特还提出了关于全球营销的两个基本假设:国际市场的同质化和顾客偏好的一致性。时至今日,通过学者们的孜孜以求,关于全球营销的内容得到了极大的丰富和完善。关于全球营销战略的观念概括起来有三种观念。

标准化观念:以莱维特为代表的标准化战略成为全球营销战略的组成部分。标准化观点认为通讯和交通的飞速进步已经使全球市场出现同质化趋势,不同国家的消费者具有相同的需求偏好。因此,企业应该通过制定标准化战略获得规模效应,包括批量生产高质量低成本的标准化产品,制定价格、促销、渠道的标准化结构,统一管理职能上的标准,等等。

适应性观念:包括产品适应性战略、定价适应性战略、促销适应性战略、渠道适应性战略等。就产品适应性战略而言,公司可以根据各个国家的特殊情况对产品和战略进行修正,以扩展本土市场基地和开发新的细分市场。企业有必要将价值链中采购、生产、研发等各项具体活动根据比较优势在全球范围内进行配置,发掘要素成本差异,从而协调各市场的活动来构筑跨国企业的竞争优势。

整合观念:标准化和适应性之间并不是非此即彼的关系,企业应该在两者之间寻求一种平衡,成功的关键是要同时进入世界上所有的主要市场以获取竞争力量,并且在这些市场上对竞争活动进行合理有效的整合。

文献来源:

向媛媛.新兴市场跨国企业营销战略研究[J].合作经济与科技,2017(8):66-67.

A. Please summarize the steps to create a successful global marketing campaign.

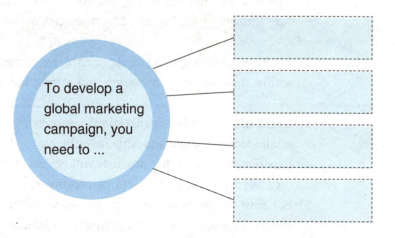

B. According to the text, fill in each of the following blanks with an appropriate word or phrase.

1) Global marketing can be defined as marketing on a _____ scale, in different countries, reconciling or taking commercial advantage of _____ operational differences, similarities, and opportunities in order to meet global objectives.

2) Managers shouldn't be bound by any _____, however; they should find creative ways to prepare a product for global marketing.

3) The driving factor in moving toward global marketing should be the efficient worldwide use of good marketing ideas rather than any economies of scale from _____.

4) Large markets with strong local managements are _____ willing to accept global programs.

5) Marketers often find themselves at the _____ of a company's global expansion.

6) Research into local markets has to be aimed at understanding the market _____, the challenges customers face, the solutions they currently have, and where your product can fit in.

7) _____ data sources don't know your customer or understand your brand — only you can answer these types of questions.

8) Marketers need to consider different _____ strategies for markets that are predominantly cash-based versus credit card-oriented.

9) The biggest challenge companies face with incorporating local insight tends to be _____.

10) As business continues to become more global, companies can gain _____ by focusing their marketing efforts on targeting the right international markets and adapting their products and strategies to appeal to _____.

C. Read the text and decide whether the following statements are True (T) or False (F).

1) Global marketing can be considered as a product strategy to increase sales through promotion and advertisements to the international market. ( )

2) All the businesses have a global presence. Even companies doing business within their homes can market and attract business internationally. ( )

3) Currently, only big organizations can reach a global audience in a small amount of time and little investment. ( )

4) Experience suggests that products will be less culture-bound if they are used by young people whose cultural norms are not ingrained. ( )

5) For most products, the appropriate degree of standardization remains almost the same for each marketing mix element. ( )

6) Executives need to think about overseas markets in clear country-based terms. ( )

7) Developing a global marketing strategy requires more complex and specialized market research. ( )

8) Marketers need to change up their own channels according to the behaviors of each market, and this can vary across countries within the same region. ( )

9) Global marketers need to ensure how to display local currency, to be able to email customers in their time zone, and to support the languages customers speak. ( )

10) Marketers can do a better job of utilizing external data to prioritize their global marketing decisions. ( )

Discussion 讨论

1) How can a company benefit from global marketing?

_____

_____

2) What does "culture-bound products" mean? Can you list two such products?

_____

_____

3) How can standardizing elements of the marketing mix contribute to economies of scale?

_____

_____

4) Can you give an example of a successful global marketing campaign? Discuss with your partner.

_____

_____

5) How do you think a company can avoid the pitfalls in global marketing?

_____

_____

Analyzing the Case
案例分析

Case Story

ByteDance

TikTok, a mobile app developed by ByteDance, allows users to post short videos of usually 15 seconds, contributing to what is known in the industry as "fast entertainment". It has an impressive 500 million active monthly users, is available in 155 countries and has teenagers who have downloaded the app spending an average of 52 minutes using it every single day.

Most noteworthy of all, is that TikTok is the first app from a Chinese company to take the world by storm. Its owner is ByteDance which has suddenly shifted from being a top Chinese online company to a top global player, rubbing shoulders with the likes of Youtube and Facebook. "TikTok democratized video content creation", says Michael Norris, strategy and research manager at AgencyChina, a marketing and sales agency. "Just like photo-editing apps before it, TikTok made complicated video effects and transitions simple. This gave a huge range of would-be content creators the tools and freedom to make the type of video content they wanted, without the hassle of cutting, editing and re-touching."

The app is all about providing users with an endless stream 15-second "brain bursts" — cute, pretty, weird, funny or strange video snippets that superficially stimulate and fill up time. Users compete to produce and post small videos of themselves dressing up, putting on makeup, doing outrageous things and generally trying to impress their peers.

TikTok crossed 1 billion downloads on Apple's App Store and Google Play in February 2019. Around 633 million of these downloads occurred in 2018, compared to 711 million for Facebook and Instagram's 444 million. In August 2019, TikTok was the world's most downloaded social media app with nearly 63 million downloads. India accounts for around a quarter of all downloads of TikTok to date, but TikTok was also the second most common non-gaming app download in the U.S. that month with 4.2

million installs — a 54% year-on-year increase.

"There are two reasons why TikTok has gained great success in such a short time", says Zhang Mengmeng, a research analyst at Counterpoint Research. "First of all, before launching TikTok, its Chinese variant Douyin, already gained wide popularity and proved to be a successful product locally. ByteDance was able to carry its experience from Douyin into TikTok. Secondly, ByteDance acquired a competing video sharing site called Musical.ly, which has most of its user base in the United States. By acquiring Musical.ly, it was able to expand its user base for TikTok quickly."

Fandango

Former Microsoft engineer Zhang Yiming, now aged 36, founded the parent company ByteDance in 2012. The first app he launched was Jinri Toutiao, which supplies AI-curated news content personalized for users. Douyin launched in 2016 with the international version TikTok following in 2017. ByteDance really went international in 2017, after it acquired the U.S.-founded app Musical.ly, and then merged it with TikTok in 2018.

Although ByteDance now operates in more than 100 countries, Norris says that beyond China the company concentrates on India, Japan and the United States. "Outside those three markets, it's had a hard time converting downloads to active users. Earlier this year, it was alleged that ByteDance spent $3 million per day on existing social media platforms to encourage downloads, but these rarely resulted in loyal users", he says.

Breakdancing

ByteDance is one of a new wave of Chinese tech companies challenging the older and more established Chinese players, led by BAT (Baidu, Alibaba, Tencent). The founders of these new companies are all at least 10 years younger than those of BAT and are also focused on mobile rather than computer-based platforms.

"It rode the wave of mobile internet brought on by the wide adoption of smartphones as well as the rapid economic growth of the past decade in China", says Zhang. "Other new Chinese tech companies like Didi, Kuaishou and Meituan also emerged at around the same time. These new founders are not only more ambitious but also have a better international perspective."

With the huge popularity of TikTok globally, ByteDance is the first Chinese tech company with a serious chance when it comes to competing with the American social media giants such as Facebook and Instagram. It has been able to gain traction internationally in a way that the BAT companies so far have not.

"Seen through the lens of user experience and product design, the emergence of ByteDance — and Douyin in particular — represents a seismic shift in the Chinese startup space", says Kendra Schaefer, Trivium China Head of Digital Research. "Alibaba, Tencent, and many of China's other tech giants are good at creating products that meet the needs of their local market, but they started out imitating, and then gradually employed their user data to hone those products. Douyin jumped out of the gate with a largely original interface that not only spoke to Chinese users, but had a more universal appeal."

For many young Chinese people, Douyin is a way of killing time. "When you're waiting for buses or the subway, you can use the app", says Versa Yang, a user of Douyin. And it seems that this, plus its ease of use and entertainment factor, is what makes it popular. While Douyin manages to appeal to a wide range of age groups in China, internationally TikTok largely appeals to young people, particularly teenagers.

Last Waltz

A key feature of this kind of app is the high potential for it to fade as fast as it grows. ByteDance is not waiting around for that to happen and is spending substantial amounts on research and development.

"We already see stagnating growth for ByteDance's Jinri Toutiao news app, with growth for Douyin also likely to hit a ceiling at some point", says Zhang. "Therefore, ByteDance has been putting a lot into R&D to incubate the next hit product and diversify its current business."

Despite having one of the world's most popular apps, the company doesn't even feature anywhere close to the top of list of global apps in revenue terms. Encouragingly, however, TikTok's in-app purchases reached $11.7 million in July, a 290% increase from the same time a year before.

"Douyin's foray into e-commerce is an important part of ByteDance's monetization efforts, and I'm sure that they're pleased with the domestic brand uptake of the integration between short video and e-commerce", says Norris. Vine, an app similar to TikTok founded in 2012 and bought by Twitter, ceased operations in 2016 due partly to an inability to monetize its offering.

In anticipation of the ceiling and as a means of becoming even bigger, ByteDance has already set its sights on other potential areas that it can expand into.

"ByteDance is considering becoming a bigger contender in the music streaming service and strengthening its social media position by launching its own smartphone", says Derval. "Combining hardware and AI sounds like a smart world domination plan." The company has also tried to diversify through the purchase of two gaming companies and various smartphone patents, along with the creation of other business units such as education oriented Gogo Kid, and workplace tool Lark.

Byte Back

Some experts see ByteDance's massive growth as being not so much a failure of Western tech companies as indicative of China's rise. "ByteDance's success shows that Chinese tech companies are capable of making hit products and achieving scales on par with and sometimes even surpassing Silicon Valley companies", says Zhang, going on to cite leadership in mobile payments and AI-based facial recognition.

The big challenge now for ByteDance is how to monetize its apps to justify its current valuation. Internationally, Zhang actually sees the popularity of TikTok amongst teens as a hindrance to this.

"ByteDance is quite promising from a financial perspective as it generates sizable income through advertising", says Zhang. But according to Norris, much of this advertising is being poached from Baidu and ByteDance will need more revenue streams to support its multiple business units. Most of the income comes from Douyin and Jinri Toutiao, and "the rest, at this point in time, is ecosystem building".

While ByteDance may be facing challenges, it is now a major player globally. "Douyin and TikTok will remain important growth drivers for ByteDance", says Zhang. "However, ByteDance knows that it cannot sit on its current glory and is very aggressive in overseas expansion and finding the next 100 million (user) product."

Case Discussion

1) Why does Norris think TikTok has demoncractized video content creation?

   _____

   _____

2) Why did TikTok gain great success in such a short time?

   _____

   _____

3) What is the big challenge for ByteDance according to Zhang?

   _____

   _____

Case Summary

字节跳动旗下产品抖音是中国公司推出的第一款风靡全球的应用。基于此,字节跳动正从一家中国顶级网络公司转变为一家全球顶级企业,与Youtube 和 Facebook 等公司同台竞争。

抖音是一款移动应用，允许用户发布长度为15秒的短视频，为业界所称的"快娱乐"做出贡献。它在155个国家拥有每月5亿的活跃用户。随着抖音在全球的人气日益增长，字节跳动成为了第一家真正拥有巨大潜力和机会，与包括Instagram在内的美国社交媒体巨头进行竞争的中国企业。

字节跳动已在国际上大获成功，而互联网巨头BAT公司（百度、阿里巴巴、腾讯）目前尚未所及。创始人张一鸣强调，虽然面临各类全球化挑战，抖音仍将是公司的首要增长动力。他还表示，字节跳动正在非常积极地海外扩张并寻找下一个1亿（用户）产品。

Reading
Expansion
拓展阅读

Reading I

Benefits of a Global Marketing Strategy
—Why Is Developing a Plan Important?

Is a global marketing strategy really necessary for your business? If you were to develop an ad campaign in the United States, do you think the same campaign would be effective in France?

Here we examine why it's important to create a global marketing strategy for your business, no matter the size, and the benefits of crafting one.

First, it's important to note what global marketing isn't. It's not a standardized process that you take to a global level. Some aspects can be standardized, such as a logo or a brand name, but others, such as packaging or advertising strategy, may or may not be effective in a global marketing strategy.

A global marketing strategy is one component of a total global strategy. It must incorporate all functional aspects of a business from finance to operations to R&D. It must also carry a well-defined objective because without officially declaring where you are going, you will never get there.

To do that, be honest with yourself and your team. Ask: What are we trying to accomplish in an overseas market? What are the weaknesses and strengths in that market? How will we overcome them? What upside potential do we have? Together with your team, answer the questions to draft a global marketing strategy.

The more detailed the objective, the clearer and more focused the global marketing strategy becomes. For example, when a target market is selected (e.g., France), the market mix comprising of price, package, and promotion, that is already in place must be evaluated to determine what parts can be standardized and what parts must be adapted to meet the target overseas market requirements. Don't think for a moment that you can minimize country-to-country differences. Embrace them and develop your strategy in such a way as to complement the differences.

If a global marketing strategy is done right, it can have many benefits for an organization. Here are four.

Improved Product and Service Effectiveness

The more you grow, the faster and more you learn, the more effective you become at rolling out new and improved product and service offerings. With Facebook's IPO, the company did a remarkable job servicing the needs of the North American market and making money. Its next expansion effort was in India. What Facebook had discovered was that Internet advertising made up just 3 percent of India's advertising market, compared to 17 percent in the United States. For Facebook to develop a global marketing strategy in India, it required improving on their already existing North American strategy to monetize all the users in India in terms of their revenue base.

Stronger Competitive Advantage

Many companies are naturals at competing locally, but how many companies can compete globally? If you do business on a global basis, but your local competitors can't or don't, you become a force they can't compete with.

As you move forward with your global strategy, if it's well-articulated, everyone gets on board, allowing for a better-informed and more focused organization as a whole worldwide. Further, it allows you to adapt quickly wherever needed based on customer demands or trends in the global marketplace.

Heightened Customer Awareness

With the Internet, customers can track the progress, or lack thereof, of a product all over the world. Apple has a uniform and consistent message with its products: deliver exceptional design and experience through superb user interfaces. The "WOW" factor also plays into the heightened customer awareness throughout the world.

Cost Reduction and Savings

By focusing on new markets, you can achieve economies of scale and scope through standardization in some areas. Not to mention the savings from leveraging the Internet globally. Customers from all corners of the world can find you, and you can reach potential customers with one single point of contact, such as a website, blog, or Facebook page. The cost savings can help you serve customers better worldwide.

Whether you run a one-person shop or an organization with 300 employees, open and honest conversations with yourself and your team about your goals will help you create a global marketing strategy, build collective commitment, and achieve an enduring global enterprise.

Second Thoughts

For each of the following statements, choose one (or more than one) answer to fill in the blank.

1) The _____ of a product may NOT be standardized in global marketing.
   A. logo
   B. packaging
   C. advertising
   D. brand name

2) To draft a global marketing strategy, you need to think about the elements including _____.
   A. goals
   B. strengths
   C. weaknesses
   D. solutions to potential problems

Reading II

Global Marketing vs International Marketing

Global marketing and international marketing, I have noticed, are perceived the same by several marketers worldwide. However, they are definitely not the same. International marketing involves the marketing tactics adopted by knowledgeable marketers in different countries specific to the markets of those countries. Global marketing, on the other hand is a marketing concept which involves the marketing efforts put in for the unique worldwide market.

We can understand that these two terms sometimes sound similar to most people most of the time but actually they are not. They aren't analogous by any means. In the words of Oxford University Press, global marketing is when an organization utilizes an exact promotional tactic all over the world — like Nike or Wal-Mart. Under its purview, the entire world is deemed one market and does not adjust the products or services, distribution channels or the communication to regional requirements.

Alternatively, international marketing refers to a situation wherein a company opens a subsidiary in a new country and permits that subsidiary to look after the market in that region and pay consideration to local customs like religion, dietary and lifestyle habits. Here are some of the key differences between the two terms that show that these are not similar:

Service or Product Offering

In global marketing, a company provides the exact product or service offerings to the customers in all countries that it operates. For example, banks, insurance companies and big retail chains such as Wal-Mart. In international marketing, however, each of the individual market is served with specific tailored products especially suited to the customers in that market only.

Marketing Personnel

The marketing staffs of companies employing the global marketing strategy work at the company's head office and are generally quite different from each other in terms of ethnicity, age, gender and also nature of work. They have distinct skills from each other which when combined produce effective results for the company and its global view.

On the other hand, in international marketing, there is much less dissimilarity amongst the team members and hail generally from the country of origin of the company itself.

Marketing Budget

The marketing budget of a company adopting the global marketing policy is finalized and approved from the corporate headquarters. For example, Nike finalizes a said amount of budget at its headquarters which then drops down to local branch offices subsequently.

However, in international marketing, the budget gets segregated into each of the subsidiary offices which can also formulate its own budget as well. For example, McDonald's runs ads in local languages and according to local traditions that can be found in those regions only.

Promotion Tactics

In global marketing, the company tries to make and air (on TV and radio) ads that are in sync with the worldwide audience and similarly does other marketing efforts. An appropriate example for this would be the ads that were aired on television during the 2014 FIFA World Cup. It was a mix of all: global event, passionate viewers and the game of football.

In international marketing, all the marketing efforts including television commercials are tailored for the local market.

Marketing Autonomy

In global marketing, every marketing strategy is devised and implemented from the corporate headquarters whereas in international marketing the marketing efforts are generated from within the domestic markets.

Use of Social Media

Just by reviewing their social media pages, one can contemplate as to what type of marketing policy the company has adopted. For example, brands like McDonald's have separate Facebook pages for numerous countries such as Malaysia, Brazil, Italy and Spain. Whereas, companies like Nike and Caterpillar have just a solitary Facebook page for their customers irrespective of any region or country.

Customers' Engagement

Customers' engagement is more visible in international marketing. A company can better connect with its customers by installing in place better communication channels. Global marketing is also as effective when it comes to customers' engagement only the international marketing strategies are little different. However, it is proved that international marketing seems to create greater amount of engagement than global marketing does.

Advertising

In the global marketing concept the advertisements are typically aired on worldwide mediums; however in international marketing companies tend to air the advertisements in local markets or markets with similar characteristics. There are some global marketing products which respond well to global advertising, however there are others that which cannot exist in certain countries due to legal restrictions.

R&D and Marketing Research

In real terms, marketing research and R&D are as thorough and widespread in global marketing as they are in international marketing. There are some instances when companies don't do their international marketing research properly and thus their products fail miserably in the global market. For example, the Ben-Gay Aspirin, McDonald's Arch Deluxe, and Redux Beverages' Cocaine Energy drink.

Hybrid Structure

This point is not a direct comparison between global and international marketing but it emphasizes the fact that a hybrid structure of the two forms of marketing can be very useful for companies. For example, in the early days Coca-Cola successfully adopted this tactic and now every company seems to be following it. For example, Frito-Lay, Proctor and Gamble, McDonald and Mercedes Benz, all have taken to this approach.

Second Thoughts

1) Can you give definitions to global marketing and international marketing in your own words?

_____

_____

2) Do you think the one-page-for-all strategy on social media will effectively function to promote consumer goods brand?

_____

_____

Global Human Resource Management

CHAPTER 15

全球人力资源管理

本章概要

本章主要介绍全球人力资源管理的含义、特点和挑战,以及以联合利华、IBM、劳斯莱斯等为代表的全球人力资源管理案例。

学习指南

全球人力资源管理意味着创建有效的全球劳动力队伍,并熟知何时使用"外派人员",何时雇佣"本地人员",以及如何创造新的员工阶层——"全球外派人员"。缺乏合格的管理人员已成为制约跨国公司扩大全球营销的主要因素。知识社会的发展和开放新兴市场的压力,使得全球尖端企业认识到:在建立可持续竞争优势方面,人力资源和智力资本十分重要。

通过本章学习,希望大家能够实现以下目标:

(1)基本目标(Text-based Goals)

- 掌握本章涉及话题的基本专业术语及词汇,如外派人员、绩效评价等;
- 掌握本章的主要知识点,即全球人力资源管理的含义、特点及挑战。

(2)拓展目标(Extended Goals)

- 思考本章引言,为什么安娜·埃莉诺·罗斯福认为"人力资源是世界上最宝贵的资产"?
- 通过学习背景知识、拓展阅读、案例分析进一步了解全球人力资源管理的机遇、挑战及影响。

Global Human Resources

Creating an effective global workforce means knowing when to use "expats", when to hire "locals" and how to create that new class of employees — the "glopats".

The scarcity of qualified managers has become a major constraint on the speed with which multinational companies can expand their international sales. The growth of the knowledge-based society, along with the pressures of opening up emerging markets, has led cutting-edge global companies to recognize now more than ever that human resources and intellectual capital are as significant as financial assets in building sustainable competitive advantage. To follow their lead, chief executives in other multinational companies will have to bridge the yawning **chasm** between their companies' human resources rhetoric and reality. HR must now be given a prominent seat in the boardroom.

Good HR management in a multinational company comes down to getting the right people in the right jobs in the right places at the right times and at the right cost. These international managers must then be **meshed** into a cohesive network in which they quickly identify and leverage good ideas worldwide.

Such an integrated network depends on executive continuity. This in turn requires career management to ensure that internal qualified executives are readily available when vacancies occur around the world and that good managers do not jump ship because they have not been recognized.

Very few companies come close to achieving this. Most multinational companies do not have the leadership capital they need to perform effectively in all their markets around the world. One reason is the lack of managerial mobility. Neither companies nor individuals have come to terms with the role that managerial mobility now has to play in marrying business strategy with HR strategy and in ensuring that careers are developed for both profitability and employability.

Ethnocentricity is another reason. In most multinationals, HR development policies have tended to concentrate on nationals of the headquarters country. Only the brightest local stars were given the career management skills and overseas assignments necessary to develop an international mindset.

The chief executives of many United States-based multinational

创建一支有效的全球劳动力队伍意味着熟知何时使用"外派人员",何时雇佣"本地人员",以及如何创造新的员工阶层——"全球外派人员"。

缺乏合格的管理人员已成为制约跨国公司扩大全球营销的主要因素。知识社会的发展,和开放新兴市场的压力,使得全球尖端企业认识到:在建立可持续竞争优势方面,人力资源和智力资本与金融资产同等重要。

Word Study

chasm /ˈkæzəm/ n. 裂口,裂隙
mesh /meʃ/ v. 匹配,适合

companies lack confidence in the ability of their HR functions to screen, review and develop **candidates** for the most important posts across the globe. This is not surprising: HR directors rarely have extensive overseas experience and their managers often lack business knowledge. Also, most HR directors do not have adequate information about the brightest candidates coming through the ranks of the overseas subsidiaries. "HR managers also frequently lack a true commitment to the value of the multinational company experience", notes Brian Brooks, group director of human resources for the global advertising company WPP Group Plc.

The consequent lack of world-wise multicultural managerial talent is now biting into companies' bottom lines through high staff turnover, high training costs, stagnant market shares, failed joint ventures and mergers and the high opportunity costs that inevitably follow bad management selections around the globe.

Companies new to the global scene quickly discover that finding **savvy**, trustworthy managers for their overseas markets is one of their biggest challenges. This holds true for companies across the technology spectrum, from software manufacturers to textile companies that have to manage a global supply chain. The pressure is on these newly globalizing companies to cut the trial-and-error time in building a cadre of global managers in order to shorten the leads of their larger, established competitors, but they are **stymied** as to how to do it.

Global Human Resource Management of Unilever and IBM

The solution for multinationals is to find a way to **emulate** companies that have decades of experience in recruiting, training and retaining good employees across the globe. Many of these multinational companies are European, but not all. Both Unilever and the International Business Machines Corporation (IBM), for example, leverage their worldwide HR function as a source of competitive advantage.

Anglo-Dutch Unilever has long set a high priority on human resources. HR has a seat on the board's executive committee and an organization that focuses on developing in-house talent and hot-housing future leaders in all markets. Since 1989, Unilever has redefined 75 percent of its managerial posts as "international" and doubled its number of managers assigned abroad, its expatriates, or "expats".

IBM, with 80 years' experience in overseas markets, reversed its HR policy in 1995 to deal with the new global **gestalt** and a new business strategy. Instead of cutting jobs abroad to reduce costs, IBM is now focusing on its customers' needs and increasing overseas assignments. "We are a growing service business — our people are what our customers are buying from us", explained Eileen Major, director of international mobility at IBM.

When managers sign on with these companies, they know from the start that overseas assignments are part of the deal if they wish to climb high on the corporate ladder. These multinational companies manage their HR talent through international databases that, within hours, can provide a choice of Grade-A in-house candidates for any assignment. Even allowing for company size, few United States-based multinationals come close to matching the bench strength of a Unilever.

A GLOBAL HR ACTION AGENDA

全球人力资源行动纲领

　　此部分以联合利华、IBM等知名跨国公司为例，介绍全球人力资源管理的行动纲领，旨在通过吸引并培养优秀管理人才，为公司建立持续的竞争优势。

　　行动纲领包含十个步骤，可助公司在三四年的时间内建立有效的全球人力资源管理体系。

In this part, we'll outline a global HR action agenda based on the approaches used by leading multinational companies. The goal is to build sustainable competitive advantage by attracting and developing the best managerial talent in each of your company's markets.

The strategy demands global HR leadership with standard systems but local adaptation. The key underlying ideas are to satisfy your company's global human resources needs via feeder mechanisms at regional, national and local levels, and to leverage your current assets to the fullest extent by actively engaging people in developing their own careers.

Implementing these ideas can be broken down into 10 steps. By taking these steps, a company should be able to put into place an effective global human resources program within three to four years.

1. Break all the "local national" glass ceilings

The first, and perhaps most fundamental, step toward building a global HR program is to end all **favoritism** toward managers who are nationals of the country in which the company is based. Companies tend to consider nationals of their headquarters country as potential expatriates and to regard everyone else as "local nationals". But in today's global markets such "us-versus-them" distinctions can put companies at a clear disadvantage, and there are strong reasons to discard them:

Ethnocentric companies tend to be **xenophobic** — they put the most confidence in nationals of their headquarters country. This is why more nationals get the juicy assignments, climb the ranks and wind up sitting on the board — and why the company ends up with a skewed perception of the world. Relatively few multinational companies have more than token representation on their boards. ABB is one company that recognizes the danger and now considers it a priority to move more executives from emerging countries in eastern Europe and Asia into the higher levels of the company.

Big distinctions can be found between expatriate and local national pay, benefits and bonuses, and these differences send loud signals to the

Word Study

favoritism
　/ˈfeɪvərɪtɪzəm/ *n.*
　偏袒
xenophobic
　/ˌzenəˈfəʊbɪk/ *adj.*
　排外的，仇外的

brightest local nationals to learn as much as they can and move on.

Less effort is put into recruiting top-notch young people in overseas markets than in the headquarters country. This leaves fast-growing developing markets with shallow bench strength.

Insufficient attention and budget are devoted to assessing, training and developing the careers of valuable local nationals already on the company payroll.

Conventional wisdom has defined a lot of the pros and cons of using expatriates versus local nationals. But in an increasingly global environment, cultural sensitivity and **cumulative** skills are what count. And these come with an individual, not a nationality.

After all, what exactly is a "local national"? Someone who was born in the country? Has a parent or a spouse born there? Was educated there? Speaks the language(s)? Worked there for a while? All employees are local nationals of at least one country, but often they can claim a connection with several. More frequent international travel, population mobility and cross-border university education are increasing the pool of available hybrid local nationals. Every country-connection a person has is a potential advantage for the individual and the company. So it is in a multinational company's interests to expand the definition of the term "local national" rather than restrict it.

2. Trace your lifeline

Based on your company's business strategy, identify the activities that are essential to achieving success around the world and specify the positions that hold responsibility for performing them. These positions represent the "lifeline" of your company. Typically, they account for about 10 percent of management.

Then define the technical, functional and soft skills needed for success in each "lifeline" role. As Ms. Major of IBM notes, "It is important to understand what people need to develop as executives. They can be savvy functionally and internationally, but they also have to be savvy inside the organization."

This second step requires integrated teams of business and HR specialists working with line managers. Over time, they should extend the skills descriptions to cover all of the company's executive posts. It took 18 months for IBM to roll out its worldwide skills management process to more than 100,000 people in manufacturing and development.

A good starting point is with posts carrying the same title around the globe, but local circumstances need to be taken into account. Chief financial officers in Latin American and eastern European subsidiaries, for example, should know how to deal with volatile exchange rates and high inflation. Unilever circulates skills profiles for most of its posts, but

Word Study

conventional
/kən'venʃənl/ *adj.*
传统的
cumulative
/'kjuːmjʊlətɪv/ *adj.*
积累的，渐增的

298

expects managers to adapt them to meet local needs.

Compiling these descriptions is a major undertaking, and they will not be perfect because job descriptions are subject to continuous change in today's markets and because perfect matches of candidates with job descriptions are unlikely to be found. But they are an essential building block to a global HR policy because they establish common standards.

The lifeline and role descriptions should be revisited at least annually to ensure they express the business strategy. Many companies recognize the need to review the impact of strategy and marketplace changes on high-technology and R&D roles but overlook the fact that managerial jobs are also redrawn by market pressures. The roles involved in running an emerging market operation, for example, expand as the company builds its investment and sales base. At IBM, skills teams update their role descriptions every six months to keep pace with the markets and to inform senior managers which skills are "hot" and which the company has in good supply.

3. Build a global database to know who and where your talent is

The main tool of a global HR policy has to be a global database simply because multinational companies now have many more strategic posts **scattered** around the globe and must monitor the career development of many more managers. Although some multinational companies have been compiling worldwide HR databases over the past decade, these still tend to concentrate on posts at the top of the organization, neglecting the middle managers in the country markets and potential stars coming through the ranks.

IBM has compiled a database of senior managers for 20 years, into which it feeds names of promising middle managers, tracking them all with annual reviews. But it made the base worldwide only 10 years ago. Now the company is building another global database that will cover 40,000 competencies and include all employees worldwide who can deliver those skills or be **groomed** to do so. IBM plans to link the two databases.

Unilever has practiced a broader sweep for the past 40 years. It has five talent "pools" stretching from individual companies (e.g., Good Humor Breyers Ice Cream in the United States and Walls Ice Cream in Britain) to foreign subsidiaries (e.g., Unilever United States Inc. and Unilever U.K. Holdings Ltd.) to global corporate headquarters. From day one, new executive trainees are given targets for personal development. Those who show the potential to move up significantly are quickly **earmarked** for the "Development" list, where their progress through the pools — company, national, business group and/or region, global, executive committee — is guided not only by their direct bosses but by managers up to three levels above. "We want bigger yardsticks to be applied to these

Word Study

scatter /ˈskætə/ v. 分散
groom /ɡruːm/ v. 使做好准备，培养
earmark /ˈɪəmɑːk/ v. 指定

Word Study

remuneration
/rɪˌmjuːnəˈreɪʃən/ *n.*
报酬，薪水
pyramid /ˈpɪrəmɪd/ *n.*
金字塔
coordinator
/kəʊˈɔːdɪneɪtə/ *n.*
协调员

people and we don't want their direct bosses to hang on to them", explains Herwig Kressler, Unilever's head of **remuneration** and industrial relations. To make sure the company is growing the general management talent it will need, the global HR director's strategic arm reaches into the career moves of the third pool — those serving in a group or region — to engineer appointments across divisions and regions.

4. Construct a mobility pyramid

Evaluate your managers in terms of their willingness to move to new locations as well as their ability and experience. Most HR departments look at mobility in black-or-white terms: "movable" or "not movable". But in today's global markets this concept should be viewed as a graduated scale and constantly reassessed because of changing circumstances in managers' lives and company opportunities. This will encourage more managers to opt for overseas assignments and open the thinking of line and HR managers to different ways to use available in-house talent.

IBM uses its global HR database increasingly for international projects. In preparing a proposal for a German car manufacturer, for instance, it pulled together a team of experts with automotive experience in the client's major and new markets. To reduce costs for its overseas assignments, IBM has introduced geographic "filters": a line manager signals the need for outside skills to one of IBM's 400 resource **coordinators**, who aims to respond in 72 hours; the coordinator then searches the global skills database for a match, filtering the request through a series of ever-widening geographic circles. Preference is often given to the suitable candidate who is geographically closest to the assignment. The line manager then negotiates with that employee's boss or team for the employee's availability.

5. Identify your leadership capital

Build a database of your company's mix of managerial skills by persuading people to describe the information in their cvs, their management talents and their potential on standard personal-profile templates. Jump-start the process by having your senior managers and those in the lifeline posts complete the forms first. Add others worldwide with the potential to move up. Include functional specialists who show general management potential.

Require over time that every executive join the global HR system. This makes it harder for uncut diamonds to be hidden by their local bosses. Recognizing that people's situations and career preferences shift over time, hold all managers and technical experts responsible for updating their cv and reviewing their personal profiles at least once a year.

Companies should make it clear that individual inputs to the system are voluntary but that HR and line managers nevertheless will be using the data to plan promotions and international assignments and to assess training needs. Be mindful of the personal privacy provisions in the European Union's new Data Protection directive and similar regulations forthcoming in Japan that basically require employee consent to gather or circulate any personal information.

6. Assess your bench strength and skills gap

Ask each executive to compare his or her skills and characteristics with the ideal requirements defined for the executive's current post and preferred next post. Invite each to propose ways to close any personal skills gaps — for example, through in-house training, **mentoring**, outside courses or participation in cross-border task forces.

Compare the skills detailed in the personal **assessments** with those required by your business strategy. This information should form the basis for your management development and training programs and show whether you have time to prepare internal candidates for new job descriptions.

Unilever uses a nine-point competency framework for its senior managers. It then holds the information in private databases that serve as feeder information for its five talent pools. The company **thoroughly** reviews the five pools every two years and skims them in between, always using a three- to five-year perspective. In 1990, for example, its ice cream division had a strategic plan to move into 30 new countries within seven years. Unilever began hiring in its current markets with that in mind and set up a mobile "ice cream academy" to communicate the necessary technical skills.

IBM applies its competency framework to a much broader personnel base and conducts its skills gap analyses every six months. Business strategists in every strategic business unit define a plan for each market and, working with HR specialists, determine the skills required to succeed in it. Competencies are graded against five proficiency levels.

Managers and functional experts are responsible for checking into the database to compare their capabilities against the relevant skills profiles and to determine whether they need additional training. Their assessments are reviewed, discussed and **validated** by each executive's boss, and then put into the database. "Through the database, we get a business view of what we need versus what we have", explains Rick Weiss, director of skills at IBM "Once the gaps are identified, the question for HR is whether there is time to develop the necessary people or whether they have to be headhunted from the outside."

7. Recruit regularly

Search for new recruits in every important local market as regularly as you do in the headquarters country. Develop a reputation as "the company

Word Study

mentor /'mentɔː/ v.
指导
assessment /ə'sesmənt/
n. 评估
thoroughly /'θʌrəlɪ/
adv. 彻底地
validate /'vælɪdeɪt/ v.
认可,批准

stellar /'stelə/ *adj.* 优
秀的
perpetuate /pə'petʃueɪt/
  v. 使持续,使延续
status quo
  /ˌsteɪtəs'kwəʊ/ *n.*
  现状
succession /sək'seʃən/
  n. 继任

to join" among graduates of the best universities, as Citibank has in India, for example. The best way to attract **stellar** local national recruits is to demonstrate how far up the organization they can climb. Although many Fortune 500 companies in the United States derive 50 percent or more of their revenues from non-domestic sales, only 15 percent of their senior posts are held by non-Americans.

There may be nothing to stop a local national from reaching the top, but the executive suite inevitably reflects where a company was recruiting 30 years earlier. Even today, many multinational companies recruit disproportionately more people in their largest — often their longest-established — markets, thereby **perpetuating** the **status quo**.

8. Advertise your posts internally

Run your own global labor market. In a large company, it is hard to keep track of the best candidates. For this reason, IBM now advertises many of its posts on its worldwide Intranet. Unilever usually advertises only posts in the lower two pools, but this policy varies by country and by business unit.

IBM used to hire only from the inside, but several years ago it began to recruit outsiders — including those from other industries — to broaden thinking and add objectivity. Unilever is large enough that it can garner a short list of three to five internal candidates for any post. Yet it still fills 15 percent to 20 percent of managerial jobs from outside because of the need for specialist skills and because of the decreasing ability to plan where future growth opportunities will occur.

9. Institute succession planning

Every manager in a lifeline job should be required to nominate up to three candidates who could take over that post in the next week, in three months or within a year, and their bosses should sign off on the nominations. This should go a long way toward solving succession questions, but it will not resolve them completely.

The problem in large multinational companies is that many of today's successors may leave the company tomorrow. In addition, managers name only those people they know as successors. Third, the chief executives of many multinational companies keep their succession plans — if they have any — only in their heads. This seems to overlook the harsh realities of life and death. A better approach is that of one European shipping magnate who always carries a written list with the name of a successor for the captain of every boat in his fleet.

10. Challenge and retain your talent

Global networks that transfer knowledge and good practices run on people-to-people contact and continuity. Executive continuity also cuts down on turnover, recruitment and opportunity costs. As international competition for talent intensifies, therefore, it becomes increasingly important for companies to retain their good managers. Monetary incentives are not sufficient: the package must include challenge, personal growth and job satisfaction.

A policy should be adopted that invites employees to grow with the company, in every market. In addition, a career plan should be drawn up for every executive within his or her first 100 days in the organization. And plans should be reviewed regularly to be sure they stay aligned with the business strategy and the individual's need for job satisfaction and employability.

Overseas assignments and cross-border task forces are excellent ways to challenge, develop and retain good managers. They can also be awarded as horizontal "promotions". This is particularly useful since the flat organizations currently in fashion do not have enough levels for hierarchical promotions alone to provide sufficient motivation.

Unilever has long had a policy of retentive development and manages to hold on to 50 percent of its high-flyers. As an integral part of its global HR policy, it develops the "good" as well as the "best". Unilever reasons realistically that it needs to back up its high-flyers at every stage and location with a strong bench of crisis-proof, experienced supporters who also understand how to move with the markets.

MANAGING OVERSEAS POSTINGS

Overseas assignments are an essential part of the 10-step program. Yet the track record at most United States-based multinational companies is poor. One study found that up to 25 percent of United States expats "black out" in their assignments and have to be recalled or let go. Between 30 percent and 50 percent of the remainder are considered "brown-outs": they stay in their posts but underperform. The failure rates for European and Japanese companies were half those of American multinational companies.

Although the average annual cost of maintaining a United States employee abroad is about $300,000, and the average overseas assignment lasts about four years, United States multinational companies have been accepting a one-in-four chance of gaining no long-term return on this $1.2 million investment. The way around this problem is to manage an expat's exit and re-entry as you would any other major appointment by adopting these strategies:

✓ Accord overseas postings the same high priority as other important business assignments.
✓ Match the candidates' hard skills, soft skills, cultural background and interests with the demands of the post and location. An

管理海外职位

　　海外任务是上述行动纲领的重要组成部分。然而，多数美国跨国公司的表现不佳。研究发现，多达25%的美国外派人员在任务中"停电"，必须被召回或终止职务。其余的30%至50%则被视为"电力不足"。他们留在自己的职位上，但表现不佳。欧洲和日本公司的失败率是美国跨国公司的一半。

American manager who studies tai chi and Asian philosophy, for example, is more likely to succeed in China than one who coaches Little League.

✓ Give internal applicants the edge, with personal and company training if needed.

✓ Spend on some insurance against blackouts and brownouts, especially with medium- to long-term assignments in the company's "lifeline". Send the final candidates to visit the country where the post is based, preferably with their spouses, and give the local managers with whom they will work input into the final selection.

✓ Give the **appointee** and his or her family cultural and language-immersion training.

✓ Assign a mentor from headquarters who will stay in touch with the manager throughout the posting. Ideally, the mentor will have similar overseas experience and can alert the appointee to possible pitfalls and opportunities.

✓ Set clear objectives for the appointee's integration into the local business environment. IBM, for example, traditionally expects a country general manager to join and head the local American Chamber of Commerce and to entertain a government minister at home once a quarter.

✓ Continue developing the manager while he or she is overseas. Do not make it an "out of sight, out of mind" assignment.

✓ Discuss "next steps" before departure and again during the assignment.

Unilever used to have big problems with expat appointments and would lose 20 percent to 25 percent on their return. The problems occurred partly because executives who could not make it in the most important markets were sent on overseas assignments. According to Mr. Kressler of Unilever: "When they were ready to come back, nobody wanted them. It took two years to get the message out that we would not post anyone who wouldn't have a fair chance of getting a job in-house on their return. Now, our rate of loss is well under 10 [percent]."

Unilever's overseas postings now have two equally important objectives: to provide the local unit with needed skills, technical expertise or training and to develop general management talent. Unilever prefers to have its foreign operations run by local nationals, supported by a multinational mix of senior managers, so most expats report to local nationals. Only 10 percent are sent to head a unit — either when no local national is available or when the assignment is important to a manager's career development.

A manager who is sent on overseas assignment remains linked to a company unit that retains a career responsibility for him or her. The unit must include the manager in its annual performance reviews and career-planning system. Responsibility is given to the unit rather than to an individual manager to provide continuity and is included in the performance assessment of the unit and its director.

Career development is a factor in managerial bonuses in emerging markets, where Unilever is trying to train and develop local people, and in established markets, which help supply young expatriate managers to emerging markets.

HOW LONG IS ENOUGH?

The duration of any overseas appointment has to make sense for the individual, the company and the country. Three-year assignments are typical for the regional and global levels on the mobility pyramid, but they are not always enough. The cultural gap between a Western country and Japan, for example, is especially large, so a Westerner appointed as country manager will probably need to stay six years to make a significant impact.

Even when the culture gap is narrower, three-year assignments may be too short, except for the skilled glopat. Usually the first year is spent unpacking, the third year is spent packing up and anticipating the next move, leaving only the second year for full attention to the job. Most Unilever expat assignments last three to four years, although Mr. Kressler believes four to five years would be preferable in many cases.

MATCHING COMPLEMENTARY SKILLS

One **caveat** — overemphasizing individual development planning can lead to trying to turn every executive into a superman or superwoman. In fact, organizational effectiveness depends mainly on leveraging complementary skills of team members. The mobility pyramid can be a great advantage here. Using a variety of information technology groupware and mobile assignments, companies can partner managers from domestic and international markets in complementary and mutually supportive assignments to transfer ideas, skills and technology.

This is done particularly in high-technology industries, where it often takes time and training to bring newly hired local nationals up to speed on highly technical product lines. In such cases, an experienced manager can be sent to the market on a short-term assignment both to build initial sales and to train the local nationals while learning about the local market from them.

Given the shortage of true glopats, many multinational companies find it useful to pair a headquarters-oriented executive from outside the market with an executive familiar with the local market as the two

海外任命期限多久足够呢?

任何海外任命的期限对个人、公司和国家来说都必须是合理的。从区域和全球层面来说,驻外工作期限通常是三年,但这并不总是足够的。

即使在文化差距较小的情况下,三年的期限也可能太短。通常第一年花在打开行李上,第三年花在收拾行李上,只剩下第二年来全神贯注于这项工作。联合利华的大多数外派任务都是三到四年。

Word Study

caveat /ˈkeɪvɪˌæt/ *n.*
警告,告诫

most senior managers in an operating subsidiary. These two often have complementary skills, and their pairing permits a "good cop, bad cop" approach to certain customers. The expat knows the product line and company well, and his or her lack of detailed knowledge about the local culture can actually help provoke a fresh and open approach to local obstacles. The insider then provides the well of country knowledge and connections for the expat to draw upon.

Once a beachhead is established, further penetration of the local market favors the executive with local knowledge. The outsider can then mentor from behind the scenes, staying in touch with headquarters to guarantee the transfer of good ideas.

In the event of a financial crisis, the home office often elects to tighten controls and appoint a financially savvy general manager with strong ties to headquarters. A major strategy change or acquisition may also require such leadership to implement it. Once the situation is under control, however, leadership may revert to a manager with deep local knowledge.

Conclusion

总结

现在，大多数跨国公司都很好地实现了基本原材料供应链的全球化，但人力资源除外。

人才竞争加剧，需求远远大于供给。为了应对全球化和知识经济带来的挑战，企业必须实事求是地将人力资源视为其最重要的资源，在其所有市场实施招聘、培训和留住管理人员的计划。

Most multinational companies now do a good job of globalizing the supply chains for all their essential raw materials — except human resources. Players in global markets can no longer afford this blind spot. Competition for talent is intensifying, and demand far outstrips supply. To have the multicultural skills and vision they need to succeed, companies will have to put into place programs that recruit, train and retain managers in all their markets.

If companies are to handle the challenges of globalization and shift to a knowledge-based economy, they must develop systems that "walk their talk" that people are their most valuable resource. The purpose of a global HR program is to insure that a multinational company has the right talent, managerial mobility and cultural mix to manage effectively all of its operating units and growth opportunities and that its managers mesh into a knowledge-sharing network with common values.

Key Terms
专业术语

global human resource management 全球人力资源管理

expatriate 外派人员　　　　　　　　career management 职业生涯管理

overseas assignments 海外外派任务　　local nationals 本地人员

glopats 全球外派人员　　　　　　　staff turnover 员工流动率

managerial posts 管理岗位　　　　　bench strength 后备力量

performance assessment/review 绩效评价　cultural sensitivity 文化敏感性

全球人力资源管理中的"跨文化"因素

企业国际化使人力资源管理活动变得更加复杂。在多元化的文化背景下,差异文化观念容易带来跨文化冲突,这给国际人力资源管理活动带来了极大的挑战。跨文化人力资源管理强调在不同文化背景下企业人力资源管理活动的文化性,能够有效的解决因文化差异而引起的跨文化冲突问题。

随着企业国际化战略的开展和深入,企业面临的经营环境越来越复杂和动态,其中文化的多元性(multiculturalism)成为跨国企业经营管理过程中必须要面对的挑战。人力资源管理活动作为企业重要的管理实践在国际化背景下也面临着多元文化的冲击,跨国企业由于处在不同"文化边际领域"所产生的文化冲突下,其人力资源管理变得更为复杂和动态。有效的进行跨文化的人力资源管理是跨国企业成功运营的有效保证。在跨文化人力资源管理中,应当着重考虑跨地域、跨民族、跨企业的文化体系的冲突与多元。如何选择全方位、全系统、全过程的跨文化人力资源管理活动,成为跨国公司人力资源管理的重中之重。

企业走出国门,国家与地区之间的文化差异也给跨国公司及其管理者的传统思维和管理理念提出了新的挑战,特别是对于人力资源管理,文化多元性和地理扩散带来了国际人力资源管理低效的新挑战,国际人力资源管理的复杂性在于其管理对象变成具有更多文化背景的复杂的员工,跨文化管理成为新的管理主题。

文献来源:

张婧,王丹,吴华.打造跨文化人力资源管理能力——以阿里巴巴为例[J].中国人力资源开发,342(24):27-32.

A. Please summarize the potential problems of human resources management under a global background.

Potential Problems of Global HR Management

① _____

② _____

③ _____

B. According to the text, fill in each of the following blanks with an appropriate word or phrase.

1) HR must now be given a _____ seat in the boardroom.

2) International managers must be meshed into a _____ network in which they quickly identify and leverage good ideas worldwide.

3) The consequent lack of world-wise _____ managerial talent is now biting into companies' bottom lines through high staff turnover and other elements.

4) Insufficient attention and budget are devoted to assessing, training and developing the careers of valuable local nationals already on the company _____.

5) More frequent international travel, population mobility and cross-border university education are increasing the pool of available _____ _____ local nationals.

6) The main tool of a global HR policy has to be a global _____ simply because multinational companies now have many more strategic posts globally.

7) Most HR departments look at _____ in black-or-white terms: "movable" or "not movable".

8) Overseas assignments and cross-border task forces are excellent ways to challenge, develop and _____ good managers.

9) The expats' lack of detailed knowledge about the local culture can actually help provoke a fresh and open approach to local _____.

10) The outsider can _____ from behind the scenes, staying in touch with headquarters to guarantee the transfer of good ideas.

C. Read the text and decide whether the following statements are True (T) or False (F).

1) Most multinational companies have the leadership capital they need to perform effectively in all their markets around the world.　　(　　)

2) In most multinationals, HR development policies have tended to concentrate on nationals of the headquarters country.　　(　　)

3) Very few distinctions can be found between expatriate and local national pay, benefits and bonuses.　　(　　)

4) Executives can be savvy functionally and internationally, and they don't have to be savvy inside the organization.　　(　　)

5) The lifeline and role descriptions should be revisited at least annually to ensure they express the business strategy.　　(　　)

6) Some multinational companies have been compiling worldwide HR databases over the past decade, concentrating on posts at the top of the organization, the middle managers in the country markets and potential stars coming through the ranks.　　(　　)

7) Monetary incentives are not sufficient: the package must include challenge, personal growth and job satisfaction.　　(　　)

8) Career plans should be reviewed regularly to be sure they stay aligned with the business strategy and the individual's need for job satisfaction and employability.　　(　　)

9) Three-year assignments are typical for the regional and global levels on the mobility pyramid, and that's enough in most cases.　　(　　)

10) Using a variety of information technology groupware and mobile assignments, companies can partner managers from domestic and

international markets in complementary and mutually supportive assignments to transfer ideas, skills and technology.　　　（　　）

1) Please explain the term "glopats" in your own words.

_____

_____

2) Why are human resources recognized as significant as financial assets for global companies?

_____

_____

3) Why do the chief executives of many United States-based multinational companies lack confidence in the ability of their HR functions?

_____

_____

4) "The best way to attract stellar local national recruits is to demonstrate how far up the organization they can climb." Do you agree with this statement?

_____

_____

5) Why does the author hold the opinion that 3-year overseas appointment may be not long enough?

_____

_____

Case Story

Rolls-Royce

A companywide, global HR implementation conducted in one single overnight deployment might sound like a scary prospect for some. But that's exactly what Workday customer Rolls-Royce did in October 2015, when the business deployed a cloud-based HR system Workday, covering employees across 46 countries.

We caught up with Mark Judd, HRIT director at Rolls-Royce, at the HR Tech World event in London last month to learn more about the move to the cloud and get his tips for other businesses looking at similar projects.

What were the business and technology challenges that prompted Rolls-Royce to deploy a new HR system?

Our ability to "see" the organization we are growing with a significant global footprint was inhibited by the underlying technology. We're talking about things such as management of capability and deployment of the right resources, including the ability to deploy the right people when and where we need them.

We had relied on a legacy system to manage HR records and payroll for employees in our five largest territories, which was about 85% of the workforce. Elsewhere we had a combination of smaller HR and payroll systems and a vast array of spreadsheets and PowerPoint files. As you can imagine, it was difficult for managers to generate an accurate picture of the workforce worldwide, or to produce reports on the skills and talents of our employees.

You clearly did your homework — why did Workday come out on top?

We looked for vendors that had conducted similar large-scale implementations and only three met that criteria: Workday, SuccessFactors, and Oracle. When we heard the response from the market, the enthusiasm and high level of excitement about Workday, it seemed right for us.

Our project team decided at an early stage to work with a standard configuration of Workday Human Capital Management. The plan was to keep variations in different regions to a minimum. We liked the idea of going back to basics, and really challenging what we wanted to do with HR.

How important was the strength of the Workday community, including all customers being on the same version of Workday?

It is a differentiator in the quality of the Workday concept. Workday doesn't compromise on that. When we first looked at the options, we saw how other customers valued the quality of being at the same place at the same time. In all honesty, Workday didn't sell to us, the other customers did. We valued the community and saw the empowerment of it.

Do you have any advice on managing project stakeholders?

Find a stakeholder who is respected and seen as a leader, and spend time earning his or her trust and support. We had a passionate business leader and someone everyone listens to. He is uncompromising in quality, and that's what is expected of Rolls-Royce in the products we produce. We invested a lot of time with that stakeholder.

Very early on, we went in front of lots of people and were told, "This new system needs to be as good, if not better than the European retailer John Lewis's website." So someone on the Workday team managed to track down the guy who developed the John Lewis website, interviewed him, and showed him the Workday application. He filmed the website developer saying Workday was "one of the most effective forms of technology he'd seen". That went down very well with the business.

What are your top tips for businesses looking to replace their aging HR systems?

First, don't sell the HR system — sell the right business idea. You have to think beyond the technology itself and sell the vision of what it will do for the business. Get it across to your business that you are buying an idea ... you are buying something that is changing all the time.

Next, acknowledge that you're choosing a different path. This isn't an upgrade, it's a transformation. You're not moving from your old typewriter to the latest and greatest typewriter. Think of it as moving from the best typewriter to the newest laptop. As such, think ahead and plan your integration strategy. Make sure the structure is there. Invest heavily in thinking of the big picture and how it will all work together.

Then, standardize, harmonize, and galvanize. We had technology in place that was complex, difficult, and not agile to change. This caused trouble because there were different processes everywhere across the business. If you're trying to get to a similar place that we were, then you should follow a common set of principles, and harmonize processes. Workday allowed us to do this and it was galvanizing for the organization.

Case Discussion

1) What did Rolls-Royce do in October 2015?

_____

_____

2) Why did Mark Judd say "it was difficult to generate an accurate picture of the workforce worldwide"?

_____

_____

3) What advice did Mark Judd give to businesses planning to replace their old HR system?

_____

_____

Case Summary

劳斯莱斯于1906年成立于英国。作为超豪华汽车厂商,其出产的轿车是顶级汽车的杰出代表,以其豪华而享誉全球,是欧美汽车的主要代表之一。

该公司曾利用旧系统来管理员工记录和薪资，这大约占员工总数的85%。同时，也结合了各种各样的电子表格和幻灯片文件来进行管理。这对于了解全球范围内的员工队伍情况十分不利。

劳斯莱斯于2015年在全公司范围部署全球人力资源管理。该公司采纳了基于云端的人力资源系统Workday，覆盖了46个国家/地区的员工，这有利于促成更高效、全面的人力资源管理。

Reading
Expansion
拓展阅读

Reading I

Seven Characteristics of Highly Effective International HR Professionals

Working as an international HR professional is a challenge in so many ways. How can you best prepare for success in your role? Here are some tips which I refer to (with apologies to the late Dr. Steven Covey) as the "Seven Characteristics of Highly Effective International HR Professionals".

Flexibility

Everyone knows HR is burdened with a lot of processes and guidelines. Companies strive for standardization across their entire enterprise. A good international HR pro understands that flexibility is a key to success. Every country is different and the standard approach that HQ designed might not work perfectly in every country. So be flexible about the application of global standards and processes.

Be Comfortable with Uncertainty

International HR staff are often faced with situations they have not encountered before and for which there is no precedent. You need to analyze the situation and create a solution, even if there are no clear cut answers. A real pro finds a solution that works for the client group, and satisfies corporate at the same time. Uncertainty simply comes with the territory, so learn to deal with it.

Cultural Awareness and Sensitivity

Each nation of the world is different, and it doesn't matter if they speak your language or share a border — each country is separate, distinct and unique. Learn how to embrace cultural differences and turn them into competitive business advantages. Listen to your people in-country before telling them what they should do. Learn what is happening in-country and how the history and culture influence how business is conducted. There are obvious things to avoid — such as holiday celebrations that are not part of the national culture. But it is the subtle things that are often overlooked.

For example, it is common in Kenya for managers to have company cars. However, many companies shy away from cars and extend that shyness to Kenya. Not a good idea. It's a cultural thing — a status symbol, too. Think about it — no one sees a car allowance in your wallet but your neighbors see that company car in your driveway.

Performance management is another area to watch. Frank, direct feedback is not a part of many Asian cultures. Hierarchy and respect for seniority prevent frank exchanges, especially in front of others, which could be embarrassing to a senior manager. So take this into account when seeking, offering and interpreting feedback. Always check the cultural aspects that impact such discussions.

Try and learn a few words of the local language. It's not that hard, and goes a long way towards establishing your credibility. It may be true that most international business people speak English but it doesn't matter. You can practice your Spanish, French or Chinese and your hosts can practice their English.

Adaptability

You are working in areas which require adaptability to the situation on the ground. It's often different from HQ. The roles of labor unions in Europe and Latin America, for example, create requirements that are very different from the U.S. If you start applying U.S.-style labor relations in Europe you will embarrass yourself and your company. So learn the rules and adapt your style as needed.

In developing countries there may be limitations due to infrastructure. Go with the flow instead of comparing to other places where it may have been easier or more convenient to conduct business. You will also encounter many aspects of compensation that are different. Don't assume they should be ignored just because you are not familiar with them — adapt your package to the local norms instead.

Be Agnostic — Good Answers Come from Many Sources

There are always many solutions to a problem. Depending on the country, the locally-recommended solution might be the best. Don't reject these ideas because they are unfamiliar or not from your usual global supplier. Perhaps the local solution is OK. Explore it, evaluate it, engage with your colleagues to fully understand and then decide.

Curiosity

It is not a coincidence that the NASA Mars Rover is called Curiosity. This trait is imperative for success in international business, and international HR is certainly part of that! Explore the differences you encounter, get to know your local colleagues and demonstrate genuine interest in learning new things. Ask questions — a lot of questions — so you can understand why things are the way they are in different countries.

Have some free time during a business trip? Explore the local sights. Shop in the local market (the one where the locals go — not the one for expats and tourists). Taste the local specialties and pick up some unique souvenirs. I traveled a lot when my daughter was young. I picked up a doll in a traditional dress in each country I visited. Now she has a great collection of dolls from all over the world, and a real appreciation of how big the world is.

Sharing and Listening

Over the years I have worked with people from many countries. One of the most striking things I've noticed is how easily people from around the globe are willing to share their ideas with others, and how many great ideas people have that I may not have encountered before.

So listen to your international colleagues and embrace their ideas. Share your experiences and ideas in return. Work on solutions collaboratively. You will benefit from their ideas and have a friend in every country!

Second Thoughts

For each of the following statements, choose one (or more than one) answer to fill in the blank.

1) To be culturally aware means _____.
   A. learning to embrace the cultural differences
   B. turning cultural differences into business advantages
   C. telling the local people what they should do
   D. avoiding holiday celebrations that are not part of the national culture
2) According to the passage, the international HR professionals should learn to _____.
   A. be willing to share ideas
   B. pick up some local language
   C. engage with colleagues
   D. stay curious

Reading II

Factors Affecting Global HR Management

Managing human resources in different cultures, economies, and legal systems presents some challenges. However, when well done, HR management pays dividends. A seven-year study in Britain of over 100 foreign companies showed that good HR management, as well as other factors, accounted for more of the variance in profitability and productivity than did technology, or research and development.

The most common obstacles to effective HR management are cross-cultural adaptation, different organizational/workforce values, differences in management style, and management turnover. Doing business globally requires that adaptations be made to reflect these factors. It is crucial that such concerns be seen as interrelated by managers and professionals as they do business and establish operations globally.

Legal and Political Factors

The nature and stability of political systems vary from country to country. U.S. firms are accustomed to a relatively stable political system, and the same is true in many of the other developed countries in Europe. Although presidents, prime ministers, premiers, governors, senators, and representatives may change, the legal systems are well-established, and global firms can depend on continuity and consistency.

However, in many other nations, the legal and political systems are turbulent. Some governments regularly are overthrown by military coups. Others are ruled by dictators and despots who use their power to require international firms to buy goods and services from host-country firms owned or controlled by the rulers or the rulers' families.

International firms may have to decide strategically when to comply with certain laws and regulations and when to ignore them because of operational or political reasons. Another issue involves ethics. Because of restrictions imposed on U.S.-based firms through the Foreign Corrupt Practices Act (FCPA), a fine line exists between paying "agent fees", which is legal, and bribery, which is illegal.

HR regulations and laws vary among countries in character and detail. In many Western European countries, laws on labor unions and employment make it difficult to reduce the number of workers because required payments to former employees can be very high. Equal employment legislation exists to varying degrees.

In some countries, laws address issues such as employment discrimination and sexual harassment. In others, because of religious or ethical differences, employment discrimination may be an accepted practice.

All of these factors reveal that it is crucial for HR professionals to conduct a comprehensive review of the political environment and employment-related laws before beginning operations in a country. The role and nature of labor unions should be a part of that review.

Economic Factors

Many lesser-developed nations are receptive to foreign investment in order to create jobs for their growing populations. Global firms often obtain significantly cheaper labor rates in these countries than they do in Western Europe, Japan, and the United States. However, whether firms can realize significant profits in developing nations may be determined by currency fluctuations and restrictions on transfer of earnings.

Also, political instability can lead to situations in which the assets of foreign firms are seized. In addition, nations with weak economies may not be able to invest in maintaining and upgrading the necessary elements of their infrastructures, such as roads, electric power, schools, and telecommunications. The absence of good infrastructures may make it more difficult to convince managers from the United States or Japan to take assignments overseas.

Economic conditions vary greatly. Cost of living is a major economic consideration for global corporations. In many developed countries, especially in Europe, unemployment has grown, but employment restrictions and wage levels remain high. Consequently, many European firms are transferring jobs to lower-wage countries, as Mercedes-Benz did at its Alabama plant. In addition, both personal and corporate tax rates are quite high. These factors all must be evaluated as part of the process of deciding whether to begin or purchase operations in foreign countries.

Cultural Factors

Cultural forces represent another important concern affecting international HR management. Culture is composed of the societal forces affecting the values, beliefs, and actions of a distinct group of people. Cultural differences certainly exist between nations, but significant cultural differences exist within countries also. One only has to look at the conflicts caused by religion or ethnicity in Central Europe and other parts of the world to see the importance of culture on international organizations. Getting individuals from different ethnic or tribal backgrounds working together may be difficult in some parts of the world. Culture can lead to ethical differences among countries.

One widely used way to classify and compare cultures has been developed by Geert Hofstede, a Dutch scholar and researcher. Hofstede conducted research on over 100,000 IBM employees in 53 countries, and he identified five dimensions useful in identifying and comparing culture. A review of each of those dimensions follows.

Power distance

The dimension of power distance refers to the inequality among the people of a nation. In countries such as Germany, the Netherlands, and the United States, there is a smaller power distance — which means there is less inequality — than in such countries as France, Indonesia, Russia, and China. As power distance increases, there are greater status and authority differences between superiors and subordinates.

One way in which differences on this dimension affect HR activities is that the reactions to management authority differ among cultures. A more autocratic approach to managing is more common in most other countries, while in the United States there is a bit more use of participatory management.

Individualism

Another dimension of culture identified by Hofstede is individualism, which is the extent to which people in a country prefer to act as individuals instead of members of groups. On this dimension, people in Asian countries tend to be less individualistic and more group-oriented, whereas those in the United States score the highest in individualism. An implication of these differences is that more collective action and less individual competition is likely in those countries that deemphasize individualism.

Masculinity/femininity

The cultural dimension masculinity/femininity refers to the degree to which "masculine" values prevail over "feminine" values. Masculine values identified by Hofstede were assertiveness, performance orientation, success, and competitiveness, whereas feminine values included quality of life, close personal relationships, and caring. Respondents from Japan had the highest masculinity scores, while those from the Netherlands had more femininity-oriented values. Differences on this dimension may be tied to the role of women in the culture. Considering the different roles of women and what is "acceptable" for women in the United States, Saudi Arabia, Japan, and Mexico suggests how this dimension might affect the assignment of women expatriates to managerial jobs in the various countries.

Uncertainty avoidance

The dimension of uncertainty avoidance refers to the preference of people in a country for structured rather than unstructured situations. A structured situation is one in which rules can be established and there are clear guides on how people are expected to act. Nations high on this factor, such as Japan, France, and Russia, tend to be more resistant to changes and more rigid. In contrast, people in places such as Hong Kong (China), the United States, and Indonesia tend to have more "business energy" and to be more flexible. A logical use of differences on this factor is to anticipate how people in different countries will react to changes instituted in organizations. In more flexible cultures, what is less certain may be more intriguing and challenging, which may lead to greater entrepreneurship and risk taking than in the more "rigid" countries.

Long-term orientation

The dimension of long-term orientation refers to values people hold that emphasize the future, as opposed to short-term values, which focus on the present and the past. Long-term values include thrift and persistence, while short-term values include respecting tradition and fulfilling social obligations. People scoring the highest on long-term orientation were in China, while people in Russia, the United States, and France tended to have more short-term orientation.

Differences in many other facets of culture could be discussed. But it is enough to recognize that international HR managers and professionals must recognize that cultural dimensions differ from country to country and even within countries. Therefore, the HR activities appropriate in one culture or country may have to be altered to fit appropriately into another culture or country.

Challenges of the Expatriate Assignments

It is a big challenge for an international organization to effectively manage its expatriate workforce.

The ratio of the failure of the assignments of the expatriate workforce is estimated to lie in between 20% to 40%. Following are the six factors that are responsible for such failures.

- Career blockage;
- Culture shock;
- Lack of cross-cultural pre-departure training;
- Overemphasis on technical qualifications;
- Family problems;
- Difficulties on return.

There are some additional issues that are faced by the expatriates on arrival at home. These problems are as follows.

- Lack of respect for obtained skills;
- Loss of status;
- Improper planning for return position;
- Reverse culture shock.

The global human resource management should develop and implement those policies and procedures that cover the fundamental issues of the expatriate assignments. These effective HR policies must be related to the selection, training, career development and compensation.

Selection

The selection of a suitable employee for the expatriate assignment is a sensitive decision. The management should select the best employee for the international assignment. Following are the guidelines for the management in this regard.

- The cultural sensitivity should be emphasized as a criterion of selection;
- A selection board should be established for expatriates;
- The previous international experience is required;
- The foreign-born employees are focused to hire;
- The spouses and families of the candidates are screened out.

Training

People belong to different cultures and countries respond differently to the same symbols, images and slogans. So the cross-cultural training is provided to the selected candidates that should cover the local customs, culture, tax laws, language and government.

Career development

The career development opportunities offered by the management of the organization also serve as a basis for the motivation of the expatriate employee to perform well on his or her given assignment.

Compensation

The effectiveness of the expatriate employees is enhanced through attractive compensation packages by the management of the organization. However, in certain cases, these special compensation packages for expatriate employees create conflict in the local employees of the organization. When local employees compare their compensation packages with the packages of expatriate employees, the local employees consider this policy of the management as unfair and hence conflict is generated in the organization.

Second Thoughts

1) What are the obstacles to effective global HR management?

_____

_____

2) Can you give three other possible reasons for the failure of the expatriate assignments?

_____

_____

Accounting and Finance in International Business

国际商务中的会计与金融

本章概要

本章主要介绍国际商务的背景下的会计与金融的含义、作用等，并基于中国企业在美上市趋势的报道，展开会计与金融案例分析。

学习指南

会计是一种跟踪和记录企业活动的系统，它必须符合时代标准且准确无误。会计有时被称为"企业的语言"。如何在国际会计准则变革时期，认识到国际会计准则的原则导向及未来发展方向，进而调整自身发展，以期在未来国际会计准则变革中争取话语权，其重要性不言而喻。另一方面，国际金融指跨越国界发生的任何金融交易。它也可以被视为一种分析潜在业务国家经济状况、判断国外市场、比较通货膨胀率并以外币支付账单的方法。国际商务中的会计和金融有着多方面的联系。

通过本章学习，希望大家能够实现以下目标：

（1）基本目标（Text-based Goals）

● 掌握本章涉及话题的基本专业术语及词汇，如财务会计、管理会计、商业融资等；

● 掌握本章的主要知识点，即国际商务中会计与金融的含义、作用等。

（2）拓展目标（Extended Goals）

● 思考本章引言，为什么沃伦·巴菲特认为"会计数字是商业估值的开始，而非结束"？

● 通过学习背景知识、拓展阅读、案例分析进一步了解国际商务中会计与金融的联系。

> Managers and investors alike must understand that accounting numbers are the beginning, not the end, of business valuation.（管理者和投资者都必须明白，会计数字是商业估值的开始，而非结束。）
>
> —Warren Buffett（沃伦·巴菲特）

The Role of Accounting in Business

会计在企业活动中的作用

For small business owners, accounting can be both a headache and an indispensable tool. Understanding the role of accounting in business can help you develop a friendlier relationship with the process, which is both a legal requirement and a source of objective feedback about your company's financial performance and overall **viability**.

会计是一种跟踪和记录企业活动的系统。该系统可简单，可复杂，但它必须符合时代标准且准确无误。

Some people start businesses because they are interested in marketing, financial ratios and long-term planning. Many other small business owners come to the world of entrepreneurship because they have a skill or a passion, or they want more autonomy over their schedules and work lives. Business owners who are more interested in their craft than their balance sheet still need to perform basic accounting tasks to stay legal and **solvent**.

会计的重要性在于其阐明短期和长期活动的能力。会计有时被称为"企业的语言"。

Accounting is a system of tracking and documenting business activities. Your system can be simple or complex, homegrown or standardized by a software company, but it must be reasonably current and accurate, or your company could run into practical and even legal difficulties. A well-maintained accounting system doesn't just keep you out of trouble. It also provides information that will help make your company into a better business.

Word Study

viability /ˌvaɪəˈbɪlətɪ/ n. 可行性，生存能力
solvent /ˈsɒlvənt/ adj. 有偿付能力的
accrue /əˈkruː/ v. 积累（钱款或债务）

The importance of accounting lies in its capacity to shed light on short-term and long-term activities. Accounting is sometimes referred to as the "language of business" because it connects the dots in meaningful ways, expressing observations in terms that are consistent and structured. Not all accounting information follows traditional formats, but these methods do give you a leg up in organizing your data to extract answers to questions that are common to all businesses, such as whether you are losing or making money.

Functions of Accounting

会计的功能
① 记账
② 生成报告
③ 审计
④ 规划预测

RECORDING

Accounting processes document business expenditures, allowing you to see and compile the many pieces of information that describe your business processes. These include outgoing expenditures for operations and infrastructure, incoming revenue from sales of products or services and other sources, such as the interest you **accrue**.

Word Study

shortfall /ˈʃɔːt.fɔːl/ *n.*
差额,缺口
auditor /ˈɔːdɪtə/ *n.* 审
计员

GENERATING REPORTS

Accounting information is typically compiled into statements using streamlined and widely understood formats such as profit and loss statements, balance sheets and cash flow statements. These reports summarize financial activities, providing a broader perspective than you'd get by simply looking over a list of transactions.

AUDITING

Accounting information should be double checked to verify its consistency and accuracy. By doing periodic audits, you can have a backup system to flag dishonesty, carelessness or faulty systems that provide questionable results. An audit can be as intensive as hiring an outside company to evaluate your work, or it can be as simple as another staff member looking through your accounting information with a fresh set of eyes.

PROJECTING

Although you'll never be able to predict future sales and expenses with complete accuracy, it is still useful to forecast future business activity based on past and present patterns. These projections can show you when you may need to borrow money to cover **shortfalls** or when you'll have extra cash to invest in capital improvements.

Objectives of Accounting

ACCURACY

Your accounting system should faithfully reflect your business activity for both legal and practical reasons. Tax reporting requires that you provide information that is accurate to the best of your knowledge. If your accounting is sloppy, and your numbers don't correspond with the flow of money in and out of your bank account, this can be a red flag for a tax **auditor**. Accuracy is important for internal purposes as well because better information helps you to make better strategic decisions.

COMPLETENESS

An accounting system that is missing key pieces of information will be neither accurate nor useful. To ensure completeness, your system should have solid systems in place for receiving information about all transactions from your staff, your vendors and your bank accounts. You should also have regular internal methods for double checking whether all of your revenue and expenditures have been entered.

RELEVANCE

If your accounting staff devotes a disproportionate share of its attention to tracking down **negligible** inaccuracies from previous years at the expense of entering information from the current year, you may lose sight of truly useful information by neglecting the big picture. It is important to prioritize tasks that keep your information relevant so you can complete your tax forms on time and understand your company's current financial picture.

USEFULNESS

Aside from being used for tax forms, loan applications and reports for investors, your accounting system should also yield information that your company can use for planning and evaluating. This may include data about production efficiency and sales reports by month, region or sales representative. The usefulness of different types of accounting information varies from business to business and even within the same business over time.

Financial Accounting vs Management Accounting

FINANCIAL ACCOUNTING

Accounting processes can be broken down in terms of the roles of accounting information for your business. Financial accounting concerns itself with compiling the reports and forms that your company uses to report to outside entities, such as tax agencies, banks and investors. The formats and processes it uses tend to be standardized, and your business should follow generally accepted accounting principles when preparing this information.

Most agencies and investors who review your financial accounting information will expect to see three basic reports:

Profit and loss statement. This financial report tracks your company's earnings and expenditures over a specific period of time, such as a month or a year. It shows your cost of goods sold, or the amount spent on direct costs such as materials and production labor. It also calculates your gross profit, or the amount left over after subtracting these direct costs from your gross revenue, and your net profit, or the amount left over after also subtracting generalized infrastructure expenditures, such as rent and utilities.

Balance sheet. Your balance sheet provides a snapshot of how much your business owns and owes at a particular point in time. It lists assets such as cash on hand, inventory and real property such as real estate. It also breaks down **liabilities** into categories such as long-term loans, credit

Word Study

negligible /'neglɪdʒəbl/ *adj.* 微不足道的
liability /ˌlaɪə'bɪlɪti/ *n.* 债务

财务会计与管理会计

会计流程可以按照会计信息在业务中的作用进行细分。

财务会计关注的是编制公司用来向外部实体（如税务机构、银行和投资者）汇报的报告和表格。它使用的格式和流程趋于标准化，企业在准备这些信息时应遵循公认的会计原则。

相比之下，管理会计处理的信息将有助于内部目的，如评估盈利能力和规划未来的投资。

管理会计不必遵循任何传统的格式，尽管财务会计报告中收集的信息通常也对管理会计有用。除了评估损益外，管理会计还研究不同产品的成本核算、总体利润率和盈利能力以及与一系列变量相关的销售数字。

card debt and accounts payable to vendors. In addition to showing the sums your company owns and owes, your balance sheet also shows how these amounts are distributed and whether your assets are sufficiently liquid to finance business activities.

Cash flow statement. This accounting report shows how funds are flowing in and out of your business and whether you will have money available to meet your current financial obligations. It is not required for tax reporting, but it is extremely important to lenders and investors who need to evaluate whether you will be able to meet loan payments and whether you will have the capital you need to operate and expand.

MANAGEMENT ACCOUNTING

While financial accounting is used to keep your business in good standing with outside stakeholders, management accounting provides essential information for making strategic decisions. It works with information that will be useful for internal purposes, such as evaluating profitability and planning future ventures. Management accounting need not follow any traditional format, although the information collected in financial accounting reports is often useful for management accounting as well.

Management accounting may include data about the profitability of each of your products and services and a more detailed and nuanced accounting than the generalized cost of goods sold figure that appears on your profit and loss statement. By identifying the products that earn the highest margins and those that are easiest to produce, your business can focus its manufacturing and marketing resources in areas that will yield the highest returns.

Management accounting can also help you plan for upcoming product launches and equipment investments by creating cash flow projections. The information on a cash flow pro forma can't be completely accurate because there's no way to precisely **foretell** the future, but you can use past accounting numbers to forecast future patterns.

This information can tell you whether you can expect a cash flow shortfall at a particular time and, if so, approximately how much you'll be short. It can also give you a sense of whether you can afford a new project you're **contemplating** and, if not, how much you'll need to borrow to make it happen.

Standards of Accounting

In addition to its usefulness for individual businesses, the field of accounting has been instrumental in creating standards and protocols that facilitate communication about financial matters.

Word Study

foretell /fɔːˈtel/ v. 预言
contemplate
 /ˈkɒntempleɪt/ v.
思考

会计标准
    会计不仅对企业有帮助，在促进财务事项沟通标准和协议的建立方面发挥着重要作用。

The fact that the vast majority of businesses use comparable formats for balance sheets and profit and loss statements allows stakeholders to understand the information in these reports through filters that zero in on answers to questions that are particularly urgent, such as whether the company in question has the resources and the track record to pay its bills.

Although standardized accounting practices make it easier to grasp an overview of a company's financial situation, they certainly lend themselves to abuse and fraud. In addition, the institution of accounting practices makes it easy to overlook idiosyncrasies that may make a company especially resilient, such as a resourceful and tenacious manager. When evaluating accounting information, it's important to keep in mind both the discipline's strengths and its limitations.

INTERNATIONAL ACCOUNTING STANDARDS (IAS)

International Accounting Standards (IAS) are older accounting standards issued by the International Accounting Standards Board (IASB), an independent international standard-setting body based in London. The IAS were replaced in 2001 by International Financial Reporting Standards (IFRS).

International accounting is a subset of accounting that considers international accounting standards when balancing books.

Globally comparable accounting standards promote transparency, accountability, and efficiency in financial markets around the world. This enables investors and other market participants to make informed economic decisions about investment opportunities and risks and improves capital allocation. Universal standards also significantly reduce reporting and regulatory costs, especially for companies with international operations and subsidiaries in multiple countries.

MOVING TOWARD NEW GLOBAL ACCOUNTING STANDARDS

There has been significant progress towards developing a single set of high-quality global accounting standards since the IASC was replaced by the IASB. IFRS have been adopted by the European Union, leaving the United States, Japan (where voluntary adoption is allowed), and China (which says it is working towards IFRS) as the only major capital markets without an IFRS mandate. As of 2018, 144 jurisdictions required the use of IFRS for all or most publicly listed companies, and a further 12 jurisdictions permit its use.

The United States is exploring adopting international accounting standards. Since 2002, America's accounting-standards body, the Financial Accounting Standards Board (FASB) and the IASB have collaborated on a project to improve and converge the U.S. generally accepted accounting principles (GAAP) and IFRS. However, while the FASB and IASB have

国际会计准则（IAS）是国际会计准则理事会（IASB）发布的较旧的会计准则。2001年，国际会计准则被国际财务报告准则（IFRS）取代。

issued norms together, the convergence process is taking much longer than was expected — in part because of the complexity of implementing the Dodd-Frank Wall Street Reform and Consumer Protection Act.

The Securities and Exchange Commission (SEC), which regulates U.S. securities markets, has long supported high-quality global accounting standards in principle and continues to do so. In the meantime, because U.S. investors and companies routinely invest trillions of dollars abroad, fully understanding the similarities and differences between U.S. GAAP and IFRS is crucial. One conceptual difference: IFRS is thought to be a more principles-based accounting system, while GAAP is more rules-based.

The Role of Finance in Business

Business finance is the art and science of managing your company's money. It guides you to make **shrewd** and prudent decisions about cash flow and longer-term funding strategies. As you develop skills and strategies for using the funds you have and for accessing additional capital when needed, you'll improve your company's profitability and increase your potential for leveraging new opportunities. The role of finance in business is to make sure there are enough funds to operate and that you're spending and investing wisely. The importance of business finance lies in its capacity to keep a business operating smoothly without running out of cash while also securing funds for longer-term investments.

BUSINESS FINANCE AND MANAGEMENT ACCOUNTING

Finance relies on accounting, but while accounting is mainly descriptive, finance is active, using accounting information to manifest tangible results. The way business finance functions in an organization depends on management accounting reports. These documents should be current and accurate enough for your finance department to find them relevant and useful. There are also the three reports you should be looking at: the profit and loss statement, balance sheet and cash flow statement.

SOURCES OF FINANCE AND WORKING CAPITAL

In a perfect world, your business would always have enough money coming in from sales of goods and services to pay for daily operations. In the real world, most businesses need some kind of funding to cover short-term expenses, which don't always correspond with incoming revenue streams. Your business may be seasonal, earning enough money over a couple of months to cover long periods during the rest of the year when you operate at a loss. Or your business may be very busy late in the month or late in the week, but you still need to make ends meet during the slower times.

Financing for working capital is easier to obtain than financing for major purchases and investments. Many banks offer unsecured credit cards and business credit lines. You can use these options to cover business expenses without staking personal collateral or filling out long loan applications requiring extensive documentation. However, interest rates for unsecured financing options tend to be **considerably** higher than for business-lending products that are harder to obtain, such as secured term loans. Because of these high interest rates on credit cards and credit lines, it's prudent to use these loan products only for short-term needs and to pay off balances as soon as possible.

If your company operates with a monthly cycle where it accrues most of its expenses early in the month and earns most of its income later in the month, a high-interest credit card isn't such a bad option. You'll pay the money back quickly, so you won't be seriously hurt by the interest rate.

If your business operates at a loss from January until November and then earns enough in December to offset these losses, it's worth doing extra research and paperwork to secure a lower-interest credit option because you'll be paying interest for a longer period of time.

BUSINESS FINANCE AND CAPITAL INVESTMENTS

When your business makes purchases of equipment or property with lasting value, finance comes into play as you evaluate whether you're ready for the expense and then find the best way to pay for it. It is common for long-term capital investments to require loans, so you'll need to consider interest expense and **principal** payments. Your business needs to earn enough to cover these upcoming expenditures.

A cash flow pro forma is an indispensable tool for forecasting and planning. You can plug in the amounts of anticipated principal and interest amounts and also tinker with other variables to find ways of making these extra payments. For example, if you're investing in a piece of equipment that will reduce labor costs, your pro forma will show how far these savings in labor will go toward meeting the payments on the equipment.

MAKING CAPITAL PURCHASES

When you're making capital investment purchases, you'll also use business finance to weigh the pros and cons of different **repayment** options. Let's say you have a choice between a lower-interest loan with a high monthly payment and a quick repayment period versus a higher-interest option with lower monthly payments over a longer period of time. Of course, a lower-interest option is the best option, provided you have the cash flow to pay for it. But if your cash flow is tight and the equipment upgrade will save you enough money to cover some added interest, you may actually decide that the option with higher interest and a lower monthly payment is better. Lower payments help cash flow, and good cash flow puts you in a position to take advantage of opportunities.

There is no set, reliable formula for evaluating all the costs and benefits of a long-term financing option. However, if you consider all the ways that a purchase will affect your income and expenses, you'll probably make a better decision than if you focus on the interest rate alone.

Another variable that will affect the long-term costs and benefits of a purchase is the value of the money you spend and the way it changes due to inflation. When you make a loan payment in the future, you'll use capital that is worth less than the capital you borrowed because inflation decreases the value of money over time. Accountants and finance professionals use a formula called "return on investment" to calculate all of the quantifiable benefits that an investment will bring in over time and then compare these benefits with the total cost.

THE ROLE OF DEPRECIATION

Finance decisions for major capital improvements should also take depreciation into account. When you make a large investment, such as a van, computer or building, your business must follow a set of tax conventions for reporting the purchase. The way you log this expense into your bookkeeping system has **ramifications** for your income and cash flow. Instead of being able to deduct the entire cost of the major asset in the year you bought it, you are required to declare a period of time for that asset's useful life and then deduct a percentage of its initial cost during each subsequent year.

The IRS stipulates specific depreciation periods for certain types of equipment, such as vehicles and computers. Other investments, such as lease hold improvements, come with more leeway. The depreciation period you choose affects your tax liability. The more quickly you can depreciate an item, the more of its cost you can deduct each year, decreasing the taxable income that you report to the IRS. It's prudent to speak to a tax professional before making decisions about how to depreciate an especially large purchase, such as a building.

BUSINESS FINANCE AND RETAINED EARNINGS

The term "finance" is used as a noun describing the process of managing your company's money, but it is also used as a verb meaning to secure capital from an outside source through a loan or investment. Despite this association with borrowing, you can also use business finance to manage the funds you have available from regular business activities, such as sales of products or services or rent on property you own.

These retained earnings are an appealing source of operating or investment capital because you don't have to pay interest on them. You also don't have to convince a banker or investor that your project is worthwhile, and you don't have to do all the paperwork required for a loan application.

BEWARE OPPORTUNITY LOSSES

If you rely exclusively on retained earnings for short-term cash flow and longer-term investments, you may lose out on opportunities you could have leveraged if you'd had more money available. You may get a **lucrative** order that requires more of a capital **outlay** than you can make with your available cash. The cost of losing the business can be higher than the interest you would have paid if you borrowed the money. Similarly, if you own a retail location and you're keeping strictly to a cash budget, you may be unable to buy enough inventory to offer enough of a selection to lure potential customers.

A finance strategy of working primarily or strictly with capital from retained earnings is a prudent approach, but it can also make you overly cautious. You may hesitate to buy a piece of equipment you need because you don't have the cash on hand, but you would have saved more in labor over time than you would have spent on the equipment. It's a good idea to use retained earnings whenever you can do so comfortably, but line up backup sources of financing so your business doesn't suffer on the occasions when your available capital just isn't enough to make a smart move or to recover from an emergency.

International Finance

International finance may sound like a complex, grandiose concept to some but it's quite the opposite. The phrase simply refers to any financial transaction that takes place across national borders. If money leaves one country and arrives in another, for whatever reason, the transaction falls under international finance.

International finance is a monetary transaction that occurs between two or more countries. This sounds simple enough but in reality, transacting across national borders raises issues of currency exchange rates and the exploitation of developing economies. International finance is a way to analyze the economic status of the countries you may wish to do business with, judge the foreign markets, compare inflation rates and pay bills in a foreign currency. Without international finance, you would not be able to compare currency exchange to figure out the cost of doing business abroad.

WHY DO WE HAVE INTERNATIONAL FINANCE?

In a nutshell, we have international finance because we live in an era of globalization. Businesses buy and sell goods abroad, countries often borrow money from each other and organizations increasingly operate on

Word Study

lucrative /'luːkrətɪv/ *adj.* 有利可图的
outlay /'aʊtˌleɪ/ *n.* 开支,费用

国际金融

国际金融是在两个或多个国家之间发生的货币交易。实际上,跨境交易引发了货币汇率问题和对发展中经济体的剥削问题。

国际金融是一种分析潜在业务国家经济状况、判断国外市场、比较通货膨胀率并以外币支付账单的方法。

Word Study

mediation /ˌmɪdrˈeɪʃən/
n. 调解，斡旋
precautionary
/prɪˈkɔːʃənərɪ/ adj.
预防的

an international scale. An international system of finance helps to keep the peace between nations in this globalized world. Without a system of regulating cross-border financial transactions, each nation would act in its own self-interest. The chance of international conflict is high. Much of the economics underpinning international finance is concerned with keeping the flow of money in a disciplined state.

WHO'S INVOLVED IN INTERNATIONAL FINANCE?

The International Finance Corporation, the World Bank, the National Bureau of Economic Research and the International Monetary Fund play pivotal roles in the **mediation** of international finance. The World Bank, for example, provides finance and advice to assist middle-and-poor-income countries, while the IMF provides advice, policy recommendations and loans to its 189 member countries to promote economic stability. If a country needs a **precautionary** loan to stop it from falling into an economic crisis, it would approach the IMF.

In the private sector, the Institute of International Finance helps the international financial industry to manage risks prudently, and advocates for the type of regulation that fosters global financial stability and sustainable economic growth. Members of the institute include investment and commercial banks, insurance companies and hedge funds.

WHAT DOES INTERNATIONAL FINANCE MEAN FOR SMALL BUSINESSES?

If you have a branch in another country, then it's likely you'll be conducting international finance. An example would be sending money from your U.S.-based head office to your factory in Mexico City. Even though the money never changes hands — it still belongs to the company — it did cross borders. So, it's a form of international finance. Buying your raw materials abroad or selling your inventory abroad also requires an international finance transaction in the form of buying and selling. Exchange rates are mission-critical in these examples. International finance lets you discover the relative values of currencies and strike the right balance of trade.

Key Terms
专业术语

financial accounting 财务会计   management accounting 管理会计
profit and loss statement 损益表   balance sheet 资产负债表
cash flow statement 现金流动表
International Accounting Standards (IAS) 国际会计准则
International Financial Reporting Standards (IFRS) 国际财务报告准则
business finance 企业融资   international finance 国际金融

国际准则与我国金融会计制度

经过三十多年的发展,我国金融企业会计制度完成了从计划经济会计模式向市场经济会计模式的转变,由单一经营模式会计体系向综合经营模式会计体系的转变,以集中化的信息管理、电子化的会计核算和系统化的内部控制,逐步实现了满足内外部经营管理需要,实现了与国际接轨。后危机时代,金融危机暴露出国际会计准则在资产分类、公允价值选择、模型计量等方面的缺陷,而对于处在与国际会计准则接轨并日趋一致的我国会计制度来说,如何在国际会计准则变革时期,认识到国际会计准则的原则导向及未来发展方向,进而调整自身发展,以期在未来国际会计准则变革中争取话语权,其重要性不言而喻。

目前,我国会计准则与国际准则基本接轨并趋于一致,对于金融危机暴露的国际会计准则的弊端,我们更应该关注并对未来我国会计准则的发展改革方向做准备。

- 突出会计的监督功能。从会计功能来说,涵盖预算、核算、监督等多项职能,但目前我国会计准则及管理体系过多集中于核算、预算,忽视了其监督职能。
- 提高会计准则的灵活性。目前,公允价值计量在我国由于引入时间较短,应用过程中存在获取及确认的难题,虽然金融危机暴露了公允价值存在的缺陷,但公允价值仍不失为最佳的量度规范,提高公允价值使用灵活度,具体环境具体分析是下一步会计准则改革的重点。
- 加强信息披露的准确性和全面性。为了提高对会计信息披露的透明度,应加强对计量模型、前提假设、会计判断、结果选择、数据来源等因素的披露力度,提高其对经营预测和风险判断的参考作用。
- 会计人员职业判断力和风险管控力。会计制度从规则导向向原则导向转变。

文献来源:

刘云阁.由国际准则新变化浅析我国金融会计制度的变迁及发展方向[J].金融理论与实践,2011,(11):63-65.

A. Compare the three financial accounting reports, and describe their functions.

Category	Function
profit and loss statement	
balance sheet	
cash flow statement	

B. According to the text, fill in each of the following blanks with an appropriate word or phrase.

1) _____ is a system of tracking and documenting business activities.

2) Accounting information should be double checked to verify its _____ and _____.

3) Your accounting system should _____ reflect your business activity for both legal and practical reasons.

4) Management accounting also looks at cost accounting for different products, overall margins and profitability and sales figures relative to a range of _____.

5) Your _____ provides a snapshot of how much your business owns and owes at a particular point in time.

6) The field of accounting has been instrumental in creating standards and _____ that facilitate communication about financial matters.

7) Financing for _____ is easier to obtain than financing for major purchases and investments.

8) A cash flow pro forma is an indispensible tool for _____ and _____.

9) Another variable that will affect the long-term costs and benefits of a purchase is the value of the money you spend and the way it changes due to _____.

10) Finance decisions for major capital improvements should also take _____ into account.

C. Read the text and decide whether the following statements are True (T) or False (F).

1) The accounting system must be reasonably current and accurate, or your company could run into practical difficulties, but will not be related to any legal difficulty. ( )

2) The reports including profit and loss statements, balance sheets and cash flow statements, summarize financial activities, providing a broader perspective than you'd get by simply looking over a list of transactions. ( )

3) Since you'll never be able to predict future sales and expenses with complete accuracy, it is not useful to forecast future business activities based on past and present patterns. ( )

4) The profit and loss statement shows how funds are flowing in and out of your business and whether you will have money available to meet your current financial obligations. ( )

5) The information on a cash flow pro forma can't be completely accurate because there's no way to precisely foretell the future. ( )

6) Universal accounting standards significantly increase reporting

and regulatory costs, especially for companies with international operations and subsidiaries in multiple countries.　　　　（　）

7) It is common for long-term capital investments to require loans, so you'll need to consider interest expense and principal payments.（　）

8) It is possible to create a set, reliable formula for evaluating all the costs and benefits of a long-term financing option.　　　　（　）

9) Without a system of regulating cross-border financial transactions, each nation would act in its own self-interest.　　　　（　）

10) International finance lets you discover the relative values of currencies and strike the right balance of trade.　　　　（　）

Discussion 讨论

1) Why is accounting sometimes referred to as the "language of business"?

_____

_____

2) Can you briefly explain the role of auditing?

_____

_____

3) What are financial accounting and management accounting respectively concerned about?

_____

_____

4) Under what circumstances isn't the high-interest credit card a bad idea?

_____

_____

5) What are the roles of the World Bank and IMF in international finance?

_____

_____

Analyzing the Case 案例分析

Case Story

Chinese IPOs in the U.S. Declining

Nasdaq senior vice president Bob McCooey predicts a slight slowdown in the number of Chinese companies listing in the U.S. this year. He expects the year 2019 to wind up with 35 to 38 Chinese IPOs in New York, he said at the East Tech West summit in Nansha, Guangzhou, China. That's less than the 40 he predicted earlier in the year.

Investors are worried about the underlying China-U.S. pressures, which is creating uncertainty and lower valuations. "Some will wait for certainty before going ahead with IPO plans", said McCooey, chairman for the Asian region and responsible for business development.

One possibility increasingly heard in Washington, D.C. is a ban on future listings of Chinese companies on Nasdaq or NYSE. Asked if he thinks this ongoing issue could cause those already publicly traded on Nasdaq or NYSE to delist, McCooey said he believes that is doubtful. He noted that many companies already have offshore structures in place to go public in the U.S. and suggested it would be too costly for them to restructure and relist on domestic Chinese exchanges.

But McCooey did not rule out another possible scenario — restrictions on U.S. pension funds from investing in Chinese companies that publicly trade on U.S. exchanges.

In this heated environment, it remains to be seen if more Chinese companies will follow the Alibaba recent route of a dual listing, in the U.S. and in Hong Kong, China.

The next generation of Chinese startups may opt to go public on one of China's Nasdaq-styled boards. Or they may pursue the same path as Chinese smartphone maker Xiaomi and superapp Meituan, which went public on the Hong Kong Stock Exchange in 2018 and raised $4.7 billion and $4.2 billion, respectively.

McCooey noted that going public in New York is still seen by some entrepreneurs and their venture investors as a top choice. Last year, four of the top 10 companies listing in the U.S. were from China — video streaming site iQiyi, electric vehicle maker NIO, social commerce upstart Pinduoduo, and music streaming service Tencent Music Entertainment.

To give this more context, consider that out of 190 U.S. IPOs that raised $47 billion in 2018, China scored 31 IPOs that pulled in $8.5 billion, up from 16 at $3.3 billion in 2017 — an eight-year high since Alibaba's mega $25 billion IPO in 2014.

China's tech innovation boom continues, looking for the marketplace dynamics to give Nasdaq and NYSE increased competition from China.

Case Discussion

1) What do the investors worry about according to the article?

_____

_____

2) What are the potential impacts on Chinese companies if there's a ban on future listings of Chinese companies on Nasdaq or NYSE?

_____

_____

3) McCooey noted that going public in New York is still seen by some entrepreneurs and their venture investors as the trophy. In your opinion, will this attitude change in the future?

_____

_____

Case Summary

随着中美科技和贸易之争的持续,未来中国公司在美国上市的影响已经显现出来。在当前的风口浪尖上,中国公司在美国的IPO数量呈下降趋势。

纳斯达克高级副总裁 McCooey 指出,许多公司已经拥有在美国上市的离岸结构,对它们进行重组和在中国国内交易所重新上市的成本太高。去年,在美国上市的十大公司中,有四家来自中国——视频流媒体网站爱奇艺、电动汽车制造商蔚来、社交商务新贵拼多多和音乐流媒体服务腾讯音乐娱乐公司。

投资者担心潜在的中美关系压力会造成不确定性和较低的估值。在这种背景下,是否还有更多的中国公司效仿阿里巴巴在美国和中国香港两地上市,还有待观察。

未来,中国创业公司可能会走上与小米和美团相同的道路,两者于2018年在香港证券交易所上市,分别筹集了47亿美元和42亿美元。

中国的科技创新热潮仍在继续,纳斯达克和纽交所有望看到更多来自中国的竞争力。

Reading Expansion
拓展阅读

Reading I

Amid Global Market Ambiguity, CFOs Can Still Act Decisively

Between the outbreak of the novel coronavirus, the resulting oil price war and an increasingly volatile stock market, the runup to this year's U.S. presidential election carries an extra helping of risk for companies' bottom lines, feeding into corporate uncertainty. If you're a chief financial officer, trying to navigate your company's finances through this unprecedented level of uncertainty and disruption while keeping your goals on course is no small task.

"During the last recession, CFOs could genuinely say that their lack of planning was a result of a sharp downturn that was a surprise to most", said Campbell Harvey, a founding director of The Duke University/CFO Global Business Outlook survey and Fuqua finance professor. "However, it would be foolhardy to claim that the recession in 2020 or 2021 was a surprise. Although recessions are not controlled by CFOs, the impact on their firm is, to a large degree, managed by the CFO. This time around, CFOs will be judged by their preparations."

"I'd expect uncertainty about the election itself to cause firms to slow expansion in the summer and fall of 2020", said John Graham, a finance professor at Duke University's Fuqua School of Business and the director of the survey.

Deloitte's quarterly CFO Signals survey has also indicated a preoccupation about the election-year economy. While only 3% of CFOs surveyed predict a full-blown recession, 97% of CFOs anticipate a downturn this year, explained Greg Dickinson, managing director at Deloitte LLP.

"It is safe to say that this election is a bit different from others from the perspective of the broader macro backdrop", he said. "The concurrent concerns about a global economic slowdown, trade tensions, geopolitical conflicts, U.S. political divisiveness ... that's a lot going on at the same time."

So how do CFOs remain confident and act decisively during times of market turmoil and disruption? Stay flexible, Dickinson said, and remain vigilant about market trends, shifts in demand and other potential developments. Otherwise, they risk missing out on key growth opportunities or falling behind competitors.

Achieving such agility requires gathering and analyzing large quantities of data that change rapidly, a feat that many financial tools and solutions are not adequately equipped to handle.

"CFOs are already managing a complex set of accounting and finance responsibilities", said Sara Baxter Orr, Global Head, CFO Practice at Anaplan. "Add in global market instability, the outbreak of the novel coronavirus and the unknowns of an election year, and finance leaders are under an immense amount of pressure to make strategic decisions based on constantly changing economic dynamics. As we brace for a potential recession, CFOs will rely even more on modern solutions that can streamline processes and deliver insights that strengthen their position as a strategic partner to the business."

Modeling scenarios and developing contingency plans can help CFOs react rapidly as change occurs but having accurate and relevant data can be the difference between a successful pivot versus a move that lacks impact or worsens the situation. While most companies aggregate and analyze data, the level of accuracy and efficiency is largely dependent on the tool being leveraged. For instance, manual tools like spreadsheets are often fragmented, tedious and prone to error, opening the door for data to be misrepresented and misinterpreted. At a time when every hire, capital investment and extra dollar of cash reserve counts, finance teams can't afford to spend valuable time collecting, validating and consolidating data in disparate spreadsheets.

That's where Connected Planning and analysis comes into play. By collecting data from the farthest points of the business — from your sales professionals and business modelers to product developers and supply merchants — Connected Planning creates a unified source of truth with linkages to all the functions across the enterprise and enables finance teams to align objectives with operational tactics and financial plans. Having the capability to aggregate data collaboratively and real-time across the organization, CFOs are armed with a more accurate and holistic view of the businesses' activities and outcomes.

One leading insurance provider is constantly looking for new ways to be more competitive and provide value to its customers. To do this, the company's finance organization turned to Anaplan to consolidate its tools and improve its processes, resulting in 25% faster annual planning cycle and a two week decrease in semiannual budget cycle. According to the company's CFOs, by consolidating tools and investing in Anaplan, the finance team was able to become more efficient and can now spend more time discovering new connections, formulating responses and preparing for the future.

With a 360-degree vantage point, CFOs are uniquely positioned to drive digital transformation for their organizations. Armed with a holistic view of the enterprise, strong data and the ability to model outcomes against any number of variables, CFOs who leverage Connected Planning and analysis can better anticipate external events — and feel confident shifting strategies to respond to them quickly.

"Being able to quickly 'model out' changing scenarios across the business — at a very rapid pace and have them connect to each other — is something CFOs haven't always had at their fingertips. These technology advancements have put more precise information and insights into the hands of the CFOs." said Baxter Orr.

As the election heats up, agility is key for CFOs who must assess the impact of alternative courses of actions quickly to deliver value.

Accurate, real-time insights can help CFOs mitigate risk and make smarter decisions in the face of uncertainty, and even helped one global asset-servicing provider to improve customer trust and retention.

While disruption is expected in an election year, Connected Planning arms finance teams with the visibility needed to discover trends and patterns in a quickly changing world. With fast access to actionable insights, and the agility to turn on a dime, CFOs become catalysts for transformation within their organizations.

Second Thoughts

For each of the following statements, choose one (or more than one) answer to fill in the blank.

1) During the last recession, CFOs could genuinely say that their _____ was a result of a sharp downturn that was a surprise to most.

   A. lack of funds

   B. lack of specialists

   C. lack of effective staffs

   D. lack of planning

2) The concerns that affect the U.S. presidential election include _____.

   A. global economic slowdown

   B. trade tensions

   C. geopolitical conflicts

   D. U.S. political divisiveness

Reading II

Protect Your Foreign Investments From Currency Risk

Investing in foreign securities, while a good thing for your long-term portfolio, continues to pose new threats for investors. As more people broaden their investment universe by expanding into global stocks and bonds, they must also bear the risk associated with fluctuations in exchange rates.

Fluctuations in these currency values, whether the home currency or the foreign currency, can either enhance or reduce the returns associated with foreign investments. Currency plays a significant role in investing; read on to uncover potential strategies that might downplay its effects.

Pros of Foreign Diversification

There is simply no doubting the benefits of owning foreign securities in your portfolio. After all, modern portfolio theory (MPT) has established that the world's markets do not move in lockstep, and that by mixing asset classes with low correlation to one another in the appropriate proportions, risk can be reduced at the portfolio level, despite the presence of volatile underlying securities.

As a refresher, correlation coefficients range between -1 and $+1$. Anything less than perfect positive correlation ($+1$) is considered a good diversifier. The correlation matrix depicted below demonstrates the low correlation of foreign securities against domestic positions.

Monthly Correlations 1988 to 2006

Security Type	S&P 500 Index	Russell 2000 Index	Russell 2000 Value	MSCI EAFE	International Small Cap	International Small Cap Value	MSCI Emerging Markets
S&P 500	1	—	—	—	—	—	—
Russell 2000	0.731	1	—	—	—	—	—
Russell 2000 Value	0.694	0.927	1	—	—	—	—
MSCI EAFE	0.618	0.532	0.487	1	—	—	—
International Small Cap	0.432	0.466	0.414	0.857	1	—	—
International Small Cap Value	0.41	0.411	0.414	0.831	0.97	1	—
MSCI Emerging Markets	0.59	0.634	0.586	0.582	0.53	0.512	1

Combining foreign and domestic assets together tends to have a magical effect on long-term returns and portfolio volatility; however, these benefits also come with some underlying risks.

Risks of International Investments

Several levels of investment risks are inherent in foreign investing: political risk, local tax implications, and exchange rate risk. Exchange rate risk is especially important because the returns associated with a particular foreign stock (or mutual fund with foreign stocks) must then be converted into U.S. dollars before an investor can spend the profits. Let's break each risk down.

Portfolio Risk

The political climate of foreign countries creates portfolio risks because governments and political systems are constantly in flux. This typically has a very direct impact on the economic and business sectors. Political risk is considered a type of unsystematic risk associated with specific countries, which can be diversified away by investing in a broad range of countries, effectively accomplished with broad-based foreign mutual funds or exchange-traded funds (ETFs).

Taxation

Foreign taxation poses another complication. Just as foreign investors with U.S. securities are subject to U.S. government taxes, foreign investors are also taxed on foreign-based securities. Taxes on foreign investments are typically withheld at the source country before an investor can realize any gains. Profits are then taxed again when the investor repatriates the funds.

Finally, there's currency risk. Fluctuations in the value of currencies can directly impact foreign investments, and these fluctuations affect the risks of investing in non-U.S. assets. Sometimes these risks work in your favor, other times they do not. For example, let's say your foreign investment portfolio generated a 12% rate of return last year, but your home currency lost 10% of its value. In this case, your net return will be enhanced when you convert your profits to U.S. dollars since a declining dollar makes international investments more attractive. But the reverse is also true; if a foreign stock declines but the value of the home currency strengthens sufficiently, it further dampens the returns of the foreign position.

Minimizing Currency Risk

Despite the perceived dangers of foreign investing, an investor may reduce the risk of loss from fluctuations in exchange rates by hedging with currency futures. Simply stated, hedging involves taking on one risk to offset another. Futures contracts are advance orders to buy or sell an asset, in this case, a currency. An investor expecting to receive cash flows denominated in a foreign currency on some future date can lock in the current exchange rate by entering into an offsetting currency futures position.

In the currency markets, speculators buy and sell foreign exchange futures to take advantage of changes in exchange rates. Investors can take long or short positions in their currency of choice, depending on how they believe that currency will perform. For example, if a speculator believes that the euro will rise against the U.S. dollar, they will enter into a contract to buy the euro at some predetermined time in the future. This is called having a long position. Conversely, you could argue that the same speculator has taken a short position in the U.S. dollar.

There are two possible outcomes with this hedging strategy. If the speculator is correct and the euro rises against the dollar, then the value of the contract will rise too, and the speculator will earn a profit. However, if the euro declines against the dollar, the value of the contract decreases.

When you buy or sell a futures contract, as in our example above, the price of the good (in this case the currency) is fixed today, but payment is not made until later. Investors trading currency futures are asked to put up margin in the form of cash and the contracts are marked to market each day, so profits and losses on the contracts are calculated each day. Currency hedging can also be accomplished in a different way. Rather than locking in a currency price for a later date, you can buy the currency immediately at the spot price instead. In either scenario, you end up buying the same currency, but in one scenario you do not pay for the asset upfront.

Investing in the Currency Market

The value of currencies fluctuates with the global supply and demand for a specific currency. Demand for foreign stocks is also a demand for foreign currency, which has a positive effect on its price. Fortunately, there is an entire market dedicated to the trade of foreign currencies called the foreign exchange market (forex, for short). This market has no central marketplace like the New York Stock Exchange; instead, all business is conducted electronically in what is considered one of the largest liquid markets in the world.

There are several ways to invest in the currency market, but some are riskier than others. Investors can trade currencies directly by setting up their own accounts, or they can access currency investments through forex brokers.

However, margined currency trading is an extremely risky form of investment, and is only suitable for individuals and institutions capable of handling the potential losses it entails. In fact, investors looking for exposure to currency investments might be best served acquiring them through funds or ETFs — and there are plenty to choose from.

Some of these products make bets against the dollar, some bet in favor, while other funds simply buy a basket of global currencies. For example, you can buy an ETF made up of currency futures contracts on certain G10 currencies, which can be designed to exploit the trend that currencies associated with high-interest rates tend to rise in value relative to currencies associated with low-interest rates. Things to consider when incorporating currency into your portfolio are costs (both trading and fund fees), taxes (historically, currency investing has been very tax inefficient) and finding the appropriate allocation percentage.

The Bottom Line

Investing in foreign stocks has a clear benefit in portfolio construction. However, foreign stocks also have unique risk traits that U.S.-based stocks do not. As investors expand their investments overseas, they may wish to implement some hedging strategies to protect themselves from ongoing fluctuations in currency values. Today, there is no shortage of investment products available to help you easily achieve this goal.

Second Thoughts

1) Why does the author think currency play a significant role in foreign investments?

   _____

   _____

2) Can you give one example of how fluctuation in the value of currencies can impact foreign investments?

   _____

   _____

Suggested Answers

Chapter 1

Workbook

B. 1) Globalization   2) economies
3) social relations   4) declining; rise
5) non-governmental   6) diversity
7) common ground   8) labor; manufacturing; distribution
9) offshoring   10) rich; poor

C. 1) F   2) F   3) T   4) F   5) T   6) F   7) T   8) T   9) F   10) T

Reading I

1) AD   2) B

Chapter 2

Workbook

B. 1) Observers; players   2) cultural norm
3) cultural differences   4) changes; complexities
5) values   6) goal expectations
7) collaboration; interdependence   8) disastrous
9) generalizations   10) cultural patterns

C. 1) T   2) F   3) T   4) T   5) F   6) T   7) T   8) T   9) F   10) T

Reading I

1. A   2. A

Chapter 3

Workbook

B. 1) virtue; morality   2) moral standards
3) specific culture   4) ethical action; normal practice
5) Reformation; Enlightenment   6) Protestant; Martin Luther
7) Reason   8) mission
9) loyalty; 1990s   10) desirability

C. 1) F   2) T   3) T   4) T   5) F   6) F   7) T   8) T   9) T   10) F

Reading I

1. A   2. ABC

Chapter 4

Workbook

B. 1) gold and silver   2) protectionist
3) market forces   4) Leontif Paradox

5) World War II; professors   6) preferences

7) product life cycle; marketing   8) maturing product

9) Global strategic rivalry   10) national competitive advantage

C. 1) T   2) F   3) F   4) F   5) T   6) T   7) F   8) T   9) F   10) F

Reading I

1. C   2. D

Chapter 5

Workbook

B. 1) firm or individual   2) effective control

3) same   4) third

5) unrelated   6) capital

7) mobility   8) currency fluctuations

9) recession   10) New Zealand

C. 1. F   2. F   3. T   4. T   5. T   6. F   7. T   8. T   9. F   10. T

Reading I

1) B   2) A

Chapter 6

Workbook

B. 1) decentralized   2) speculation; settlements; investments

3) price   4) fixing

5) fundamentals; technical   6) transfer

7) counter   8) spot rate

9) economic strength   10) forward

C. 1) F   2) F   3) F   4) T   5) F   6) T   7) T   8) T   9) F   10) F

Reading I

1. B   2. C

Chapter 7

Workbook

B. 1) gold   2) fixed

3) 700 B.C.   4) 1944; 44

5) International Monetary Fund/IMF; World Bank   6) Washington, D.C.

7) financial crises   8) financing; advice; research

9) forex   10) floating

C. 1) F   2) T   3) T   4) T   5) F   6) F   7) T   8) F   9) T   10) T

Reading I

1. C   2. A

Chapter 8

B. 1) savings; investments   2) hold capital
3) existing/already-issued   4) over-the-counter
5) London   6) debt securities
7) raise money   8) outside
9) eurodollar   10) Japanese yen
C. 1) T   2) F   3) T   4) T   5) F   6) T   7) F   8) T   9) F   10) T

Reading I
1. D   2. B

Chapter 9

Workbook
B. 1) maximize   2) arenas
3) multinational corporation/MNC   4) Differentiators
5) expansion risk   6) multidomestic
7) strategic asset seeking   8) Global strategy
9) international/global/foreign   10) scale and scope
C. 1) F   2) F   3) T   4) F   5) T   6) F   7) T   8) F   9) T   10) F

Reading I
1) A   2) D

Chapter 10

Workbook
B. 1) organizational structure   2) centralized
3) ineffective   4) departmentalization; formalization
5) one-to-many   6) span of control
7) conservative   8) decentralized
9) description; expectations   10) guidelines
C. 1) F   2) T   3) F   4) F   5) T   6) F   7) T   8) F   9) T   10) T

Reading I
1) A D   2) B

Chapter 11

Workbook
B. 1) foreign; overseas   2) conservative
3) Exporting   4) piggybacking
5) Joint venture   6) wholly owned subsidiary
7) strategic alliance   8) goals
9) procompetitive   10) Competitive alliance
C. 1) T   2) F   3) T   4) F   5) F   6) T   7) T   8) F   9) T   10) F

1) B   2) D

Chapter 12

Workbook

B. 1) domestic
3) individual consumers
5) costs
7) reputation
9) medium; large
2) exchangeable
4) market
6) (market) leader
8) exporting
10) innovative

C. 1) T   2) F   3) T   4) T   5) F   6) T   7) F   8) T   9) F   10) T

Reading I

1) A; D   2) C

Chapter 13

Workbook

B. 1) worldwide system
3) outposts
5) efficient
7) global value chain
9) delays
2) halt
4) waste; theft
6) thrive
8) outsourcing
10) managing; identifying

C. 1) T   2) F   3) T   4) T   5) F   6) T   7) F   8) T   9) F   10) T

Reading I

1. A   2. B

Chapter 14

Workbook

B. 1) worldwide; global
3) standardization
5) forefront
7) Third-party
9) communication
2) matrix
4) less
6) size
8) pricing
10) competitive advantage; local customers

C. 1) T   2) F   3) F   4) T   5) F   6) T   7) T   8) T   9) T   10) F

Reading I

1) BC   2) ABCD

Chapter 15

Workbook

B. 1) prominent
3) multicultural
5) hybrid
7) mobility
9) obstacles
2) cohesive
4) payroll
6) database
8) retain
10) mentor

C. 1) F   2) T   3) F   4) F   5) T   6) F   7) T   8) T   9) F   10) T

Reading I

1) ABD   2) ABCD

Chapter 16

Workbook

B. 1) Accounting   2) consistency; accuracy
   3) faithfully   4) variables
   5) balance sheet   6) protocols
   7) working capital   8) forecasting; planning
   9) inflation   10) depreciation

C. 1) F   2) T   3) F   4) F   5) T   6) F   7) T   8) F   9) T   10) T

Reading I

1) D   2) ABCD

Resources

CHAPTER 1

Steger, Manfred. *Globalization: A Very Short Introduction.*
　　Oxford University Press, Oxford UK, 2017.
Stiglitz, Joseph. *Globalization and Its Discontents Revisited: Anti-Globalization in the Era of Trump.*
　　W.W. Norton & Company, New York, NY USA, 2017.
Hansen, Valerie. *The Year 1000: When Explorers Connected the World — and Globalization Began.*
　　Scribner, New York, NY USA, 2017.

CHAPTER 2

Tuleja, Elizabeth A. *Intercultural Communication for Business.*
　　Dog Ear Publishing, LLC. Minnesota.USA. 2014.
Geert Hofstede's Cultural Dimensions Theory.
　　Health Research Funding. Bethesda. USA. 2018.
Hodgetts, Richard M. & Luthans, Fred. *International Management: Culture, Strategy and Behavior.*
　　McGraw-Hill. New York. NY USA. 2003.
Jacob, Nina. *Intercultural Management: MBA Masterclass.*
　　Kogan Page. London. UK. 2003.

CHAPTER 3

Divya, K. *Impact of Ethics on Global Business.*
　　Journal of Business and Management. Ontario. USA. 2011.
Kumar, Brij Nino. *Ethics in International Management.*
　　De Gruyter. Berlin. German. 1998.
Jackson, Terence. *International Management Ethics: A critical, cross-cultural Perspective.*
　　Cambridge University Press. Cambridge. UK. 2011.
Duarte, Alonso Raul. *Comparison of Work-Related Values and Leadership Preferences of Mexican Immigrants and Caucasians.*
　　Walden University. Minnesota. USA. 2020.

CHAPTER 4

Neuefeind, Wilhelm. *Economic Theory and International Trade.*
　　Springer. Berlin. German. 2001.
Harrod, Roy & Hague, Douglas. *International Trade Theory in a Developing World.*
　　Palgrave MacMillan. London. UK. 1962.
Feenstra, Robert C. *Advanced Interantional Trade: Theory and Evidence.*
　　Printceton University Press. Printceton. USA. 2015.
Negishi, Takashi. *Developments of International Trade Theory.*
　　Springer. Berlin. German. 2001.

CHAPTER 5

Mun, Hwi-ch'ang. *Foreign Direct Investment — A Global Perspective.*
> World Scientific Publishing Company Pte Limited, Seoul. South Korea. 2015.

Blaine, Harrison G. *Foreign Direct Investment.*
> Nova Science Publishers, New York. USA. 2009.

Moran, Theodore. *Foreign Direct Investment and Development.*
> Peterson Institute for International Economics, Washington DC. USA. 2011.

CHAPTER 6

Brian, Coyle. *Foreign Exchange Markets.*
> Financial World Publishing, London. UK. 2000.

Weisweiller, Rudi. *How the Foreign Exchange Market Works.*
> New York Institute of Finance. New York. USA. 1990.

CHAPTER 7

Genberg, Hans. *The International Monetary System: Its Institutions and Its Future.*
> Springer Berlin Heidelberg, Berlin. Germany. 2012.

Kenen, Peter B. *The International Monetary System.*
> Cambridge University Press, Cambridge. UK. 1994.

Pascal, Salin. *The International Monetary System and the Theory of Monetary Systems.*
> Edward Elgar Publishing Incorporated, Cheltenham. UK. 2016.

CHAPTER 8

Obstfeld, Mauric. *Global Capital Markets: Integration, Crisis, and Growth.*
> Cambridge University Press. Cambridge. UK. 2005.

Camfferman, Kees & Zeff, Stephen A. *Financial Reporting and Global Capital Markets: A History of the International Accounting Standards Committee, 1973–2000.*
> OUP Oxford. Oxford. UK. 2007.

Ray, Christina I. *The Bond Market: Trading and Risk Management.*
> Business One Irwin, London. UK. 1993.

CHAPTER 9

Carpenter, Mason A. *International Business.*
> Saylor Academy, Washington DC, USA. 2012.

Kim, Chan & Mauborgne, Renée. *Blue Ocean Strategy.*
> Harvard Business Review Press, MA. USA. 2005.

CHAPTER 10

Raymond, Miles. *Organizational Strategy, Structure, and Process.*
> Stanford University Press, Redwood. USA. 2003.

Alvesson, Mats. *Understanding Organizational Culture.*
> SAGE Publications Ltd, London. UK. 2002.

CHAPTER 11

Shenkar, Oded & Reuer, Jeffrey J. *Handbook of Strategic Alliances.*
  SAGE Publications Ltd, London. UK. 2005.

CHAPTER 12

Elhanan, Helpman. *Understanding Global Trade.*
  Harvard University Press, London. UK. 2011.
Entrepreneur Press. *Start Your Own Import/Export Business.*
  Entrepreneur Press, California. USA. 2003.
Onkvisit, Sak & Shaw, John. *International Marketing: Analysis and Strategy Countertrade.*
  Prentice Hall Publishing, NJ. USA. 1996.

CHAPTER 13

Matt, Drake. *Global Supply Chain Management.*
  Business Expert Press, NY. USA. 2011.
Binglian Liu, Shao-Ju Lee, Zhilun Jiao, Ling Wang. *Contemporary Logistics in China: An Introduction.*
  World Scientific Publishing Company, NJ. USA. 2011.

CHAPTER 14

Ries, Al & Trout, Jack. *Marketing Warfare.*
  McGraw-Hill, New York, NY. USA. 1985.
Ries, Al & Trout, Jack. *Positioning.*
  McGraw-Hill Education, New York, NY USA. 2001.
Ries, Al & Ries, Laura. *The 22 Immutable Laws of Branding.*
  Harper Business, New York, NY USA. 2002.
Kotler, Philip. *Kotler on Marketing.*
  The Free Press (A Division of Simon & Shuster Inc.), New York, NY USA. 2014.
Kotler, Philip & Kevin, Keller. *Marketing Management*, 15th Edition.
  Pearson, New York, NY USA. 2015.
Kotler, Philip & Armstrong, Gary. *Principles of Marketing*, 17th Edition.
  Pearson, New York, NY USA. 2017.

CHAPTER 15

Drucker, Peter. *The Practice of Management.*
  Harper Business, New York. NY USA. 2010.
Drucker, Peter. *The Effective Executive.*
  HarperCollins Publisher, New York. NY USA. 1967.
Goldratt, Eliyahu & Cox, Jeff. *The Goal.*
  Routledge, New York. NY USA. 2016.
Palmer, Helen. *The Enneagram.*
  HarperCollins Publisher, New York. NY USA. 1991.
Rosenberg, Marshall & Chopra, Deepak. *Nonviolent Communication* 3rd Edition.
  PuddleDancer Press, Encinitas. CA USA. 2015.
Ulrich, David & Younger, Jon & Brockbank, Wayne & Ulrich, Mike. *HR from the Outside In: Six Competencies for the Future of Human Resources.*
  McGraw-Hill Education, New York. NY USA. 2012.

CHAPTER 16

Mankiw, N. Gregory. *Principles of Economics* 7th Edition.
Cengage Learning, Stanford. CT, USA. 2014.
Eun, Cheol & Resnick, Bruce. *International Financial Management*.
McGraw-Hill Education, New York. NY USA. 2017.